CANADA
History in the Making

History in

COVER PHOTO BY DICK LOEK

"Tall Ships" enter the historic harbour of Quebec City in 1984. Early European settlers probably travelled to Canada on similar ships. Like these early sailing ships, the "tall ships" travelled to both coasts of Canada. They also sailed up the St. Lawrence River to enter the Great Lakes, bringing living history to many parts of Canada. The hopes and dreams which travelled with these early ships are alive today in Canada. An understanding of our history will help us see this. This history belongs to all Canadians, past, present and future.

Why do you think these ships are called "tall ships"?

You can tell this is Quebec City because of the rocky cliff climbing up from the St. Lawrence River. Do you know the name given to the land on top of this cliff?

A very significant military battle in Canadian history was fought here. Do you know the name of this battle? You can learn more about this important battle in Lesson 31.

CANADA

the Making

Gillian Bartlett
Janice Galivan

John Wiley & Sons
TORONTO NEW YORK CHICHESTER BRISBANE SINGAPORE

To Kenny G.B.

To Anne, Jason, Michael, and Vi, with thanks J.G.

Canadian Cataloguing in Publication Data

Bartlett, Gillian, 1950-
Canada: history in the making

For use in high schools.
Includes index.
ISBN 0-471-79795-2

1. Canada - History - 20th century. I. Galivan, Janice A., 1948- II. Title.*

FC170.B37 1986 971 C83-098654-5
F1026.B37 1985

Designer: Julian Cleva
Illustrator: James Loates, illustrating and Peter Grau
Typesetter: Jay Tee Graphics Ltd.

Printed and bound in Canada by T.H. Best Printing Company Ltd.

10 9 8 7 6 5 4 3 2

CONTENTS

UNIT FIVE Our Place in the World 409

TO THE TEACHER

Given the number of Canadian studies textbooks currently available on the market, it would be only natural to query the publication of yet another. However, *Canada: History in the Making* has several unique features designed to make Canadian government and history even more accessible to students.

First, the material in this book has been divided into short, easily readable lessons, each of which follows precisely the same pattern. The Introduction explains this pattern while simultaneously demonstrating to students the kinds of activities that will be expected of them. Every effort has been made to ensure that the short essay which opens each lesson is easy to read and understand: sentence structure has been kept deliberately simple; difficult terms have been kept to an absolute minimum; numerals have been used instead of written numbers. Similarly, great care has been taken to phrase all questions and material in the accompanying activities as clearly as possible.

Second, there is a strong emphasis in the text on skill development. Each lesson features a series of activities broken into four main sections. The first section involves factual recall and suggestions for basic research. The second entails questions that encourage students both to state and to discuss their opinions. Next are language-related activities emphasizing vocabulary and language skills. And, finally, there is work related to an illustration of some kind such as a map, graph, or table.

Throughout the text, every effort has been made to bring lively subject material to the students. This has been done, in part, through a broad and interesting selection of illustrations, many of them rare and unusual photographs. Intriguing points of Canadiana in the form of Maple Leaf Facts are featured in every lesson. In addition, each lesson features the biography of an appropriate figure from Canadian life. While these figures include familiar names such as Wayne Gretzky, Barbara Frum, and Pierre Trudeau, many of the people described — people like Sarah Malabar, Alex Decoteau, and Hanka Romanchych-Kowalchuck — are generally unknown to most Canadians but nonetheless fascinating individuals.

In general, we have endeavoured to make the material in this text both accessible to students and relevant to their needs. We hope that this text will help students to see themselves as part of the historical process that shapes the Canadian experience. We also hope that they will learn that a knowledge of the past helps us to understand the present and gives us the key to shape a better future.

Acknowledgements

Naturally, a text such as this could not have come into being without considerable help from others.

We received many useful comments and suggestions from a number of reviewers, whose contribution we would like to acknowledge. The reviewers are:

Gerard Boulay, Ecole Secondaire Etienne Brûlé, Willowdale, Ontario;

Steven Dart, A.Y. Jackson Secondary School, Willowdale, Ontario;

Peter Hill, Caledonia High School, Caledonia, Ontario;

Brooke Hodgins, Lakeview Secondary School, Toronto, Ontario;

Charles Kahn, Kahn and Associates, Toronto, Ontario;

Murray Locke, Albert Campbell Collegiate Institute, Agincourt, Ontario;

J.S. Milloy, D.Phil., Trent University, Peterborough, Ontario;

Patricia Saul, A.Y. Jackson Secondary School, Willowdale, Ontario;

Nancy Smith, West Toronto Secondary School, Toronto, Ontario.

We are especially grateful to Jim Rogerson for his unswerving faith in this project from its very inception and to Heather Sperdakos — not only for her consistently cheerful advice and support but also for the interminable hours she spent gamely wrestling with permissions.

In that regard, we would like to thank especially the Public Archives of Canada and the Robarts Library, University of Toronto, for their assistance in securing photographs.

We are also indebted to those involved in the actual production of this book including Pam Young for her dedicated copy-editing and Julian Cleva for his insightful design. Kathryn Dean, Joan Kerr, and Kaari Turk deserve our thanks as well for the immense energy, effort, and time they devoted to the book's publication.

Finally, we would like to thank our students and colleagues from over the years for all they have taught us about what it is to teach and to learn.

Gillian Bartlett
Janice Galivan

INTRODUCTION

Canada's Family Tree

You will find that this book is divided into 69 lessons. Each one of these lessons follows exactly the same pattern. This introductory lesson will show you just how the pattern works.

First, you will be asked to read some material such as the following short essay. You will find that some words are printed in **boldface**. *These words are explained for you in the Glossary at the back of this book.*

You will also find "Maple Leaf Facts" in the margins. These are marked with a blue maple leaf. These contain interesting bits of information about Canada.

Figure 1 Coming to Canada *Over the years, thousands of immigrants have come to Canada. They have come from many different countries. And they have come from many different backgrounds. These photographs show just a few of these immigrants who have helped to settle and build our country.*

Who in your class is a Canadian? Most of you are probably Canadian citizens. But all of you come from different backgrounds. Some of your families may have been living in Canada for a long time. Others may have been here for only 1 or 2 **generations**. Still others may have arrived here very recently.

(1.a.) *John Ware and family helped settle western Canada, 1896*

(1.b.) *Doukhobor immigrant women pulling a plough, 1899*

(1.c.) *German immigrants to Quebec, 1911*

(1.d.) *English war brides, 1946*

(1.e.) *East Indians on their way to Canada, c. 1906*

(1.f.) *Ukrainian immigrants working in the fields, c. 1915*

(1.g.) *Young immigrants from the Orient*

(2.a.) *A Native high school student using a microcomputer.*

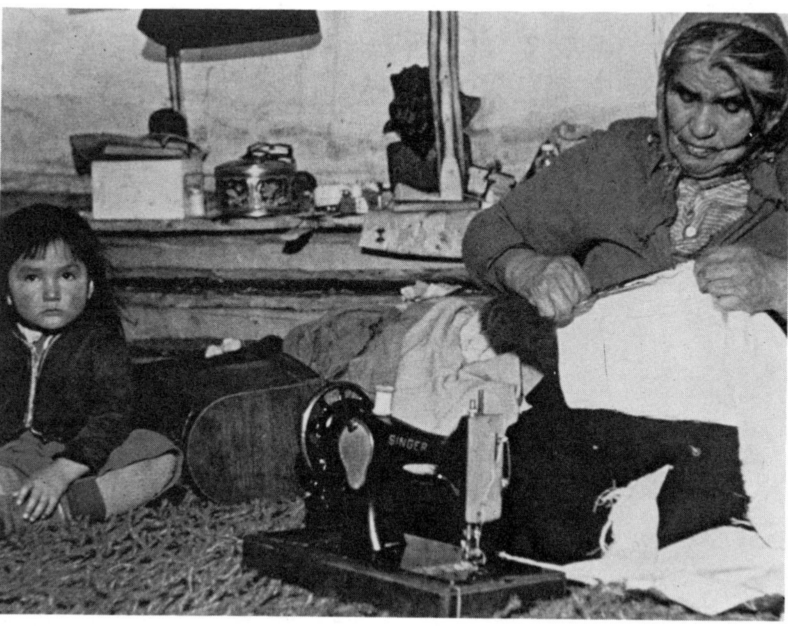

(2.b.) *A Cree woman sewing*

Figure 2 Canada's original peoples *The ancestors of these Native people may have been immigrants to Canada many thousands of years ago.*

Some historians think that the **ancestors** of our Native people began to come to Canada about 40 000 years ago. These ancestors possibly came from the land we now call the Soviet Union. The Soviet Union is separated from Alaska by a strip of water called the Bering Strait. These historians think that the ancestors of our Native people crossed this water when it was frozen. Then they travelled across North America in search of food.

In a sense, then, every Canadian could be considered either an **immigrant** or the **descendant** of an immigrant. Immigrants are people who come from other countries.

We do know for sure that thousands of years later, in the 1600s, French settlers immigrated to Canada. Most French Canadians today can trace their families all the way back to these early French immigrants.

Some British immigrants had been living in Newfoundland since the late 1600s. But the first large groups of British immigrants came to Canada in the late 1700s. This was after the American Revolution when many of the Loyalists came to Canada. Later, in the 1840s and 1870s, many more immigrants came to Canada from Britain.

The French and the British began this country as we know it today. A quarter of Canadians today do not have a Native, French, or British background. As you can see from the Canadian family tree in Figure 3, Canadians come from many different **ethnic** backgrounds.

Canada is 18 times the size of France and 40 times larger than Great Britain.

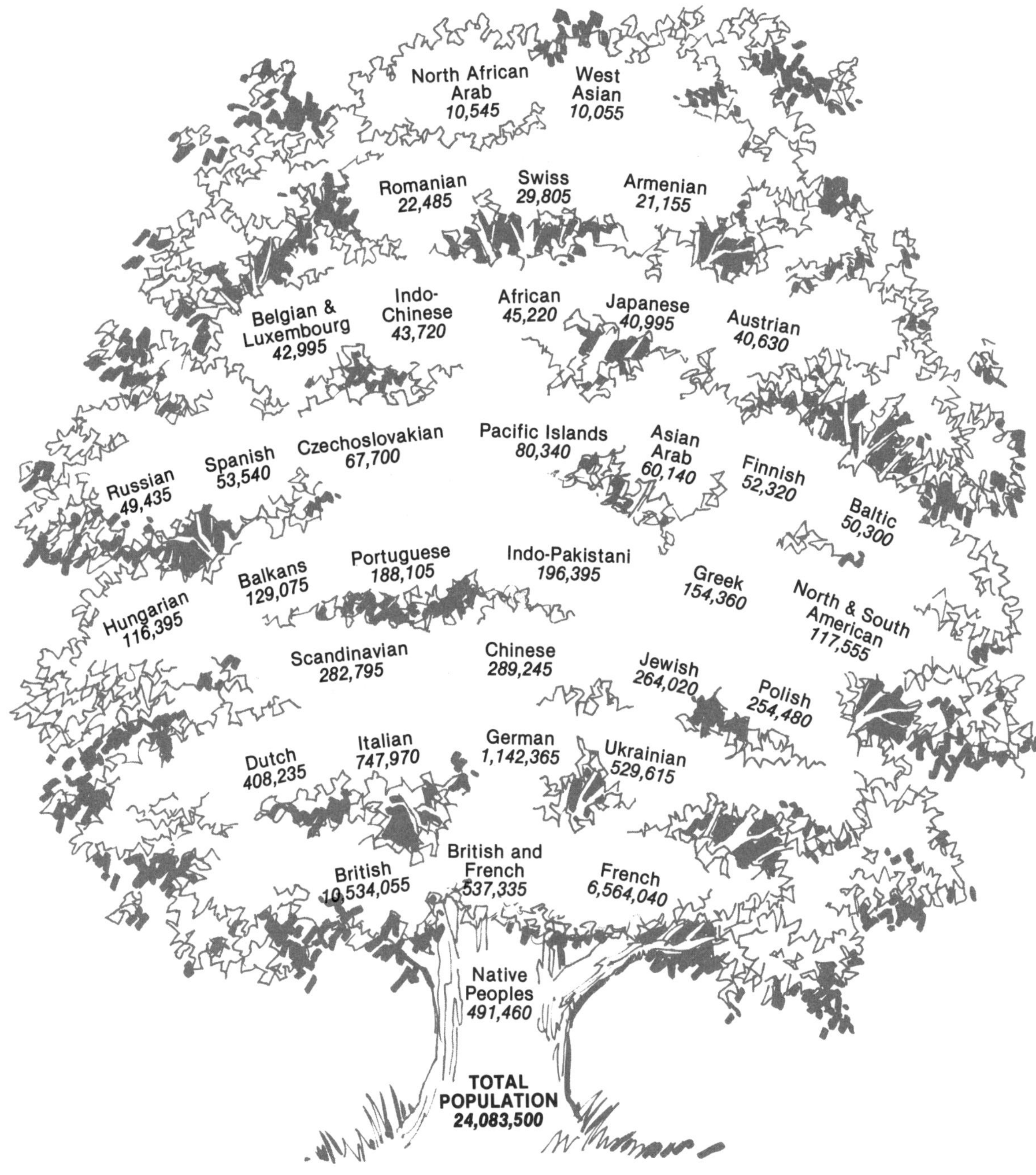

Notes: 1. The numbers for "British" and "French" include those people who are only half British or half French.
2. 414 605 people are not on the tree. They were in categories of "other" or "mixed".

SOURCE: 1981 Census of Canada

Figure 3 The Canadian family tree *This family tree shows the different ethnic backgrounds of Canadians. It also shows the number of Canadians who come from each background. Where do you fit on the tree?*

Figure 4 *New Canadians taking the oath of citizenship*

The fact that Canadians come from so many different backgrounds has had a big effect on our country. It helps to explain how our country is run. And it also helps to explain the important issues in Canada today.

Note: You will be learning about our system of government in Unit I of this book. In Unit II you will learn about our system of law.

Our system of government — how we agree to run our country — and our system of law — the rules we all agree to obey — were set up when the British controlled Canada. So they are based on the British systems of government and law.

Note: You will be learning more about relations between French-speaking and English-speaking Canadians in Unit III of this book.

Even though the British controlled Canada after the mid-1700s, there were many Canadians of French background. Many of these French Canadians disliked being ruled by the British. Very often in the history of Canada, the Canadians of French background have disagreed with the Canadians of British background. Even today this is an important issue in Canada.

Note: You will learn about relations between Canada and the United States in Unit IV of this book.

Many of the first British immigrants to Canada came from the United States. For a long time after that, Canadians and Americans were enemies. Now, of course, Canadians and Americans are friends. But whether we have been enemies or friends, our relationship with the Americans has had a big effect on Canada.

Note: You will be learning about Canada and important world issues in Unit V of this book.

Finally, as you have learned, many Canadians do not have either a British or a French background. Instead, they come from all around the world. This is one reason why it is so important to understand Canada's place in the world today.

The maple leaf is a symbol of Canada everywhere in the world today. The lessons in this book explain a lot of what this symbol stands for. They will help explain what it means when you say you are a Canadian.

All Canadian.

Figure 5 A multicultural Canadian flag *This Canadian flag is made up of smaller flags from different countries around the world. Do you recognize any of these smaller flags?*

THE FACTS

After each lesson you will be asked about the facts. As you know, facts are things that are true. They are things that have happened.

First, you will be asked to remember facts from the lesson. Then, you will be asked to find out some new facts related to the lesson.

Remembering Facts

1. Where do some historians think the Native people of Canada first came from?
2. When did the French settlers first come to Canada?
3. When did the first large group of British settlers come to Canada?
4. How many Canadians today do not have a Native, British, or French background?
5. What does the maple leaf mean?

Finding Facts

Look carefully at Canada's family tree in Figure 3. There are 35 different groups on this family tree. Make a list of these 35 groups. Start with the group with the biggest number, and end with the group with the smallest number.

YOUR OPINIONS

Next, you will be asked to give your opinions. Opinions are the ideas you have about a subject. They are not right or wrong. They are just your own feelings.

First, you will be asked to state your opinions in a few sentences. Then you will be asked to discuss your opinions with other people in the class.

Try to bring in facts to explain your opinions. But don't be afraid to change your ideas about the subject. Other people might convince you that their opinions are more sensible.

Stating Opinions

Are you happy living right now? Or would you like to have lived at some other time in history? Explain your opinion in a few sentences.

Discussing Opinions

Today some Canadians don't want to let more people come into our country. They want to keep Canada to themselves.

Do you think we should stop more people from coming into Canada? Or do you think that anybody who wants to should be allowed to come here? Discuss your opinions with the rest of the class.

NEW WORDS

In each lesson, you will also be asked to work with words. First, you will learn 5 words that are in the lesson. Then you will be given a language activity. Sometimes it will teach you spelling or punctuation rules. Sometimes it will teach you how words are put together. And sometimes it will teach you something unusual about the English language.

Learning Words

In your notebook, write the title Vocabulary: Introduction. Then write down the following words in a list. Using the Glossary or a dictionary, write the meaning beside each word.

When you are finished, write a short note telling what you have learned in this lesson. Try to use all 5 of these words in your note.

ancestor	**descendant**	**ethnic**
generation	**immigrant**	

Examining Words

The following 4 words were used in this lesson. There is 1 sound that is the same in each word. What is the sound? How is the sound spelled in each word?

class	trace
descendant	history

AN ILLUSTRATION

Sometimes things are easier to understand if you can look at a picture, or illustration, of them. These illustrations don't have to be photographs. They can also be maps, graphs, charts, or tables.

In this section of each lesson, you will be asked to work with an illustration. Sometimes you will be asked to study an illustration. Sometimes you will be asked to make the illustration yourself.

Look at a globe or map of the world. Find the following places on this globe or map:

(a) the place where the French settlers came from;
(b) the place where the British settlers came from;
(c) two places where other immigrants to Canada have come from.

Giulia Iannucci

Each lesson in this book is followed by a short biography. These biographies tell about the lives of important or interesting Canadians. They come from many different backgrounds and professions. Half of them are men, and half of them are women. Some of them are from the past, and some are still alive.

After each biography, you will be asked 2 questions. One question will be about facts related to this biography. The other question will ask you to give your opinions.

Claim to fame: She represents the thousands of immigrants who have helped to make Canada a better place to live.

Born: 1929 in Casalvieri, Italy

Married: 1944 to Pompilio Iannucci. She met Pompilio during a bomb raid in World War II. They eloped on a bicycle when Giulia was 15. Two years later, they had a son named Amilcare. Their son Fernando was born 4 years after that.

Career: The Iannuccis could not afford to educate their sons in Italy. They had heard that Canada was a country full of opportunities. Giulia and Pompilio did not speak English, or French. Also, there were not many Italians in Canada at that time. Still they decided to come here.

They made a down payment on a small house. The first years were very difficult. Giulia almost died from thyroid disease and had to stay in bed for many months. There was no health insurance then. It was hard to find money for the doctor's visits as well as for food and the house payments. Then, just when Giulia was feeling better, Pompilio hurt his back and could not work for a year.

Giulia set up a catering business. That way, she could look after the children while she worked. She would often get up before dawn to cook food for weddings that had as many as 500 guests! Once the children were older, Giulia went out to work as a seamstress.

Life was not always easy for Giulia and Pompilio in Canada. But their dream did come true: both their sons were able to go to school. Fernando is now a school teacher. And Amilcare is a university professor.

Figure 6 *Pictures from the Iannucci family album*

- **Find Italy on a globe. How far is it from where you live?**
- **What kinds of food would you cook for a wedding?**

UNIT ONE

Government in Canada

We all talk about the government. We all have opinions about what the government should and shouldn't do. But sometimes we talk about the government as though it was a machine that we have no control over.

In reality, the government is made up of people just like you and me. The lessons in this unit will help you understand how these people work together to make a government. You will also learn how the government can be changed if enough people want it to change.

You will find that each unit in this book has its own sign, or symbol. The sign for Unit I is based on the Parliament Buildings in Ottawa.

CHAPTER ONE

The Structure of Government

If your garbage hasn't been collected as usual, who can you complain to? If you think that teenagers should be allowed to drive when they're 14, who can you talk to? If you're having trouble getting a Social Insurance Number, who can you ask for help?

In all these cases, you could go to the government representative who looks after the area you live in. But the problem is, there will be more than one person who represents your area. There will be a different one for each level of government.

This chapter will help you understand the 3 main levels of government in Canada and how they share responsibilities. By the end of the chapter, you will be able to tell which person could help you in each of the situations described above.

On page 13 you will find a picture of an imaginary street in an imaginary town. Look carefully at the picture. Can you find at least 3 things that governments do?

When you have finished Chapter 1, look at this picture once again. Now how many things can you find that governments do?

POLICE
PROVINCIAL COURT
RADIO
CKYX
1060
DRUG STORE
LIBRARY
POST OF
POLICE
WEST PARK
TELEPHONE
LITTER

1 Confederation

Look at the map of North America in Figure 1.1. If you compare it with a modern map, you can see many differences. Before 1867, the area we now call Canada was broken into **separate** units called colonies. These colonies belonged to Britain. All the colonies together were called British North America.

Figure 1.1 *North America before Confederation*

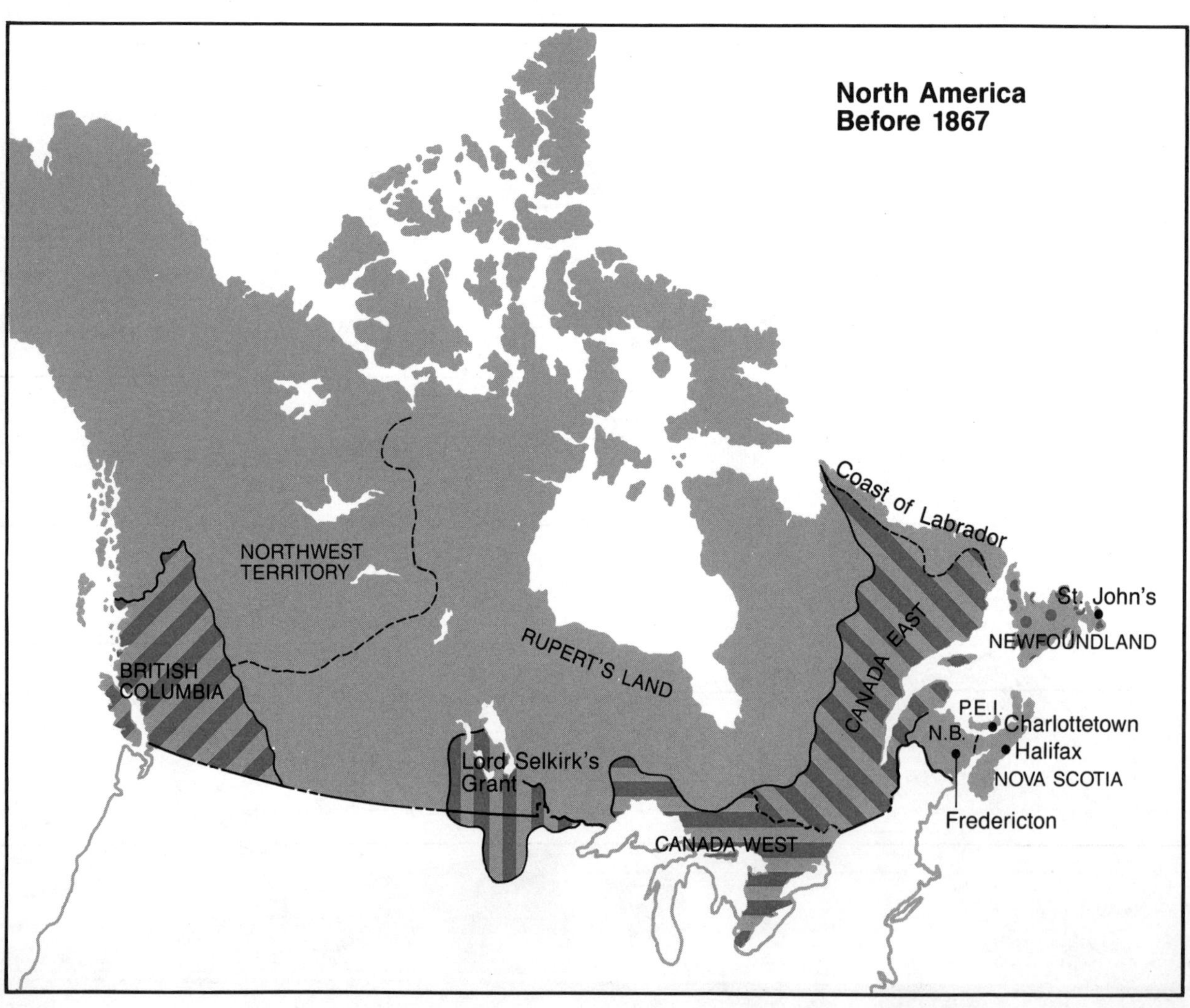

Most people in British North America lived in the colonies in the east. These were Canada West (now Ontario), Canada East (now Quebec), New Brunswick, Newfoundland, Nova Scotia, and Prince Edward Island.

In 1864, leaders from these colonies met in Charlottetown, Prince Edward Island. They wanted to discuss the idea of joining together as a single country. Many of the leaders thought that this was a good idea. If all the colonies joined together, they said, then they could help each other in times of trouble. They would also be able to share each other's **wealth**.

Life expectancy at the time of Confederation was just 40 years. Today it is more than 70 years.

Figure 1.2 Some of the activities in Canada in the late 1800s *If you compared these photographs with modern photographs of the same kinds of activities, what differences would you see?*

(1.2.a.) *Shipping lumber in Ontario, 1872*

(1.2.b.) *Making horse-drawn carriages in New Brunswick, 1893*

(1.2.c.) *Haying in Quebec, c. 1900.*

Robert Harris's famous picture of the Fathers of Confederation wasn't painted until 30 years ***after*** **Confederation.**

But there were 2 main problems. First, the colonies were very far apart. In 1864, it took 2 full days to travel by steamer from Quebec City to Charlottetown. Second, each colony had its own special interests. For example, Upper Canada depended on farming, while Nova Scotia depended on fishing. Some of the leaders wondered whether 1 government for the whole country could possibly work.

At Charlottetown, and later at Quebec City, the leaders drew up a plan for the new country that was to be called Canada. They decided to solve the problems by having 2 main levels of government: federal and provincial.

The federal government would be in Ottawa. It would include **representatives** from across the country. It would take care of things that concerned the whole country. For example, the federal government would be in charge of building railways.

Each colony that joined Canada would be called a province. Each province would then have its own provincial government. The provincial government would take care of the things that concerned only that province.

In 1864, the leaders took the plan back to their colonies. There was a lot of **debate** about the plan in each colony. Finally Canada West, Canada East, Nova Scotia, and New Brunswick decided to accept the plan and join together as a single country. They called this joining together a "confederation".

Since colonies in Canada were ruled by Britain, they did not have the power to make themselves into a country. Instead, the plan was sent to Britain to be approved by the British government. In March of 1867, the British Parliament passed the plan, calling it the British North America Act (or the BNA Act, for short).

Confederation took place on July 1, 1867. Ottawa was named the capital of Canada. John A. Macdonald was selected as its first leader, or prime minister. The new country was made up of only 4 provinces in the east. But the leaders of Canada were sure that many more colonies would join. That is why they made Canada's **motto** *A Mari Usque ad Mare*, or "From sea to sea".

In fact, the leaders were quite right. Six more provinces were added over the years:

Manitoba	1870	Saskatchewan	1905
British Columbia	1871	Alberta	1905
Prince Edward Island	1873	Newfoundland	1949

In the end, the new country did stretch from sea to sea.

Figure 1.3 The Canadian coat of arms *This is the official symbol for Canada. Where do you see this coat of arms used?*

Figure 1.4 *John A. Macdonald and his wife are standing on the right. They are looking at a lake in the wilderness on their first journey by train to British Columbia.*

THE FACTS

Remembering Facts

1. Why did some leaders of the British colonies want to join together?
2. What 2 problems were there with joining together?
3. How did the leaders try to solve these problems in their plan for Confederation?
4. Why didn't the colonies pass the BNA Act themselves?
5. What is Canada's motto?

Finding Facts

In 1864 it took over 48 hours to travel from Quebec City to Charlottetown. Call a travel agent or airline to find out how long it takes to make the same journey by air today. If you were going to travel from your own home to Charlottetown, what would be the best way to go? How long would the journey take?

Stating Opinions

Look again at the map of North America in Figure 1.1. What do you think is the biggest difference between the way North America looked then and the way it looks now? Write a few sentences to explain your opinion.

Discussing Opinions

The leaders made their plan for joining together in 1864. But the Dominion of Canada did not come into being until 1867. Discuss why you think it took 3 years for this to happen.

Learning Words

In your notebook, write the title Vocabulary: Lesson 1. Then write down the following words in a list. Using the Glossary or a dictionary, write the meaning beside each word.

When you are finished, write a short note telling what you have learned in this lesson. Try to use all 5 of these words in your note.

debate **motto** **representative**
separate **wealth**

Examining Words

If something belongs to *Britain* it is called *British*. For example, the colonies in North America were *British* colonies. And a ship belonging to Britain is called a *British* ship. What word do we use if something belongs to each of the following countries?

Canada France
America Russia

Draw or trace an outline map of Canada. Draw in the boundaries of the provinces. Then print on the map the name of each province. Under each name, write the date that the province joined Canada.

John A. Macdonald

Figure 1.5 *John A. Macdonald at work in his office*

Claim to fame: He was the first prime minister of Canada.

Born: 1815 in Glasgow, Scotland

Married: 1843 to his cousin, Isabella Clark. Their first son died at 13 months of age. The second son, Hugh John Macdonald, became premier of Manitoba in 1900. Isabella was bedridden for 12 years before she died in 1857.

Ten years later, Macdonald married Susan Agnes Bernard. They had 1 daughter, Mary, who had to use a wheelchair all her life.

Career: John A. Macdonald was trained as a lawyer. He was a member of the government of Canada West and East before Confederation. At the 1864 Charlottetown Conference, he was the first of all the leaders to speak about joining the 2 Canadas with the other colonies.

He led the first government of the Dominion of Canada from 1867 to 1873. This government began building the Canadian Pacific Railway to join Canada to a new province, British Columbia.

The Pacific Scandal (relating to the building of the railway) forced Macdonald to resign in 1873. He was re-elected in 1878 and remained prime minister until his death in 1891.

Died: Macdonald died in 1891 after campaigning to be re-elected. Macdonald's death was caused by several strokes after months of overworking. Sadly, he died without learning that his party had won the election.

- **Who was the prime minister of Canada between 1873 and 1878?**
- **Macdonald had many problems in his private life. Do you think these could have affected his work?**

2 Our Changing Constitution

Figure 2.1 Newfoundland joins Canada *This picture was taken at the special ceremonies when Newfoundland joined Canada. Canada's prime minister, Louis St. Laurent, is helping to carve the Newfoundland coat of arms into the arch of the Parliament Buildings in Ottawa. What year was this picture probably taken?*

As times change, new rules must be made to suit new situations. For example, when the first cars were built in Canada, drivers didn't have to have licences. Anyone could just buy a car and drive it. This was not very dangerous because there were only a few cars on the roads.

But as time passed, more and more people bought cars. This made driving more difficult. So new rules were made. People now had to pass special tests before they could drive.

This same sort of change has happened with the Canadian **constitution**. A constitution is a set of rules for how a country is to be run. When Canada first started in 1867, its constitution was the British North America Act (BNA Act). However, there have been many changes in Canada since 1867. For example, new provinces have joined. Therefore, new rules have been added to the BNA Act.

In fact, between 1867 and 1982 over 20 rules were added to the BNA Act. These new rules were called **amendments**. And each amendment became a part of Canada's constitution.

But there was a problem with this arrangement. Every time the Canadian government wanted to make an amendment, it had to ask the British Parliament for **permission**. This was because the BNA Act had been passed when Canada was still a British colony. Therefore, all amendments or changes to the Act had to be passed by the British Parliament.

Over the years this system became embarrassing. Canada was the only **independent** country in the world that had to go to the government of another country to change its constitution. It was like a 30-year-old having to get his or her parents' permission to change jobs.

Leaders of the federal and provincial governments held many meetings to see whether they could solve this problem. They wanted to "bring the constitution home" so

The beaver first appeared on the Canadian nickel in 1936.

that Canada wouldn't have to go to the British Parliament to make new rules.

However, this was not so easy. The federal government and the provinces could never seem to agree on an amending **formula**. This was a plan for how new rules could be added to the constitution after it had been brought home. There had to be a way to make sure that most of the people agreed with any new rule before it was added to the constitution.

The problem was that the provinces couldn't agree on how many of them needed to like a rule before it could be made part of the constitution. Also, some provinces wanted to be able to say no to any new rule they didn't like. Other provinces thought this was unfair.

Finally, in 1980, Prime Minister Pierre Trudeau decided that something had to be done. It seemed as though the provinces would never agree about bringing the constitution home. So he said that the federal government would act on its own.

The federal government did go ahead and make plans to bring home the constitution. Most of the provinces were furious that the federal government would do this without their permission. So they agreed to meet one last time in November, 1981, to see if they could all come to an agreement.

Our motto and the name *Dominion* of Canada came from the Bible, Psalm 72: "He shall have dominion also from sea to sea."

Figure 2.2 The Constitution comes home to Canada *Queen Elizabeth II signed the Constitution Proclamation in Ottawa on April 17, 1982, while Prime Minister Pierre Trudeau looked on. It was cold and wet that day, and the rain spoiled Queen Elizabeth's signature. The other official copy of the constitution that Queen Elizabeth signed later when she was indoors was damaged afterwards with red paint by a peace protestor.*

The Trans-Canada Highway was officially opened on September 3, 1962.

It took many hours of talking and arguing. But finally there was a breakthrough. The federal government and 9 of the provinces agreed to a new plan for bringing the constitution home. The Premier of Quebec, René Lévesque, would not accept it. (*There were many reasons why Lévesque refused to accept the plan. You will learn more about them in Chapter 6.*)

Many people were very upset about Quebec. They thought that the federal government should wait until Quebec also agreed to the plan. However, the federal government decided to go ahead. It asked the British Parliament to pass the Canada Act. This Act became law on April 17, 1982.

The Canada Act explains Canada's constitution. It says that Canada should be run using almost the same rules as before. But 2 major changes were made.

First, the Canada Act explains how new rules can be added to our constitution. It explains the amending formula that the federal government and the 9 provinces agreed on. Now Canada can change its own constitution without going to Britain.

THE AMENDING FORMULA
The Canada Act states that any amendment to the constitution must be passed by the federal government. At least 7 provinces also have to agree to the amendment. And at least half of all Canadians must be living in these 7 provinces.

It is possible that a province might not like an amendment. For this reason, the Canada Act states that any province that disagrees with an amendment does not have to obey it.

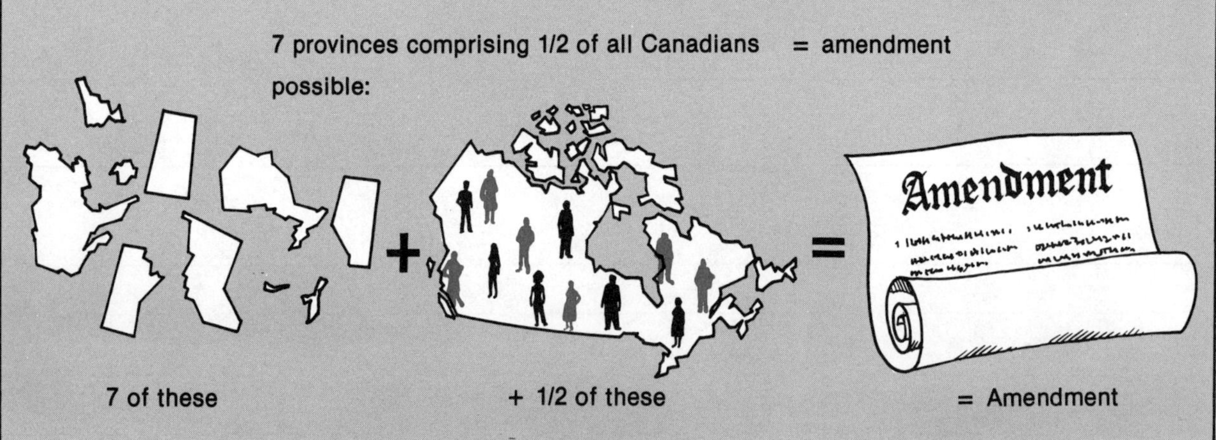

Figure 2.3 *The amending formula*

Second, the Canada Act explains the rights and freedoms of all Canadians. There is a summary of this charter in the box on page 24. Is there a copy of the Charter of Rights in your library?

Figure 2.4 Canadian rights and freedoms *Which important Canadian rights and freedoms are shown in this picture?*

The idea of private, or individual land ownership was foreign to the Native peoples of America.

THE CANADIAN CHARTER OF RIGHTS AND FREEDOMS

Like most Canadians, you probably take for granted the fact that you can practise your own religion — or that you can move to another province — or that you can express your own feelings about the government.

However, in many countries in the world, you wouldn't be allowed to do these things. Therefore the charter lists the rights and freedoms that every Canadian has. The most important rights and freedoms are as follows.

Fundamental Freedoms

- Freedom of conscience and religion
- Freedom of thought, and expression, including freedom of the press and other media of communication
- Freedom of peaceful assembly
- Freedom of association

Democratic Rights

- The right to vote
- The right to run for election

Mobility Rights

- The right to enter, remain in, and leave Canada
- The right to move to, live in, and work in any Canadian province

Legal Rights

- The right to "life, liberty, and security of the person"
- Security from unreasonable search or seizure
- Security from arbitrary arrest or detention
- The right not to be subjected to cruel and unusual punishment

Equality Rights

- The right to equality before the law regardless of race, national or ethnic origin, colour, religion, sex, age, or mental or physical disability

Language Rights

- The equal status for the use of English and French in the government and courts of Canada
- The right to education in English or French wherever there are reasonable numbers of Anglophone or Francophone students

THE FACTS

Remembering Facts

1. Which government made the amendments to the BNA Act from 1867 to 1982?
2. Why did it take so long to "bring the constitution home"?
3. Who is Pierre Trudeau?
4. Which province did not agree to the new amending formula?
5. What is the Canada Act?

Finding Facts

Table 2.1 shows how many people were living in each province in Canada in 1981. Look carefully at this table. Next, read the rules for the amending formula on page 22. Then decide whether an amendment could still be made in the following situations:

1. The province you live in does not agree.
2. Quebec and Ontario do not agree.
3. Prince Edward Island, Newfoundland, and Alberta do not agree.
4. Quebec does not agree.
5. New Brunswick and the federal government do not agree.

PROVINCE	POPULATION
Alberta (AB)	2 237 725
British Columbia (BC)	2 744 470
Manitoba (MB)	1 026 245
New Brunswick (NB)	696 405
Newfoundland (NF)	567 680
Northwest Territories (NT)	45 740
Nova Scotia (NS)	847 445
Ontario (ON)	8 625 110
Prince Edward Island (PE)	122 510
Quebec (PQ)	6 438 400
Saskatchewan (SK)	968 310
Yukon Territory (YT)	23 150
TOTAL POPULATION	24 343 190

SOURCE: *1981 Census of Canada*

Table 2.1 *The populations of Canada's provinces and territories*

YOUR OPINIONS

Stating Opinions

Read the summary of the Charter of Rights and Freedoms on page 24. Which right or freedom do you think is most important? Write a few sentences to explain your opinion.

Discussing Opinions

Some people do not like the amending formula. They think that every province should have to accept an amendment if it is passed.

Do you think it is a good thing that a province can decide not to obey an amendment? Or do you think this is a bad thing? Discuss your ideas with the other students in your class.

NEW WORDS

Learning Words

In your notebook, write the title Vocabulary: Lesson 2. Then write down the following words in a list. Using the Glossary or a dictionary, write the meaning beside each word.

When you are finished, write a short note telling what you have learned in this lesson. Try to use all 5 of these words in your note.

amendment **constitution** **formula**
independent **permission**

Examining Words

The word *amendment* can be broken into 2 parts. The first part is *amend* which means "to change". The second part is *ment*.

Find another word in this lesson which ends in *ment*. What is the first part of this word? Can you explain what it means?

AN ILLUSTRATION

The graph in Figure 2.5 is not finished. It shows the populations of only 2 provinces. Copy this graph into your notebook. Then finish the graph using the numbers in Table 2.1.

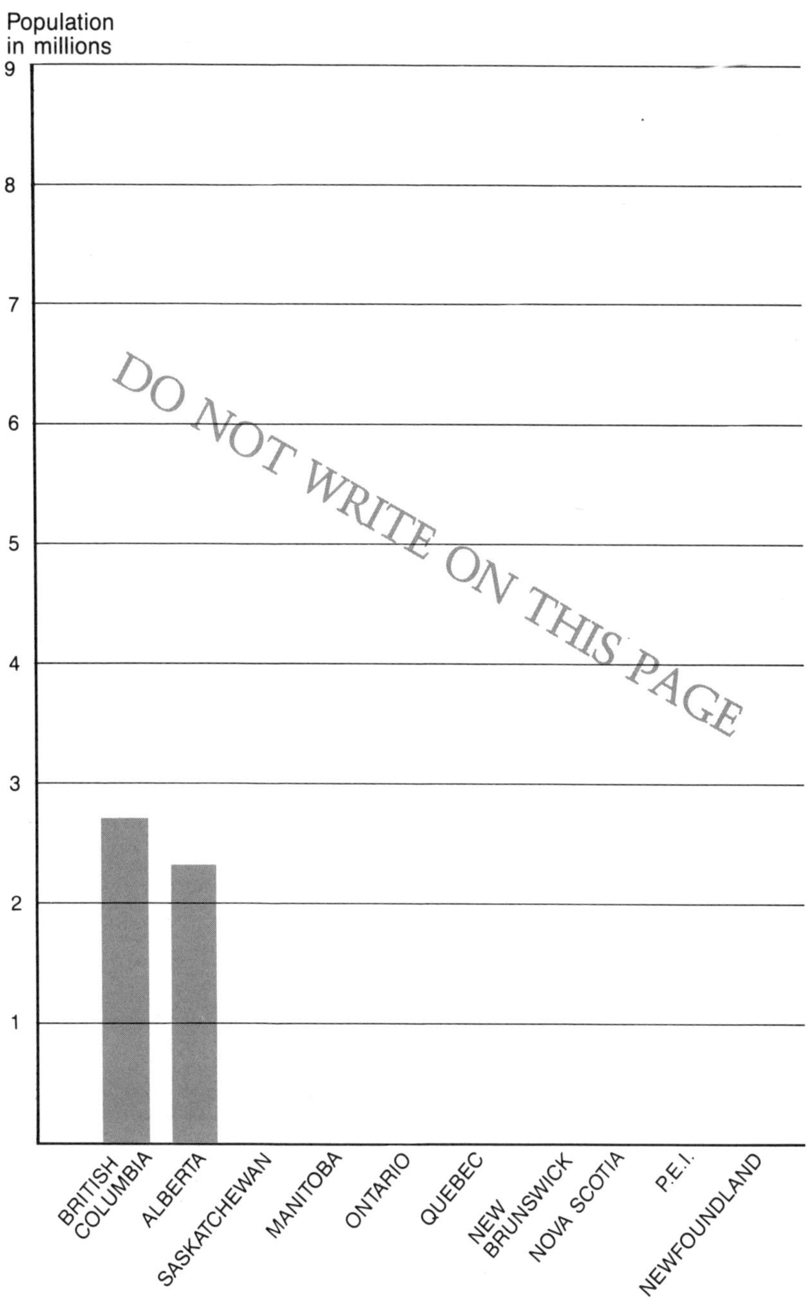

Figure 2.5 *The populations of Canada's provinces*

Pierre Elliott Trudeau

Figure 2.6 *Pierre Trudeau signing papers in his office*

Claim to fame: He was the prime minister who brought home the Canadian constitution.

Born: 1919 in Montreal, Quebec

Married: 1971 to Margaret Sinclair in a secret wedding. They had three children — Justin, Sacha, and Michel. Justin and Sacha were each born on a Christmas day. The couple separated in 1977. They were divorced in 1984.

Career: Pierre Elliott Trudeau was trained as a lawyer and became a professor of law at the University of Montreal in 1951. He wrote several books about politics and the role of Quebec in Canada.

He was first elected to the House of Commons in 1965. In 1968, he became leader of the Liberal Party. At the same time he became prime minister and held the office until 1979. After a year out of office his government was re-elected and he became prime minister once more.

On February 29, 1984, Trudeau announced he was retiring as leader of the Liberal Party. By the time he was replaced by John Turner on June 30, 1984, he had become the longest serving French Canadian prime minister in Canada.

Trudeau will be remembered as the prime minister who brought the constitution home. He dared to act alone without the agreement of the provinces. And he insisted that there be a Charter of Rights and Freedoms.

- **Who was the prime minister who defeated Trudeau in the 1979 election?**
- **You were probably alive when Trudeau was still prime minister. What memories or opinions of him do you have?**

The Division of Powers

3

Everyone knows it is the **duty** of police officers to make sure that laws are obeyed. To do this, police officers are given certain **powers**. For example, they have the power to arrest people who are caught breaking the law. They also have the power to put these people in jail.

Governments also have duties and powers. In Canada, these are explained in the constitution. They are divided between the 2 main levels of government: the federal government and the provincial government. In general, the federal government is in charge of matters that affect all Canadians. Provincial governments, on the other hand, are in charge of matters that affect only the people in their provinces.

For example, the constitution says that the federal government has the duty to defend Canada. This means that the federal government has the power to recruit men and women to serve in the armed forces. It has to equip and train these soldiers. It has to buy defence materials such as weapons, tanks, ships, and planes. It also has to decide whether to send troops to help other countries in trouble.

Of course the federal government does much more than defend Canada. The other duties and powers of the federal government are listed in Section 91 of the BNA Act. This section has been reprinted for you on page 30. If you read through the list, you will recognize some of the services that our federal government performs for all Canadians:

> Number 5 on the list gives the power to the federal government to run our postal system, Canada Post. It is a federal duty to see that your letters are delivered to the correct address.
>
> Number 6 refers to Statistics Canada. This is the agency that collects the statistics you hear every month on the radio about how many people are unemployed or how much the inflation rate has changed.

Quebec's Emma Casgrain became Canada's first woman dentist in 1898.

In 1907, the fare to travel by the Canadian Pacific Railway was 2¢ a kilometre.

Numbers 14 to 16 refer to our system of money and banking. It is the federal government that decides what kind of coins and paper money we will use or whether a new bank can be opened.

FEDERAL POWERS IN THE BNA ACT: Section 91

The BNA Act lists 30 different subjects or areas controlled by the federal government. Only the federal government can make laws concerning these subjects: the provincial governments are not allowed to interfere without the federal government's permission.

1. The public debt and property
2. Setting the rules for trade and commerce
3. Raising money through taxes
4. Borrowing money on the public credit
5. Postal service
6. The census and statistics
7. Defence, including militia, military and naval service
8. The salaries of civil servants
9. Beacons, buoys, lighthouses and Sable Island
10. Navigation and shipping
11. Quarantine and the setting up and running of marine hospitals
12. Sea coast and inland fisheries
13. Ferries between a province and any foreign country, or between two provinces
14. Currency and coinage
15. Banking, incorporation of banks, and the issue of paper money
16. Savings banks
17. Weights and measures
18. Bills of exchange and promissory notes
19. Interest rates
20. Legal tender
21. Bankruptcy and insolvency
22. Patents of invention and discovery
23. Copyrights
24. Native people and lands reserved for the Native people
25. Naturalization and aliens
26. Marriage and divorce
27. Criminal law
28. The setting up and running of penitentiaries
29. Any other subject or area not specifically controlled by the provinces
30. Unemployment insurance

The Grey Cup was donated to Canadian football in 1909 by Governor General Lord Grey.

Figure 3.1 Federal powers *How many federal powers can you see in this picture?*

The constitution also explains the duties and powers of the provincial governments. These duties and powers affect only the people in each province. For example, the constitution says that provincial governments are in charge of education. In this way, a student in New Brunswick doesn't have to study exactly the same things as a student in Quebec or British Columbia.

The duties and powers of the provincial governments are listed in Section 92 of the BNA Act. This has been reprinted for you on page 32. Read through the list. You might recognize a few of your province's duties and powers.

In May in British Columbia you can swim in Deep Cove or throw snowballs on Seymour Mountain, just a 20-minute drive away.

Number 2 gives your province the power to charge you a sales tax on all the items you buy.

Number 5 is an important regulation that gives your province the power to control the forests and **resources** (such as uranium or oil) that are found in the province.

Number 7 gives your province the duty to provide health care. The hospitals, doctors, and nurses in your province are all controlled by your provincial government.

PROVINCIAL POWERS IN THE BNA ACT: Section 92

The BNA Act lists 16 different subjects or areas controlled by the provincial governments. Only the provincial governments can make laws concerning these subjects.

1. Amendment of the provincial constitution, except concerning the Lieutenant-Governor
2. Direct taxes within the province in order to pay for provincial projects
3. Borrowing money on the sole credit of the province
4. The appointment and salaries of provincial civil servants
5. The management and sale of the public lands belonging to the province, and of the timber on those lands
6. The setting up and running of provincial prisons
7. The setting up and running of hospitals, asylums, and charities for the province
8. Municipal governments in the province
9. Liquor and similar licences in order to raise money for provincial or municipal purposes
10. Local works such as railways *except* those that join the province to another province or those works that the federal government decides are important for Canada as a whole
11. The incorporation of businesses and companies
12. The rules for marriage ceremonies in the province
13. Property and civil rights in the province
14. The administration of justice in the province
15. Setting the punishment for breaking the laws of the province
16. Any matters of a local or private nature in the province

Figure 3.2 Provincial powers
How many provincial powers can you see in this picture?

One of the problems with Sections 91 and 92 is that it can sometimes be very difficult to decide which level of government has control of an area. For example, number 26 of Section 91 and number 12 of Section 92 seem to **overlap**: they both concern marriage.

Because duties and powers can seem to overlap, there is sometimes **tension** between the federal and provincial governments. For example, in the 1970s, Alberta and the federal government argued about which government had the power to tax oil from Alberta. Later, Newfoundland and the federal government argued about which government had the power to control the oil found in the ocean off the Newfoundland coast.

Canada has a long history of dealing with such problems. It isn't always easy. But the federal and provincial governments have always managed to solve their differences in the past. The important thing is that our system of government meets the needs of all Canadians.

GOVERNMENT DEFINED

"A federation requires a very delicate balance" - Prime Minister Trudeau

Figure 3.3 Balancing federal and provincial powers *Former prime Minister Trudeau — who is shown here in the middle — once said that "a federation requires a very delicate balance." Do you think the cartoonist agrees with this statement? Explain your answer.*

THE FACTS

Remembering Facts

1. Where are the duties and powers of the federal government and provincial governments written down?
2. Which level of government has the power to decide the following? (Look at Section 91 and Section 92 of the BNA Act to find out.)
   (a) whether we will have a new coin worth $1
   (b) how many doctors and nurses will be hired to run a new hospital
   (c) how much it will cost to post a letter
   (d) how much sales tax you will have to pay on a shirt you want to buy
3. Why is there sometimes tension between the federal and provincial governments?

Finding Facts

In the 1970s, the federal government decided that Canada should change to the metric system. Instead of using measures like pounds and miles, Canadians had to start using kilograms and kilometres.

Read the list of responsibilities in Section 91 on page 30. Find the number in the list that gave the federal government the power to make Canada metric.

YOUR OPINIONS

Stating Opinions

Which level of government do you think is the most important in your life — the federal or the provincial? Write a few sentences to explain your opinion.

Discussing Opinions

The leaders of our country decided to make education a provincial power. Do you think it is a good thing that students in different provinces get different educations? Or do you think that all Canadian students should have the same educational system?

NEW WORDS

Learning Words

In your notebook, write the title Vocabulary: Lesson 3. Then write down the following words in a list. Using the Glossary or a dictionary, write the meaning beside each word.

When you are finished, write a short note telling what you have learned in this lesson. Try to use all 5 of these words in your note.

duty	**overlap**	**power**
resource	**tension**	

Examining Words

When you look in the dictionary to find the meaning of a word, you often find that there is more than 1 meaning. How many meanings can you think of for the word *train*? Check in your dictionary to see whether you missed any meanings.

AN ILLUSTRATION

Look closely at a map of your province in an atlas. The capital city of your province will be marked with a special sign, or symbol, on the map.

Look for this special sign on the maps of 2 other provinces. Name the capital cities of these 2 other provinces.

Wilfrid Laurier

Figure 3.4 *Wilfrid Laurier speaking to supporters*

Claim to fame: He was the Canadian prime minister who helped unify Canada and make Canadians proud of their nation.

Born: 1841 in St. Lin, Canada East

Married: 1868 to Zoë Lafontaine. They had no children.

Career: After working as a lawyer, Laurier entered provincial politics and won a seat in the Quebec Assembly in 1871. He soon switched to federal politics when he won a seat in the House of Commons in the 1874 elections. Ten years later, he was chosen leader of the Liberal Party.

Laurier served as the leader of the Opposition until the Liberals won the election in 1896. The major issue in the election was the Manitoba Schools Question (see Lesson 37). Laurier did not like the plans of Manitoba for its school system. But he said that the federal government had no right to interfere with a province's educational system. He believed strongly in the division of powers between the provincial and federal governments.

Laurier solved the schools issue with charm and "sunny ways". He was a popular prime minister until 1911, when the Liberals lost the election. However, during World War I, Laurier gave his party's full support to the Conservative government.

Died: Laurier died in 1919. The whole country mourned the death of this great Canadian.

- **How many French Canadian prime ministers have there been?**
- **Many of our politicians are lawyers. Do you think this is a good thing or not?**

The House of Commons

4

Canada is a **democracy**. In a democracy, all of the people help make the laws and rules they will live by. But with nearly 25 million Canadians, it would be impossible for everyone to vote on every law. Think how long it would take to **discuss** one single law!

Therefore, Canadians are divided into groups. Each group chooses a representative to express the people's views and to make laws for them. People vote for these representatives in elections.

For the federal government, all of Canada has been divided into ridings or constituencies. Each riding has about the same number of voters. And each riding elects just 1 representative.

Today, there are 282 federal ridings in Canada. That means that there are 282 representatives, or Members of Parliament. These Members of Parliament (or MPs, for short) meet in the House of Commons in Ottawa. Their job is to vote on every law for all the people, or constituents, in their ridings.

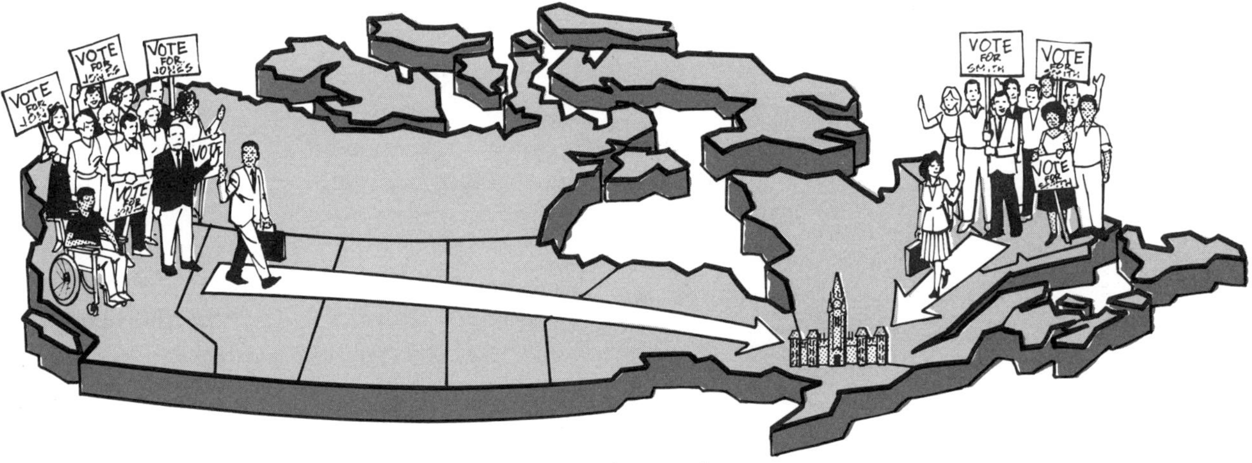

Figure 4.1 Sending a representative to Ottawa *The people in each federal riding send just 1 person to the House of Commons to represent them.*

Figure 4.2 A party leader is chosen *Ed Broadbent won the leadership of the New Democratic Party in 1976. Here he is congratulated by one of his opponents, Rosemary Brown. It is never easy to win the leadership of a party. Usually several people would like the job. This is because the leader of the party has the chance to become either the prime minister or the leader of the Opposition. Who is the leader of the New Democratic Party today?*

Most of the 282 elected members of Parliament belong to a political party. The 3 main political parties in Canada are the Liberal Party, the New Democratic Party, and the Progressive Conservative Party.

The political party that has the **majority** of the 282 elected MPs forms the government. In other words, the party with the largest number of MPs decides what laws should be voted on and how the country will be run. The leader of the party with the majority becomes the prime minister. For example, if most of the MPs belonged to the New Democratic Party, then the New Democratic Party would form the government and the leader of the New Democratic Party would become the prime minister.

The political party that elects the second-largest number of MPs is called the **Opposition**. And the leader of this party is called the leader of the Opposition. Because Canada is a democracy, the Opposition plays a very important role. Its job is to watch what the government does. The Opposition points out when the government does something it thinks is wrong.

The prime minister has the most important job in our government. He or she chooses MPs to become the heads of different government departments. These MPs are called ministers.

Canada's youngest-ever prime minister was Joe Clark, who took office on June 4, 1979, at the age of 39.

Each minister takes care of different federal duties or powers. For example, you will remember that the federal government is in charge of defending the whole country. Therefore there is a minister in charge of national defence.

06:30 Rises to dress for the day. Eats working breakfast with senior advisers to discuss upcoming issues.

08:00 Arrives at office. Checks the day's schedule with staff. Reads summary of news stories in previous day's papers.

09:00 Keeps a series of appointments with politicians, experts, and important citizens.

10:30 Attends weekly caucus meeting (a meeting of all the MPs who belong to the same party).

12:00 Talks over lunch with party organizers and campaign managers.

13:00 Leads Cabinet meeting to discuss new legislation.

15:00 Attends question period in House of Commons to answer questions from Opposition MPs.

17:00 Hosts reception for officials visiting from prime minister's home riding.

19:30 Arrives at a dinner in honour of new ambassadors.

21:00 Gives a speech of welcome. Chats for a short time with the crowd.

22:00 Returns home to read memos and reports for following day.

24:00 Lights out.

Figure 4.3 A day in the life of the prime minister *The prime minister has a lot of power. But being the prime minister is not an easy job. There are long working days, as you can see from this illustration.*

Figure 4.4 The House of Commons *Inside the House of Commons are seats for all the members of Parliament. The government MPs sit on one side of the room. The Opposition MPs sit on the other side facing them.*

The single seat up on a platform to the left is for the Speaker. The Speaker of the House of Commons has an extremely important job. The Speaker controls the debate between the MPs. For example, the Speaker decides whose turn it will be to ask a question or make a speech.

Lester Pearson, a former Canadian prime minister, once played semi-professional baseball.

The prime minister and the ministers meet together regularly to discuss the business of the country. When they meet like this, they are called the Cabinet. This explains why you sometimes will hear or read about *Cabinet* ministers.

The most important job of the Cabinet is to decide what laws should be made. To do this, the ministers write **bills**. A bill is a suggestion for a new law. These bills are presented to the MPs in the House of Commons, which is pictured in Figure 4.4.

The steps a bill must go through before it can become law are shown in Figure 4.5. You can see that there are many steps. This has been done on purpose. It gives everyone a lot of time to think carefully about the suggestion for a law and decide whether it is a good one.

If a majority of MPs votes against the bill, the bill will be defeated. This means that the bill will not become law. If the bill passes all the steps in the House of Commons, it will probably become law. But there are still more steps ahead before this can happen. You will learn more about this in Lesson 5.

Problem:
Acid rain is becoming a serious problem. Scientists say car pollution is causing a lot of this acid rain. People and the press seem to be worried about this issue.

Minister's Solution:
The Minister of Transport asks for advice from the workers in the department. They suggest that car makers should be made to add better pollution controls.

Cabinet Discussion:
The Minister introduces the idea at a Cabinet meeting. The Cabinet discusses whether this is a good idea. The Cabinet also discusses whether the people will like this idea.

First Reading:
A bill is written by the Minister. It says that car makers have to add better pollution controls by a certain date. This bill is read in the House of Commons to let all the MPs know the government wants to make a new law.

Second Reading:
Once they have had a chance to think about the bill, then the MPs discuss it. They vote whether to accept the main idea that there should be better pollution controls on cars.

Committee Discussions:
The bill is then discussed by a small group of MPs representing all the parties. They go through the bill line by line and suggest changes. For example, they might change the date when these controls must be added.

Third Reading:
The bill with all the changes made is sent back to the House of Commons for a third reading. The MPs discuss this revised bill. Then they vote whether or not to make it a law.

(on to Part 2 in Lesson 5)

Figure 4.5 Making a law — Part 1 *This is the first part of a diagram showing the steps a bill must go through before it becomes law. In our example, the law involves pollution control on cars.*

THE FACTS

Remembering Facts

1. What is a democracy?
2. Name the 3 main political parties in Canada.
3. Match the name on the left with the correct phrase on the right. For each one, write the letter and the number together in your notebook.

(a) prime minister	(1) heads a government department
(b) minister	(2) all ministers meeting together
(c) Member of Parliament	(3) leader of the political party with the second-largest number of MPs
(d) Cabinet	(4) place of meeting for Members of Parliament
(e) House of Commons	(5) a person who represents the voters in a riding
(f) leader of the Opposition	(6) leader of the political party with the most MPs

Finding Facts

Do you know the names of the following people and parties? Use a newspaper or some other source to help you fill in the names you don't know.

(a) the prime minister
(b) the political party that the prime minister leads
(c) the leader of the Opposition
(d) the political party that the leader of the Opposition leads

YOUR OPINIONS

Stating Opinions

Would you like to be the prime minister of Canada? Write a few sentences to explain why you would or would not.

Discussing Opinions

Television cameras are now set up in the House of Commons so that people all over the country can see what their representatives are doing and saying. At first, many MPs did not want the cameras to be there. Do you think it is a good idea that we can see these debates on television?

If it is possible in your area, watch some of the broadcasts from the House of Commons on television. Discuss your opinions about how the MPs behave and the jobs they are doing.

NEW WORDS

Learning Words

In your notebook, write the title Vocabulary: Lesson 4. Then write down the following words in a list. Using the Glossary or a dictionary, write the meaning beside each word.

When you are finished, write a short note telling what you have learned in this lesson. Try to use all 5 of these words in your note.

bill **democracy** **discuss**
majority **Opposition**

Examining Words

The word *prime* means "first" or "most important". That is why the head of all the ministers is called the *prime* minister. Knowing this, can you explain why the 4 hours of television shows in the evening are called "prime time"?

AN ILLUSTRATION

Your teacher will tell you the name and boundaries of the federal riding your school is in. Draw a sketch map showing the main streets in this riding. Mark where your school is located. If you live in this riding, also mark where your home is located.

Jeanne Sauvé

Figure 4.6 *This photograph of Jeanne Sauvé was taken when she was still Speaker of the House of Commons.*

Claim to fame: Jeanne Sauvé was the first woman Speaker of the House of Commons.

Born: 1922 in Prud'homme, Saskatchewan

Married: 1948 to the Honourable Maurice Sauvé, a businessman, politician and former Liberal cabinet minister. They have 1 son, Jean-François, who followed his mother's first career and became a journalist.

Career: After graduating from university, Jeanne Sauvé wrote articles for newspapers and magazines. She also worked as an interviewer and political commentator on television.

Sauvé decided to enter politics directly instead of just commenting on political issues. In the election in 1972, she won a seat in the House of Commons. That same year she was appointed to the Cabinet, becoming Minister for Science and Technology. Over the next 8 years she held several different Cabinet posts.

Then in 1980, Sauvé was chosen as the first woman Speaker of the House of Commons. She began a program to modernize and streamline the business of Parliament.

In 1984, Sauvé resigned as Speaker of the House of Commons. She did this in order to accept an even more important appointment as Governor General of Canada. As Governor General, she became the first woman to represent the Crown in Canada.

- **Is there still a Minister for Science and Technology today?**
- **Which would you like best — being a politician, or being a journalist who comments on what politicians do?**

The Senate and the Governor General

5

The real work of making the laws for Canada is done in the Cabinet and the House of Commons. However, before a bill can become law it has to go through the Senate. It also has to be signed by the Governor General.

The Senate is a group of 102 politicians. Each of these senators, as they are called, represents the people in a whole province. The prime minister decides who will become senators. The **appointments** are **permanent**. Senators are replaced only if they turn 75, decide to resign, or die.

There are several rules about who can become a senator. The person must be a Canadian citizen who lives in the province he or she will represent. The person must be between the ages of 30 and 75. And the person must own **property** worth at least $4000.

Figure 5.1 The opening of Parliament *By tradition, when the Queen or the Governor General opens Parliament, the ceremony is held in the Senate. In this picture, Queen Elizabeth and Prince Philip are sitting at the front of the Senate chamber. They are looking on as the Speaker asks for the members of the House of Commons to come to the Senate for the ceremonies. What symbols of Canada can you find in this picture?*

Figure 5.2 When women became persons *Prime Minister Mackenzie King is shown here after unveiling a bronze plaque just outside the Senate chamber. In the back row are standing two of the first women senators, the Honourable Senator Fallis and the Honourable Senator Cairine Wilson.*

The plaque is in honour of the 5 Alberta women who fought for the right of women to become senators. You can read more about this struggle in the biography about Emily Murphy at the end of this lesson.

After a bill has been passed by the MPs in the House of Commons, it is sent to the Senate. Then the whole voting process is repeated. The bill has 3 more readings before the senators give their final vote.

By law, the Senate has the power to change or defeat a bill. But this does not happen very often at all. Most Canadians would be angry if a bill was refused. After all, the bill was passed by the people who were elected to represent Canadians. The senators were not voted into office themselves.

Once a bill has been passed by the Senate, it still has to go through 1 more step before it can become law. The bill has to be signed by the Governor General. The person who is Governor General could refuse to sign a bill. But in reality, the Governor General never does this.

The Governor General is the representative of the queen or king of Canada. The prime minister decides who will become Governor General and the **monarch** to make to appointment. The Governor General acts as the head of state. He or she takes part in all the ceremonies that are a necessary part of government.

Because the Senate and the Governor General have very little effect on the laws that are made these days, many Canadians feel we don't need them. In fact, when the Senate held up a money bill for several weeks in 1985, many Canadians said the Senate should be **abolished**. However, there are some good reasons for keeping both the Senate and the office of Governor General.

The first official visit to Canada by a member of the Royal Family was made by George V (then Duke of York) in 1901.

The Senate:
The bill is given 3 readings, just as in the House of Commons. The Senators can send the bill back to the House of Commons for slight changes. But usually the Senate will pass the bill without trouble.

The Governor General:
Once the bill has been passed by the Senate, it goes to the Governor General. When the Governor General signs the bill, it becomes law.

Figure 5.3 Making a law — Part 2 *This is the second part of a diagram showing the steps a bill must take before it becomes law. You can find the first part in Figure 4.5 in Lesson 4.*

It is true that senators don't usually change bills when they go through the Senate. But many senators are older politicians who can give wise advice to MPs.

Senators can also serve as ministers in the Cabinet. This can be important when the government wants to make sure that every province is represented in the Cabinet. Sometimes the government does not have any MPs elected from a certain province. Then the prime minister can ask a senator from that province to be in the Cabinet. That way, the views of the province are not left out.

The Governor General plays an extremely important role. He or she does all the ceremonial things that a head of state has to do in a country. For example, the head of state has to entertain representatives sent by other countries. If there were no Governor General, the prime minister would have to do all these things. And they can take a lot of time. Because there is a Governor General to attend the ceremonies, the prime minister can get on with the job of running the country.

Even more important, the Governor General is neutral. This means that he or she does not take the side of one political party against the other. Therefore the Governor General does not divide Canadians. He or she can help to unite us all.

James Gladstone was Canada's first treaty Indian to become a senator — February 1, 1958.

Figure 5.4 Governor General Vincent Massey *Vincent Massey was the first Canadian-born Governor General. He is shown here with his grand-children in the gardens of Government House. This is the official home of the Governor General in Canada. Which Canadian city do you think this home is in? Why?*

THE FACTS

Remembering Facts

1. What has to happen before a bill passed by the House of Commons can become law?
2. Whom does a senator represent?
3. How does a person become a senator?
4. Whom does the Governor General represent?
5. How does a person become Governor General?

Finding Facts

Besides Vincent Massey (Figure 5.4) and Jeanne Sauvé (Figure 4.6), the following Canadians have served as Governor General.

Georges Vanier
Roland Michener
Jules Léger
Edward Schreyer

Choose one of these Governors General. Then use an encyclopedia or history book to find out the following facts:

(a) when this person was born;
(b) when this person became Governor General;
(c) what province this person came from;
(d) one important thing this person did.

YOUR OPINIONS

Stating Opinions

The Governor General represents the king or quecn of Britain. That means Canada is a kind of monarchy, a country with a king or queen. Some Canadians don't like this tie with Britain. Others feel that it is a good idea.

What are your feelings about the Governor General? Write a few sentences explaining your opinion.

Discussing Opinions

Read through the rules on page 45 for becoming a senator. These days, many millions of Canadians can fit these rules. If you were prime minister, how would you decide who should become a senator? Discuss your ideas with the rest of the class.

NEW WORDS

Learning Words

In your notebook, write the title Vocabulary: Lesson 5. Then write down the following words in a list. Using the Glossary or a dictionary, write the meaning beside each word.

When you are finished, write a short note telling what you have learned in this lesson. Try to use all 5 of these words in your note.

abolish	**appointment**	**monarch**
permanent	**property**	

Examining Words

Some people think it sounds bad to say that a person has died or is dead. They would rather say "passed away" or "passed on." They think these are nicer and kinder words to use. These nicer expressions for bad situations are called *euphemisms*.

Can you think of a euphemism, or nicer way of saying, for each of the following sentences?

1. I have a *bellyache*.
2. Where is the *toilet*?
3. That person is *drunk*.

AN ILLUSTRATION

In the past few lessons, you have been reading about Members of Parliament, the prime minister, senators, the Governor General and so on. Look through old newspapers and magazines to find pictures of real people who have held these jobs. Make a poster using these pictures to show some of the different jobs in government.

Emily Murphy

Figure 5.5 *Emily Murphy presiding over Juvenile Court in Edmonton in 1918.*

Claim to fame: She forced the government to recognize that women were "persons" and therefore could be appointed to the Senate.

Born: 1868 in Cookstown, Ontario

Married: the Reverend Arthur Murphy of Chatham, Ontario. They had 3 daughters: Kathleen, Evelyn, and Doris.

Career: Emily Murphy devoted herself to social work. She also wrote under the pen name of "Janey Canuck". Her books and articles made her famous across Canada.

In 1904 she and her family moved to Alberta, where she campaigned for women's rights, especially for the right to vote. In 1916 she became the first woman ever to be appointed a judge in Canada.

In 1919 Murphy became president of a national women's group. This group asked the government to appoint a woman to the Senate. But the government refused because the BNA Act only talked about "persons" becoming senators. The government said that only men were "persons" — not women!

Murphy and four other women decided to fight back. They took their case to the highest court in Britain before it was settled. In the end it was decided that women were "persons".

Died: Many people were angry that Murphy was never appointed as a senator. Instead, she continued to work in western Canada. She died in Edmonton in 1933.

- **Persons Day is celebrated each year in Canada. Find out when this day is.**
- **Can you think of any reason why the government never appointed Murphy as a senator?**

Our National Capital

6

The government meets in Ottawa, the **capital** city of Canada. Queen Victoria named Ottawa as the capital of Canada East and Canada West in 1857. Ten years later, at Confederation, the leaders decided to keep Ottawa as the capital of the new Dominion.

In 1857, Ottawa was a small town. It was not nearly as well known as Toronto (in Canada West) or Montreal (in Canada East). In many ways this helped make Ottawa the best choice.

Ottawa was not far from either Toronto or Montreal. Ottawa was on a river, so there could be easy transportation. And most important, Ottawa was very far from enemies in the United States. On hearing that Ottawa was to be made the capital, one American said: "Ottawa is safe from attack during a war: no invading army will ever find it."

Today Ottawa is a large city in Ontario, right on the Quebec **border**. Just across the border in Quebec is a city called Hull. Together these 2 cities are called either Ottawa-Hull or the national capital region. If you count all the people of Ottawa and Hull together, they make the fourth-largest city in Canada.

Every year thousands of tourists come to visit Ottawa. The main attraction is Parliament Hill. This is where all the Parliament buildings are. The House of Commons and the Senate meet in these buildings. There are also offices in these buildings for all the MPs and their staffs.

Since the federal government meets in Ottawa, the leaders of Canada have **official** homes there. The prime minister always lives at 24 Sussex Drive. The leader of the Opposition lives in a house called "Stornoway". And the Governor General lives in Rideau Hall (or "Government House", as it is sometimes called).

Figure 6.1 Celebrations on Parliament Hill *This huge fireworks display took place on Parliament Hill on July 1, 1967. What is important about that date?*

The first bridge between Ottawa and Hull was opened on January 17, 1881.

The first meal ever cooked completely by electricity was served at the Windsor Hotel in Ottawa in 1892.

There are also thousands of other government workers who live in the area of Ottawa-Hull. These people are called civil servants. Their job is to make sure that all the laws are understood and obeyed.

Once a law has been signed by the Governor General, it has to be put into effect. The first step in putting a law into effect is to **inform** the people who will be affected by it. For example, a law about changes in meat processing would have to go to all farmers, meat packaging plants, supermarket butchers, delicatessens, restaurants, health inspectors, and anyone else who is involved.

(6.2.a.) *24 Sussex Drive, home of the prime minister*

(6.2.b.) *Stornoway, home of the leader of the Opposition*

Figure 6.2 The official residences in Ottawa *Which of these official homes do you think you would like to live in? Explain your reasons.*

(6.2.c.) *Rideau Hall, home of the Governor General*

Therefore, the federal government has civil servants whose job is to let everyone know about new laws. Free pamphlets are printed to explain changes. Ads are placed in newspapers and magazines. Commercials are aired on radio and television. In this way, as many people as possible find out about the changes.

New laws also have to be **enforced**. That is, somebody has to make sure that the laws are obeyed. When you think of law enforcement, you probably think first of the police. But the police play only a small part in law enforcement. Thousands of civil servants such as building inspectors, tax collectors, and immigration officers also enforce the laws each day.

Most of these federal civil servants are bilingual. This means that they can speak both English and French. Bilingual civil servants are important because Canada has 2 official languages: English and French. If you visit Ottawa, you will also find bilingual street signs and stores with bilingual signs. Because of this, more Canadians can feel comfortable in their national capital. Ottawa truly represents both the English and the French parts of Canada.

Figure 6.3 An Ottawa street sign *One street in Ottawa was named after Paul Anka, a popular Canadian singer. Notice that the signs are bilingual. What do you think the abbreviations CH. and PROM. stand for in French?*

THE FACTS

Remembering Facts

1. Name 1 reason why Ottawa was chosen as the capital of Canada.
2. Which level of government meets in Ottawa?
3. What kind of worker is a civil servant?
4. What 2 important jobs do civil servants have?
5. Why are many civil servants in Ottawa bilingual?

Finding Facts

If you put Ottawa and Hull together, they make the fourth-largest city in Canada. Can you guess which cities are first, second, and third? Use an atlas or encyclopedia to check whether you are right.

YOUR OPINIONS

Stating Opinions

Many countries in the world have only 1 official language. On the other hand, some countries have 2 or more official languages. For example, Belgium has 2 official languages. Switzerland has 4.

Do you think it is a good thing that Canada has 2 official languages? Write a few sentences to explain your opinion.

Discussing Opinions

Imagine that Ottawa suddenly disappeared and Canada had to find a new capital. Which city in Canada do you think would make the best capital? Why do you think so?

NEW WORDS

Learning Words

In your notebook, write the title Vocabulary: Lesson 6. Then write down the following words in a list. Using the Glossary or a dictionary, write the meaning beside each word.

When you are finished, write a short note telling what you have learned in this lesson. Try to use all 5 of these words in your note.

border	**capital**	**enforce**
inform	**official**	

Examining Words

We use the word *capital* in several expressions besides *capital city*. For example, we also talk about *capital letters* and *capital punishment*. Explain the meaning of these 2 expressions. Show how the word *capital* fits in each case.

AN ILLUSTRATION

Table 6.1 shows the distances by road between Montreal, Ottawa-Hull, and Toronto. Look carefully at this table. Then use it to answer the following questions.

1. How far is it from Montreal to Ottawa-Hull?
2. How far is it from Ottawa-Hull to Toronto?
3. How far is it from Montreal to Toronto?
4. Which 2 cities in Table 6.1 are farthest apart?
5. Which 2 cities in Table 6.1 are closest together?

	MONTREAL	OTTAWA-HULL	TORONTO
Montreal	—	190 km	539 km
Ottawa-Hull	190 km	—	399 km
Toronto	539 km	399 km	—

Table 6.1 *Distances between 3 major Canadian cities*

Colonel John By

Figure 6.4 *This drawing shows Colonel By in uniform on the right as he supervises the construction of the Rideau Canal.*

Claim to fame: Colonel By founded the city of Ottawa.

Born: 1779 in London, England

Career: Colonel By joined the Royal Engineers, a regiment in the British Army. He was sent to Canada twice. The first time was from 1802 to 1811. During that time he worked on the fort and other defences at Quebec.

Colonel By was sent to Canada again from 1826 to 1832. His job was to direct the building of the Rideau Canal. This canal was supposed to give Canadian soldiers another way of travelling from Montreal to Lake Ontario in case the Americans attacked. Luckily, the canal never had to be used for defence.

Colonel By built his headquarters in 1826 at the spot where the Ottawa River and the Rideau River meet. A village soon grew up around the headquarters. In 1827 it was named Bytown in his honor. The town's name was changed to Ottawa in 1855 when it had reached a size of 10 000 people. But his name can still be found on maps of the Ottawa-Hull region.

Died: in 1836 back home in England.

- **Find out how a town, street, school or other place in your area got its name.**
- **Which people living today do you think will have places named after them some day?**

7 The Provincial Governments

According to the constitution, each province has its own duties and powers. This means that each province has to have its own government. Although there are some differences, the system of government in each province is very much like the federal system you have just been learning about.

The governments for the provinces are known by several names. These governments can be called the provincial **legislature**, the legislative assembly, or the provincial parliament. In Quebec, the provincial government is called the National **Assembly**. But whatever name they have, these provincial governments all serve the same purpose as the House of Commons in the federal system.

The people in each province are divided into groups, or ridings. These are usually not the same ridings as the ones for the federal elections that you read about in Lesson 4. But they work in the same way. The voters in each riding elect a person to represent them in the provincial legislature. These representatives can be called either Members of Provincial Parliament (MPPs, for short) or Members of the Legislative Assembly (MLAs, for short).

Just as in the federal government, most of the MPPs or MLAs belong to a political party. Members of the Liberal Party, the New Democratic Party, or the Progressive Conservative Party can be found in most provinces. But there are also other parties, such as the Social Credit Party and the Parti Québécois.

The party with the most people elected to the provincial legislature forms the government of the province. The leader of this party becomes the head of the government, or the **premier**.

The only private residence in Canada surrounded by a moat belongs to the Lieutenant-Governor of Newfoundland.

The premier chooses people to lead the various government departments. Just as with the federal government, these people are called ministers.

When the premier and ministers meet together, the group is also called the Cabinet. These people have the same sort of job as the members of the Cabinet for the federal government. Members of the provincial Cabinet are supposed to suggest new laws, or bills. These bills are presented to the provincial legislature.

The members discuss each bill thoroughly. Just as in the House of Commons in Ottawa, the bill has 3 readings before it can finally be passed. But at this point there is a big difference from the federal system. The provinces do not have anything like the Senate. Instead of going to the Senate, a bill that has been passed in the provincial legislature goes straight to the Lieutenant-Governor.

The CPR telegraph cable stretching from the Atlantic to the Pacific, was completed in 1885.

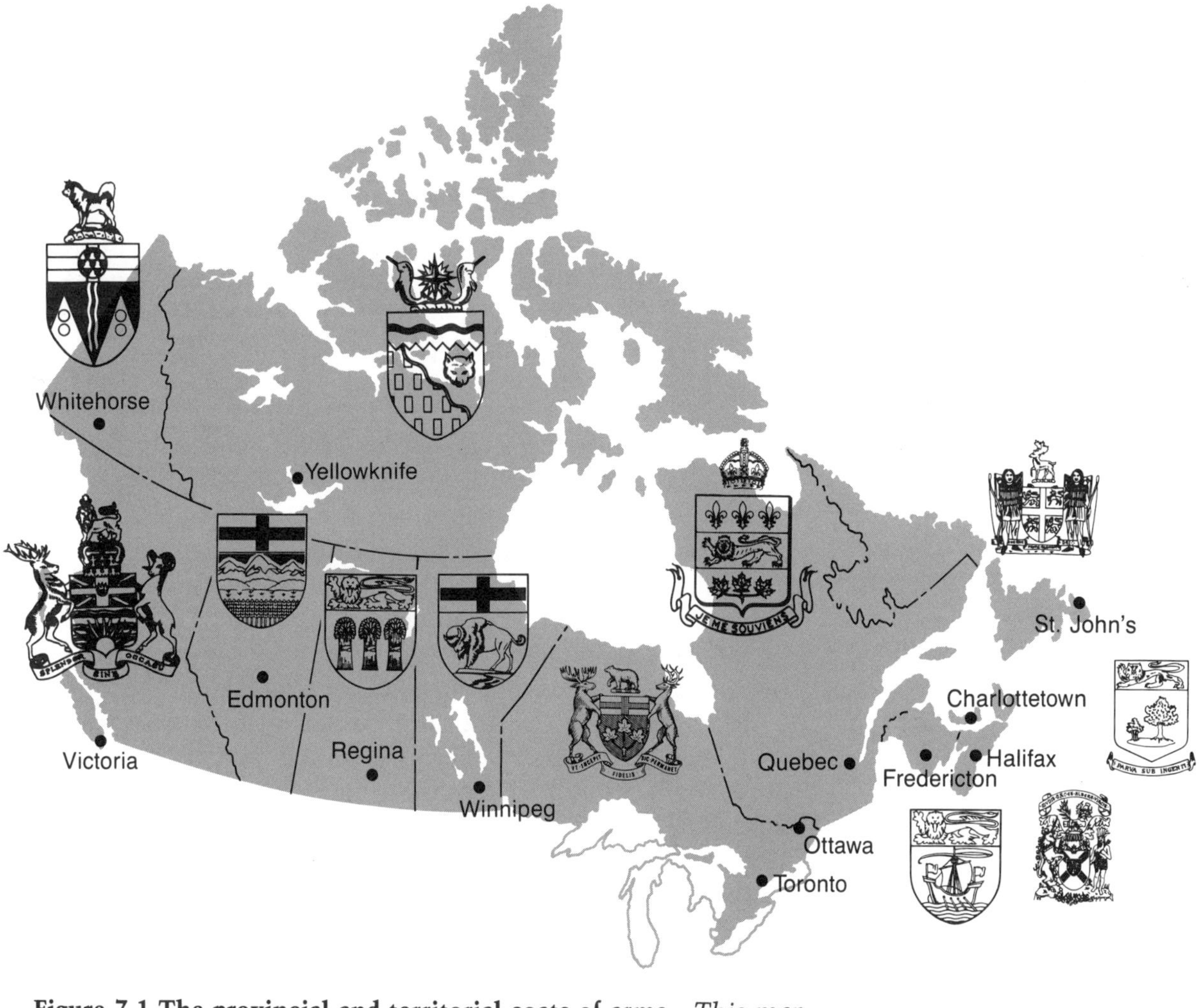

Figure 7.1 The provincial and territorial coats of arms *This map shows the coats of arms of all the provinces and territories. Look carefully at these symbols. What do these symbols tell you about each province or territory?*

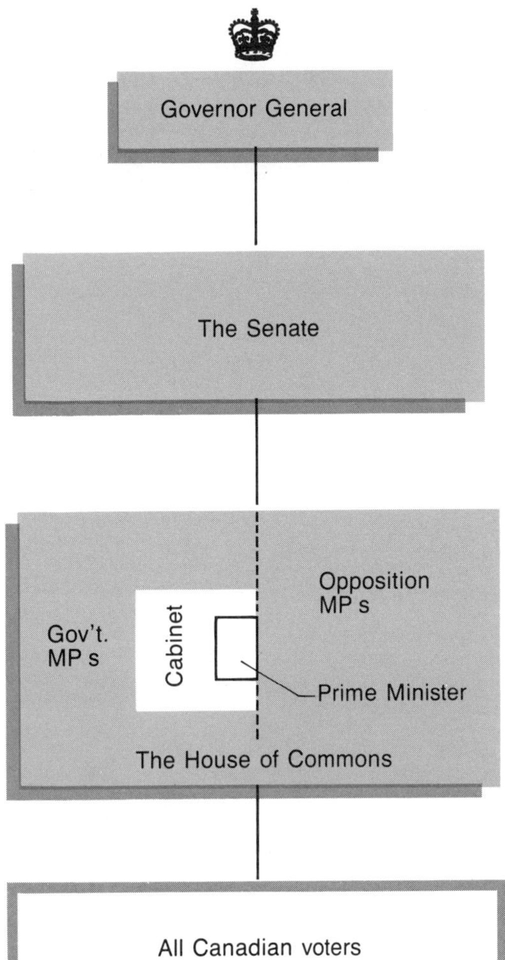

Figure 7.2 *Comparing the federal and provincial systems of government*

Like the Governor General, the Lieutenant-Governor is a representative of the British king or queen. But the Lieutenant-Governor represents the British monarch only in his or her province. The premier of the province chooses who will be Lieutenant-Governor. The announcement is always made by the prime minister of Canada.

The Lieutenant-Governor does exactly the same sorts of things as the Governor General does. This means that the Lieutenant-Governor signs bills to make them law. The Lieutenant-Governor also acts as **host** to leaders of other countries when they visit the province.

All in all, the provinces run in almost exactly the same way as the federal government. They just have different duties and powers.

There is one form of government in Canada which is quite different from the federal and the provincial forms of government. This is the government for the Yukon **Territory** and the Northwest Territories.

In 1955 Cape Breton was connected to the Nova Scotia mainland by the Canso Causeway — 2133.6 m long.

Figure 7.3 The provincial and territorial governments have many different concerns.

(7.3.a.) *The British Columbia government is trying to protect the logging industry.*

(7.3.b.) *Auto-makers in Ontario are worried about the number of foreign cars being sold in Canada.*

(7.3.c.) *Wheat farmers in Saskatchewan have always been concerned with the Crow Rate — the amount of money they have to pay to send their wheat to the East.*

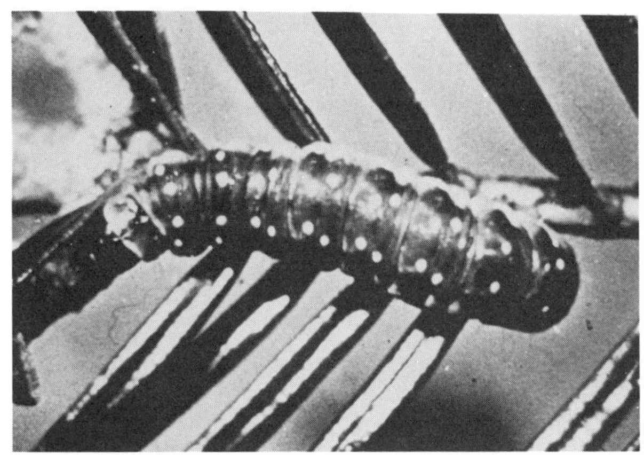

(7.3.d.) *In New Brunswick, the spruce budworm has been destroying the province's forests.*

(7.3.e.) *The Newfoundland government is concerned with off-shore oil resources.*

(7.3.f.) *Transportation has always been an important issue in Yukon and Northwest Territories.*

Before 1922, people in British Columbia drove on the left-hand side of the road.

The Yukon and the Northwest Territories are the lands which lie in the far North of Canada. These lands do not have the same powers as the 10 provinces. Instead, many of their laws are made for them and controlled by the federal government in Ottawa.

But the map of Canada has been changing ever since Confederation. It is quite possible that within a few years these territories could be changed to provinces. And then they would be governed by a system like the one used by the provinces.

THE FACTS

Remembering Facts

1. Match the provincial item on the left with the correct federal item on the right. For each one, write the letter and the number together in your notebook.

(a) premier	(1) House of Commons
(b) legislative assembly	(2) Governor General
(c) Lieutenant-Governor	(3) prime minister

2. What is the biggest single difference between the federal system of government and the provincial system of government?
3. Name two of the duties or powers of the provincial governments. If you have trouble remembering, look back at Lesson 3 to refresh your memory.

Finding Facts

Look in newspapers or other reference materials to find the answers to the following questions.

1. Are representatives for the legislature in your province called MPPs or MLAs?
2. What city is the capital of your province?
3. Who is the premier of your province?
4. What political party does your premier belong to?
5. Who is the Lieutenant-Governor of your province?

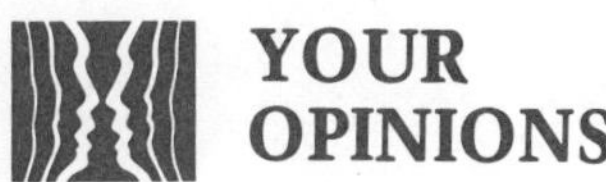

YOUR OPINIONS

Stating Opinions

Think about what you have heard about the Yukon and the Northwest Territories. Would you like to live in the North for a while? Write a few sentences to explain your opinion.

Discussing Opinions

The Governors General and Lieutenant-Governors in Canada all represent the British monarch. For over half the time since Confederation, the British monarch has been a woman. Queen Victoria had already been queen for 30 years when Canada became a country. And she reigned until she died in 1901. Queen Elizabeth II became queen in 1952.

Yet there was no woman Lieutenant-Governor in Canada until 1974. And the first woman Governor General was not appointed until 1984. Discuss why you think it took so long for women to be appointed to these positions. What is your opinion about this?

NEW WORDS

Learning Words

In your notebook, write the title Vocabulary: Lesson 7. Then write down the following words in a list. Using the Glossary or a dictionary, write the meaning beside each word.

When you are finished, write a short note telling what you have learned in this lesson. Try to use all 5 of these words in your note.

assembly	**host**	**legislature**
premier	**territory**	

Examining Words

Some people pronounce the word *lieutenant* like /*lef tenant*/. Other people pronounce it like /*loo tenant*/. Make a survey of 5 people in your community. How do *they* pronounce the words in Table 7.1? Share your results with the class.

lieutenant	/*lef tenant*/	/*loo tenant*/
either	/*ee ther*/	/*eye ther*/
clerk	/*clirk*/	/*clark*/
route	/*root*/	/*rout*/
tomato	/*to mah to*/	/*to may to*/

Table 7.1 *Everyday words that can be said in more than one way*

AN ILLUSTRATION

Most newspapers have something called an *editorial cartoon*. Many of these cartoons poke fun at politicians. Find and cut out an editorial cartoon that pokes fun at a politician in your province. Paste this cartoon in your notebook. Beneath it, write a short explanation of what the cartoon is about.

Pauline McGibbon

Figure 7.4 *Pauline McGibbon was an extremely popular Lieutenant-Governor who enjoyed meeting people from across the province and the country.*

Claim to fame: She was the first woman Lieutenant-Governor.

Born: 1910 in Sarnia, Ontario

Married: 1935 to Donald McGibbon. They have no children.

Career: Pauline McGibbon has made a career of being the "first woman". In fact, she has been the "first woman" in more than a dozen important jobs.

She has worked for business and was the first woman director of IBM Canada. She has worked for the arts and was the first woman chairman of the Board of Trustees for the National Arts Centre in Ottawa. She has worked for education and was the first woman chancellor of the University of Toronto.

McGibbon's most important role, however, was as the first woman representative of the British monarch in Canada. McGibbon was appointed in 1974 as Lieutenant-Governor of Ontario. She served in this office until 1980.

- **How many female Lieutenant-Governors have there been in your province?**
- **How do you think it would feel to always be first?**

Municipal Government 8

How often do you drink a glass of water? It was probably your **municipal** government that treated it and piped it to your home. How often do you use traffic lights? It was probably your municipal government that put them in. How often do you throw something in the garbage? It is probably your municipal government that will get rid of it for you.

A municipal government is a system of government for a very small area. There is only 1 federal government. And there are just 10 provincial governments. But there are hundreds of municipal governments across Canada.

The reason is that the federal and provincial governments are too big and usually too far away to take care of services such as water and sewage, local transportation, and garbage collection. That is why our constitution says that the provincial governments can set up smaller municipal governments.

There are 2 basic systems of municipal government. One system is used for most **urban** areas. That means it is used for people living in towns and cities. The other system is used for **rural** areas. That means it is used for people living outside of towns and cities.

Urban areas are usually run by a group of politicians known as the city council. This council is led by a mayor. During elections, all the voters in the city get a chance to choose who will be mayor.

The other members of the council are called aldermen. These aldermen represent different sections of the city called wards. During elections, the voters in each ward get a chance to choose who will be their aldermen.

The municipal governments for rural areas are organized in a slightly different way. This is because in rural areas people are scattered over many square kilometres of land.

In order to set up rural municipal government, every province has been divided into small areas of land called townships. Instead of having city councils, there are township councils to take care of the people's everyday needs.

Figure 8.1 Charlotte Whitton *Charlotte Whitton was one of Canada's best known mayors. She was the popular but controversial mayor of Ottawa from 1951 to 1972. In this picture she is wearing the chain of office. This custom goes back to very old times. Does the leader of your municipality wear a chain of office?*

Via Rail began when the government took over the Grand Trunk Railway in 1923.

Township councils are usually led by a person called a reeve. This is like the mayor of a city or town. Other people called township councillors help the reeve to govern the township. They are like the aldermen in city governments.

Townships are usually very small and not many people live there. As a result, it is difficult for the people in each single township to afford expensive items like snowplows. For this reason, several townships are often grouped together.

Each group of townships is usually called a county. All the reeves in the county meet together to discuss local concerns like repairing roads or running a library. Most of the time, they will choose 1 reeve to lead them. This person is called the warden.

The urban and rural systems outlined here are the most simple forms of municipal government. In reality, there are many other systems as well. You may, for example, have heard of regional governments. You may also have heard of metropolitan governments.

No matter how these various municipal governments are organized, they all have similar duties and powers. They make decisions about such things as street parking, traffic lights, snow and garbage removal, and road repairs. The municipal governments also decide about the location of public parks, arenas, and libraries. In addition, they make by-laws to **regulate** firefighters, police officers, and local businesses.

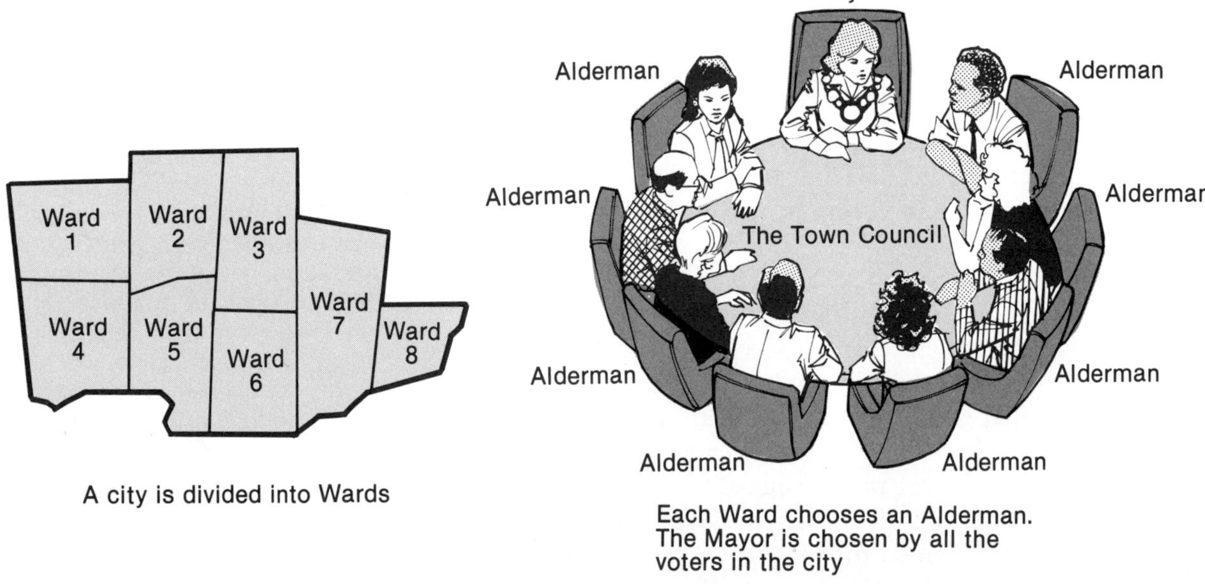

Figure 8.2 *A common system for urban municipal government.*

One of the most important services of any municipal government is education. In fact, education is so important that voters also vote for special school **trustees** during municipal elections.

The job of these trustees is to form the board of education to look after the school system in the area. This board makes decisions about schools, books, school buses, teachers' salaries, and so on. It also decides how much money the people who live in the area should pay in property tax in order to support the school system.

For it is a fact that education costs much more than any other municipal service. And all the muni' pal services taken together cost a great deal. The money has to come from somewhere. That means that people must pay taxes. There is more about taxes in Lesson 9.

The fishing schooner, *Bluenose*, was launched at Lunenberg, Nova Scotia, on March 26, 1921. A picture of the *Bluenose* is on our dime.

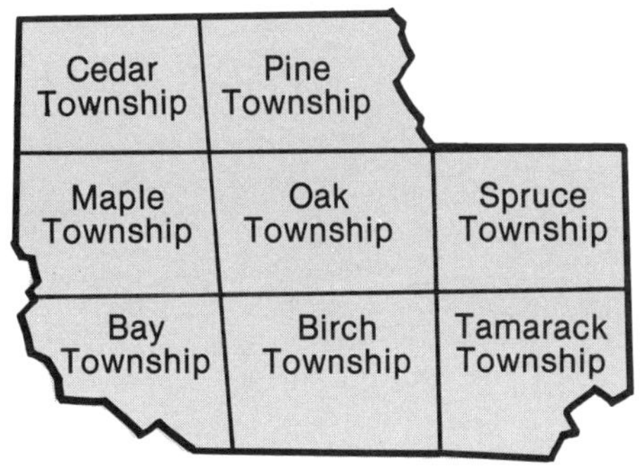

A County is divided into Townships

Each Township has a Council made up of a Reeve and Township Councillors

The County Council is made up of the Reeves. One of them is chosen to be Warden.

Figure 8.3 *A common system for rural municipal government.*

(8.4.a.) *(above) Municipal workers building a sewer in Toronto, 1912*

(8.4.b.) *The first steam fire engine for St. John's, 1885*

Figure 8.4 *Municipal governments have always had the same types of duties and powers. Which duties and powers are shown in these historical photographs?*

(8.4.c.) *An early streetcar*

THE FACTS

Remembering Facts

1. Why do we need municipal governments?
2. Match the rural title on the left with the urban title on the right. For each one, write the letter and the number together in your notebook.

(a) reeve	(1) city
(b) township councillor	(2) mayor
(c) township	(3) alderman

3. Name 4 services most municipal governments provide.
4. What job do school trustees have?
5. Which municipal service costs the most money?

Finding Facts

Find the telephone listings for your municipal government in the telephone directory. How many departments are there?

Your class should invite a municipal politician from your area to come and speak about how your municipal government is organized. Don't forget to write a note thanking the politician for spending time with your class.

YOUR OPINIONS

Stating Opinions

Would you rather live in the city or in the country? Write a few sentences to explain your opinion.

Discussing Opinions

There are examples of municipal services all around your neighbourhood. Name as many of these as you can. Then discuss whether you think your municipal government is doing a good job or not.

NEW WORDS

Learning Words

In your notebook, write the title Vocabulary: Lesson 8. Then write down the following words in a list. Using the Glossary or a dictionary, write the meaning beside each word.

When you are finished, write a short note telling what you have learned in this lesson. Try to use all 5 of these words in your note.

municipal **regulate** **rural**
trustee **urban**

Examining Words

You may have noticed when you read this lesson that the laws made by municipal governments are called *by-laws*. Can you think of any other words that begin with *by*?

AN ILLUSTRATION

Look closely at the drawings in Figures 8.2 and 8.3. Then make a similar drawing that shows how the municipal government in *your* area is set up.

William Peyton Hubbard

Figure 8.5 *William Hubbard*

Claim to fame: He was a prominent Black politician in Toronto.

Born: 1842 in Toronto, Ontario, the son of a Black refugee from the United States

Married: 1874 to Julia Luckett, a former teacher from Washington, D.C. Their son, Fred, became an authority on street railways, and worked for the city from 1930 to 1939.

Career: When he was a young man, Hubbard drove horse-drawn cabs for his uncle's company. One day he saved a passenger from falling into the Don River near Toronto. The passenger was George Brown, the famous publisher of the *Globe* newspaper, who later encouraged Hubbard to go into municipal politics.

In 1894, Hubbard was first elected as alderman. He later said he was successful because he ran as a Canadian who was an expert in real estate rather than as a Black in politics.

Hubbard spent the next 19 years in city politics. In that time, he gained a reputation as a gifted speaker, earning the nickname "Cicero of Council". His greatest success was in helping set up Toronto's publicly owned hydro-electric system.

From 1904 to 1907, Hubbard was the second most powerful politician in the city next to the mayor, for whom he often acted. When Hubbard retired in 1913, he was honoured with a gala ceremony at city hall.

Died: Hubbard died in the spring of 1935 at the age of 93.

- **Who was Cicero? What would it mean to call someone a Cicero?**
- **Blacks represent about 6% of Canada's population. Do you think there should be more Black politicians in our governments?**

Paying for Government Services

9

Until now, you have been reading about the duties and powers of the 3 levels of government: federal, provincial, and municipal. All of these duties and powers cost a lot of money to carry out.

The way governments raise money is by charging **taxes**. Everyone pays taxes. A young child buying a chocolate bar pays tax. A teenager putting gasoline in the car pays tax. An adult who earns a living pays tax.

The best-known tax is **income** tax. This is a tax on the income, or money, each person earns in Canada. Income tax is **collected** by both the federal and the provincial governments.

Every time an individual earns a paycheque, money is taken away and sent to the government. At the end of the year, everyone who has earned money sends in a form called an income tax return. Those people who have paid too much money during the year will be sent a refund. Those people who have not paid enough money have to give the government more.

Another common tax is the sales tax. This is often collected by provincial governments. Buyers must pay an extra percentage whenever they purchase something in a store. For example, you might live in a province that has an 8% sales tax. If you want to buy a pen that costs $1 you will have to pay 8% more. This means that the storekeeper will charge you $1.08. The 8 extra cents will then be sent to the government.

The federal government also charges sales tax on many things you buy. But this tax is hidden in the price of the products. For example, one reason that a diamond ring costs as much as it does is that the jeweller had to pay a federal sales tax on the cost of the diamond.

Figure 9.1 Multi-millionaire lottery winners *These people are Lillian and Stuart Kelly, who went into hiding after they won nearly $14 million in a 1984 Lotto 6-49 draw. Many people have criticized the government for running lotteries. They say that lotteries are just another form of taxation that hurts the poor.*

According to Revenue Canada, 8000 people who earned more than $150 000 in 1981 paid absolutely no income tax.

A municipal government earns most of its money from property taxes. The government decides how much tax must be paid by every person or company who owns land in the municipal area. This is called **assessing** property.

The amount of the tax that is assessed is based on a number of things, such as the size and location of the property. The owner of an apartment building will usually be asked to pay more property tax than the owner of a house. A factory owner will usually have to pay more property tax than the owner of a small store.

Income tax, sales tax, and property tax are the 3 most obvious forms of taxation. But governments have many other ways of raising money. A good example of this is the way that most oil from Alberta was taxed in 1984. Some of this oil was used to make gasoline for cars. On its way from the oil field to the gas tank, the oil was taxed 8 times.

Figure 9.2 Vancouver artist Tony Onley *In 1983, Tony Onley threatened to burn his paintings because Revenue Canada was taxing him unfairly. The publicity around his case led to changes in the way artists are taxed in Canada. What can ordinary taxpayers do if they feel they are being taxed unfairly?*

First, the owners of the oil well had to pay federal *and* provincial income tax on the profit from selling the barrel of oil. Then they had to pay a share of the money to the province because the constitution gives the provinces control of natural resources such as oil.

The people who bought the oil in order to turn it into gasoline had to pay a special federal charge for Canadian ownership *and* something called a federal compensation charge. Once the gasoline was produced, a federal excise tax was added, then a federal sales tax, then a provincial road tax.

All of these taxes can be very confusing. But it isn't important for you to know all the specific ways governments earn money from the oil that is turned into gasoline. You *should* know, however, that every time you buy something, whether gasoline or some other product, you always pay hidden taxes. And very often, you are paying taxes on taxes!

These taxes are high. One reason is that Canadians demand a lot of services from their governments. We all take it for granted that we have an army and a police force to defend us. We all take it for granted that our children will go to school. We believe that we should be able to drive on well-paved roads. We believe that we should get a pension when we retire. Very few other people in the world can expect to have these services automatically.

Most people complain about taxes. But in the end, everybody **benefits** from the government services that the taxes pay for. It has been said many times that taxes are the price we pay for civilization.

Income tax was introduced in 1917 as a *temporary* measure, but no Canadian government has ever tried to abolish it.

Figure 9.3 Canada Customs
Here a Canada Customs officer checks the papers of a truck driver crossing the Canada-United States border. Taxes, or duty, must be paid on items coming into Canada from foreign countries. But Canadians travelling outside the country are allowed to bring back a certain amount of goods without paying duty. Find out how much this amount is.

THE FACTS

Remembering Facts

1. Why do governments collect taxes?
2. What is income tax?
3. What is sales tax?
4. What is the biggest source of money for municipal governments?
5. Why do Canadians pay such high taxes?

Finding Facts

When you fill out an income tax return, the government asks you first to write down all the money you have earned. The more you earn, the more tax you must pay.

But you do not have to pay tax on your whole income. The government lets you deduct, or take away, certain items from the total amount of money you earned. This means that your taxes will be lower. For example, if you are a student in college or university you can deduct the fees you have to pay. You do not have to pay taxes on this money.

Find out about 4 other items that people can deduct from their income tax. You can telephone the local branch of the tax office or look at old income tax forms in order to find this information.

YOUR OPINIONS

Stating Opinions

Whenever a government raises taxes, you can be sure that it will raise the taxes on alcohol and tobacco. Some people say that this is only fair because alcohol and tobacco cause all kinds of problems that governments have to pay for (such as car accidents and sickness).

Other people think that the government is unfair for charging such high taxes. They say alcohol and tobacco are the main sources of entertainment for many people.

What do *you* think? Should the government charge such high taxes on alcohol and tobacco? Write a few sentences to explain your opinion.

Discussing Opinions

In Canada, we pay *graduated* income tax. This means that the higher a person's salary is, the more he or she is taxed. As an example, a single person who earns $25 000 a year will pay about 20% in income taxes. But a single person who earns $50 000 a year will pay about 30% in income taxes.

Discuss what you think of the graduated income tax system. Why do you think the federal government decided to use it? Do you think it is fair?

NEW WORDS

Learning Words

In your notebook, write the title Vocabulary: Lesson 9. Then write down the following words in a list. Using the Glossary or a dictionary, write the meaning beside each word.

When you are finished, write a short note telling what you have learned in this lesson. Try to use all 5 of these words in your note.

assess **benefit** **collect**
income **tax**

Examining Words

Someone who *assesses*, or decides on, the taxes a person will have to pay is called an assess*or*. Someone who sits on the town or county council is called a councill*or*. Someone who practices law is called a lawy*er*.

Write in your notebook what each of the following people is called:

(a) someone who acts,
(b) someone who writes,
(c) someone who is appointed to the Senate,
(d) someone who paints,
(e) someone who votes.

AN ILLUSTRATION

Figure 9.4 shows how the property tax money was spent for 1 year in an imaginary town. This type of figure is often called a pie chart. The "pie" is divided into several pieces to show you how each tax dollar was spent. For example, 12.4¢ of every $1 went to the police force.

Study Figure 9.4 carefully. Answer the questions asked.

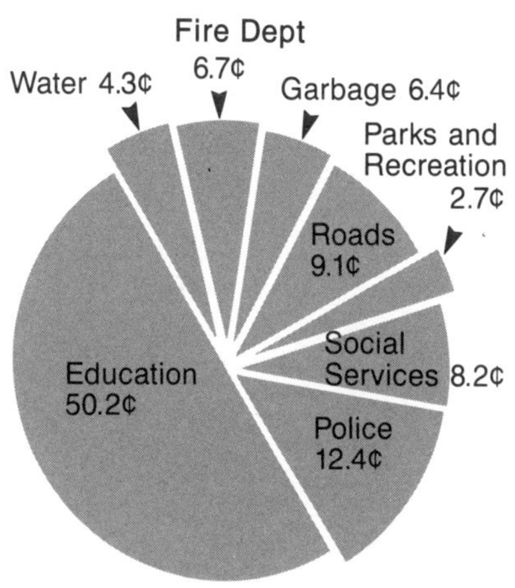

Figure 9.4 The budget of an imaginary small town

1. Which service costs the most money?

2. Which service gets the smallest "piece of the pie"?

Monique Bégin

Figure 9.5 *Monique Bégin is standing at the far left in this picture of the 5 women MPs elected to the 1974 Parliament. Standing beside Bégin, from left to right, are Flora MacDonald, Albanie Morin, Grace MacInnis, and Jeanne Sauvé.*

Claim to fame: She was the federal Cabinet minister who fought with the provinces about how they should spend their tax dollars.

Born: 1936 in Rome, Italy

Career: Monique Bégin began her public life by working in the women's movement. In 1965, she helped start an important women's group in Quebec. Two years later, she was asked to work for the Royal Commission on the Status of Women in Canada.

In 1972, Bégin ran for election as a Liberal MP. She won the seat, and thus became one of the first women from Quebec to be elected to Ottawa. In 1976, she was promoted to the Cabinet as Minister of National Revenue. In 1977, she became Minister of Health. In that same year, she earned a Ph.D. from St. Thomas University in New Brunswick.

In 1983 while she was still Minister of Health, Bégin decided to ban extra billing for doctors' and hospital services. Many of the provinces disagreed with her strongly, but she refused to give in.

When John Turner took over as prime minister from Pierre Trudeau in 1984, he wanted Bégin to stay on as Minister of Health. However, she decided not to run again in the 1984 election. Instead, she left politics to become a university professor.

- **What is a Ph.D.? What do you have to do in order to get a Ph.D.?**
- **Do you think that doctors should be paid only what the government allows? Or do you think they should be allowed to charge extra?**

QUIZ 1

The following questions are based on the lessons in Chapter 1. **DO NOT WRITE YOUR ANSWERS IN THIS TEXTBOOK.** Instead, you should write the answers in your notebook or on a separate sheet of paper.

1. There are 8 blanks in the following paragraphs about Canada. They have been labelled from (a) to (h). Write down the 8 answers in a list on your paper. Then beside each answer write the letter of the blank where it belongs.

Canada Act	July 1, 1867
Ottawa	Elizabeth II
1982	BNA Act
Confederation	John A. Macdonald

In 1864, leaders of the colonies in British North America met at Charlottetown. They wanted to discuss joining together as a single country. Britain agreed to this plan, and on (a) _____ 4 colonies officially joined together to form the country of Canada.

The action of joining together was called (b) _____. It was made legal by an act passed by the British Parliament called the (c) _____. (d) _____ was the first prime minister of the new country. Its capital was (e) _____.

For over 100 years, Canada could only change its constitution by going to the British Parliament. Finally, in (f) _____, this embarrassing situation was ended. (g) _____ came to Canada from Britain to proclaim the (h) _____. Canadians now had complete control over their constitution.

2. Match the item in the list on the left side with the correct item from the list on the right side. For each one, write the letter and the number together on your paper.

(a) sales tax	(1)	money paid to the government based on how much you've earned
(b) property tax	(2)	money paid to the government based on how much something you buy costs
(c) income tax	(3)	money paid to the government based on the value of the land you own

3. Match the item in the list on the left side with the correct item from the list on the right side. For each one, write the letter and the number together on your paper.

(a) prime minister	(1) place of meeting for all members of Parliament
(b) leader of the Opposition	(2) leader of the political party with most members elected to the House of Commons
(c) minister	(3) representative of the British king or queen in Canada
(d) Cabinet	(4) all ministers and the prime minister meeting together
(e) House of Commons	(5) a person who has been *appointed* to discuss and vote on laws
(f) senator	(6) head of a government department
(g) Governor General	(7) leader of the party with the second-largest number of members in the House of Commons

4. Find the correct answer from the list given after each statement. Then write the whole statement on your paper.

(a) The leader of a provincial government is called the _____.
Cabinet
premier
Provincial Assembly
minister

(b) The Cabinet is a meeting of the premier with _____.
the queen
the premiers of other provinces
ministers
news reporters

(c) The king or queen of Britain is represented in the provincial government by _____.
the Governor General
no one
the premier
the Lieutenant-Governor

5. Write the letters from (a) to (e) on your paper. Then write a T if the statement is TRUE. Write an F if the statement is FALSE.

(a) Municipal governments look after local services like garbage removal and fire protection.
(b) Mayors are usually elected by the people in a single ward.
(c) A reeve represents all the people in the township.
(d) Laws passed by municipal governments are called by-laws.
(e) A ward is the section of a city that elects a warden.

CHAPTER TWO

Electing a Government

In Chapter 1, you learned about our 3 systems of government. You learned about how they were set up and what duties and powers they have. In this chapter, you will learn about how we elect our governments. You will read about how we choose the people to represent and lead us.

You can learn a lot about elections just by reading these lessons. But you will learn even more if you actually run an election in your class. This election could be a real one: you could elect a class president or other officer. Or the election could be role playing: you could pretend to be running a federal election campaign.

10 The Voters

Sometimes people complain about the government's power. But the government didn't get power on its own. It was given that power by the voters.

The right to vote is the most important right in a democracy. It means that the people can choose who will make laws for them. And it means that the people can take that power away. They can give the power to someone else if they want to.

These days almost every Canadian citizen over the age of 18 can vote in federal elections. But it wasn't always this way.

In the early days of Canadian history, only men who owned a piece of land or who earned $300 a year could vote. Men didn't worry too much about this rule. Most of them had these **qualifications**, so most men could vote.

However, women were not allowed to vote at all. Many people believed that "nice" women didn't want to vote.

Figure 10.1 *Many people believed that when women were given the vote they would simply vote the way their fathers or husbands did. This is not true for the husband and wife pictured in this cartoon. When you are able to vote, do you think you will be influenced by the way other members of your family vote?*

They thought women should stay at home, raise children, and **ignore** the outside world. They felt that women couldn't understand politics and government.

About the time of Confederation, women in Britain and Canada began to **demand** the right to vote. The right to vote is called **suffrage**. So these women called themselves suffragists.

The suffragists in Britain did many dangerous things to let people know they wanted the vote. They threw acid in mailboxes. They tied themselves to lamp-posts. They jumped in front of race-horses.

The suffragists in Canada wanted the vote just as badly. But they used **legal** methods. They gave public speeches. They asked people to sign petitions. They held meetings with politicians.

Their first victory was in Manitoba. The Manitoba Liberal Party agreed that women should be allowed to vote. In the provincial election in 1915, the Liberals won. And in 1916, women were given the right to vote in Manitoba elections.

Very soon, the rest of the country followed Manitoba's example. In 1918, women won the right to vote in federal elections. And by 1922, they had won the right to vote in elections in every province but Quebec.

Once they had won the right to vote, women also were allowed to run for office. In 1921 Agnes Macphail became the first woman elected to the House of Commons. In 1957, Ellen Fairclough became the first woman member of the federal Cabinet.

Jeannie Snowball, an Inuk from Kujuuak Quebec, made the first Ookpik. This Arctic owl is the symbol of the Canadian North.

Figure 10.2 A juvenile temperance parade in 1909 *Most of the early suffragists were also part of the temperance movement. In other words, they wanted to ban alcohol. They felt that there was a strong link between drinking alcohol, child abuse, and wife beating. In this picture, the women and children are protesting against the sale of alcohol. Do you think that alcohol, child abuse, and wife beating are problems today?*

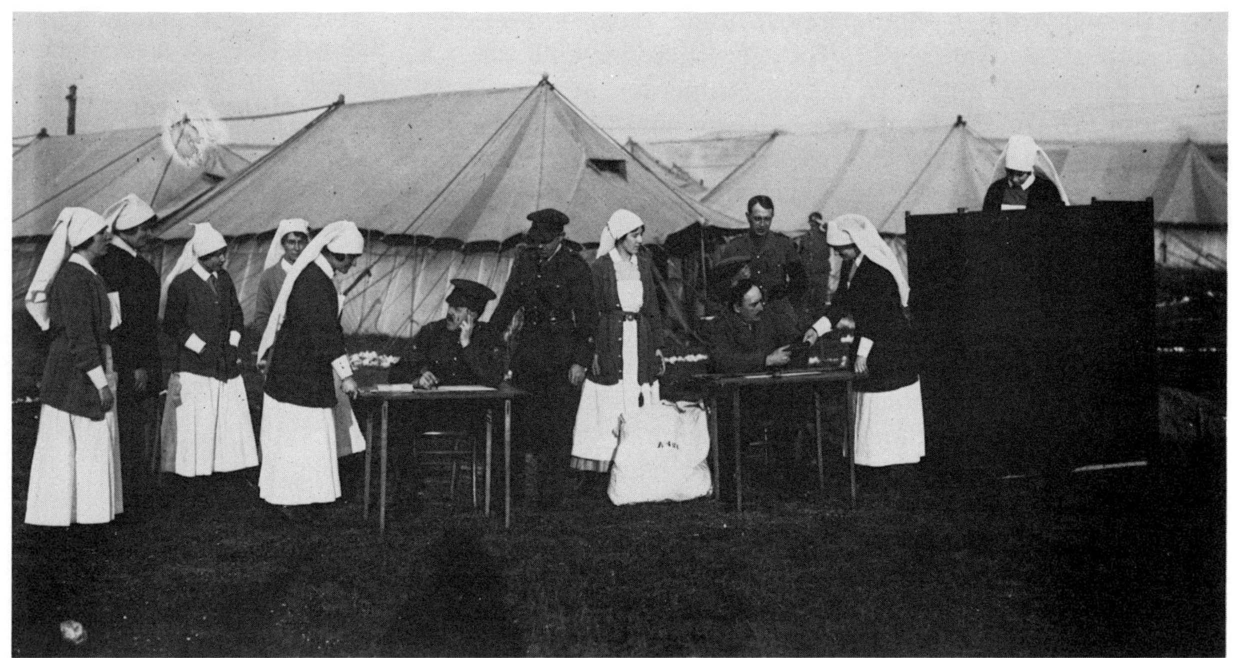

Figure 10.3 Canadian nurses overseas voting in 1917 *Not all women were given the vote in 1917. Only those who had some connection with the war were allowed to vote. You can find out why in Lesson 38.*

But so far there have been no women in Canada elected to lead a province. There have been no women elected to be prime minister of the whole country. And even today there are only a few women in our government compared to the number of men.

Of course, this situation can be changed. And the way it can be changed is through the vote. This is true of all things in government. If people want to make a change, they can vote for representatives who want to make the same change.

Unfortunately, many Canadians do not use their right to vote. In most federal elections, a third of the people who are allowed to vote just don't bother.

Why don't people use their right to vote? Sometimes they find it difficult to understand what the issues are. Sometimes they find it difficult to decide who will be a good representative for them. And sometimes they just don't care.

Actually, it's not too hard to find out what the issues are in an election. And once you have this information, it is easier to decide who to vote for. The most important thing is that you should care. After all, your vote allows *you* to tell the government just how you think the country should be run.

In the next 5 lessons, you will learn about how elections are run. You will also learn how to use your right to vote wisely.

In 1947, Canadian people became recognized officially as *Canadian* citizens and not just as *British* citizens.

THE FACTS

Remembering Facts

1. What is the most important right in a democracy?
2. Why weren't women allowed to vote in the early days?
3. Name 2 methods Canadian women used to win the right to vote.
4. When did women first get the right to vote in Canada?
5. Why is the right to vote so important?

Finding Facts

Women in every province except Quebec had the right to vote by 1922. Can you find out when women got the right to vote in the following provinces? Use an encyclopedia or other history textbook to help you find the dates.

(a) Quebec
(b) Newfoundland
(c) one other Canadian province

YOUR OPINIONS

Stating Opinions

Women in Britain used many dangerous and sometimes illegal methods to win the right to vote. Canadian women used only legal methods.

What do *you* think about people who use dangerous and illegal methods to get what they want? Write a few sentences to explain your opinion.

Discussing Opinions

Over half of the people in this country are women. But even today there are only a few women elected to the federal and provincial governments.

What do you think of this situation? Why do you think there are only a few women in government? Is it a problem that there are so few women in government? How would you react to a woman prime minister?

Discuss your opinions about these questions with your classmates.

NEW WORDS

Learning Words

In your notebook, write the title Vocabulary: Lesson 10. Then write down the following words in a list. Using the Glossary or a dictionary, write the meaning beside each word.

When you are finished, write a short note telling what you have learned in this lesson. Try to use all 5 of these words in your note.

demand	**ignore**	**legal**
qualification	**suffrage**	

Examining Words

Suffragists were also called *suffragettes*. The word *suffragette* is made from two parts: *suffrage* and *ette*.

The ending *ette* means either "feminine" or "small". Can you explain why the ending *ette* was used in each of the following words?

cigarette	majorette
dinette	roomette

AN ILLUSTRATION

Look through old newspapers or magazines to find 2 photographs that are related to important political events. Cut out these photographs and paste them on a sheet of paper. Beneath each photograph, write the following information:

(a) the number of women who are in the picture;
(b) the number of men who are in the picture;
(c) the number of women who have leading roles in the picture;
(d) the number of men who have leading roles in the picture;
(e) the number of women who have support roles in the picture;
(f) the number of men who have support roles in the picture.

Share your pictures with the rest of the class. Did you all have the same information about women in the pictures? Why do you think this is so?

Nellie McClung

Figure 10.4 *Nellie McClung outside her home with her son and the family dog*

Claim to fame: She was a leader of the Canadian suffragists.

Born: 1873 in Chatsworth, Ontario

Married: in 1898 to Robert W. McClung. They had 5 children.

Career: McClung moved from Ontario to become a teacher in Winnipeg, Manitoba. While there, she decided that her family needed more money. So she began her career as a writer. When her first novel was published in 1908, it became a great success. She continued to write, producing more than 15 other major works in her lifetime.

Nellie McClung was also a talented speaker. She became a leader of the women's suffrage movement in both Manitoba and Alberta. She worked closely with another suffragist, Emily Murphy (see Lesson 5), and was one of the 5 women who forced the Canadian government to recognize that women were ''persons''.

McClung was also one of the first women elected to a provincial legislature. She won a seat in Alberta in 1921.

As well as fighting for women's rights, McClung also fought against the sale of alcohol in Canada. This belief that alcohol should be banned caused problems for McClung. Because of it, she was defeated in the Alberta elections of 1926.

Died: Nellie McClung died in Victoria, British Columbia, in 1951.

- **Does your library have any copies of books by Nellie McClung?**
- **Do you think that your province's liquor laws should be changed?**

11 The Candidates

Figure 11.1 A Conservative nomination meeting in Edmonton, Alberta *Not all nomination meetings are as rowdy as the one in this picture. But politicians often use loud music, banners, hats, and buttons to advertise themselves. This is what is known as "hoopla". Do you think this hoopla has any effect on how people vote?*

In an election, voters say who they want to represent them in the government. But it would be very confusing if voters just voted for anyone they knew. That is why our election system uses **candidates**.

Candidates are the people who are running for office. In other words, they want to be elected as government representatives. As long as a person can vote in the election, that person can also be a candidate. There are just 2 other **requirements**.

First, the person who wants to be a candidate has to be **nominated**. In other words, other voters have to say they would like that person to run for office.

The person who wants to be a candidate has to fill out special forms called nomination papers. There are spaces on these forms for people's signatures. These spaces must be signed by the people who would like the candidate to run for office.

Second, the person who wants to be a candidate almost always has to pay some money. The amount is usually about $100 or $200. This money is called a **deposit**. If the candidate wins a certain number of votes in the election, then he or she will get the deposit money back.

Anyone who is a voter can become a candidate. But in federal and provincial elections it is almost impossible to be elected without belonging to one of the political **parties**. Therefore, most of the candidates are chosen by members of the political parties.

A political party is a group of people who have similar ideas about how the government should be run. As you learned in Lesson 4, there are 3 major political parties today in Canada. These are the Progressive Conservative Party, the Liberal Party, and the New Democratic Party.

Political parties are something like clubs. People join them by paying a small membership fee. This means that they can go to the regular party meetings where the members discuss what is happening in politics.

The "Miss Canada" beauty pageant began in 1946. "Miss Teen Canada" came along in 1968.

When party members think there will be an election soon, they hold nomination meetings. All the party members in a riding get together. They talk about who should be the party's candidate in that riding.

Sometimes several party members would like to be the candidate. They explain their views to the other party members. And then there is a small election. The person who wins becomes the party's candidate.

All the party members in the riding then work together to help get their candidate elected. This includes even the people who would have liked to run for office themselves. The fact is that people can make changes in government much better if they work in groups rather than working on their own.

But this doesn't mean that you have to belong to one of the 3 main political parties. There are many other parties in Canada, such as the Social Credit Party and the Parti Québécois.

In fact, any group of people with similar ideas about government can get together and form a party. This happened in Alberta in the early 1980s.

A man called Gordon Kesler decided that the West should be separate from the rest of Canada. Other Westerners agreed with him. They met together and decided

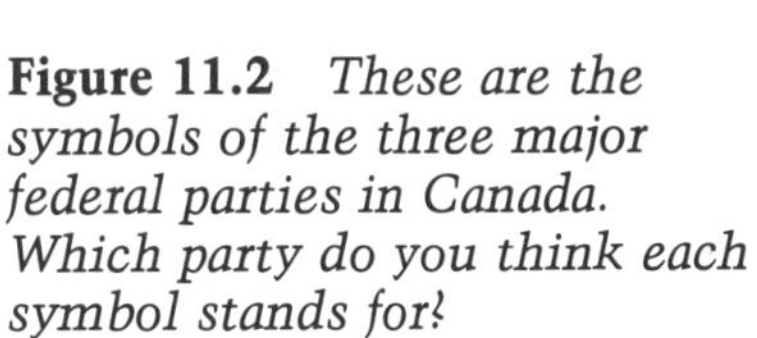

Figure 11.2 *These are the symbols of the three major federal parties in Canada. Which party do you think each symbol stands for?*

Figure 11.3 *Not all political parties and their candidates are serious about winning elections. Here, members of the Rhinoceros Party, which lasted from 1964 to 1985, hold up a picture of their mascot. Members of the Rhinoceros Party thought that Canadians are too serious about elections. Do you think parties like this are a good or a bad thing for our country?*

In the 1984 federal elections, there were 11 registered political parties. A total of 1449 candidates ran for 282 seats.

Early Canadian farmers wore straw hats in summer. These were called *cow's breakfasts* since they were often eaten by cattle.

to call themselves the Western Canada Concept Party. At one point they had nearly 1000 members. They ran candidates in the Alberta provincial elections. And one of their candidates was even elected.

So you can see that anyone who has strong ideas about what the government should be doing can make a difference. That person just needs to get together with other people who share the same ideas.

THE FACTS

Remembering Facts

1. Who can be a candidate in an election?
2. What are nomination papers?
3. What is a deposit?
4. What do members of political parties do?
5. How many candidates does a political party nominate in each riding?

Finding Facts

Divide the class into groups. Each group should be responsible for a party, either at the federal level or the provincial level. For example, one group should be responsible for the *federal* Liberal Party. Another group should be responsible for the *provincial* Liberal Party (if there is one).

Find out the following information for every party in your area:

(a) how much it costs to join the party;
(b) where the party members meet;
(c) whether there is a special branch of the party for young people.

If possible, invite representatives of the different parties to talk to your class.

Stating Opinions

Would you be interested in joining a political party? Write a few sentences to explain your opinion.

Discussing Opinions

Candidates who do not belong to a political party are called *independents*. Independent candidates almost never win in federal and provincial elections. Why do you think this is so?

NEW WORDS

Learning Words

In your notebook, write the title Vocabulary: Lesson 11. Then write down the following words in a list. Using the Glossary or a dictionary, write the meaning beside each word.

When you are finished, write a short note telling what you have learned in this lesson. Try to use all 5 of these words in your note.

candidate	**deposit**	**nominate**
party	**requirement**	

Examining Words

The verb *elect* can be turned into the noun *election*. In the same way, the verb *nominate* can be turned into the noun *nomination*. In both cases, the letters *ion* turn the verb into the noun.

Use the letters *ion* to turn the following verbs into nouns.

direct	exhibit	inflate
pollute	subtract	

AN ILLUSTRATION

In every election campaign, there will be losers and winners. In some ridings, it is not clear who will win until the very end of the election. But there are other ridings that are known as "safe" seats. In other words, the people in the riding tend to vote the same way in election after election.

Table 11.1 shows the history of elections in a riding called Central Nova, in Nova Scotia. In 1983, the Conservative MP for the riding stepped down. He did this so that Brian Mulroney, who had just been elected as party leader, could run for a seat in the House of Commons.

Look carefully at Table 11.1. Why do you think Brian Mulroney chose to run for election here? Would you want to be a candidate in Central Nova for one of the other parties?

Table 11.1 *Percent of votes won by candidates in federal elections in Central Nova*

ELECTION	LIB	NDP	PC	SC/IND	GOV'T
1968	33.27	8.16	58.57	n/a	Lib
1972	28.97	12.84	56.95	1.24	Lib
1974	36.30	8.86	53.94	0.90	Lib
1979	29.89	13.53	56.58	n/a	PC
1980	34.26	17.71	48.03	n/a	Lib

Key: LIB = Liberal Party; NDP = New Democratic Party; PC = Progressive Conservative Party; SC/Ind = Social Credit Party or Independent candidate; Gov't = the party which formed the government after this election

SOURCE: Derived from *Canadian Parliamentary Guide*

John Shaver Woodsworth

Figure 11.4 *J.S. Woodsworth in front of the Parliament Buildings, 1923*

Claim to fame: He was the first leader of the CCF Party of Canada. This party later became the New Democratic Party of Canada.

Born: 1874 in Etobicoke, Ontario

Married: 1904 to Lucy Staples. They had 6 children. One daughter, Grace MacInnis, herself held a seat in the House of Commons for 11 years.

Career: Woodsworth became a Methodist minister in 1896. During his years as a minister, he became interested in living conditions for the working poor in Canada.

Woodsworth wanted to work more actively to help workers and labourers. Therefore he resigned from the church in 1918. At first he worked as a longshoreman in Winnipeg. Then in 1919 he became involved in the Winnipeg General Strike. He was arrested, but the charges against him were dropped.

In 1921, Woodsworth was elected to the House of Commons. Ten years later, he joined with other social reformers to form a new political party called the Co-operative Commonwealth Federation, (or the CCF, for short). The party's goal was to help Canadian workers. Woodsworth became its first leader.

Died: Woodsworth died in 1942. At the time of his death he was still an MP for the Winnipeg riding he had first won in 1921.

- **What kind of work does a longshoreman do?**
- **Do you think Canadians are generally better off now than they were in J.S. Woodsworth's time?**

Calling an Election

12

Elections are called for different reasons, depending on the level of government involved.

Municipal elections are normally **automatic**. In other words, the law says that municipal elections must be held on certain dates. In Ontario, for example, municipal elections are held every 3 years on the second Monday in November.

This means you can almost always tells when the next election will be in your town or county. But you can't always tell when the next provincial or federal election will be.

The constitution says that there must be a federal election at least once every 5 years. Most provinces have the same sort of rule. But federal and provincial elections are usually held sooner than the law says.

Sometimes the government has tried to pass a law, but the law was defeated. If the law was an important one, then this is a serious problem. We say that the government has "lost the **confidence**" of the Members of Parliament. This means that the government has to call an election immediately.

At other times, the prime minister may decide that his or her party is very popular at that moment. If the prime minister is right, there is a good chance that the party will be re-elected. So the prime minister may decide to call an election even though it isn't really necessary.

Once an election is called, there are thousands of details that need to be taken care of. Lists have to be made of all the voters. Ballots have to be printed with the candidates' names on them. Places for voting have to be arranged. There even have to be enough pencils ready for the voters to mark their ballots with.

Elections are run in almost exactly the same way for all 3 levels of government. There are some differences, but these aren't very important. Therefore, the rest of this section will describe what happens in federal elections only.

Figure 12.1 *Joe Clark's government collapsed after only 7 months in office. The budget was defeated in the House of Commons. Therefore Clark's government lost the confidence of the House and he had to call a new election. What happened to Joe Clark after this election in 1980?*

The first official portrait of Pope John Paul II was painted in 1983 by Canadian artist André Durand.

Alberta-born folk star Joni Mitchell got her start singing in Toronto coffee houses in 1964.

Just remember that the elections for your provincial and municipal governments may be run a little differently.

All the rules for running federal elections are stated in the Canada Elections Act. The Canada Elections Act says that for every riding there needs to be a person who is in charge of the election. This person is called the returning officer.

The biggest job of the returning officer is to prepare a list of all the people in the riding who can vote. The returning officer couldn't possibly do this alone. There are sometimes as many as 90 000 voters in a single riding.

Therefore the returning officer divides the riding into smaller areas called **polls**. Each poll has no more than 300 voters. The returning officer appoints people called **enumerators** to go from door to door in each poll.

At each house or apartment, the enumerators ask for the names of people who are **eligible** to vote. These names are put together in a big list for each poll. This list is called the voters' list.

If no one is at home the first time the enumerators call, they will try again later. Sometimes there is still no one at home the second time. In those cases the enumerators leave a notice. This notice tells the people in the house how to make sure their names are put on the voters' list.

Figure 12.2 Jean-Marc Hamel, Canada's Chief Electoral Officer since 1968 *Between elections, the Chief Electoral Officer heads a staff of approximately 50 full-time employees. By election night, however, there are more than 110 000 employees at work to make sure the election runs smoothly. How many ballot boxes do you estimate are in the pile of boxes behind M Hamel?*

As a rule, your name has to be on the voters' list for you to vote. In some special cases, you will be allowed to vote even if your name is not on the list. But in these cases, voting is very complicated. Therefore it is always wise to make sure your name is on the voters' list.

The returning officer also sets the date when nominations are closed. Anyone who wants to be a candidate in the election has to inform the returning officer by this date. The candidate does this by handing in the completed nomination papers.

The nomination date is usually 3 weeks before election day. This gives the returning officer time to have the ballots printed with the candidates' names.

Normally, it takes about 2 months between the time when a federal election is called and election day itself. During this time, the candidates try to impress as many voters as possible. This is called the campaign. You will learn more about election campaigns in the next lesson.

Canada's longest river is the Mackenzie. It runs 4240 km from Great Slave Lake, Northwest Territories, right to the Arctic Ocean.

Figure 12.3 *An employee with the office of the Chief Electoral Officer in Ottawa checks the bags of election materials that will be sent out to all the ridings across Canada. Estimate the floorspace that is taken up by the bags in this photograph.*

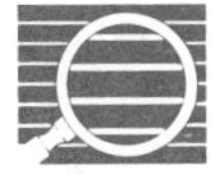

THE FACTS

Remembering Facts

1. How often does there have to be a federal election in Canada?
2. What does it mean when the government has "lost the confidence" of the Members of Parliament?
3. Who is in charge of the election in each riding?
4. What is a poll?
5. Why is it important to have your name on the voters' list?

Finding Facts

Find out the dates of each of the following elections. Use the newspaper or an encyclopedia yearbook to help you. Or you could call your government representatives for this information.

(a) the last municipal election
(b) the next municipal election
(c) the last election in your province
(d) the last federal election in Canada

YOUR OPINIONS

Stating Opinions

A prime minister can call a federal election any time he or she wants to as long as there is one at least every 5 years. Therefore, most prime ministers try to call an election at the time they think their party will have the best chance of winning.

Do you think this is a fair way to call elections? Or do you think that the dates for federal elections should be set for a regular period such as once every 4 years?

Write a few sentences to explain your opinion.

Discussing Opinions

What do you think it would be like to be an enumerator? What kind of problems might you have in trying to get all the right names for the voters' list?

After you have discussed these questions, divide the class into groups. One student should act as the enumerator for each group. Ask for the names of all the people who are allowed to vote in each student's home. Make a list of these names and addresses and post it in the classroom. Let the students check the list to see that it is accurate.

NEW WORDS

Learning Words

In your notebook, write the title Vocabulary: Lesson 12. Then write down the following words in a list. Using the Glossary or a dictionary, write the meaning beside each word

When you are finished, write a short note telling what you have learned in this lesson. Try to use all 5 of these words in your note.

automatic **confidence** **eligible**
enumerator **poll**

Examining Words

We used 2 meanings of the word *call* in this lesson. The first time it was used in the phrase "to *call* an election". The second time it was used in the phrase "people *called* enumerators".

Call means something different in each of these examples. To call an election means "to command" that there will be an election. To call somebody an enumerator means "to give the name" of enumerator to that person.

Call has many more meanings than this. In fact, one dictionary lists 17 different meanings. Can you explain the different meanings of *call* in the following sentences?

(a) "You had 4 *calls* during lunch," said the secretary.
(b) The baseball game was *called* at 15:00 because of rain.
(c) The audience enjoyed the play so much that there were 6 curtain *calls*.
(d) It was Dave's turn to *call* trump.

Table 12.1 lists the dates of federal elections in Canada over a 30-year period. Work out how many years and months have passed between each election. What is the shortest time between elections? What is the longest time? What seems to be the average length of time?

Table 12.1 *Federal election dates in Canada, 1953-1984*

Election Date	Winning Party
August 10, 1953	Liberal
June 10, 1957	Progressive Conservative
March 31, 1958	Progressive Conservative
June 18, 1962	Progressive Conservative
April 18, 1963	Liberal
November 8, 1965	Liberal
June 25, 1968	Liberal
October 30, 1972	Liberal
July 8, 1974	Liberal
May 22, 1979	Progressive Conservative
February 8, 1980	Liberal
September 4, 1984	Progressive Conservative

SOURCE: Canadian Parliamentary Guide

John Turner

Figure 12.4 *John Turner is shown here greeting some young supporters during the 1984 election campaign.*

Claim to fame: Some politicians feel that he made a mistake in calling a quick election when he replaced Pierre Trudeau as prime minister.

Born: 1929 in Richmond, England

Married: Geills McCrae Kilgour in 1963. They have 1 daughter, Elizabeth, and 3 sons, Michael, David, and Andrew.

Career: Turner was brought to Canada when he was a very young child. At the time, his stepfather was the Lieutenant-Governor of British Columbia.

Turner went to the University of British Columbia. Then he won a Rhodes scholarship to attend Oxford University. After university, he qualified as a lawyer in both England and Quebec.

In 1962, John Turner became a Liberal MP in Ottawa. He served in many cabinet posts, including as Minister of Finance. But in 1975, Turner resigned from the Cabinet and the House of Commons. People said that he had argued with the prime minister at the time, Pierre Trudeau.

Turner returned to private life. But when Trudeau retired in 1984, Turner decided to run for the leadership of the Liberal Party. He won the leadership in June and thus became the prime minister of Canada, even though he was not an MP at the time.

Turner took a big chance: he called an election almost as soon as he became prime minister. But he lost the gamble. He was badly defeated by the Conservatives, led by Brian Mulroney.

- **What is a Rhodes scholarship?**
- **Should a person be allowed to become the prime minister of Canada even if that person is not a member of Parliament?**

The Campaign 13

As soon as the candidates have been nominated, they start **campaigning**. They try to **convince** the voters that their ideas about how the government should be run are the best.

One way the candidates do this is by canvassing the riding from door to door. In other words, the candidates try to visit every home in the riding. They knock on the doors, talk to the people inside, and ask for their votes.

The candidates also have a chance to explain their ideas when they attend all-candidates meetings. At these meetings, all the candidates in the riding debate with each other and try to show that they are better than their opponents.

Voters in the riding come to watch the debates. Sometimes the voters are allowed to ask the candidates questions to see where they stand on important **issues**. This way the voters can compare the candidates' ideas and make wiser decisions about which candidate to vote for.

Candidates may have excellent ideas. But in order to win, candidates also need **publicity**. They need to make sure that the voters recognize them. They need to give the impression that lots of people are voting for them.

The candidates could not possibly do this alone. That is why they have workers to help them during the campaign. Sometimes these workers are just friends of the candidates, or people the candidates have hired. But normally these workers are members of the candidates' political parties.

The candidates' workers usually canvass the riding several times during the campaign. They leave leaflets for the voters in each home. These leaflets explain the candidates' qualifications and ideas about important issues.

The party workers also ask householders for permission to put up election signs. These signs advertise the candidates' names. Householders who put signs on their lawns or in their windows are showing their support for a candidate.

Figure 13.1 Lucille Broadbent during her husband's campaign *Politicians' families usually become very involved in election campaigns. For example, in all the years Ed Broadbent has been a politician, Lucille has worked by his side. People say that the families of politicians can make a real difference. Do you think that the families of the candidates are important in a campaign?*

Figure 13.2 An election sign with a difference *Many voters put election signs on their lawns to show their support for the party of their choice. But few voters go as far as Ken Riddell (on right). He had the whole side of his house painted in support of the Progressive Conservative candidate. It took 2 volunteer campaign workers just 3 hours to complete the job.*

The election signs are an important way of advertising the candidates. But candidates do many other things in order to get publicity and to attract voters. For example, they may hold a pancake breakfast or a barbecue for people in the riding. Then they will invite reporters to cover these events.

All candidates want news coverage. They want their names to be in newspapers, on the radio, and on television. They hope that this free publicity will lead to more votes.

But most of the news coverage in an election is about the *leaders* of the parties. Party leaders are extremely important in Canadian elections. In fact, many people vote according to party leaders, not according to the candidates.

For example, if the voters prefer the leader of the Liberal Party, they will vote for the Liberal candidate. They will vote this way even if the New Democratic or Progressive Conservative candidates in their riding are better qualified.

So you can see that it isn't easy to get elected. An election campaign involves a lot of time and hard work. And it also costs a lot of money. The bills for election signs, leaflets, advertisements, and travelling around the riding can quickly add up to thousands of dollars.

More than 500 000 kg of election supplies were needed for the federal election in 1984.

Some of this money comes from party membership dues.

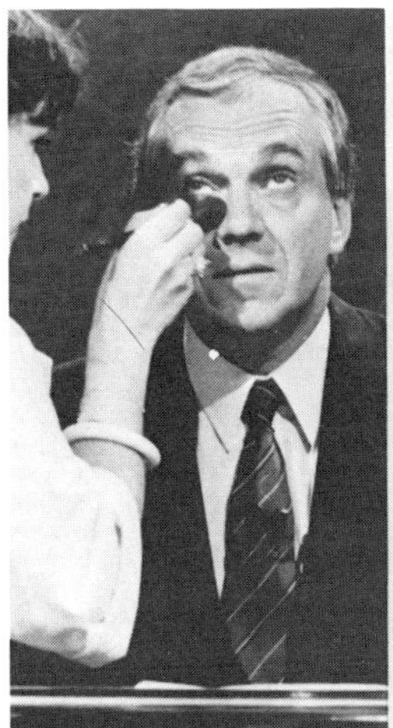
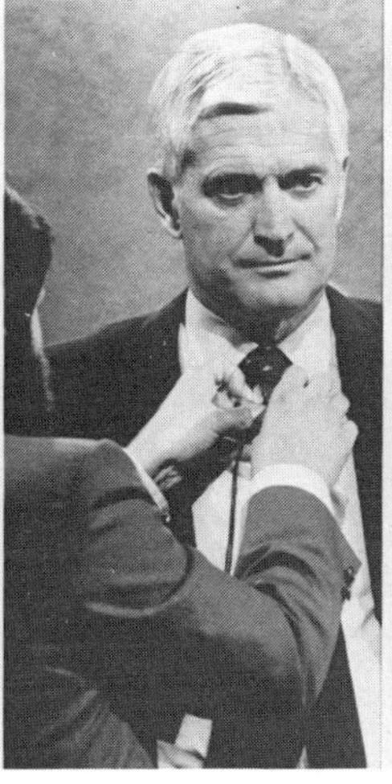
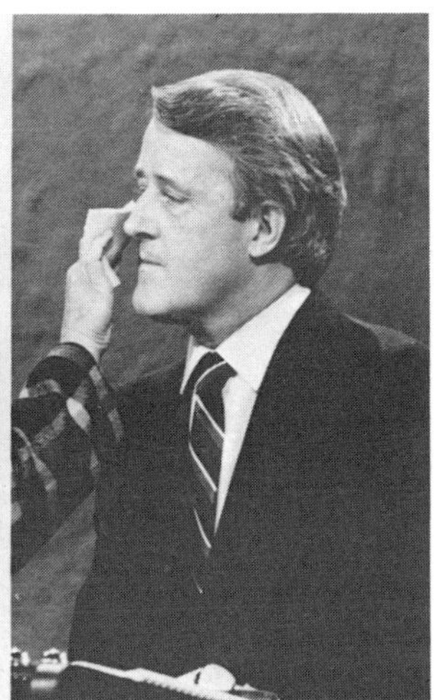

Figure 13.3 The leaders debate *In most modern election campaigns, the party leaders debate with each other on television for a cross-Canada audience. The parties take these debates very seriously. In the top photo Ed Broadbent, John Turner and Brian Mulroney are being made up before going in front of the television cameras. In the bottom photo they are shown during a debate on women's issues held in the 1984 election campaign. Can you identify the leaders in the bottom photograph and the parties they belong to?*

More of it is **donated** by businesses or by wealthy individuals. And usually several thousand dollars come straight from the candidate's own pocket.

For candidates who do not belong to one of the main parties, the money is much harder to find. These candidates have to pay for almost all the costs themselves. Normally this means that they can't afford to run a very effective campaign.

It is no wonder, then, that very few people ever try to win a federal or provincial election without belonging to a political party. Winning an election requires a total team effort.

Glenn Gould, Canada's world-famous classical pianist who died in 1982, always hummed along in the background on his records.

THE FACTS

Remembering Facts

1. What is an all-candidates meeting?
2. Who are the workers who help the candidates in their campaigns?
3. Name 2 ways that candidates can have publicity.
4. Do voters always vote for the best candidate in a riding?
5. Where does the money for election campaigns come from?

Finding Facts

Imagine that you are a candidate in a riding with 50 000 voters. Find out how much it would cost for the following items:

(a) 50 000 1-page leaflets, printed on both sides in black and white;
(b) 50 000 1-page leaflets, printed on both sides in black and white and one other colour;
(c) 10 000 election signs printed in black and white on pieces of carboard approximately 1 m by 0.5 m;
(d) 10 000 election signs printed in black and white and one other colour on pieces of cardboard approximately 1 m by 0.5 m;
(e) 2 000 pointed wooden stakes approximately 1.5 m tall for putting election signs on lawns;
(f) 10 000 heavy-duty staples for stapling election signs and stakes together.

YOUR OPINIONS

Stating Opinions

There are many things you can do to get involved in an election campaign. You can simply put a candidate's sign on your lawn. Or you can agree to deliver leaflets to homes in your neighbourhood. Or you can help staple together signs and put them on people's lawns. Or you can go from door to door and ask people to vote for your candidate.

Do you think that *you* would ever get involved in an election campaign? Write a few sentences to explain your opinion.

Discussing Opinions

There are laws that limit the amount of money that candidates can spend on their election campaigns. There are also laws that say the candidates must tell where they got their money from.

Imagine that you are the owner of a business. You give $5000 to one of the candidates in your riding. What reasons could you have for giving this money? How do you think you would feel about other people knowing you have given this money?

Discuss your answers to these questions with your classmates.

NEW WORDS

Learning Words

In your notebook, write the title Vocabulary: Lesson 13. Then write down the following words in a list. Using the Glossary or a dictionary, write the meaning beside each word.

When you are finished, write a short note telling what you have learned in this lesson. Try to use all 5 of these words in your note.

campaign	**convince**	**donate**
issue	**publicity**	

Examining Words

The word *canvass* with a double *s* means "to ask for votes". The word *canvas* with a single *s* means "a heavy cloth".

There are other pairs of words where doubling one letter makes a difference in meaning. Can you explain the differences between the following pairs of words?

(a) desert / dessert	(b) fury / furry
(c) in / inn	(d) lose / loose
(e) of / off	(f) to / too

AN ILLUSTRATION

In modern times, election campaigns seem to be controlled by polls. Each of the main parties hires people to find out the voters' opinions on a number of issues. Newspapers publish polls that try to forecast how the election will turn out.

All of these polls are based on samples. The pollsters predict what will happen based on the answers of only a few thousand people. These people are chosen very carefully from across the country.

As a result, the polls are often very accurate. A Gallup Poll just before the federal election in 1984 predicted that the Progressive Conservatives would win 50% of the votes, the Liberals 28%, and the New Democrats 19%. And that is exactly what happened in the election.

Try taking your own poll. You and your classmates should each ask 5 different people in the community the following question:

> If there were an election today,
> which party would you vote for?

Write down the answers from everyone, including those who don't know who they'd vote for.

Pool your results together with those of the rest of your class. Make a table that shows the result of your poll. Were you surprised at these results? Do you think these results would be accurate for the whole country?

Barbara Frum

Figure 13.4 *Barbara Frum at her desk on* The Journal

Claim to fame: She is a national television host with the CBC.

Born: 1937 in Niagara Falls, New York

Married: 1957 to dentist and real estate developer, Murray Frum. They have 3 children.

Career: Barbara Frum was always a very clever student. She went to the University of Toronto when she was only 17 to study modern history. While she was a student there, she met and married her husband.

After her first child was born, Frum started to work as a writer and journalist. Her big break came when she was hired to host the CBC Radio show *As It Happens* in 1971. Millions of Canadians tuned in every night to hear her interviewing people in the news. She became famous for her hard-hitting questions. And she won several awards for her work.

Then, in 1982, she became the host for CBC's new national television news program, *The Journal*. She continues to interview people on this program. She also acts as an interviewer on programs covering important events, such as Canadian federal elections.

- **Is the CBC radio show *As It Happens* still on the air?**
- **Do you think it makes a difference whether the person who reads the television news is male or female? (or young or old?)**

Election Day

14

In the early days in Canada, people didn't vote secretly. They used to vote in front of everybody. They did this by raising their hands when the returning officer called out a candidate's name. Or they would just go up to the returning officer and announce the name they wanted to vote for.

This system was simple. But it caused problems. Sometimes gangs would beat up a voter if they didn't like the way that person had voted. Sometimes employers would watch how their employees voted. If the employer didn't like the way an employee voted, then the employee could be fired.

Sometimes candidates would pay people to vote for them. Because the vote was in the open, the candidates could make sure that the people voted the way they promised.

All these problems meant that elections weren't always fair. People would sometimes be afraid to vote the way they really wanted to. That was why the government decided in 1874 that voting should be secret. This was done by using **ballots**.

Ballots are the pieces of paper used by people for voting. In most elections, these ballots have the names of the candidates printed on them. Beside each name is a space. To vote, people just have to put a mark in the space beside the name of the candidate they want to win.

In a secret ballot, the voter makes this mark in **private**. Today there are many steps taken to make sure that nobody else sees how another person votes.

First of all, the returning officer decides on places where the people in each poll will vote. These places are called polling stations. Each polling station is located as close as possible to where most of the people in the poll live. Sometimes the polling station will be in a school. Sometimes it will be in a community centre. Sometimes it will even be in an apartment lobby.

The 1984 federal elections cost $38 million just to record people's votes.

Figure 14.1 A polling booth in 1874 *Why are there only men in this picture?*

Normally, 2 people work at each polling station on election day. One of these people is called a poll **clerk**. This person's job is to mark off voters' names from the voters' list. This is done to make sure that nobody tries to vote more than once.

The other worker is called the **deputy** returning officer. This person is in charge of the ballot box where people leave their votes.

The process of voting is really quite simple. Usually you just go to the polling station and tell the poll clerk your name and address. Once the poll clerk is sure you are on the voters' list, then the deputy returning officer will give you a ballot.

You then take your ballot to one of the voting booths. Usually these are tables and chairs that are surrounded by screens. On the table you will find a pencil and instructions about how to mark your ballot.

You can take all the time you want to mark your ballot. Just be sure to follow the directions carefully. For example, in some provinces you are only allowed to make an X, while in other provinces any kind of mark is all right.

As soon as you have made your mark, you fold up your ballot so no one can see how you have voted. Then you give your ballot to the deputy returning officer. This person will put your ballot into a locked ballot box. Once that is done, you are finished. You have voted, or, as people also say, you have cast your ballot.

In 1983, Canadians went through 120 million ball-point pens and 32 million pencils.

Figure 14.2 A voting station in a Quebec provincial election
On the table are lists of voters, blank ballots, the ballot box, and a Bible. Why do you think there is a Bible? Who is the man voting?

When the poll closes, the poll clerk and deputy returning officer open the ballot box and count the votes. Then they telephone the results to the returning officer. The ballot box is sealed up and taken to the returning officer for safe-keeping.

There are many **precautions** taken to make sure that everything is done fairly and according to the rules. For example, each candidate is allowed to have a worker present on election day. These workers are called scrutineers. Their job is to make sure that nobody votes more than once. They also make sure that there are no mistakes made in counting the votes.

As you can see, it is almost impossible now for people to cheat in an election. And nobody needs to be afraid to vote for a candidate. Elections certainly have improved a lot since Canada's early days.

In the 1984 federal election, there were 70 000 polling stations in 282 ridings.

THE FACTS

Remembering Facts

1. How did people vote in the early days in Canada?
2. Describe 2 problems that were caused by this system.
3. Match the word on the left with the correct description on the right. For each one, write the letter and the number together in your notebook.

(a) ballot	(1) a person who marks voters' names off the voters' list
(b) polling station	(2) a person who takes care of the ballots and the ballot box
(c) deputy returning officer	(3) the place where the people in a poll vote on voting day
(d) poll clerk	(4) a piece of paper printed with the names of the candidates
(e) scrutineers	(5) a person who is sent by the candidate to make sure the election is run properly

Finding Facts

This lesson has described what happens on election day for most people. However, there are always special cases that need to be taken care of during elections. Use the encyclopedia or contact the nearest government office to find out about 1 of the following:

(a) how people who are going to be out of the country on election day can vote in a federal election;
(b) how students who are away at university or college can vote in federal elections;
(c) how blind people vote in federal elections;
(d) how people in the armed forces vote in federal elections;
(e) who *isn't* allowed to vote in a federal election.

YOUR OPINIONS

Stating Opinions

In the early days in Canada, everyone knew how a person voted. How would you feel if everyone knew how you voted? Would you mind everybody knowing? Or would you be pleased because you wanted to show that you supported the candidate?

Write a few sentences to explain your opinion about this.

Discussing Opinions

In 1874, not everyone liked the idea of having a secret ballot. Many people felt that if you wanted to support a candidate, you should be brave enough to do this in public.

Think about the elections you have in class for offices like the class president. Would you vote differently if everyone could see how you voted? Discuss this problem with your classmates. Is the secret ballot the best way of voting?

NEW WORDS

Learning Words

In your notebook, write the title Vocabulary: Lesson 14. Then write down the following words in a list. Using the Glossary or a dictionary, write the meaning beside each word.

When you are finished, write a short note telling what you have learned in this lesson. Try to use all 5 of these words in your note.

ballot	**clerk**	**deputy**
precaution	**private**	

Examining Words

To be an employ*er* means "to employ somebody". To be an employ*ee* means "to be employed by someone". In the same way, to be a nominat*or* means "to nominate somebody". To be a nomin*ee* means "to be someone who has been nominated".

In English, the *er* or *or* ending often means "the person who is doing this". The *ee* ending often means "the person this is being done to".

Use the information to explain the difference in meaning between the following pairs of words.

payer	payee
interviewer	interviewee
trainer	trainee

AN ILLUSTRATION

Elections in Canada take place across 6 different time zones. Use the map in Figure 14.3 to help you answer the following questions:

1. What time is it in your home when the polls open at 08:00 in Newfoundland?
2. What time is it in your home when the polls close at 20:00 in British Columbia?

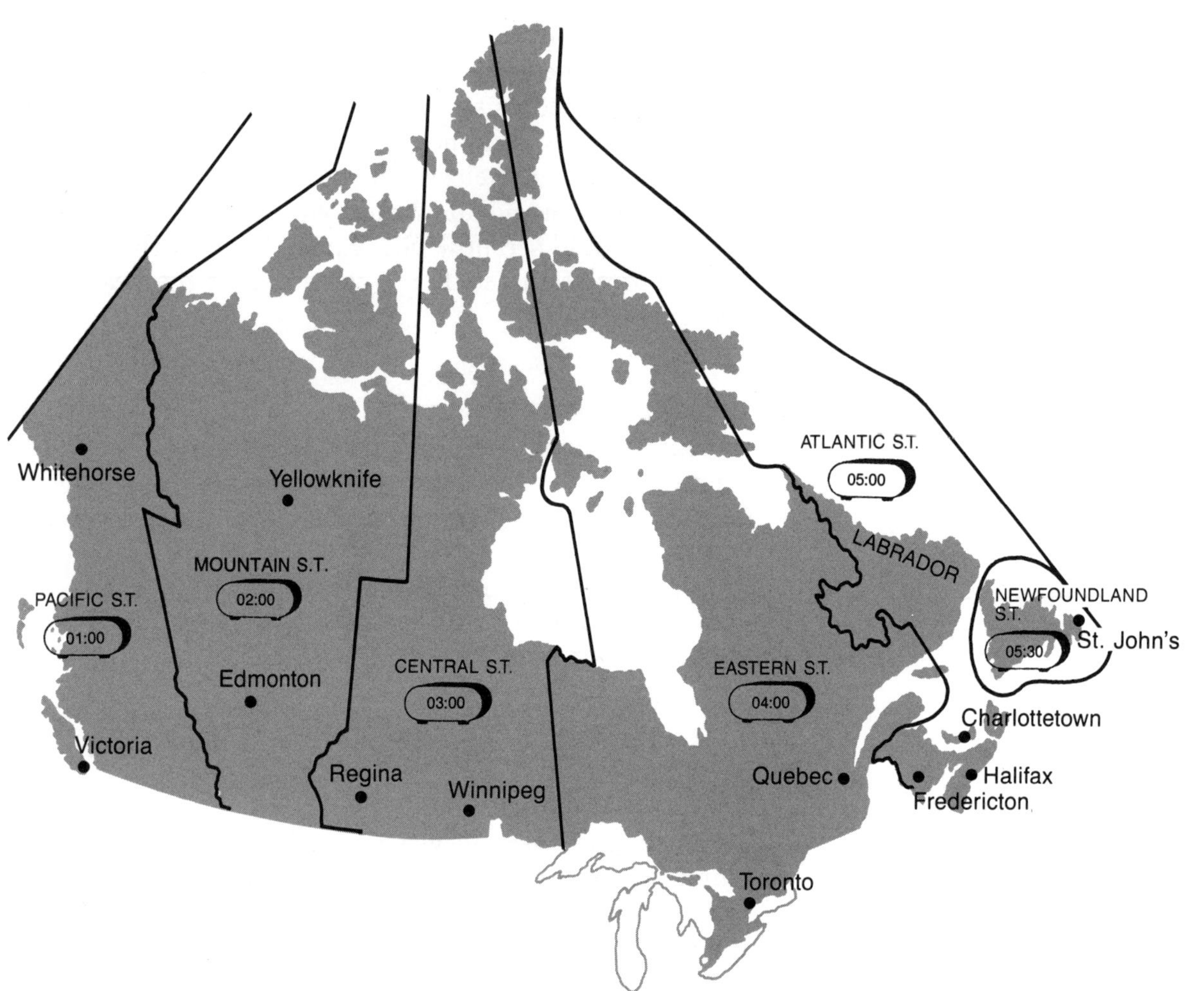

Figure 14.3 *A map of Canada's time zones.*

Flora MacDonald

Figure 14.4 *Flora MacDonald*

Claim to fame: She was a candidate for the leadership of the Conservative Party. She also became the first woman Minister for External Affairs.

Born: 1926 in North Sydney, Nova Scotia

Career: Flora MacDonald was first elected to the House of Commons in 1972. In 1976 she became a candidate for the leadership of the Conservative Party.

Many people from across Canada supported MacDonald's bid for the leadership. They sent her donations to help with her campaign. And many of the delegates at the leadership convention promised that they would vote for MacDonald.

Everyone thought MacDonald had a good chance of winning the leadership. But when they cast their secret ballots, only a few of the people who had promised to vote for her actually did. Everyone was very surprised when they heard how few votes there were for MacDonald.

It was clear that MacDonald could not win. So she decided to support Joe Clark. As a reward, he made her the first woman Minister for External Affairs when he became prime minister in 1979.

MacDonald remained loyal to Clark even after the election defeat in 1980. When the Conservatives held another leadership convention in 1983, she refused to run herself and instead supported Clark.

- **Is Flora MacDonald still a member of Parliament?**
- **Do you think it is right to tell a lie just because you don't want to hurt a person's feelings?**

15 The Results

Election night in Canada is full of excitement and tension. It sometimes seems as if the whole country has come to a stop. People sit in front of their television sets. They are eager to find out who has won the election.

Results are flashed on the television screen as soon as they come in from the polls. But it can take hours before all the votes in a riding have been counted.

The candidates wait tensely at their party **headquarters** with their workers. The results from each poll in the riding are written on giant chalkboards. As the numbers are written down, the workers cheer or groan, depending on who is winning.

Figure 15.1 Watching the 1926 election results *Winnipegers stand in the street watching the* FREE PRESS *bulletin board as the results come in from across the country. Which would you prefer: to watch the election results at home on your own television, or to watch the election results along with a huge crowd of people?*

The greatest tension is in the ridings where the vote is very close. Sometimes the vote can see-saw back and forth all night. Sometimes one candidate is winning by a few votes. Then another one pulls ahead.

What every candidate wants, of course, is to win by a big **margin**. In other words, each wants to have many more votes than the other candidates. Then he or she can feel confident in representing the riding in the government.

This does not happen for a candidate who wins by only a few votes. If there are 3 candidates in the riding, sometimes the winner is picked by fewer than half the voters. For example, imagine an election with the results in Table 15.1.

The Canadian branch of the Society for the Prevention of Cruelty to Animals (SPCA) was set up in 1869.

Political Party	Number of Votes
Conservatives	7 423
Liberals	6 789
New Democrats	5 788
Total	20 000

Table 15.1 *Possible election results for a riding*

The Conservative candidate has the most votes. So the Conservative has won the election.

But look at the results carefully. Only 7423 out of 20 000 people voted for the Conservative. That's fewer than half the voters. In fact, only 37% of them wanted the Conservative. More than half the other voters, or 63%, wanted someone different.

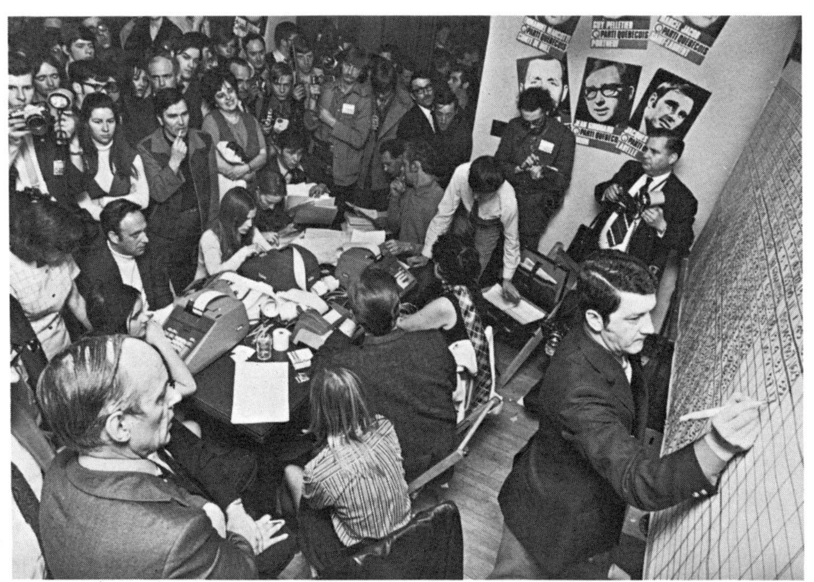

Figure 15.2 Party headquarters on election night *This photograph was taken during the Quebec provincial elections in 1970. René Lévesque is in the bottom left corner of the photograph. You can find out the results of this election in Lesson 43.*

As of 1984, the Liberals have won 19 federal elections in Canada, the Conservatives 14.

There is another similar problem when you think about all the MPs together. As you learned in Lesson 4, the party with the most seats will become the government. There are 282 seats in the House of Commons. If a party wins at least 142 seats, then it has won more than half the seats. The party has something called a clear majority.

But many times the party with the most seats in the House of Commons has fewer than 142 seats. For example, look at Table 15.2.

Political Party	Number of Seats
Conservatives	136
Liberals	114
New Democrats	26
Other parties	6
Total	282

SOURCE: Canadian Parliamentary Guide

Table 15.2 *Results of the 1979 federal election*

Because the Conservatives won the most seats, they became the government in 1979. But as you can see from Table 15.2, they did not have at least 142 seats. Therefore, they did not have a clear majority. In this case they had something called a **minority** government.

The party that runs a minority government can find it difficult to govern. It has to **rely** on other parties in order to pass laws.

In 1979, for example, the Conservatives wanted to pass a law about taxes. They needed at least half of the MPs to vote for the law. But the Conservatives did not have half of the MPs. Therefore they needed the help of MPs from some other party.

The MPs from the other parties didn't like the Conservatives' law. So they voted against the law. And the Conservatives lost. That meant there had to be another election.

Sometimes people talk about making changes in our election system to take care of these problems. But there are no easy **solutions**. The trouble is that no system is perfect.

What is important is that the people believe the system is as fair as possible. These days most Canadians seem happy with the way the government is elected. But there have been changes in the past. And there can always be changes in the future. It's up to the Canadian people to decide

Members of Canada's first Parliament, which opened on Nov. 6, 1867, were paid $6 for every day the House was in session.

Figure 15.3 Barrels of beef and pork are delivered to a Newfoundland store, c. 1900
You may have heard the phrase "pork barrel" politics. This is an old expression from an old political practice. The representative for a riding will push for laws that do special favours for the riding. It does not matter whether these laws will hurt the rest of the country. In this way, the representative hopes to be re-elected.

This is similar to political patronage. With political patronage, winning politicians make sure that their friends and supporters get government jobs. Do you think there is much political patronage today?

THE FACTS

Remembering Facts

1. Why do the winning candidates in an election want to have many more votes than the other candidates in the riding?
2. What does it mean when a government has a clear majority?
3. What is a minority government?
4. What problem does a minority government have?
5. Can the election system in Canada be changed?

Finding Facts

Find out the following information about the last federal election in the riding you live in. You can do this by going to the library and reading old newspapers. Or you could telephone or write to the MP for your riding.

(a) How many people voted for your MP?
(b) How many people voted in your riding?

Once you have these 2 numbers, you can use them to find out what percent of the voters actually voted for your MP. (Just divide the answer you have for part (a) by the answer you have for part (b), then multiply by 100.)

Does your MP represent more than half of the voters in your riding? Report what you have found to the rest of the class.

YOUR OPINIONS

Stating Opinions

Imagine that you are a candidate in a close election. The vote goes back and forth all night. Sometimes you're winning; sometimes another candidate is winning.

How do you think you would feel in this situation? What thoughts would be going through your mind? Write a few sentences that describe what you think your feelings would be.

Discussing Opinions

A problem with our election system showed up in the 1980 federal election. The Liberal Party won this election with a clear majority.

The trouble was that Canada was split almost down the middle. The Liberals won almost all their seats in the East and in Quebec and Ontario. There was only 1 Liberal elected from the 4 western provinces of Manitoba, Saskatchewan, Alberta, and British Columbia. The rest of the MPs from the West were either Conservatives or New Democrats.

This meant that the people in the West felt left out of the government. Can you think of any way we can change our election system to take care of problems like this? Discuss your ideas with the rest of the class.

NEW WORDS

Learning Words

In your notebook, write the title Vocabulary: Lesson 15. Then write down the following words in a list. Using the Glossary or a dictionary, write the meaning beside each word.

When you are finished, write a short note telling what you have learned in this lesson. Try to use all 5 of these words in your note.

headquarters	**margin**	**minority**
rely	**solution**	

Examining Words

A *minority* is the opposite of a *majority*. In the same way, *up* is the opposite of *down*. And *then* is the opposite of *now*.

State the opposite of each of the following words.

first	more	near
over	stop	that

AN ILLUSTRATION

The pie charts in Figure 15.4 show the results of 4 federal elections in Canada. For each chart, decide which party formed the government. In each case, was the government a majority or a minority?

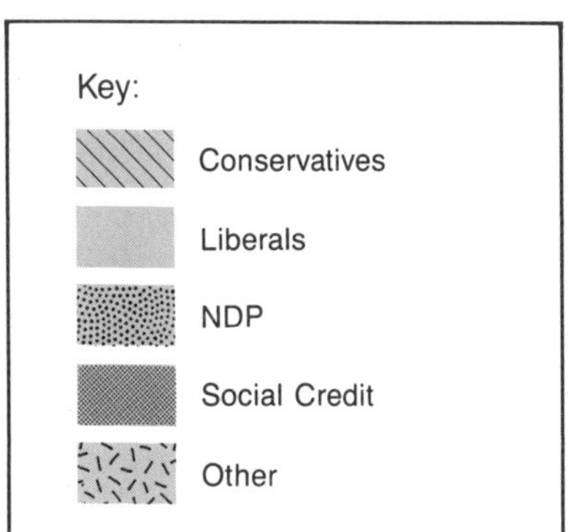

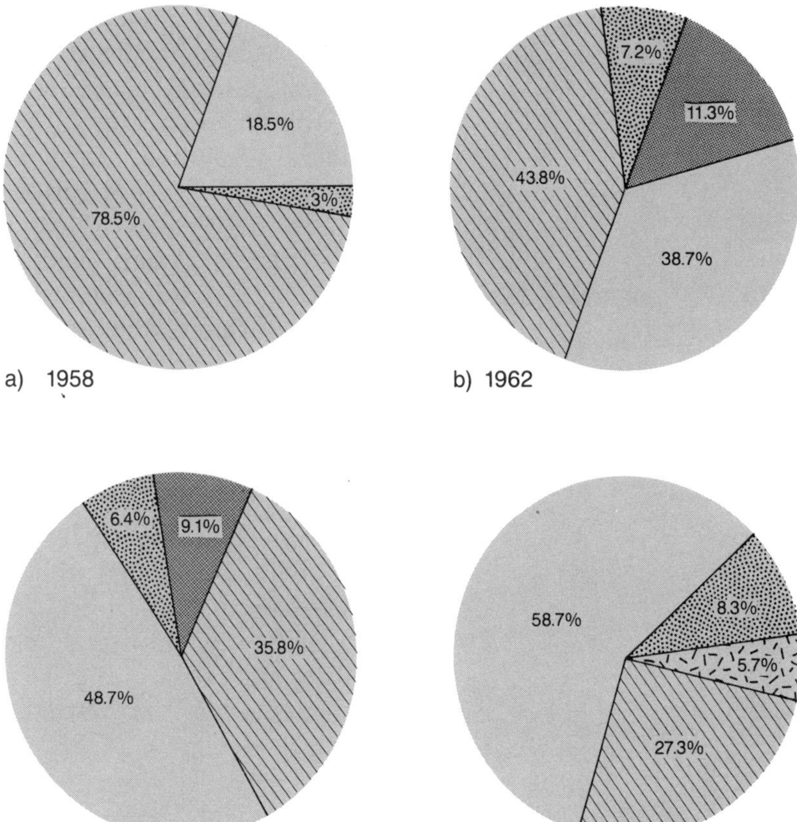

Figure 15.4 *The percent of seats won by the different political parties in 4 federal elections*

Iona Campagnolo

Figure 15.5 *Iona Campagnolo explaining some documents to John Turner, leader of the Liberal Party*

Claim to fame: She is National President of the Liberal Party.

Born: 1932 in Prince Rupert, B.C., the daughter of a cannery worker and the oldest of four children

Married: 1952 to a fisherman, Louis Campagnolo. They raised 2 daughters before their divorce in 1972.

Career: Campagnolo started her political career in 1966 when she became a school trustee. She spent 8 more years in municipal politics. Then, in 1974, she ran for the federal Liberal Party in a Vancouver riding. She won the seat with one of the biggest majorities a Liberal candidate has ever had in the West.

Two years later, Campagnolo was appointed to the Cabinet. She was made the Secretary of State for Fitness and Amateur Sport. She became well known across the country.

But the voters in her riding became angry with one of the policies of the Liberal government. So Campagnolo was defeated in the 1979 election.

At the time, she said she would never go back to politics. She started work as a television host. But in 1982 she was elected as the Liberals' first full-time party president. She did so well at this job that she was re-elected in 1984.

In 1984, Campagnolo also ran to become MP for her old riding of Skeena. But she and dozens of other Liberals were defeated when the Conservatives won 211 out of the 262 seats.

- **What kind of work is done in a cannery?**
- **Do you think that the government should make rules about amateur sports?**

QUIZ 2

The following questions are based on the lessons in Chapter 2. **DO NOT WRITE YOUR ANSWERS IN THIS TEXTBOOK.** Instead, you should write the answers in your notebook or on a separate sheet of paper.

1. Find the correct answer from the list given after each statement. Then write the whole statement on your paper.

   (a) The women who wanted the right to vote were called ______.
   suffragees
   suffragors
   suffragists

   (b) Canadian women first got the right to vote in ______.
   Quebec
   Manitoba
   Ontario

   (c) Women won the right to vote in federal elections in ______.
   1895
   1918
   1945

   (d) The last province to give women the vote was ______.
   Quebec
   Manitoba
   Ontario

2. Write the letters from (a) to (e) on your paper. Then write a T if the statement is TRUE. Write an F if the statement is FALSE.

   (a) People have always voted in secret in Canada.
   (b) Most Canadian citizens over the age of 18 are allowed to vote in federal elections.
   (c) Ballots are the pieces of paper voters use in an election.
   (d) To be elected, a candidate needs to win at least half of the votes in his or her riding.
   (e) In a minority government, the ruling party wins fewer than half the seats.

3. There are 10 blanks in the following paragraphs. They have been labelled from (a) to (j). Write down the 10 answers in a list on your paper. Then beside each answer write the letter of the blank where it belongs.

canvass	candidates	voters' list
deposit	political party	enumerators
polls	returning officer	
campaign	nomination papers	

The person in charge of the elections in each riding is called the (a) ______. This person divides the whole riding into smaller groups called (b) ______. The returning officer also appoints people called (c) ______ to go from home to home and ask for the names of voters. They put these names all together in a (d) ______ for each poll.

Usually there are several people who want to run for office. These people are called (e) ______. Usually they are chosen by the members of a (f) ______. Before they can run for office, the candidates need to fill out special forms called (g) ______. They also need to pay a small (h) ______.

The candidates work hard in order to win votes. They (i) ______ the riding from door to door and ask for votes. Their workers also help them in the (j) ______ by asking people to put up signs.

UNIT TWO

Law in Canada

Try to imagine a world with no rules: no rules about school; no rules about working; no rules about driving; no rules about anything at all. The world would be in a terrible mess.

Rules and laws are an important part of our daily lives. You can prove to yourself how important rules and laws are. Just take 5 minutes right now to list all the laws you and your classmates can think of. You may be surprised at how many you already know.

The sign for Unit II is a drawing of the scales of justice. Why do you think justice is represented by scales?

CHAPTER THREE

The Law in Principle

Have you ever heard the expression, "Ignorance of the law is no excuse"? It means that if you break a law, you will have to pay the penalty. It doesn't matter if you didn't *know* you were breaking the law at the time.

This is just one of the principles, or main ideas, on which our system of justice is based. This chapter will teach you more about these principles.

Rights and Responsibilities 16

Do you expect your parents or guardians to feed you? Do you expect them to pay for the roof over your head? Do you expect them to buy you clothes? You probably think of these as your **rights**.

Do you have to be home by a certain time each night? Do you have to keep your radio turned down? Do you have to do chores like washing the dishes? These are your **responsibilities** at home.

Rights and responsibilities depend on each other. They are always tied up together. For example, imagine that you were responsible for shovelling the sidewalk and you didn't do it. Your parent or guardian might take away your right to eat dessert.

In the same way, imagine that you decided it was time to help out at home by doing the weekly grocery shopping. Because you'd taken on this responsibility, you might be given more rights. For example, you might be allowed to choose what foods you would be eating.

We have rights and responsibilities in all parts of our lives. But there can be problems when people's rights come into **conflict** with each other.

For example, it is your neighbours' right to have a party in their home. But they are also responsible for keeping the noise level down. This is because it is also your right to sleep undisturbed.

If your neighbours' party is very loud and goes on until after midnight, your right to a quiet night has been taken away. In this case, your neighbours have **infringed** on your rights.

The chances are that in a situation like this you would just call your neighbours and ask them to be more quiet. However, if they didn't stop the noise, you might then call the police.

Figure 16.1 *In 1886, Indian chiefs from western Canada, including Crowfoot (middle row, centre), met in Ottawa to discuss treaties with the Canadian government. The rights of Indians and the responsibilities of the Canadian government for Native people are still important issues today.*

Figure 16.2 *The signs above involve both rights and responsibilities. Explain the rights and responsibilities for each.*

You can call the police because there is a law about people disturbing the peace. Laws are the rules that help us solve the problems that occur when people's rights come into conflict. They are also the rules that help us solve the problems that come up when people don't live up to their responsibilities.

For example, a person with a driver's **licence** has the right to drive. But that person also has the responsibility to drive safely according to the rules of the road. If a driver is drunk, then that driver is not acting responsibly. For this reason, the law says that drunk drivers can have their licences taken away from them.

But it isn't always so easy to decide what should be done when a person's rights have been infringed on. And it isn't always so easy to decide what should be done when a person has not acted responsibly.

For example, think about a bad car crash. One of the drivers is knocked unconscious. The police need to know whether this driver has been drinking. If the driver is unconscious, then the only way to tell is by taking a blood sample.

The trouble is, you normally can't take a blood sample from a person without his or her permission. If you do, you are infringing on that person's rights. But then the other people in the accident have the right to know whether the unconscious driver was drunk. Should the law allow a doctor to take a blood sample without permission?

Because of questions like this, making laws can be difficult. There are many situations where the answers to the problem are not clear.

The first Black player in the NHL was Willy O'Ree, born and educated in Fredericton, New Brunswick.

THE FACTS

Remembering Facts

1. What do rights and responsibilities have to do with each other?
2. Describe a situation in which people's rights come into conflict with each other.
3. What 2 main problems do laws help solve?
4. When can we take away a person's rights?
5. Is it always easy to decide when to take away a person's rights?

Finding Facts

In Canada, all of us have the right to say what we think. But we also have the responsibility to tell the truth. If a person tells a lie about someone else, that person can be taken to court and fined.

In lesson 2, you stated your opinion on one of the rights from the Canadian Charter of Rights and Freedoms. Go back and read this again. Can you think of a *responsibility* that goes with this right?

YOUR OPINIONS

Stating Opinions

In this lesson, you read about a bad car crash where a driver was knocked unconscious. The question was whether or not a doctor should be allowed to take a blood sample from an unconscious driver.

This is an important question. Government officials and human rights groups are arguing about this issue. What do *you* think?

Explain your answer to this question in a few sentences.

Discussing Opinions

Should students have more rights? Many students think so. For example, there are always students who would like the right to skip classes.

What they don't always realize is that with every right comes a responsibility. If they had the right to skip classes, then they would also have the responsibility to catch up on the work they missed.

Working with your classmates, make a list of the rights you would like to have. Then make a list of the responsibilities you would have if you got those rights.

NEW WORDS

Learning Words

In your notebook, write the title Vocabulary: Lesson 16. Then write down the following words in a list. Using the Glossary or a dictionary, write the meaning beside each word.

When you are finished, write a short note telling what you have learned in this lesson. Try to use all 5 of these words in your note.

conflict **infringe** **licence**
responsibility **right**

Examining Words

The words *rights* and *responsibilities* are a common pair. You hear and see them together often.

There are many other common pairs of words in the English language. Do you know the missing item from each of the following pairs? Write (a) to (i) in your notebook and fill in as many missing items as you can.

black and ______ (a) bread and ______ (b)
cats and ______ (c) life and ______ (d)
meat and ______ (e) pork and ______ (f)
salt and ______ (g) table and ______ (h)
town and ______ (i)

Can you think of another common pair of words? Test this pair on your classmates. Do they agree that it is a common pair?

AN ILLUSTRATION

Copy Table 16.1 into your notebook. Be sure to leave plenty of space for writing. Then fill in each section of the chart. You will need to think of 3 major rights and 3 major responsibilities you have both at home and at school. **DO NOT WRITE YOUR ANSWERS IN THIS TEXTBOOK.**

	RIGHTS	RESPONSIBILITIES
At Home	1. 2. 3.	1. 2. 3.
At School	1. 2. 3.	1. 2. 3.

Table 16.1 *My rights and responsibilities*

Dan Hill

Figure 16.3 *After a busy day at work, Dr. Dan Hill likes to relax by working in his garden.*

Claim to fame: He has spent a lifetime working for human rights in Canada.

Born: 1923 in Independence, Missouri. His father was a Methodist minister. His grandfather (on his father's side) was born a slave.

Married: Donna Bender, a sociologist. They have 3 children: Karen, Larry, and Dan, jr. Dan Hill, jr. is the famous singer and songwriter who has made several platinum and gold record albums.

Career: When he was a boy, Dan Hill travelled from one small town to another with his parents in the western United States. His father was often sent to poor parishes, and Dan was very upset by the poverty of many of the people that he met. He vowed that he would also spend his life trying to help the poor.

Hill served in the United States Army in World War II. Then he came to Canada to study sociology at the University of Toronto, where he earned his Ph.D.

As a sociologist, Dan Hill has written 3 books and many articles on human rights and the history of Blacks in Canada. For a time, he also ran a private consulting firm on human rights.

For 11 years, Dan Hill was head of the Ontario Human Rights Commission. His most recent appointment was in 1984 as the Ontario ombudsman. In this new job, he fights for the rights of ordinary citizens who think they have been unfairly treated by the government.

- **What is sociology? What does a sociologist do?**
- **The government pays the salary of the ombudsman. Do you think this could have an effect on the way the ombudsman works?**

17 Making Laws

Figure 17.1 *This picture was taken in 1890. People would pay the owner of the bear to watch the animal dance. Do you think a person would be allowed by law to do this on a city street today?*

What would it be like if you lived alone on a tropical island? You might be lonely, but you could eat whenever you wanted to. You could go fishing whenever you wanted to. You could go to sleep and wake up whenever you wanted to. You wouldn't have to worry about anybody but yourself.

If someone else lived with you on that island, you wouldn't be quite so free. You would have to agree about sharing responsibilities such as fishing and cooking. You would have to agree about when to eat and when to sleep. In other words, you would have to make some rules and agree to follow them.

Of course, if there were only 2 of you on the island, these rules would be quite simple. And these rules could also be changed very easily. You would just have to agree to eat dinner later or to wake up earlier if that was what you wanted.

But imagine what would happen if there were 20 or 30 of you. You would need many more rules to **protect** everyone's rights and explain everyone's responsibilities. And it would be much harder to get everyone to agree when someone wanted to change a rule.

In fact, the more people you have trying to live together **peacefully** in a group, the more rules you need. And the more difficult it becomes to change or bend the rules that you already have.

You can see this in your own life. At home there are probably several rules you have to follow. Perhaps you have to help with household chores. Perhaps you have to be in by a certain time at night.

But if something special comes up, the chances are that you will be allowed to skip your chores for the night. Or you will be allowed to come home later than usual. Because there are only a few people involved, it's not so difficult to bend the rules.

At school, where many more people are trying to live and work together peacefully, there are many more rules. There are rules about getting to class on time. There are rules about smoking on school property. There are rules about the proper clothing for gym class.

As you may have found out, these rules are harder to change. But if you talk with the students' council and teachers in your school, sometimes these rules can be changed or **modified**.

The school rules that are hardest to modify are the rules that have been written for all the schools in a province. There are thousands of people involved in the school system in every province. Therefore, any changes to these rules have to be thought out very carefully.

These rules are really laws, such as the law that children and young teenagers have to attend school. These laws have been discussed and approved by government representatives and have been written down.

If you think about it, you can see that laws are just very formal rules passed by governments. The major difference is the number of people involved. Laws are made by many more people. And laws apply to many more people.

One of the world's greatest optical illusions is at Magnetic Hill near Moncton, New Brunswick, where cars appear to coast *up*hill.

Figure 17.2 *One of the first steps in trying to change a law is to show that many people are against it. One way of doing this is by organizing protest marches and demonstrations. What law did the people in this picture want changed?*

Bartholomew Green set up the first printing press in Canada at Halifax in 1751.

In a country as big as Canada, we need many laws. That is why we have people whose main job is to make rules or laws that help us get along with each other. These people are the representatives we elect to our governments. The main job of any government is to **legislate**. That means the government's job is to make laws.

Everyone in Canada is expected to obey the laws that are made. No one is above the law. The only **exceptions** are for young children. Children who are under 12 years of age in Canada cannot be charged with breaking the law.

Sometimes people disagree with laws that are made. However, they still have to obey them. The only way they can get the law changed is by proving to the government that many other people also want the law changed. And this can be a long, slow process.

THAT'S THE LAW

There is usually a very good reason behind every law. But sometimes laws can seem quite strange. Read, for example, the following Canadian laws.

— Women's hairdressers in British Columbia are not allowed to give haircuts to boys who are over 7 years old.
— In Alberta restaurants it is illegal to dry dishes with a cloth dishtowel.
— The doors have to be left open during civil marriage ceremonies in Saskatchewan.
— You have to have a licence to sell garter snakes or elks' teeth in Manitoba.
— It is illegal in Ontario to sleep in a bakeshop.
— In Quebec it is a crime to hunt while in disguise.
— When ice fishing in New Brunswick, you must surround the hole with 4 pine trees at least 2 m in height.
— In Halifax, Nova Scotia, it is forbidden to wash windows after 8 o'clock in the morning.
— In Prince Edward Island, it is against the law to drop surplus potatoes on a garbage dump.
— Professional laundries in Newfoundland are not allowed to use wooden tubs.
— In the Yukon, it is an offence to catch a fish with an unbaited hook.
— In the Northwest Territories, it is against the law to keep chickens in the same shed as a milk cow.

SOURCE: Adapted from Nigel Napier-Andrews, *This Is the Law!*

No plants could grow in the far North without permafrost. It stops precious rain from sinking into the ground.

THE FACTS

Remembering Facts

1. Why do we have rules?
2. What is the difference between a rule and a law?
3. Who makes the laws in Canada?
4. Who has to obey the laws in Canada?
5. What can you do if you disagree with a law?

Finding Facts

Every province has laws about how the school system should be run. These laws are called Acts of education.

Find a copy of the Education Act for your province. Then copy out one of the rules or laws in this Act. Try to explain what this rule or law means.

YOUR OPINIONS

Stating Opinions

Have you ever heard someone say "There ought to be a law!"? Or have you ever thought there should be a law about something?

Write a few sentences describing a law that you think should be made. If you can't think of a new law, write about a change you would like to make in an already-existing law.

Discussing Opinions

Governments make laws about almost every part of our lives. Some people feel that there are too many laws. They think the government has no business making laws about things like wearing seat belts, for example.

Other people feel that such laws are necessary. These people would like to see even more laws that help to protect us all.

Working with a small group of students, write a list of 5 laws that affect your lives. When you are finished, discuss these laws. Why do you think they were made? Do you think they are needed?

NEW WORDS

Learning Words

In your notebook, write the title Vocabulary: Lesson 17. Then write down the following words in a list. Using the Glossary or a dictionary, write the meaning beside each word.

When you are finished, write a short note telling what you have learned in this lesson. Try to use all 5 of these words in your note.

exception **legislate** **modify**
peaceful **protect**

Examining Words

The word *formal* suggests something that is done according to exact rules. The word *informal* means just the opposite. Something that is *informal* is done without exact rules.

Thc letters *in* at the beginning of a word can make it mean the opposite.

Three words and their meanings follow. Make the opposite of each of the words by adding *in*. Then write down what you think the meaning of the new word is.

When you are finished, check the dictionary to see if your answers are correct.

visible (can be seen)
sane (mentally healthy)
secure (safe)

AN ILLUSTRATION

Make a poster to illustrate an important rule in your school, or an important law in your province or in Canada. It could, for example, be a rule about smoking, or it could be a law about wearing seatbelts while driving.

Emily Stowe

Figure 17.3 *Emily Stowe*

Claim to fame: She helped change the laws for Canadian women.

Born: 1831 in South Norwich, Upper Canada

Married: 1856 to John Stowe. Their daughter, Dr. Augusta Stowe Gullen, became president of the Canadian Suffrage Association and was the first woman to receive a medical degree in Canada.

Career: Emily Stowe began working as a school teacher. But she really wanted to be a doctor. At that time, women were not allowed to go to medical school in Canada. So she went to study in New York and became a doctor in 1867.

When she came back to Canada, she was told that women were not admitted to the College of Physicians and Surgeons. This is the organization that gives doctors a licence to practise. Stowe fought their rules, and they gave in. In 1880 she was given a licence. She became the first woman to practise medicine in Canada. Through her efforts, the University of Toronto finally admitted women students in 1886.

Dr. Stowe and her supporters also worked for other legal rights for women. As a result of their efforts, Parliament passed the Married Woman's Property Act. Because of this act, married women were finally allowed to control some of their own property.

Died: Emily Stowe died in 1903.

- **Survey 10 people. Ask them whether their family doctors are men or women. Share your results with other students in your class.**
- **What do you think it would be like to be a doctor?**

Enforcing Laws

18

When our government representatives make a law, that is just the first step. Then the law has to be enforced or put into action. In the federal and provincial governments, this is done by cabinet ministers.

Of course, cabinet ministers couldn't possibly do this alone. They need workers to do the job for them. These workers, who are hired and paid by the government, are called civil servants.

One group of civil servants helps **interpret** the laws. This is an extremely important job. For example, the law says that people who run a business can work out their income tax in a special way. Many times this leads to tax savings. But what is a business?

Figure 18.1 *When dial telephones were first invented, the public had to be given lessons on how to use them. In this photograph, police officers are being given instructions on how to dial a call on the new machines. What new machines do we have today that you think will be as common as the telephone in the future?*

The official motto of the RCMP is not *They always get their man* but *Maintiens le droit* (Uphold the right).

Clearly companies like Eaton's and Imperial Oil Limited are businesses. But is a hockey player who advertises products on television running a business? Is an artist who sells 5 or 6 paintings a year running a business?

The people who must make these decisions are the civil servants. They write rules to cover this sort of situation and many others. These are the rules that people sometimes call "red tape". And these rules and decisions often have a big effect on people's lives.

Another special group of civil servants is the police. The job of these civil servants is to make sure that the laws are obeyed. In fact, just the presence of police officers makes a difference. Have you noticed how drivers are more careful as soon as a police car comes into sight?

One of the powers of the police is to **arrest** anyone they have "reasonable and probable grounds" to believe is about to break the law. For example, imagine that a police officer sees a person holding a baseball bat and looking in a store window. If this is in the afternoon (16:00, for example), then it would not be reasonable to think a crime was being planned. But if this was in the early morning (04:00, for example), then the officer might have "reasonable and probable grounds" for thinking that a robbery was being planned.

The police also have the right to arrest people they catch in the act of breaking the law. And they can arrest anyone who they feel has just broken the law. In order to arrest the person, the police can chase him or her into any building or area, including a private home. This is because they are in "fresh **pursuit**" of the criminal.

However, the police often need to arrest someone for a crime committed some time earlier. In this case, they have to have a document called a **warrant** for arrest. In certain cases, the police will also want to search a place for stolen or illegal property. In these cases, they have to have a document called a search warrant.

A warrant is a document signed by a judge. This document gives the police special powers. In the case of a warrant for arrest, the document says that the police have reason to believe that the person named is guilty of a crime. Therefore this person can be arrested and taken to the police station.

The famous RCMP Musical Ride was first performed in 1876 as part of the officers' regular training.

In the case of a search warrant, the document says that the police believe there are stolen or illegal items in a certain place. The search warrant allows the police to search that place at the date and time mentioned in the warrant.

Figure 18.2 *Police officers do many things besides enforcing the law. Here, Ontario Provincial Police escort Terry Fox during his run across Canada to raise money for cancer research. Terry Fox never managed to finish his run, but in 1985 another teenager who had lost a leg to cancer ran across Canada. Who was he?*

The police also have the power to search people, photograph them, and fingerprint them if they have been charged with a serious offence. The police also have the right to question an arrested person, although the arrested person does not have to answer the questions. Instead, an arrested person can demand to see a lawyer before answering questions.

Many people are worried about how much power the police forces have. And many people are worried about how much power civil servants have in general.

The problem is that unlike politicians, no civil servants are elected. Politicians can lose their jobs in an election. But most civil servants keep their jobs, even when one party loses power and another party forms the government. That means the voters have no direct **control** over civil servants.

But Canadians demand many different services from their governments. There has to be a large group of civil servants to make sure we get these services. The important thing to remember is that civil servants have to obey the elected representatives. They cannot just make up rules or take special powers on their own.

Elmer the Safety Elephant was first drawn in 1949 by Winnipeg artist Charles Thorson.

A University of Saskatchewan student once threw an egg 68 m to a classmate — and the egg didn't even crack!

SOME RIGHTS FOR PEOPLE WHO HAVE BEEN ARRESTED

The Canadian Charter of Rights lists a number of rights to protect people who have been arrested. The most important of these rights are explained here.

A person who has been arrested

(a) must be told *why* he or she has been arrested;

(b) must be brought to trial within a reasonable time;

(c) cannot be forced to testify at his or her own trial;

(d) is considered to be innocent until proven guilty;

(e) has the right to a trial by jury for serious charges;

(f) cannot be tried a second time for the same crime once he or she has been found innocent or has been punished.

THE FACTS

Remembering Facts

1. What is a civil servant?
2. What is red tape?
3. What does the phrase "reasonable and probable grounds" mean?
4. What is a warrant?
5. Civil servants aren't elected. Why could this be a problem?

Finding Facts

People are sometimes surprised to find out that police officers, fire fighters, and teachers are civil servants.

Make a list of all the adults you know who work outside their homes. Then find out who these people work for. Ask them whether they are civil servants.

When you are finished, look carefully at your list. How many people are on your list? How many of these people are civil servants? Share the results of your survey with the rest of the class.

YOUR OPINIONS

Stating Opinions

There is a constant debate about police powers in this country. Many people feel that the police have too much power. But many other people feel the police don't have enough power. What is your opinion?

Write a sentence that explains your ideas about police power.

Discussing Opinions

Some rules seem very clear and simple: *No one under the age of 19 can drink alcohol*, or *Everyone who has a job must pay unemployment insurance*. The trouble is, even the simplest rules can be very hard to enforce. They take up a lot of time and effort on the part of many people.

Imagine that your principal agreed to the following rule:

Students will get homework in only 1 subject each night.

What would be necessary in order to enforce this rule?

Discuss with your classmates how you would go about putting this rule into action. How would you decide what subject could be given for homework each night? How would you make sure the rule was followed? How would you handle special requests by teachers?

NEW WORDS

Learning Words

In your notebook, write the title Vocabulary: Lesson 18. Then write down the following words in a list. Using the Glossary or a dictionary, write the meaning beside each word.

When you are finished, write a short note telling what you have learned in this lesson. Try to use all 5 of these words in your note.

arrest	**control**	**interpret**
pursuit	**warrant**	

Examining Words

The expression *red tape* has a long history. Old documents and laws used to be written down and sealed with red tape. So long ago people started calling government rules *red tape*.

The phrase "to be caught *red-handed*" also has a long history. It used to be used in murder cases. Can you guess what the word *red* refers to in this phrase? Check your dictionary to see how we use this phrase today.

AN ILLUSTRATION

Table 18.1 shows how many women were working as civil servants for the federal government in 1983. Look carefully at this table. Then answer the following questions.

1. In 1983, how many federal civil servants were women?
2. In 1983, what percentage of federal civil servants were women?
3. What percentage of management and professional staff in 1983 were women?
4. What percentage of support staff in 1983 were women?
5. What is your opinion about the figures in this table? What do these figures seem to show about women in the federal civil service?

Occupation Level	Men	Women	Total	% Women
Management & Professional Staff	81 564	27 326	108 890	25.1
Support Staff	50 231	62 752	112 983	55.5
Total	131 795	90 078	221 873	40.6

SOURCE: Public Service Commission of Canada, *Annual Report 1983*

Table 18.1 *Employment in the Canadian civil service by sex in 1983*

Alex Decoteau

Figure 18.3 *This is the team picture of the Battleford Indian Industrial School Soccer Team of 1903. Alex Decoteau is standing third from the left.*

Claim to fame: He was a championship runner and the first full-blooded Indian to serve on a police force in Canada.

Born: 1887 on the Red Pheasant Reserve, south of Battleford, Saskatchewan, 2 years after Louis Riel was hanged

Career: Alex Decoteau spent his early life attending school on the Indian reserve where he had been born. Few people paid attention to the fact that he could outrun and outjump anyone of his own size.

But this all changed in 1909 when Decoteau went to live in Edmonton with his sister and brother-in-law. In May of that year, he entered a race at Fort Saskatchewan. He astonished the crowd by coming in second, just behind one of the best runners in Canada.

Decoteau went on after that first race to win dozens of important races across Canada. At a provincial meet in 1910, he won 4 races in a single day. He set many Canadian records and became the only Albertan to serve on the Candian team for the Olympics at Stockholm in 1912.

When he wasn't running, Decoteau was working as a police officer for the Edmonton Police. He was promoted to the rank of sergeant in 1914. But he resigned in 1916 in order to join the Canadian Army. Decoteau was sent overseas to fight in the trenches of France.

Died: Alex Decoteau died in 1917, in the terrible battle of Passchendaele in which 15 654 Canadians lost their lives.

- **Tom Longboat is another famous Native Canadian athlete. What was he famous for?**
- **Which do you think was hardest for Decoteau — to win races or to be the first full-blooded Indian policeman?**

19 The Adversary System

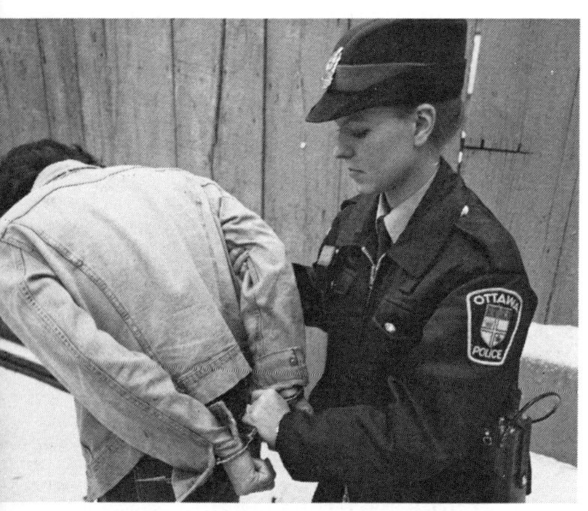

Figure 19.1 A police officer makes an arrest *Most police work involves public law. The police are responsible for protecting the public and for upholding the Criminal Code. This is an Act passed by Parliament that describes the most common criminal offences.*

Our system of justice is based on one party or person accusing another party or person of doing something wrong. The parties involved are somewhat like enemies who are having a fight. Another word for enemy is **adversary**. That is why our system of justice is called the adversary system.

You have probably watched American police dramas on television. In these shows there is often a character called the district attorney, or the D.A. This person is always a lawyer who has been hired by the government to fight criminals.

In Canada we also have lawyers who are hired by the government to fight criminals. But they are not called *district* attorneys. As you know, Canada is headed by a monarch — a queen or a king. So the lawyers hired by our government are called *crown* attorneys.

Whenever a crown attorney is fighting a case in court, you can be sure that the case is part of what we call public law. This is the whole area of law that involves the government on the one hand and private citizens or organizations on the other. In these cases, the government is always the adversary that is accusing the other party of doing something wrong.

There is more than one kind of public law. The kind you have probably heard most about is criminal law. This is the kind of law that involves crimes like murder and driving dangerously. But it doesn't matter what kind of crime is involved. In public law it is always the government that accuses another party or person of doing something wrong.

In addition to public law is private law. For example, you will have heard about divorced couples who take each other to court to get custody of their children. Or perhaps you have read in the newspaper about a patient suing a doctor for giving the wrong treatment.

Front Page Challenge, **Canada's longest-running television entertainment show, began on June 24, 1957.**

Both these cases involve private citizens. In both examples one person is taking the other to court. The government is not directly involved. So there will be no crown attorney. The cases are part of private law.

In private law, the person who accuses someone else of doing something wrong is called the **plaintiff**. It is possible for a single person to act as the plaintiff on his or her own. But most people who go to court hire lawyers to do the work for them. In this case, the lawyers are called the lawyers for the prosecution.

Sometimes the plaintiff isn't a single person but a whole company. For example, this might happen if a person was caught shoplifting from a store. The store would act as the plaintiff, and it would be represented by its lawyers.

The person who is being accused of doing something wrong is called the **defendant**. This is true for both private and public law. It is possible for the defendant to be a single person, an organization, or even the government.

For example, if someone thought that a food store was pretending to sell hamburger when it was really selling ground pork, that person might take the store to court. In this case, the food store would be the defendant.

In the same way, a group of citizens might be angry that the government was dumping garbage close to their homes. They might take the government to court in order to stop the dumping. In this case, the government would be the defendant.

It is possible for a defendant to represent him or herself in court, but very few do. Most defendants hire lawyers to do the work for them. In this case, these lawyers are called the lawyers for the defence.

In every court case, the two parties, or adversaries, come together in front of a judge for the **trial**. It is the judge's job to decide who is right.

Most court cases are tried by a single judge. The 2 parties explain their sides to the judge. Usually they do this by answering lawyers' questions. They will also call **witnesses** to support them. Witnesses are people who know something about the case. They can appear of their own free will. Or they can be forced to come to court. When witnesses are forced to come to court, we say they have been subpoenaed.

The judge listens carefully to this testimony, as it is called. Then the judge must come to a verdict, or decision. In other words, the judge has to decide whether the defendant is innocent or guilty. If the judge decides that the defendant is guilty, then the judge must also decide what penalty or sentence to give.

The E.B. Eddy Company of Hull, Quebec, is one of the world's largest matchmaking companies. It introduced book matches in 1928.

Figure 19.2 *Before speaking in court, witnesses are always asked to swear an oath. In this oath, they promise to tell the truth. Usually, the oath is sworn on the Bible. But if the witness does not believe in the Bible, the Bible does not have to be used.*

The Calgary Stampede, famous for its annual rodeo events for 10 days each July, was founded in 1912.

These steps may sound quite simple. But in fact they involve a lot of time, effort, and thought. It is not always easy for one person to decide whether someone else is guilty. And it is even harder for one person to decide what would be a fair penalty.

That is why our system of justice involves 3 safeguards: common law, trial by jury, and appeals. You will learn about these safeguards in the following lessons.

PUBLIC LAW

This involves a crown attorney who represents the government. In the name of the government, the crown attorney accuses the other party of doing something wrong.

Criminal Law *This involves actions that are forbidden by law such as assault or theft.*

Constitutional Law *This involves decisions about which government has the right to pass certain laws. It also involves decisions about whether laws are correct according to the Canadian constitution and Charter of Rights and Freedoms.*

Figure 19.3 *There are several different kinds of public law, and there are several different kinds of private law. The most important kinds are shown in this illustration. Whenever you listen to the news or read a newspaper about a court case, try to decide first whether it involves public or private law. Then try to decide what type of public or private law is involved.*

PRIVATE LAW

This involves an argument between 2 private parties or persons.

Contract Law *This involves agreements that 2 or more people have made. Example: there is an agreement to buy a car, but the new owner does not pay all the money owing.*

Family Law *This involves the relationship between people in close family groups. Example: a divorced parent wants to be allowed to see the children more often.*

Tort Law *This involves situations when one party wrongs another. Example: someone has hit you and you want to get money, or compensation, for the pain you have suffered.*

Property Law *This involves the selling and renting of property of any kind. Example: you are renting an apartment but the landlord refuses to fix the ceiling.*

THE FACTS

Remembering Facts

1. Why is our system of justice called the adversary system?
2. Who does the crown attorney represent?
3. What is the main difference between public and private law?
4. Are the plaintiff and defendant always just single people?
5. What is the job of the judge?

Finding Facts

Generally, it is not wise to go to court without a lawyer. And as a rule, you should always hire the best lawyer possible.

The trouble is that most lawyers, especially the best, cost a lot of money to hire. Therefore, the government has set up a legal aid program for people who cannot afford a lawyer.

Telephone the nearest legal aid office to find out who can get legal aid and how the legal aid system works. Ask them to mail you any information pamphlets they have. If possible, invite a lawyer from legal aid to explain to the class how the system works.

YOUR OPINIONS

Stating Opinions

If you had to appear in court, would you rather be the plaintiff or the defendant? Explain your opinion in a few sentences.

Discussing Opinions

Judges are very powerful. In the case of a major crime like murder or armed robbery, judges have the power to send people to jail for 20 years.

Try to imagine the perfect judge. Then discuss with your classmates what qualities you think good judges should have.

NEW WORDS

Learning Words

In your notebook, write the title Vocabulary: Lesson 19. Then write down the following words in a list. Using the Glossary or a dictionary, write the meaning beside each word.

When you are finished, write a short note telling what you have learned in this lesson. Try to use all 5 of these words in your note.

adversary	**defendant**	**plaintiff**
trial	**witness**	

Examining Words

The word *safeguard* is made up of 2 common words: *safe* and *guard*. Therefore, the word *safeguard* means "something which guards us and keeps us safe".

The following words are also made up of 2 common words. Say which 2 common words each longer word is made of. Then explain how these 2 common words fit the meaning of the longer word.

fireplace	football	handstand
notebook	overcoat	waterfall

It costs millions of dollars each year to run our system of justice. The pie chart in Figure 19.4 shows where the money goes in cases involving criminal law. Are you surprised by any of these figures? Do you think more money should be spent in certain areas?

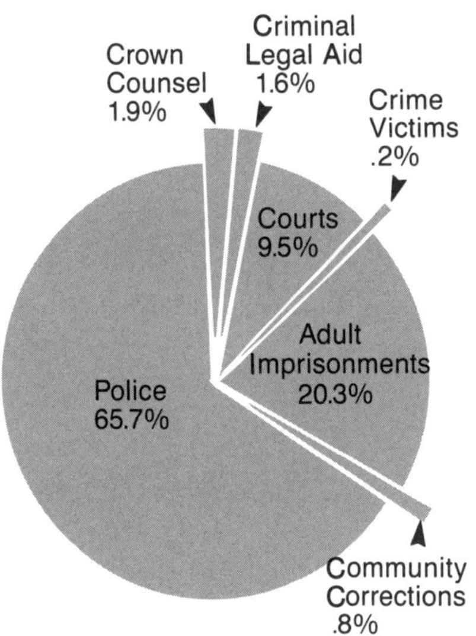

SOURCE: The Criminal Law in Canadian Society, August 1982, Government of Canada

Figure 19.4 *Average spending on penal justice programs in Canada: 1977/78*

Clara Brett Martin

Figure 19.5 *Clara Brett Martin*

Claim to fame: She was the first woman lawyer in Canada.

Born: 1874 in Toronto, of Hungarian and Irish parents

Career: Clara Brett Martin was educated privately at home before entering Trinity College in Toronto. She shocked her professors by insisting on studying mathematics instead of English literature like most other young women of that period.

After spending a few years as a teacher, Martin decided to become a lawyer. However, the Law Society refused to admit her as a student because a woman was not considered a "person" at the time.

Luckily, Oliver Mowat, the premier of Ontario, supported Martin. He arranged to pass a law that said the Law Society was allowed to admit women. But the Law Society still refused to admit Martin.

This time, Mowat threatened to *force* the Law Society to admit women as students. After a heated debate, the Law Society agreed to accept Clara Brett Martin as a student by a vote of 12 to 11.

In 1897, Martin became the first woman to become a lawyer, not only in Canada, but also in the entire British Empire. She had a brilliant legal career. She built a large legal practice and also served on the Toronto Board of Education.

Died: Clara Brett Martin died suddenly of heart failure in 1923.

- **What was the British Empire? Name 4 countries in this empire.**
- **Which would you prefer — going to a regular school, or being taught at home by tutors?**

Common Law 20

A **statute** is a law that has been written down. All laws made by Canadian governments are written down. Therefore, the laws that are made by the different levels of government are called statute law.

This is important because there is a whole other area of law called **common** law. Common law is based on all the cases that have ever been taken to court. It is easiest to explain the difference between statute law and common law by giving an example.

Imagine that a person has been charged with stealing a valuable diamond ring. After hearing all the evidence, the judge decides that this defendant is guilty. Then the judge has to decide what penalty to give.

The statute law passed by the government says that a person who steals can be put in jail for up to 10 years. But perhaps it is the first time this defendant has ever been caught stealing. Ten years seems like a long time. So before

Figure 20.1 Inuit children in a Roman Catholic school at Fort Resolution, N.W.T. *In the days when this picture was taken, the Canadian government tried to force a different culture and way of life on the Native people. They did this through education and through the law. This has now changed, as you will find by reading about John Howard Sissons at the end of this lesson.*

Figure 20.2 *There are many different kinds of evidence. Here, watches, jewellery, guns, and other stolen items lie on a table at the police station. They have been neatly organized and tagged, ready to be used as exhibits in a court case. Find out what happens to objects like this after the court case is over.*

deciding on the **penalty**, our judge would be sure to think about the **precedents**.

Precedents are similar cases that have been tried in court before. The judge in this example would look at cases from the past in which someone was caught stealing for the first time.

Probably our judge would find that most other first-time thieves were not sent to jail for 10 whole years. In most of the past cases, these thieves were sent to jail for only a few months. Therefore, the judge in our example would probably send the defendant to jail for just a few months.

Canada's Sandford Fleming was the inventor of standard time zones.

This is an example of common law at work. By statute law, our judge could have sent the diamond thief to jail for 10 years. But using common law, our judge gave a much lighter penalty.

Judges also use common law to decide what kind of **evidence** they will accept in court. For example, think again about the example of the stolen diamond ring. The police might have given the defendant a lie detector test. And this test might have shown that the defendant was guilty. Naturally, the police would like to use the test as proof that the defendant was the thief.

But back in 1967, a precedent was set that lie detector tests could not be used as evidence. In 1967, the Supreme Court of Canada — the most powerful court in the whole country — refused to accept the results of a lie detector test as evidence in a murder trial.

A precedent is a brand-new decision made by an important judge. It is a decision that sets the pattern (precedent) for all similar court cases. That is why, from 1967 on, all other Canadian judges have said that lie detector test results could not be used in court. So in the example of the stolen diamond ring, the judge would probably not allow the police to use the lie detector test as evidence.

This does not mean that Canadian courts will *never* accept lie detector evidence. In fact, a Canadian judge in 1984 decided that a lie detector test could be used as evidence in a trial. The judge allowed this on the grounds that the defendant *wanted* the test results to be used. If the Supreme Court goes along with this idea, then there will be a new precedent for the use of lie detector tests in Canadian courts.

As you can see, this system of precedents can be quite complicated. But common law has 2 big advantages. First, it lets people know what to expect. By looking at similar cases from the past, a person can have a good of idea of what will happen in his or her own court case.

Second, common law is fair. It helps make sure that people are treated fairly in court. If a person's penalty is almost the same as the penalty given to someone else in a similar case, then we can all feel that the judge's decision was fair.

Figure 20.3 *It takes a lot of time to read and learn precedents. That explains why people who have to go to court usually hire lawyers. Lawyers have spent many years in school reading books of cases and memorizing the decisions made by earlier judges. Before every trial a good lawyer will review all the similar cases in order to prepare for court.*

The second digit in a telephone area code is always a 0 or a 1. Check in the phone book to prove it.

THE FACTS

Remembering Facts

1. What is statute law?
2. What is common law?
3. Why are precedents important?
4. How is a precedent set?
5. What are the two advantages of common law?

Finding Facts

Common law has been used in Britain for many centuries. Therefore when the first settlers came from Britain to Canada, they used the common law system for justice. That is why common law is used in Canada today.

However, the people in France do not use common law. So when the French settlers came to Canada, they used a different system of law. Even today, parts of this French system are still used in Quebec.

Use an encyclopedia or textbook to find out how the law used in Quebec is different from the common law used in the rest of Canada.

YOUR OPINIONS

Stating Opinions

Do you think that first-time thieves should be given lighter sentences than thieves who have been caught many times? Explain your opinion in a few sentences.

Discussing Opinions

Some judges feel that public figures like politicians or entertainers should be given harsher penalties. They say that this sets a good example for ordinary people. It also shows that just because people are famous, it doesn't mean they don't have to obey the law.

Others say that this is wrong. They say that everyone should be treated equally under the eyes of the law.

What do you think? Should public figures be treated more harshly? Discuss your opinions with your classmates.

NEW WORDS

Learning Words

In your notebook, write the title Vocabulary: Lesson 20. Then write down the following words in a list. Using the Glossary or a dictionary, write the meaning beside each word.

When you are finished, write a short note telling what you have learned in this lesson. Try to use all 5 of these words in your note.

common **evidence** **penalty**
precedent **statute**

Examining Words

You may have heard of something called a "common law marriage". Now that you know what *common law* is, can you explain what a common law marriage is in comparison to a legal marriage?

AN ILLUSTRATION

Even though our system of justice is based on common law, there still can be big differences from one judge to another. For example, look closely at Table 20.1. It gives information about the sentences given by 5 different judges in one province. In every case, the defendant was found guilty of "creating a disturbance".

Discuss this chart with your classmates. What does this chart show? If you were the defendant, which judge would you prefer to hear your case? Which judge would you *not* like to hear your case?

Judge	Number of Defendants Found Guilty	Number of Defendants Sent to Jail	Average Number of Days in Jail
Judge A	65	1	31
Judge B	26	3	13
Judge C	26	0	0
Judge D	46	29	40
Judge E	29	0	0

SOURCE: D.L. Gibson, F. Jarman, and T.G. Murphy, *All About Law* (Toronto: John Wiley and Sons Canada Limited, 1984)

Table 20.1 *The record of 5 provincial judges in trying cases of "disturbing the peace"*

John Howard Sissons (Ekoktoegee)

Figure 20.4 *John Howard Sissons*

Claim to fame: He was the judge in the Northwest Territories who adapted Canadian laws to suit the lives and customs of the Native people in the far North.

Born: in 1892 in Orillia, Ontario

Career: John Sissons had polio at age 4. This left him with a permanent limp. But he refused to let it stop him.

Sissons studied law and then set up a practice in Grand Prairie, Alberta. He stayed in the area for 25 years. During that time, he ran for election and became the Liberal MP for Peace River in 1940.

While he was in Parliament, Sissons gained a reputation for helping the Native people of the area. They trusted him. So in 1955 he was appointed as the Justice of the first Court of the Northwest Territories.

During his 11 years as justice, Sissons won the respect and love of the Native people. They called him "Ekoktoegee" — the man who listens. This was because Sissons always tried to fit Canadian law to the lives of the Inuit.

For example, in one famous case an Inuk had been charged with shooting a muskox out of season. Sissons ruled that the Native people depended on hunting for their meals. Therefore, he decided that this Inuk should not have to be bound by the Canadian laws that had been written to stop sports hunters.

Died: Sissons died in 1969, 3 years after his retirement.

- **Chief Justice Berger was another important judge in the far North. What was his job?**
- **Do you think it would be easy or difficult to be a judge?**

Trial by Jury 21

Many court cases are for minor crimes such as disturbing the peace. These minor crimes are called summary **offences**. In these cases it isn't such a big responsibility for one person — the judge — to decide whether or not the defendant is guilty.

But some court cases are for major crimes such as murder or armed robbery. These major crimes are called indictable offences. In these cases the defendant could be sentenced to prison for a very long time. This is a major decision for one person to have to make.

That is why our system of justice allows most defendants who are accused of indictable offences to choose how they want to be tried. They can ask to be tried by a judge alone. Or they can choose to be tried by a judge and a **jury** made up of 12 ordinary people. In some cases, however, they must be tried by a jury.

Figure 21.1 Riel addressing the jury, Regina, 1885 *Louis Riel's trial is probably the most famous jury trial in Canadian history. You can read more about Riel and the trial in Lesson 36.*

In 1922, Canadian Moses Cardin patented a special rocking chair that churned butter while you rocked.

When a defendant is tried by a jury, the court officials take a computer list of all the people who live in the county. Then they choose 75 to 100 names at random from the list.

These people are sent a letter telling them they have been chosen to serve on a jury. And they are told that they have to come to the courtroom on a certain day. This is the law. Only a few special people can be **excused** from serving on a jury.

On the day the people come to court, their names are put on cards and mixed up in a box. Then cards are pulled out, one at a time. The people whose names are on the cards have to come to the front of the room and answer questions. This is because the lawyers for the defence and the lawyers for the prosecution both have the right to turn down a certain number of people as jurors.

First the defence lawyers ask questions. The defence lawyers want to make sure that the person has not already decided that the defendant is guilty. This might have happened if the person had read a newspaper report about the case.

Then the crown attorney or the lawyers for the prosecution ask the person questions. They want to make sure that the person has not already decided that the defendant is innocent. They also want to make sure that the person is not against the law or the police.

After they have questioned several of the people, the lawyers agree on 12 people who will be the jury. These 12 people are expected to listen to the evidence during the trial.

At the end of the trial, the jury listens to summaries made first by the defence lawyers and then by the lawyers for the prosecution. Afterwards, the judge gives the jury members instructions about what they have to do. During this time, the judge will explain what the *law* is for this case.

Then the jury will be **sequestered**. This means that the jury members will not be allowed to read or hear any news reports. They will not be allowed to speak to their friends or families. They will not even be allowed to go home. If necessary, they will have to stay overnight in a hotel and be guarded by court officers.

While these 12 people are sequestered, they have to discuss the evidence they have heard in the trial. It is important that they listen only to each other. They must not be influenced by anyone else. It is their job and their job alone to decide whether or not the defendant is guilty.

Canadians make 27 billion local phone calls annually, plus 100 million phone calls to other countries.

The jury's decision must be **unanimous**. This means that all 12 members have to agree either that the defendant is guilty or that the defendant is innocent. If the jury members cannot agree, then the jury is called a "hung jury". In this situation, the case has to be tried all over again with a new jury.

Once the jury has reached a decision, it goes back to the courtroom to tell the judge. If all 12 say the defendant is innocent, then the defendant is allowed to go free. If all 12 say the defendant is guilty, then the judge has to give a sentence.

Even after the trial, the members of the jury are not allowed to talk to reporters or friends or family about what happened when they were sequestered. This protects the defendant, and it also protects the members of the jury themselves.

Serving on a jury can take a lot of time and emotional energy. But serving on a jury is also one of the most important jobs a citizen can do. It shows that in our country we all have a say in the law. Every person has the right and the responsibility to take part in our system of justice.

In 1903, 100 people in the town of Frank, Alberta, were killed when 63 million tonnes of rock came crashing down from Turtle Mountain.

Figure 21.2 Dr. Henry Morgentaler *The most famous modern jury trials are those of Dr. Henry Morgentaler. Dr. Morgentaler has been tried in both Ontario and Quebec for performing abortions illegally. He has been acquitted by juries 4 times; that is, he has been found not guilty. But Dr. Morgentaler still faces more trials. This raises an important legal question: should the decisions of juries be final, or should jury decisions be changed if lawyers and judges think they are wrong?*

THE FACTS

Remembering Facts

1. What is the difference between a summary offence and an indictable offence?
2. How is a jury chosen?
3. What is the job of a jury?
4. Why are juries sequestered?
5. What is a hung jury?

Finding Facts

In very early times, people weren't tried by jury. They were tried by ordeal. An ordeal is a really bad experience.

Look in the dictionary, encyclopedia, and other books to find out exactly how a trial by ordeal was run.

YOUR OPINIONS

Stating Opinions

There is a very good chance that some time in your life you will be asked to serve on a jury. Explain in a few sentences what you think it would be like to serve on a jury.

Discussing Opinions

There are 2 reasons why you can be excused from serving on a jury. First, you can get permission to be excused if it would be a hardship. For example, many students are excused because it might be impossible for them to catch up on the school they have missed.

The Lieutenant-Governor
Members of the House of Commons and the Senate in Ottawa
Members of the provincial legislature
Judges
Members of the Armed Forces
Lawyers to the Supreme Court
People who work full time as officers in the courts
Police officers
Doctors
Dentists
Ministers or priests or rabbis
People whose job is to choose members of the jury

SOURCE: Consolidated Statutes of Nova Scotia, Vol 10, 1979

Table 21.1 *Those people in Nova Scotia who are automatically excused from jury duty*

Second, you can get permission to be excused if you have a special job. The specific jobs change a bit from province to province. But the list in Table 12.1 is typical.

Discuss with your classmates why you think each of the people listed in Table 21.1 can be excused from jury duty. What other jobs do you think should be added to the list? Do you think some of the jobs on the list should be taken off?

NEW WORDS

Learning Words

In your notebook, write the title Vocabulary: Lesson 21. Then write down the following words in a list. Using the Glossary or a dictionary, write the meaning beside each word.

When you are finished, write a short note telling what you have learned in this lesson. Try to use all 5 of these words in your note.

excuse	**jury**	**offence**
sequester	**unanimous**	

Examining Words

The word *indict* rhymes with kite. You don't pronounce the letter *c* in indict.

There are other words like this in English. What letters are silent in the following words?

campaign	island	knife
lamb	salmon	subtle

AN ILLUSTRATION

Table 21.2 compares summary offences and indictable offences over a 20-year period in Canada. It gives the number of actual convictions. It also gives the *rate* of convictions; that is, the number of convictions for every 100 000 people in the population. Look carefully at the figures in Table 21.2. Then answer the following questions.

1. Does the number of summary offences appear to be increasing?
2. Does the rate of summary offences appear to be increasing?
3. Does the number of indictable offences appear to be increasing?
4. Does the rate of indictable offences appear to be increasing?

5. Are there more summary offences or more indictable offences each year?

Year	Summary Offences: Number of Convictions	Summary Offences: Rate per 100 000	Indictable Offences: Number of Convictions	Indictable Offences: Rate per 100 000
1950[1]	1 183 991	8 634.7	31 385	228.9
1960	1 106 532	6 192.1	35 443	198.3
1970[2]	1 451 943	10 488.6	45 880	215.8

[1]1950 statistics do not include Newfoundland

[2]1970 statistics do not include Alberta and Quebec (Statistics for indictable convictions were not collected in Canada after 1973.)

SOURCE: The Criminal Law in Canadian Society, August 1982, Government of Canada

Table 21.2 *A comparison of summary and indictable offences in Canada, 1950-1970*

Donald Marshall

Figure 21.3 *Donald Marshall celebrates his release from prison.*

Claim to fame: He spent 11 years in prison for a murder he did not commit.

Born: 1954 in Sydney, Nova Scotia. His father is a lifetime religious leader for the Micmac Indians of Nova Scotia.

Career: On May 28, 1971, 17-year-old Donald Marshall and his friend, 16-year-old Sandy Seale, were walking in a park in Sydney, Nova Scotia. They tried to rob another man. But instead, the man stabbed Seale to death and wounded Marshall.

Marshall called for help. But he never told anyone that he and Seale had set out to rob the man. Therefore, the police didn't believe Marshall's story. Instead, they charged him with the murder.

Marshall was tried by jury. Two witnesses had been scared into saying they had seen Marshall kill Seale. The evidence seemed uncertain. But the jury convicted Marshall. He was sentenced to life imprisonment.

For 11 years, Marshall lived behind bars. But through it all, he kept saying he was innocent. Finally, in 1983, the witnesses came forward and said that they had not told the truth. A new trial was called. And Marshall, at age 29, was set free.

The government paid Marshall $270 000 as compensation for his time behind bars. But nothing could ever make up for his 11 lost years.

- **What is perjury?**
- **What do you think should happen to the witnesses who lied about Marshall?**

22 Sentencing

Figure 22.1 Polly, Carleton County Jail, 1895 *The living conditions in early jails were terrible. The cells were dirty, cold, and dark. Often people who were mentally ill were locked up as common criminals. What happens today to criminals who are found not guilty by reason of insanity?*

It can be very difficult for a judge or jury to convict a person; that is, to say that a person is guilty. But it is usually even more difficult to decide what sentence to give to that person.

Before giving a sentence, a judge normally considers a lot of different things. Of course the judge will have to think about the crime itself and about other sentences that have been given. But the judge will also consider the person's past record.

The judge may even ask an expert such as a psychiatrist to interview the offender and write a report. The report will explain how the offender feels about the crime. It will describe the offender's personality. And it will discuss the offender's chances of becoming a law-abiding citizen.

All of these things are very important. This is because a sentence isn't given just to punish someone for breaking the law. There are 3 other main reasons for sentences.

First, sentences are meant to act as **deterrents**. A deterrent is something that stops people from doing something. For example, if people know they will be put in jail for armed robbery, then they won't be as likely to do it.

Second, sentences are meant to **rehabilitate** offenders. This means that offenders will change and become law-abiding citizens. That is why our prison system employs doctors and ministers and teachers to help people in jail.

Third, sentences are meant to **segregate** offenders. If offenders are put in jail, then they can't repeat their crimes. This helps to protect other citizens.

Once the judge has taken all of these things into account, he or she will decide on a sentence. Sometimes it will be a suspended sentence. In this case, the offender is not given a sentence right away. Instead, the offender is released on **probation** for a certain period of time.

During probation, the offender has to keep in regular contact with a social worker called a probation officer. Normally they meet once a week or so to discuss what the offender has been doing.

Offenders on probation must be sure to obey all the laws. Normally there will also be other special rules for the offender. For example, the offender may be given a curfew and may have to be at home by a certain time each night. Or the offender may not be allowed to meet people that the probation officer thinks will be a bad influence.

As long as the offender does this for the whole period of probation, then he or she will never be sentenced. However, if the offender breaks any of these rules, then he or she will have to appear before the judge and be sentenced.

The right to appeal a conviction was first granted to Canadians in 1923.

Figure 22.2 A modern detention cell *This modern cell looks quite comfortable and pleasant, especially compared with the cell in Figure 22.1. But how do you think a person would feel about being locked up here?*

Marie-Josephe Corriveau's body was displayed for a month after she was hanged in Quebec in 1763. She was thought to be a witch.

Figure 22.3 Mary Dawson, Warden of Kingston Penitentiary *In 1984, Mary Dawson became the first female warden of a Canadian maximum security prison. Do you think it makes any difference whether the person in charge of a prison is a man or a woman?*

However, most offenders are given a sentence right from the start. This sentence can be as minor as paying a small fine, or sum of money. But it can also be as major as being sent to jail for several years.

Sometimes the people involved in a court case feel that the judge's decision was wrong or unfair. Therefore our system of justice sometimes lets people **appeal** court decisions that they disagree with. In other words, they can have a more senior judge consider their case again.

Either the defendant or the prosecutor can ask for an appeal. This is done by going to a special court of appeal that is made up of several experienced judges. Normally this has to be done within 30 days after the sentence is given.

Not all convicted people are given an appeal when they ask for it. They have to have good reasons. For example, they have to be able to prove the judge made an error and did not follow the law correctly. Or they have to prove that there was an error in the facts given in evidence.

The judges in the appeal court can change the verdict. They can change the sentence. They can even order a new trial. If there is a new trial, the case will be tried by a higher court. Sometimes cases are appealed and tried several times until they reach the highest court of all — the Supreme Court of Canada.

THE FACTS

Remembering Facts

1. Name 3 things a judge will consider before deciding on a sentence.
2. Why are sentences given?
3. What happens when a person is on probation?
4. Why would someone ask for an appeal?
5. Does everyone always get an appeal?

Finding Facts

There are many different kinds of jails that prisoners are sent to. Some of these are run by the provinces. Many others are run by the federal government.

The federal prisons are divided into four groups:

(a) community correction centres,
(b) minimum-security prisons,
(c) medium-security prisons,
(d) maximum-security prisons.

Find out about one of these prisons. Why does it have this name? What kind of prisoners are sent there? What is life like for these prisoners while they are in jail?

YOUR OPINIONS

Stating Opinions

When prisoners have been in jail for one-third of the time they were sentenced to, then they are eligible for parole. Parole is very much like probation. The prisoners who are given parole have to keep in touch with social workers called parole officers. As long as they do not break any laws or rules, they are allowed to live outside of prison. If they do break the law, then they must go back to prison.

About 75% of the prisoners who are released on parole manage to stay out of difficulty. But about 25% commit more crimes and have to be taken back to prison.

Some Canadians think that too many prisoners are released on parole. Others think that parole is a very good way to help rehabilitate a prisoner.

What do you think about parole? Explain your ideas in a few sentences.

Discussing Opinions

By statute, a person who steals something from the mail can be sentenced for up to 10 years in jail. But in common law, people are not often given such a big penalty.

Discuss each of the following cases with your classmates. Which person do you think deserves the biggest penalty? Which person deserves the smallest penalty?

1. Susan works at the postal plant sorting mail. A letter jams in the machine and Susan pulls it out so the other mail can go through. The letter has been ripped and Susan can see that there are 5 $20 bills inside. At the moment she is having trouble supporting herself and her 2 small children. She takes the bills out for herself and sends the letter on its way. Later she feels guilty but doesn't know how to return the money.
2. Carol takes the elevator downstairs to the mailroom in her apartment building. She notices that the mailbox for her neighbour has been left open. Inside, Carol finds a copy of her favourite magazine. She takes the magazine

for herself even though it is addressed to her neighbour. Carol feels that it was her neighbour's fault for being careless. And anyway, it's easy enough for the neighbour to go out and buy another copy of the magazine.

3. Gord and his friends have been making a lot of money by forging credit cards. Gord breaks into mailboxes on the street and steals the letters inside. He takes any letters addressed to credit card companies and opens them. Then he uses the account numbers and names inside in order to make false credit cards. This is the fifth time Gord has been caught by the police. But in this case he doesn't feel guilty. He figures that the individual people won't be hurt by his actions. The credit card companies' insurance will pay.

NEW WORDS

Learning Words

In your notebook, write the title Vocabulary: Lesson 22. Then write down the following words in a list. Using the Glossary or a dictionary, write the meaning beside each word.

When you are finished, write a short note telling what you have learned in this lesson. Try to use all 5 of these words in your note.

appeal	**deterrent**	**probation**
rehabilitate	**segregate**	

Examining Words

The word *supreme* means "the highest or most powerful possible". That is why you will often hear the word *supreme* in advertisements.

For the next week, watch for examples of advertisers using the word *supreme*. These advertisements could be on the radio, in newspapers, on billboards, or on television. Write down every time you see or hear the word *supreme* used and the product it is describing.

At the end of the week, bring your list of advertisements using the word *supreme* to class. Discuss your list with your classmates. Do you think it was right for the word *supreme* to be used in each case?

AN ILLUSTRATION

Figure 22.4 shows the number of people in prisons for every 100 000 people in a country. This is called the rate of imprisonment in a country. Look closely at the graph. Then answer the following questions.

1. Which country has the highest rate of imprisonment?
2. Which country has the lowest rate of imprisonment?
3. Which country has almost the same rate of imprisonment as Canada?

When you have finished answering these questions, discuss Figure 22.4 with your classmates. Can you think of any explanations for why the rates of imprisonment are so different?

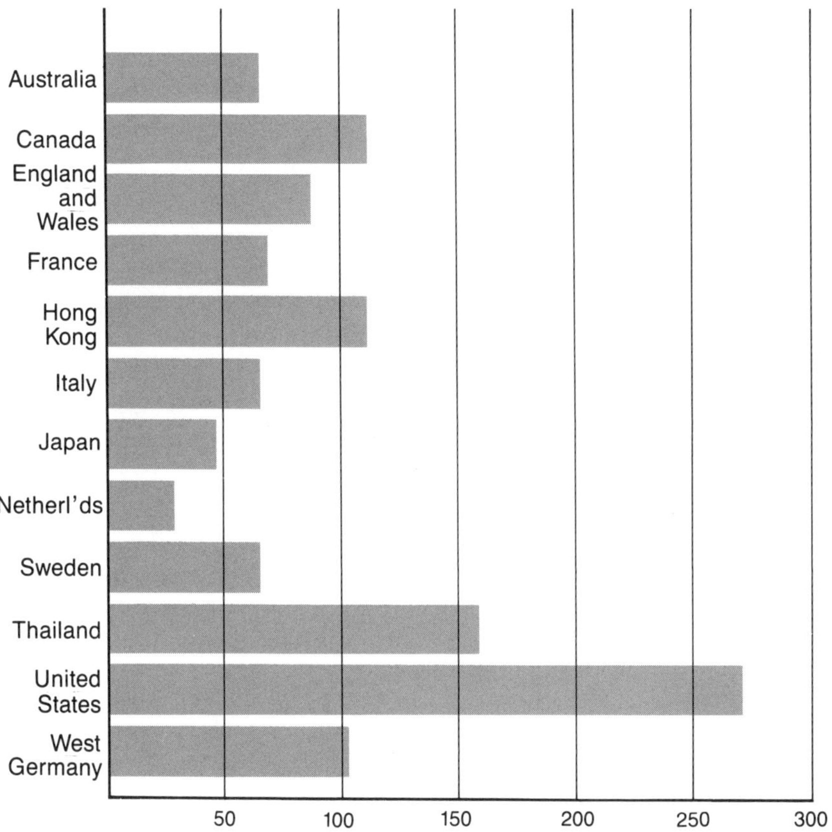

SOURCE: the Communications Branch, The Correctional Service of Canada, *Basic Facts 1984*

Figure 22.4 *Rates of imprisonment in 12 different countries per 100 000 population*

Agnes Macphail

Figure 22.5 *Agnes Macphail*

Claim to fame: She was the first woman in Canada elected to Parliament.

Born: 1890 in Grey County, Ontario

Career: Agnes Macphail began her career as a school teacher. She also became active in farm organizations and learned a lot about farmers' problems. In 1921 she ran for a seat in Parliament as a representative of the United Farmers of Ontario.

Macphail won the election. By doing this, she became the first woman ever elected to Parliament in Canada. Unfortunately, while she was in Parliament most people, including her fellow MPs, treated her like an outcast. They found it very strange for a woman to be in Parliament. Nevertheless, she fought hard for social issues, especially for help for farmers.

Macphail was most interested in prison reform. She fought for this cause for many years even though most people were opposed to the idea. Her efforts were not in vain. Finally, in 1936, a commission was set up to investigate the state of Canadian prisons.

Macphail was defeated in 1940 because she believed in peace. Canada was fighting in World War II, so many people did not like pacifists like Macphail. But then in 1943 she was elected to the Ontario legislature.

Died: Agnes Macphail stayed in political life until 1951. She died just 3 years later, in 1954.

- **How many women MPs are there in the House of Commons today?**
- **Do you think that an MP would lose an election today just because he or she was a pacifist?**

QUIZ 3

The following questions are based on the lessons in Chapter 3. **DO NOT WRITE YOUR ANSWERS IN THIS TEXTBOOK.** Instead, you should write the answers in your notebook or on a separate sheet of paper.

1. Write the letters from (a) to (e) on your paper. Then write a T if the statement is TRUE. Write an F if the statement is FALSE.

   (a) You do not have to obey a law if you do not agree with it.
   (b) Even a 5-year-old child can be charged with breaking the law in Canada.
   (c) Civil servants are government workers who are not elected.
   (d) The police can arrest someone if they have "reasonable and probable" grounds to think that the person is about to commit a crime.
   (e) Police can enter any house at any time of the day and whenever they choose.

2. Match the item in the list on the left side with the correct description from the list on the right side. For each one, write the letter and the number together on your paper.

(a) statute law	(1) a jury whose members cannot agree about whether the defendant is guilty or innocent
(b) common law	(2) a system of justice in which one person accuses another person of doing something wrong
(c) adversary system	(3) a document that gives the police special powers
(d) hung jury	(4) a system of law based on all the similar cases that have been taken to court
(e) warrant	(5) all the laws that are made and written down by our governments

3. Find the correct answer from the list given after each statement. Then write the whole statement on your paper.

   (a) The person who is accused of committing a crime is called the ______.

crown attorney
plaintiff
defendant
witness
judge

(b) The answers to the questions lawyers ask in a trial are called ______.
sentences
red tape
evidence
witnesses
precedents

(c) Prison sentences are given in order to ______.
punish criminals
deter criminals
rehabilitate criminals
segregate criminals
do all four of these things

4. There are 10 blanks in the following paragraphs. They have been labelled from (a) to (j). Write down the 10 answers in a list on your paper. Then beside each answer write the letter of the blank where it belongs.

appeal	twclve	trial by jury
government	crown attorney	verdict
probation	plaintiff	
sequestered	sentence	

In every court case, one party always accuses the other party of doing something wrong. In *private* law, the party that accuses someone else of doing something wrong is called the (a) ______. In *public* law, the party that does the accusing is always the (b) ______. This party is represented by a lawyer called a (c) ______.

The party that is being accused of a crime is always called the defendant. If the case involves a major crime, then the defendant can ask for a (d) ______. This means that the judge will not decide whether the defendant is innocent or guilty. Instead, (e) ______ ordinary people will decide this.

The jury will be (f) ______ until all the members can agree about whether the defendant is innocent or guilty. They will then give their (g) ______ to the judge.

It is the judge's job to (h) ______ the defendant if the verdict is guilty. But the judge may decide to give the defendant another chance. In this case, the defendant will not be given a penalty but will be put on (i) ______. If the people on either side of the case don't agree with the judge's decision, then they can ask for an (j) ______.

CHAPTER FOUR

The Law in Action

This chapter looks at the law in terms of practice rather than principles. The first 5 lessons discuss problems mostly found in private law. They show you how the law affects your daily life whether you are working, or driving, or finding a place to live, or even getting married.

The last 3 lessons deal with public law, especially the Criminal Code. These lessons discuss the criminal laws that are most often broken: laws about drugs, theft, and assault.

23 *Entering a Contract*

Almost everybody will someday receive a credit card, take a job, and rent a place to live. These all have something in common: they involve legal **contracts**. Contracts are an important part of our daily lives. As a matter of fact, whenever you buy something, even if it's just a litre of milk, you are entering into a contract.

A contract is an agreement between 2 people or sides. For example, when you buy the litre of fresh milk, you and the sales clerk agree that it is worth a certain amount of money. By paying the cash and taking the milk, you and the sales clerk have taken part in a contract.

But not all agreements are legal contracts. There are 5 conditions necessary before an agreement is considered a legal contract.

Imagine, for example, that your father has always promised to buy you a stereo system when you turn 16. This does not mean your father legally has to give you the stereo system. He has only made an agreement to give it to you.

Figure 23.1 The Canadian Pacific Railway *Not all contracts are between private individuals or companies. For example, Canada made a contract with British Columbia when it joined Confederation in 1871. The Canadian government promised that it would build a railway from Ontario to British Columbia within the next 10 years. In fact, the line was not completed until 1885. You can tell how difficult the project was from just looking at this huge trestle bridge near Schreiber, Ontario.*

On the other hand, imagine that you decide to buy yourself a used stereo system that you've seen advertised in the newspaper. You and the owner agree on a price, you pay the money, and the owner wraps the system up for you to take home.

In this case, you and the owner of the used stereo system do have a legal contract. The first thing that makes it a contract is that there is a clear offer and acceptance. The owner of the stereo system has made an *offer* to sell at a certain price and you have *accepted* the offer.

Second, **consideration** is involved. Consideration in this case means something of value. For a contract to be legal the 2 people involved have to exchange something of value. You have given money. And in exchange the owner has given you the stereo system.

Third, you both have the **capacity** to make the contract. You and the owner are both old enough to know what you are doing. And you both understand what you are doing.

Fourth, you both have **consented** to the terms of the contract. You have both agreed to the price for the stereo system without being tricked into it.

And, finally, the contract is for *legal* purposes. You aren't breaking any law by agreeing to buy the stereo system. This would not be the case, for example, if the person selling the stereo system had actually stolen it.

Once you have agreed to a legal contract, you are bound by law to go through with the terms of the contract. The contract can only be changed if *both* sides involved agree to the changes.

This is true even if the contract has not been written down. An oral contract is just as binding as a written one. However, it's normally a good idea to put important contracts into writing. This often helps prevent confusion.

You may have a legal contract, but what can you do if the other side breaks it? And what can you do if the other side doesn't follow all the conditions of the contract? In these cases, you should always first try to settle the matter directly with the other side.

For example, when you buy a litre of milk from a sales clerk, part of the contract is that the milk is fresh. If it turns out that the litre you have purchased is sour, then you simply return the sour milk to the store and ask for either a refund or a fresh litre of milk.

However, it isn't always so easy to solve the problem of a broken contract. Think back, for example, to the case of the stereo system. Perhaps the owner told you it included a

The Devonian Gardens in Calgary contain 16 000 tropical plants — all on the top 2 floors of a downtown shopping mall.

Until 1970, the Hudson's Bay Company had to give the British monarch 2 elk and 2 beaver whenever the monarch visited Rupert's Land.

The Edmonton West Mall is said to be the largest shopping mall in the world.

cassette recorder. But when you got home and unwrapped the system you discovered that the recorder wasn't there. Then what would you do?

First, of course, you would telephone and explain the mistake. But perhaps the owner would still refuse to give you the recorder. In this case, you might decide to take the owner to small **claims** court.

Each province has something called a small claims court. They are called small claims courts because the judges in these courts listen only to cases involving small amounts of money. The people involved come to the court and explain their problems to the judge. Most of the time they do this without the help of any lawyers. Then the judge makes a decision about what should be done.

Small claims courts are designed to give speedy justice for people involved in small contracts. They make justice simple for everybody involved. But to be on the safe side, if you are ever involved in a small claims court case, you would be wise to buy or borrow a book that explains what you should do to help your case.

Figure 23.2 *This article describes the more unusual demands made by famous entertainers in their contracts. If you were an entertainer, what special clauses would you put in your contract?*

Stars demand more than fries with their gravy

By Henry Mietkiewicz

TORONTO STAR

As CNE visitors chomp on cotton candy and gulp mouthfuls of greasy french fries, singer Julio Iglesias will be sitting down to an oh-so-genteel dinner of Beluga caviar and $60-a-bottle wine before his Grandstand appearance tonight.

No midway food for Iglesias — and he's got it in writing.

The demand for caviar and wine is part of a special clause in his contract and concert promoter Concert Productions International has little choice but to comply with the crooning superstar's request.

Clauses containing unusual demands are not uncommon among top acts and this summer's batch of Grandstand contracts is no exception.

According to a CPI spokesman, county singer Willie Nelson has specified "a home-style sit-down meal" for performers and crew before his Aug. 27 concert: Fresh fruit and vegetables, Perrier water, fruit juice, beef, chicken, turkey and veal are allowed on the menu.

But there's a prohibition against pork, lamb, turkey loaf, chicken loaf or chopped meats — foods that Nelson says often resemble processed junk food in the United States, even though the Canadian meats generally are of better quality.

For tomorrow's Heavy Metal Hurricane concert, members of the Scorpions rock group have asked organizers to be sure to provide at least 226 meals — enough for the musicians and crew of the Scorpions and the three other heavy metal bands, Helix, Kickaxe and Quiet Riot.

But food isn't the only concern of the Grandstand stars.

In what is probably the most commendable request, the rocking Thompson Twins have specified there must be no sexist or sexually offensive material sold or displayed in the stadium on Aug. 24. Should such articles be discovered, the group reserves the right to remove them or cover them up.

As for personal preferences, the Thompsons have asked for carnations in their dressing room and a supply of postcards and stamps to write to friends and family back home in Britain.

Rocker Rod Stewart, who appears Aug. 30, has asked for a supply of soccer balls, even though kicking the balls into the audience is not nearly as likely to be part of his stage act as it once was.

Still, a contract is a contract, and when stars like Stewart ask for perks, you don't say no.

SOURCE: The Toronto Star Syndicate

THE FACTS

Remembering Facts

1. Name 3 common situations that involve legal contracts.
2. Not one of the following situations involves a legal contract. Explain why there is not a legal contract in each case.
   (a) Louise said that she would take her best friend to the movies. But when they get to the theatre, Louise finds that she hasn't got enough money to pay for both tickets and her friend has to buy her own. Has Louise broken a contract? Explain your answer.
   (b) Nick agrees to buy a bicycle from Sam for a certain price. Nick then finds out that the bicycle was stolen. Does Nick still have go to through with the agreement and buy the bicycle? Explain your answer.
   (c) Two new Canadians who speak almost no English are pressured by a fast-talking salesman into signing a contract for classes at a local health club. The new Canadians had thought they were signing a form that would give them a free demonstration class. Could the new Canadians legally get out of the contract? Explain your answer.
   (d) Sima offered to sell Mila her bicycle for $50. Mila thought the price was too high and offered $30 instead. Sima said she thought that wasn't enough money. Was Mila's offer a contract? Explain your answer.

2. What can you do if a person breaks a legal contract that you had with that person?

Finding Facts

Almost every time you open a magazine, you will find forms inside offering things such as subscriptions. And often you will receive advertisements in the mail for certain products. These will include a form that you can sign and send back if you want to buy the product advertised.

These forms are offers to make a contract. Once you sign these and return them, then you have made a legal contract.

Find one of these forms and bring it to class. Everyone in the class should read the forms carefully. Can you explain what the terms of the contract are for each form?

YOUR OPINIONS

Stating Opinions

Many travel agencies now offer package deals for holidays that include flight, hotel, and sometimes meals. Sometimes these holiday packages promise things like first-class hotels or a hotel right on the ocean.

Unfortunately, some people have found that their holiday didn't turn out the way the travel agent promised. The hotel might have been really small and dirty. Or it might have been several kilometres from the ocean. Recently, several people who have been disappointed in this way have taken the travel agencies to court and won some of their money back.

Imagine that you signed a contract for a holiday and then it didn't turn out as promised. What would you do? Would you just shrug your shoulders and forget it? Or would you take the travel agency to court? Write a few sentences that explain how you think you would handle the situation.

Discussing Opinions

Caveat emptor is a Latin phrase that means "let the buyer beware". In other words, the law says that people who buy things have a responsibility to check out what they are paying for. For example, imagine buying a used motorcycle "as is" from someone without testing it first or having a mechanic look at it. The law says that it is your problem if you find out later that the motorcycle doesn't work.

Discuss with the rest of the class whether you think the idea of *caveat emptor* is fair.

NEW WORDS

Learning Words

In your notebook, write the title Vocabulary: Lesson 23. Then write down the following words in a list. Using the Glossary or a dictionary, write the meaning beside each word.

When you are finished, write a short note telling what you have learned in this lesson. Try to use all 5 of these words in your note.

capacity	**claim**	**consent**
consideration	**contract**	

Examining Words

The prefix *con* in the word *contract* comes from the Latin word meaning "with". Of course, a contract is something you draw up *with* someone else. Can you explain why the prefix is used in the following words?

consult	contact	contest

AN ILLUSTRATION

Almost every time you make a contract, money will be involved. Banks help you keep track of your money. If you don't already have one now, you will one day need to open a bank account.

Figure 23.3 shows just one of the many forms used by banks to keep track of your money. Get a blank form from your local bank. The form could be a withdrawal slip, or an account application form, or even a transfer slip.

No matter what type of form you get, fill it out completely (but using a made-up name and information). Paste this form on a piece of paper. Then write a short note beside it explaining what this form is for.

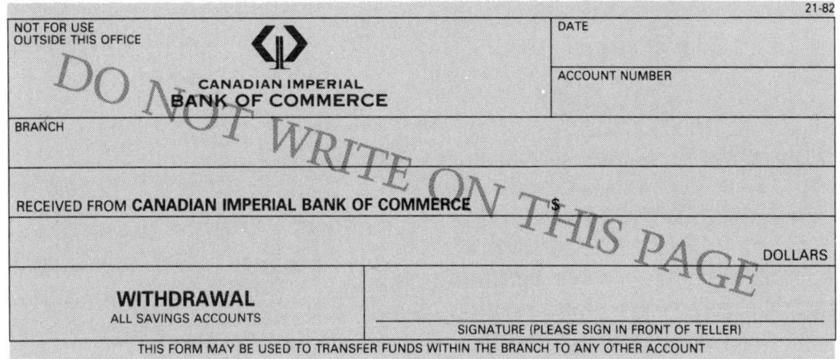

21-82

NOT FOR USE
OUTSIDE THIS OFFICE

CANADIAN IMPERIAL
BANK OF COMMERCE

DATE

ACCOUNT NUMBER

BRANCH

RECEIVED FROM **CANADIAN IMPERIAL BANK OF COMMERCE** $

DOLLARS

WITHDRAWAL
ALL SAVINGS ACCOUNTS

SIGNATURE (PLEASE SIGN IN FRONT OF TELLER)

THIS FORM MAY BE USED TO TRANSFER FUNDS WITHIN THE BRANCH TO ANY OTHER ACCOUNT

Figure 23.3 A typical cash withdrawal slip *You need to fill in a cash withdrawal slip to get money from your bank account. It is very much like writing out a cheque. Why do you think the dollar amount is written both in numbers and in words?*

Wayne Gretzky

Figure 23.4 *Wayne Gretzky holds up Veronica Tennant, a ballerina from The National Ballet of Canada. This photo was used to help raise money for the company. Gretzky did not charge the company any money for making this photograph.*

Claim to fame: He is the hockey star who signed a contract worth over $1 million a year.

Born: 1961 in Brantford, Ontario. He is the oldest child of Walter and Phyllis Gretzky, who have 4 other children.

Career: As a young boy, Wayne Gretzky was coached by his father, who flooded the back yard every winter to make an ice rink. Gretzky entered organized hockey at 6 years of age, playing with boys who were 10 and 11 years old.

By the time he was 11, Gretzky was a scoring sensation who could beat players twice his size. His reputation spread across the country. When he was only 17, he turned professional and joined the Edmonton Oilers. He went on to make and break dozens of National Hockey League records.

But the biggest record he broke involved his contract with the Edmonton Oilers. In 1982, he became the highest-paid player in hockey history.

By signing the contract, Gretzky agreed to play for the Edmonton Oilers for 15 years. In return, they agreed to pay him a total of $20 million — over $1 million a year.

- **Other famous Canadian hockey players are Gordie Howe, Bobby Orr, and Maurice ''Rocket'' Richard. Find out more about one of these players.**
- **Is it right for a hockey player to earn so much money?**

Renting 24

You're renting an apartment and accidentally break one of the windows. Who should fix it? You've been laid off and won't be able to pay this month's rent on time. Can the **landlord** force you to leave? You've been a good tenant but the landlord wants to rent the apartment to someone else. Do you have to leave the apartment when your lease is up?

Situations like these happen all the time. That is why every province in Canada has passed a law called the Landlord and Tenant Act. These Acts explain the legal rights and responsibilities of landlords and **tenants**. The acts protect these rights in case there is a disagreement.

Figure 24.1 A pioneer shack in Vancouver, c. 1910 *It would be hard to rent this shack today. But apparently it was quite a cosy home. The stump on the right was the kitchen. The lower part of the stump on the left was the living room. The bedroom was above and could be reached only by ladder.*

Figure 24.2 *The news article tells about discrimination one couple faced when trying to rent an apartment. Do you think the fine the landlord had to pay was fair? Do you think this kind of discrimination happens very often?*

Bid to keep out mixed-race pair costs landlord $350

The Ontario Human Rights Commission has fined a landlord $350 for discriminating against a young married couple by demanding $50 extra rent for an apartment when she learned one of the pair was a black West Indian.

Javuntheanball Soobiah, born in South Africa of East Indian descent, has been ordered to donate the money to the Universal African Improvement Association, a society dedicated to improving race relations.

A commission of inquiry, headed by Queen's University law professor Daniel Soberman, ruled Soobiah discriminated against Frieda and Naurice Baldwin, when they tried to rent an apartment in Soobiah's home in January, 1980.

Soberman said Soobiah jacked up rent on the apartment $50 from the $300 she had advertised and lied to Naurice Baldwin, saying she had already rented the apartment, after she discovered Baldwin was a West Indian.

A day later, when two of Baldwin's Canadian friends called Soobiah to ask about the apartment, they were told it was still available and renting for only $300.

But when a West Indian friend of Baldwin's called Soobiah about the apartment in between the two other calls, he was told the apartment was already rented at the higher rent.

As you probably know, a landlord is someone who owns property and rents it out. The person who rents the property is called a tenant. And the contract between the landlord and tenant is called a **lease**.

A lease doesn't have to be written down. As long as the lease is for less than 3 years, it can simply be an oral contract. But most people think it's a good idea to put the lease in writing anyway.

Most leases are for periods of 1 month or 1 year. The lease normally states the address of the property, the date the tenant will move in, and the amount of rent to be paid. If you ever rent property, also make sure that the lease says clearly who pays for the **utilities**. Utilities are things like electricity, water, and heat. In some cases the landlord will pay for all of these. In other cases, you will be responsible for them.

A tenant usually has 2 major rights whether or not they are stated in the lease. The first right is called quiet enjoyment and privacy. This means that the landlord cannot just barge in whenever he or she pleases. The landlord can only enter the apartment during an emergency, or after giving notice in writing at least a day before.

The second major right of the tenant is a place that is fit for habitation. That means, for example, that the heating system and plumbing have to work and that the building has to be safe.

The Hudson's Bay Company, incorporated in 1670, is one of the oldest companies in the world.

"I don't live here! I wouldn't live in a dump like that — I'm the landlord!"

Figure 24.3 *What is the cartoonist trying to say? Do you think this is an exaggeration?*

Every tenant also has responsibilities. The first of these is to pay the rent on time and in full. If you've shared an apartment with a friend, for example, and your friend decides to go back home to live, it is your responsibility to pay the full rent, not just half of it.

Some tenants pay their rent by giving post-dated cheques. For example, if the lease is for a year, then you might give your landlord 12 cheques dated for the first of each month. This is not always a good idea. The landlord may sell the building while you are still living in it. In that case, the cheques should be made out to the new landlord.

Another responsibility of a tenant is to keep the property clean and in good repair. If you break a window or burn a counter top, for example, it is your job to repair it or replace it.

As long as you are reasonably quiet and pay your rent on time, a landlord cannot force you to leave, or **evict** you. Not so long ago, landlords could evict tenants whenever they wanted to. But now there are strict legal procedures they have to go through before they can get rid of tenants they don't want.

One thing these legal procedures help prevent is discrimination. Generally it is against the law in Canada to refuse to rent a place to a person just because of something

Hoodoos are pillars of dirt found in western Canada that can stand 10 m high. Carved by erosion, they are usually topped by a large rock.

The first Eaton's catalogue was 32 pages and issued in 1884. The last one was 900 pages and issued in 1976.

like his or her race or religion or marital status. In fact, most provinces have a Human Rights Commission that will help people who have been discriminated against in this way.

These are only a few of the main points about renting property. Just remember, when you finally rent your own place, you should read the lease carefully before signing it. It would also be wise to get a book from the library in order to learn about the rights and responsibilities of tenants in your province.

THE FACTS

Remembering Facts

1. What information is usually given in a lease?
2. Why shouldn't you give post-dated cheques to your landlord?
3. In each of the following situations, who is in the wrong? Explain your answer.
   (a) Mary is surprised one day when she comes into her apartment and finds the landlord just leaving. He says he wanted to check to see whether her apartment is warm enough. Mary is angry that he has come in without her permission and tells him never to do so again.
   (b) Adam comes home from a hockey game to find his landlord in the kitchen with a plumber. A hot-water pipe in the apartment below has burst because of the cold and the plumber needs to repair it from above. Adam tells the landlord she has no right coming into the apartment without his permission.

(c) When Mr. and Mrs. Drabble move out of the house they have been renting, the landlord is shocked at the mess. Floors have been stained by pools of water. The walls are covered in holes from picture nails. The mirror on the bathroom cabinet is cracked. The landlord demands that the Drabbles pay for the repairs, but the Drabbles say the repairs are the landlord's responsibility.

(d) When Kim first rented the apartment, she didn't notice that there were cracks around one of the windows in the living room. Now it is wintertime and the room is too cold to sit in. Kim tells the landlord about the problem. But the landlord claims that it is Kim's responsibility because she agreed to rent the apartment that way.

Finding Facts

The thing most people worry about when trying to find a place to rent is how much it is going to cost them. Of course the cost will depend on how big the place is, where it is located, and whether or not there is furniture in it, such as a bed, table, and chairs.

Use the newspaper to find out how much rent people have to pay for the following kinds of accommodation in your area:

(a) a 1-bedroom apartment, unfurnished;
(b) a 1-bedroom apartment, furnished;
(c) a single room with shared bath and kitchen, unfurnished;
(d) a single room with shared bath and kitchen, furnished.

Stating Opinions

Many provinces have passed rent control laws. These laws stop landlords from raising rents beyond a certain amount each year. Tenants like these laws because they feel protected from large rent increases. However, landlords say these laws are unfair.

Because landlords can't charge what they want, there are fewer apartment buildings being built. And in many Canadian cities, there is an apartment shortage.

What is your opinion about rent control laws? Explain your ideas in a few sentences.

Discussing Opinions

Imagine the following situation.

> A young couple buys a house in a downtown neighbourhood of a large city. There is a small 1-bedroom apartment on the second floor of the house, complete with its own kitchen, bathroom, and entrance way.
>
> In order to help pay the mortgage, the young couple decides to rent the apartment. They advertise in the newspaper and receive calls from several interested people. Now they will have to interview these people to see if they are suitable.

Divide the class into 2 groups: one group will take the part of the young couple who own the house, and the other group will act the part of a person thinking of renting the apartment.

Each group should write a list of the questions that should be asked in an interview by the people or person they are representing. Then the groups should share their lists. Are any of the questions discriminatory or unfair? Are there any other questions that should be asked?

NEW WORDS

Learning Words

In your notebook, write the title Vocabulary: Lesson 24. Then write down the following words in a list. Using the Glossary or a dictionary, write the meaning beside each word.

When you are finished, write a short note telling what you have learned in this lesson. Try to use all 5 of these words in your note.

evict	**landlord**	**lease**
tenant	**utility**	

Examining Words

The plural of the word *utility* is *utilities*. You make this plural by changing the *y* to *i* and adding *es*. This method is used to make the plural for most other words that follow the same pattern. That is, you change the *y* to *i* and add *es* on words that end in a consonant plus the letter *y*.

One of the following words does not fit this pattern. Can you tell which one it is? Make the plurals for all these words.

activity	berry	copy
study	turkey	

AN ILLUSTRATION

Many people will have to sign a lease at least once in their lives. A typical lease for an apartment is shown in Figure 24.4. If your parents rent your home, ask if you can see a copy of the lease. Is your lease more or less complicated than the one in Figure 24.4?

This Indenture

MADE THE .... DAY OF ...., 19.....
in pursuance of the Short Forms of Leases Act

Between,

....
Lessor

AND

....
Lessee

Witnesseth,

that in consideration of the rents, covenants and agreements, hereinafter reserved and contained, on the part of the lessee, the lessor doth demise and lease unto the lessee, ... executors, administrators, successors and assigns, ...

....

....

....

To have and to hold the said demised premises for and during the term of .... years .... months to be computed from the .... day of .... 19...... and from thenceforth next ensuing and fully to be complete and ended on the .... day of .... 19......

Yielding and paying therefore yearly, and every year during the said term unto the said lessor, ... heirs, executors, administrators, successors, or assigns, the sum of .... dollars, to be payable on the following days and times, that is to say, on the .... day of ...., the first of such payments to become due and be made on the .... day of .... next.

The said lessee covenants with the said lessor:

a) to pay rent;
b) and to pay taxes except for local improvements;
c) and to repair reasonable wear and tear and damage by fire, lightning and tempest only excepted;
d) and to keep up fences;
e) and not to cut down timber;
f) and that the said lessor may enter and view state of repair; and that the said lessee will repair according to notice in writing, reasonable wear and tear and damage by fire, lightning and tempest only excepted;
g) and will not assign or sub-let without leave;
h) and that he will leave the premises in good repair, reasonable wear and tear and damage by fire, lightning and tempest only excepted.

Provided, that the lessee may remove .... fixtures;

Provided, that in the event of fire, lightning or tempest, rent shall cease until the premises are rebuilt;

Proviso for re-entry by the said lessor on non-payment of rent or non-performance of covenants;

....

....

....

The said lessor covenants with the said lessee for quiet enjoyment.

This lease shall be interpreted with all changes in number and gender as the context or the parties require.

IN WITNESS whereof the parties have hereunto set their hands and seals.

SIGNED, SEALED AND DELIVERED
in the presence of

.... SEAL
WITNESS TO LESSOR'S SIGNATURE — LESSOR

.... SEAL
WITNESS TO LESSEE'S SIGNATURE — LESSEE

Figure 24.4 A typical apartment lease *Read this lease carefully. Try to guess the meaning of any words or phrases you do not understand. Then check with your teacher to see whether you were right.*

Sarah Malabar

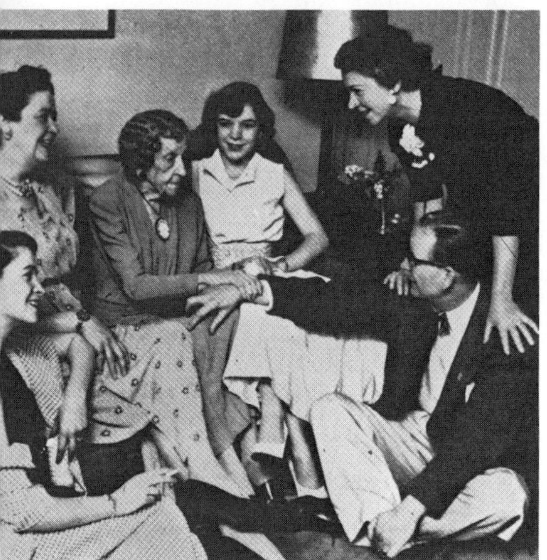

Figure 24.5 *Sarah Malabar sits surrounded by her family, including her son, Harry, and her daughter, Tanyss, who both carried on their mother's company.*

Claim to fame: She began a world-famous costume rental company.

Born: 1869 in Quebec, the oldest of 3 sisters and 2 brothers

Married: around 1887 to John Malabar. They had 4 children.

Career: When Sarah's parents died, she and her 2 sisters moved to Winnipeg to live with family friends. There she met and married John Malabar, who opened a store in Brandon.

Unfortunately, John caught tuberculosis. The Canadian climate was not good for this disease. At the time, Sarah's brothers were living in Mexico. So Sarah took John and their children to live there.

The Malabars lived happily in the warmer climate for several years. John was able to open a bicycle store. When he died in 1901, Sarah was left a widow in a foreign country with 4 young children to raise.

She came back to Winnipeg to be with her sisters. She found work in a beauty parlour. But this was not enough. Then a fortune teller told Sarah that she would work in an odd business with a lot of clothes. This gave Sarah the idea of making and renting costumes. So she started her own business, which she called Malabar.

It wasn't easy at first. Sarah often worked all through the night to finish a costume. But the hard work paid off. In the 1920s her children, Harry and Tanyss, opened 2 new Malabar stores in Toronto and Montreal.

Died: Sarah died in 1953, but her name still lives on through the company she started.

- **Tuberculosis used to be a very common disease. What is this disease? Why do so few people catch it these days?**
- **Do you believe in fortune tellers?**

Working 25

Some of the boys will get half-way up the chimney, and will not go any further. They halloo out, "we cannot get up," and they are afraid to come down. Sometimes they will send for another boy, and drag them down. Sometimes they get up to the top of the chimney, and throw down water, and drive them down. Then, when they get them down, they will begin to drag, or beat, or kick them about the house. Then, when they get home, the master will beat them all around the kitchen afterwards.

— a young boy working as a chimney sweep in England in 1819
(adapted from *The Edinburgh Review*, 1819)

Figure 25.1 Child worker, 1912 *Children were also forced to work under terrible conditions in Canada. This young child worked in the mines outside Winnipeg. Now laws protect children from such abuse. How old does a child have to be before he or she is allowed to go to work full time in your province?*

It's almost impossible to believe that such horror stories were true. But it is a fact that in the last century working conditions were horrible. Many people worked 14 hours a day for 6 days a week. Factory workers were often killed or badly injured by dangerous machinery. Working conditions today are very different from those of the early 1800s.

One of the major reasons for these changes in working conditions is the labour union. The first labour union in British North America was formed in 1812 in New Brunswick. Labour unions were banned almost everywhere else. It wasn't until 1943 that the law gave unions the right to something called **collective bargaining**.

In collective bargaining, all the people who work for a company join together to elect leaders. In other words, they collect together. These leaders then bargain with the bosses of the company. They work out a contract that makes statements about how much each worker will be paid and what the working conditions will be like.

If the union and the company cannot agree, then usually they ask for help from someone outside. This outside person is called an **arbitrator**. Sometimes the union and company representatives just want advice from the arbitrator. In other cases, they ask for binding arbitration.

Labour Day was celebrated in Canada for the first time in 1894.

Figure 25.2 Unemployment in the Depression *During the Depression in the 1930s millions of people were out of work. In this photograph, men belonging to the Single Men's Association are parading to ask for work. Unemployment is still a problem today. How many people are unemployed in Canada at this moment?*

In binding arbitration the union and company representatives are *bound* by what the arbitrator says. In other words, they agree to accept what the arbitrator decides would be the fairest contract.

Not many unions and companies agree to binding arbitration. If they can't reach an agreement with the company, most unions go on strike. In a strike, the workers all refuse to work until there is an agreement. Striking used to be illegal. But now most strikes are allowed by law.

More than 15% of Canadians do regular volunteer work. This time is equal to 200 000 people working full time for a year.

For its part, a company can lock workers out. That is, it can close down until an agreement on a contract is reached. The trouble is that both strikes and **lockouts** are very costly. They hurt everybody involved.

Even though strikes can create problems, they also can help win new rights for workers. Strong labour unions have helped create several very important laws to protect Canadian workers. For example, every province now has something called a minimum wage. This is the lowest amount of money an employer is allowed to pay a full-time worker.

There is also a minimum *age* for full-time workers. In most provinces, you have to be 16 before you can take a full-time job. If you are younger than 16, your employer needs special permission to hire you.

There are also laws to protect workers from health problems and injuries that are related to their jobs. Governments now set safety standards for most industries. For example, government inspectors regularly test the air that workers have to breathe. This way they can be sure that workers aren't breathing in poisonous chemicals.

Nevertheless, it is impossible to prevent all health problems and accidents on the job. When these occur, workers who are sick or injured because of working conditions can apply for help from the Workers' Compensation Board in their province.

The provinces also have strict laws to stop discrimination at work. Sometimes people are not hired because of their race. Sometimes they are fired because of their religion. Some workers are also **harassed**, or constantly bothered, by their bosses. Often these are women working for male bosses who want to take advantage of them.

In cases like this, workers can appeal to the Human Rights Commission, if their province has one. These commissions operate like courts. They have the power to fine any companies and their managers who are guilty of discrimination or sexual harassment.

Many of these protections have been put into law because of the strength of labour unions. Today, nearly 4 million Canadians belong to unions. It's hard to believe that not so long ago, labour unions were illegal.

THE BIGGEST CHALLENGE IN THIS PLACE IS STAYING ALIVE 'TIL QUITTING TIME.

Figure 25.3 *How many safety hazards can you spot in this cartoon?*

In the Springhill, Nova Scotia, mine disaster of 1958, 75 miners died. Another 19 were rescued after being trapped for nearly a week.

THE FACTS

Remembering Facts

1. How does a labour union work?
2. What job does an arbitrator have?
3. What is a minimum wage?
4. Where can workers who are injured on the job go for help?
5. What can workers do when they feel they have been discriminated against?

Finding Facts

Telephone or write to the department in charge of labour in your province to find out the answers to the following questions:

1. What is the minimum wage for your province?
2. How many hours are considered a regular (not overtime) work week?
3. How much must workers who work overtime be paid?
4. What can workers do when they are asked to work with machinery they think is not safe?
5. If a woman worker becomes pregnant, can she be forced to leave her job?

YOUR OPINIONS

Stating Opinions

One of the best-known protections for workers is unemployment insurance. Every worker pays into a special fund. Then, if a worker loses a job, he or she is paid money by the government while looking for another job.

Some people are against unemployment insurance. They say it just encourages workers to quit their jobs, especially if they aren't earning much money at work. Others say that this is nonsense. They say that unemployment insurance is absolutely necessary and that many unemployed workers would starve without it.

How do you feel about unemployment insurance? Write your answer in a few sentences.

Discussing Opinions

Most people believe there should be equal pay for equal work. What this means is that 2 people who are doing the same sort of job should be paid the same salary.

However, the truth is that very often equal pay is not given for equal work in Canada. In many industries, women are paid less than men for doing almost the same jobs.

Added to this, jobs that have normally been taken by women are not paid very well compared to traditional men's jobs. In fact, on the average, Canadian women earn about two-thirds the amount of money that men do.

As a class, discuss whether you think the government should force companies to give equal pay for work of equal value. Discuss whether it is fair that secretaries, nurses, and bank tellers are generally paid less than construction workers, truck drivers, and letter carriers.

NEW WORDS

Learning Words

In your notebook, write the title Vocabulary: Lesson 25. Then write down the following words in a list. Using the Glossary or a dictionary, write the meaning beside each word.

When you are finished, write a short note telling what you have learned in this lesson. Try to use all 5 of these words in your note.

arbitrator	**bargain**	**collective**
harass	**lockout**	

Examining Words

Sometimes you will see the word *labour* spelled with an *our* at the end. And sometimes you will see it spelled *or*. There are several other words in the English language that have an alternate, or other, spelling.

Each of the following words has an alternate spelling. Do you know another way each word can be spelled?

centre	cheque	curb
colour	ketchup	program

AN ILLUSTRATION

Usually when you go out looking for a job, you will be asked to fill in an application form. Most job application forms ask for the same sort of information. But some will want more information than others. Study the form in Figure 25.4. Do you have all the information you need to fill out a form like this one? What other questions do you think you could be asked on a job application form?

McDonald's

McDONALD'S RESTAURANTS

EMPLOYMENT APPLICATION

Date ______ Social insurance number ☐☐☐ ☐☐☐ ☐☐☐

PERSONAL INFORMATION

Name ______ (last / first / middle) Phone ______

Present address ______ (no. & street / city / province / postal code) How long there ______

Previous address in Canada ______ (no. & street / city / province / postal code) How long there ______

Are you presently employed? ______ Date of availability ______ Referred by ______

Have you ever worked for McDonald's before? ______ If so, where? ______

Are you presently attending school? ______ If so, at what level? ______

If you are under 15, please state your age* ______ Position applied for ______

*Please Note: You may be required to provide proof of age prior to hire.

Have you ever been convicted of a criminal offense related to the position applied for and for which you have not been pardoned? ______ Are you legally entitled to work in Canada? ______

DO NOT WRITE ON THIS PAGE

AVAILABILITY

HOURS AVAILABLE	MONDAY	TUESDAY	WEDNESDAY	THURSDAY	FRIDAY	SATURDAY	SUNDAY
FROM							
TO							

EMPLOYMENT BACKGROUND
List your PRESENT OR LAST position FIRST.

DATE MONTH & YEAR	COMPANY NAME AND ADDRESS	TELEPHONE NUMBER INCLUDING AREA CODE	NAME AND POSITION OF SUPERVISOR	YOUR POSITION	SALARY/WAGE		REASON FOR LEAVING
					START	END	
FROM							
TO							
FROM							
TO							
FROM							
TO							

As a condition of my application/employment, I authorize investigation of all statements contained in this application. I understand that McDonald's decision will be based solely on non-discriminatory considerations and that misrepresentation or omission of facts called for is just cause for the rejection of my application or dismissal. If hired, I agree that, due to labour shortages, promotions or training, I may be required to transfer from one restaurant to another. I also agree that, at all times, I will follow the rules and regulations of McDonald's restaurants in Canada.

Signature ______

This application expires at the end of 30 days.

Figure 25.4 *A simple job application form*

Grace Hartman

Figure 25.5 *Grace Hartman at work at her desk*

Claim to fame: She was the first woman to lead a major Canadian union.

Born: 1918 in Toronto

Married: in 1939 to Joseph Hartman. They have 2 sons.

Career: Grace Hartman started work as a clerk-typist for the Township of North York in 1954. By 1967, she had worked her way up to become a top-of-the-range secretary.

During this time, Hartman also became very active in the union for North York civil servants. This union joined with another small union in 1963 to form CUPE — the Canadian Union of Public Employees.

In 1967, Hartman went to Ottawa to work for CUPE. Then in 1975 she was elected president of CUPE. She won by acclamation: she was so popular that no one ran against her.

Hartman fought hard for her fellow workers, especially for women in low-paying jobs. In 1981 she organized an illegal strike for hospital workers. She had to spend 30 days in jail for this. One of those days was her 42nd wedding anniversary. But she said she would do it again if she had to.

While she was president, Hartman also travelled thousands of kilometres around the country organizing new members. She gained such a good reputation that she was elected vice president of Public Services International. She was the first woman ever to be elected to this important international group.

- **Talk to someone you know who belongs to a union. What union does he or she belong to? Is this union Canadian?**
- **Do you believe that leaders of illegal strikes should be sent to jail?**

26 Marrying

Figure 26.1 The Hollywood idea of Canadian romance *Romances and love stories have always been popular. But many people don't end up living happily ever after in real life. Do you think that love is the only way of choosing a marriage partner? Or should other things be considered too?*

Have you ever seen a wedding on a television show, or in a movie? Chances are that the bride was a beautiful young woman wearing a long white dress. And the groom was probably a tall, handsome man just a few years older than his bride. As they walked happily down the aisle together, you could hear the wedding march playing in the background.

Behind all of the romance and the beauty of any wedding ceremony is the law. The laws about marriage in Canada are part of a whole set of laws and **regulations** that we call family law.

Family law has to do with the relationships between women and men and between parents and children. In other words, family law involves marriage, separation, and **divorce**. It also involves the support, custody, and protection of children.

When 2 people marry, they are making a legally binding contract. And this means there are rules they have to follow. In the first place, the bride and groom have to prove that they are eligible to be married. And the law has a lot to say about who can get married and who can't.

For example, normally you can't be married in Canada unless you are at least 12 (for a girl) or 14 (for a boy). Most provinces also have a law that forbids teenagers to marry before they turn 16. And even then teenagers often have to have their parents' written consent.

The law also protects people by saying they cannot be married without their genuine consent. No one can be forced to marry anyone. For this reason, someone who is drunk or drugged cannot be married.

You also cannot marry a close relative: a mother cannot marry her son; a sister cannot marry her brother. The law also says that you cannot be married to 2 people at the same time.

The very first family allowance payments in Canada were made in 1945.

Once a couple has decided that they are legally allowed to be married, there are several formal **procedures** they have to follow. Normally, they need to buy a marriage licence. The wedding ceremony itself should be performed by either a judge or a religious official such as a priest or rabbi. And in all cases there must be witnesses present.

Life would be much easier if that were the end of it. Unfortunately, many couples do not stay happily married. In fact, it has been said that nearly 1 in 3 marriages in Canada ends in separation or divorce.

Just as people cannot be married without following certain legal rules, in the same way they cannot be divorced without proving in court that there are proper grounds or reasons for the divorce.

For a long time in Canada the only legal reason for divorce was adultery. But now there are many other grounds accepted by the courts. These include physical or mental cruelty. They also include marriage breakdown caused by such things as alcoholism, or imprisonment, or separation for a long period.

When a couple divorces, they need to divide the family **assets**. These assets are things like a house, furniture, car, and so on.

The first documented marriage in Canada took place in Quebec in 1654.

Figure 26.2 Newlyweds are showered with rice *Maxwell MacRae, 87, is shown escorting his bride, Martha Rose Grace, 83, after their marriage in the fall of 1984. Maxwell agreed that he and Martha were not as young as most newlyweds. But, as he also pointed out, "We are happier than some of them." Do you think that there is a perfect age for getting married?*

You can visit the actual house of Anne of Green Gables in Cavendish National Park in Prince Edward Island.

The couple also needs to come to an agreement about support payments. In some marriages, one partner has always stayed at home to raise the children and manage the household. In these cases, the other partner will have to continue supporting the one who stayed at home.

Finally, if children are involved, the partners will have to work out whom the children will live with. In other words, they will have to decide which parent will have **custody** of the children. The partners will also need to arrange visiting rights for the one who does not have custody. This can be a very painful experience for everyone involved.

There are many laws about how these arrangements should be made. But these laws are constantly changing. The reason is that people's attitudes change. For example, until recently the mother was automatically given custody of the children. Now, however, many fathers are being given custody by the courts.

Family law will keep changing in order to fit with new ideas about the relationships between men and women and children and parents.

THE FACTS

Remembering Facts

1. What is family law?
2. Name 2 situations in which people would not be legally allowed to marry.
3. What are the formal procedures needed for a marriage ceremony?
4. Explain 2 grounds for divorce that are accepted in Canadian courts.
5. Describe 1 of the items that divorced couples often fight over.

Finding Facts

Family law involves much more than marriage and divorce. For example, it is family law that protects children from being abused by their parents. Most municipalities have an agency that looks after the welfare of children. It might be called the Children's Aid Society. Or it might be called the Family and Child Services Agency. Or it might have some other name.

Whatever it is called, telephone or write to the children's welfare agency in your area. Ask them to send you information about the work the agency does. If possible, invite a member of the agency to come to your school and talk about the agency's work.

YOUR OPINIONS

Stating Opinions

Do you think young teenagers should be allowed to marry whenever they want, even if their parents don't give their permission? Explain your opinion in a few sentences.

Discussing Opinions

Many couples today who live together — whether they are legally married or not — have signed special contracts. These contracts are legal agreements that state the rights and responsibilities of the partners.

In most cases, these contracts say how the partners will agree to split up the property they own in case they separate in the future. The contracts also cover things like how each partner's salary will be spent — on house payments, heating costs, food, clothing, and so on. The contracts can also include items that say how the household chores such as cooking and cleaning will be shared. Often, as well, these contracts set out how any children will be taken care of and educated.

Do you think these contracts are a good idea? Would you want to write and sign one yourself? Discuss your opinions with the rest of the class.

NEW WORDS

Learning Words

In your notebook, write the title Vocabulary: Lesson 26. Then write down the following words in a list. Using the Glossary or a dictionary, write the meaning beside each word.

When you are finished, write a short note telling what you have learned in this lesson. Try to use all 5 of these words in your note.

asset	**custody**	**divorce**
procedure	**regulations**	

Examining Words

Many people have trouble spelling the word *separate*. They forget that it is spelled sep*a*rate. One good way to remember how to spell a word is to make up a silly story to remind you. For example, in the word *separate* the difficult part is the *par*. *Par* is also a term in golf. So you might remember how to spell se*par*ate by thinking of the couple who se*par*ated because one of them spent too much time playing golf.

Choose one of the words that you always have trouble spelling and make up a silly story to help you remember. Share your story with another student in the class.

AN ILLUSTRATION

Each province has its own marriage licence application form, but they all ask for the same sort of information. One of these forms has been reprinted for you in Figure 26.3 Read the questions on this form carefully. Do any of them surprise you?

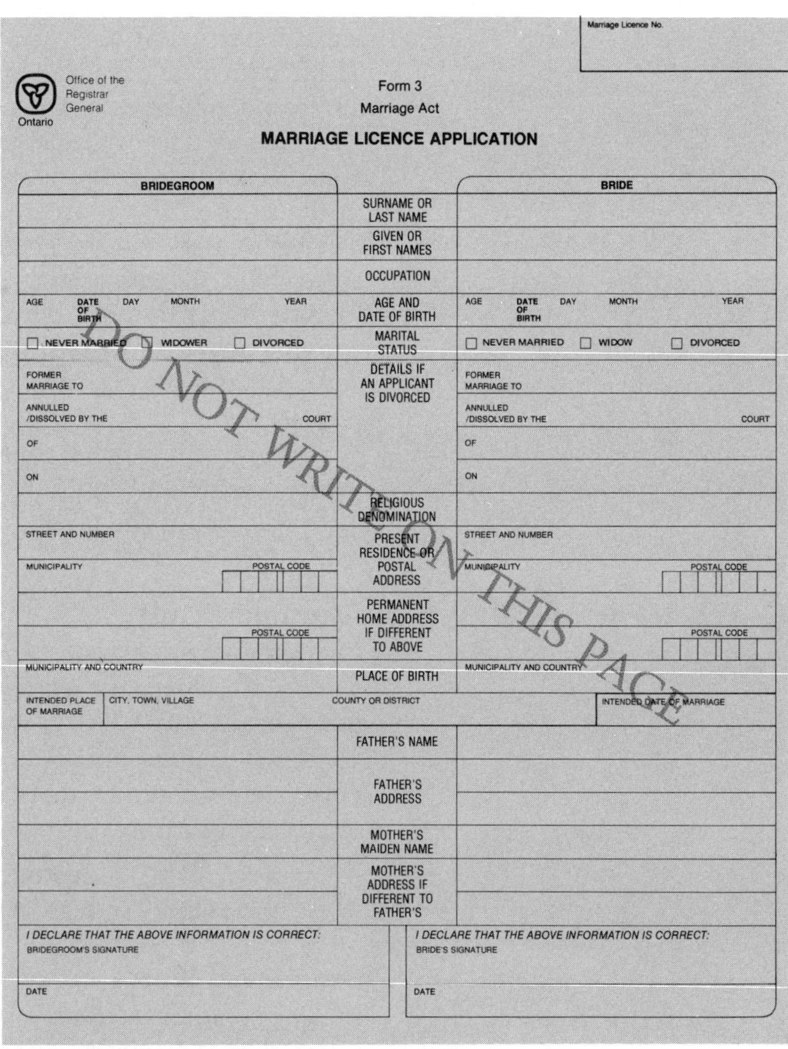

Marriage Licence No.

Ontario — Office of the Registrar General

Form 3
Marriage Act

MARRIAGE LICENCE APPLICATION

DO NOT WRITE ON THIS PAGE

BRIDEGROOM		BRIDE
	SURNAME OR LAST NAME	
	GIVEN OR FIRST NAMES	
	OCCUPATION	
AGE / DATE OF BIRTH: DAY MONTH YEAR	AGE AND DATE OF BIRTH	AGE / DATE OF BIRTH: DAY MONTH YEAR
☐ NEVER MARRIED ☐ WIDOWER ☐ DIVORCED	MARITAL STATUS	☐ NEVER MARRIED ☐ WIDOW ☐ DIVORCED
FORMER MARRIAGE TO	DETAILS IF AN APPLICANT IS DIVORCED	FORMER MARRIAGE TO
ANNULLED /DISSOLVED BY THE COURT		ANNULLED /DISSOLVED BY THE COURT
OF		OF
ON		ON
	RELIGIOUS DENOMINATION	
STREET AND NUMBER	PRESENT RESIDENCE OR POSTAL ADDRESS	STREET AND NUMBER
MUNICIPALITY / POSTAL CODE		MUNICIPALITY / POSTAL CODE
	PERMANENT HOME ADDRESS IF DIFFERENT TO ABOVE	
POSTAL CODE		POSTAL CODE
MUNICIPALITY AND COUNTRY	PLACE OF BIRTH	MUNICIPALITY AND COUNTRY
INTENDED PLACE OF MARRIAGE / CITY, TOWN, VILLAGE	COUNTY OR DISTRICT	INTENDED DATE OF MARRIAGE
	FATHER'S NAME	
	FATHER'S ADDRESS	
	MOTHER'S MAIDEN NAME	
	MOTHER'S ADDRESS IF DIFFERENT TO FATHER'S	

I DECLARE THAT THE ABOVE INFORMATION IS CORRECT:	I DECLARE THAT THE ABOVE INFORMATION IS CORRECT:
BRIDEGROOM'S SIGNATURE	BRIDE'S SIGNATURE
DATE	DATE

Figure 26.3 A marriage licence application

Irene Murdoch

"WELL, I'VE GOT TO GO TO WORK, EVEN IF YOU DON'T."

Figure 26.4 *Read the following biography of Irene Murdoch. How is this cartoon related to Irene Murdoch's situation?*

Claim to fame: When her marriage broke up in 1968, she was treated unfairly by the courts. Her case led to changes in family law right across Canada.

Born: 1925

Married: in 1943 to Alex Murdoch. They have a son, Bill.

Career: For almost 25 years, Irene Murdoch worked on a farm in Alberta with her husband. She drove tractors, branded cattle, and harvested hay. For 5 months every year, Alex would go away on business. Irene would be left completely in charge of the ranch.

In 1968 Alex decided that he wanted to sell the ranch and move somewhere else. Irene found that she had no say in the matter. During an argument about his plans, Alex hit Irene and broke her jaw. When she returned from hospital, she found he had locked her out.

Irene went to court to get what she thought was her rightful share of the property. But to her horror, she found that the courts did not support her. Even the Supreme Court of Canada declared that the farm belonged completely to Alex since it was in his name. She was left with only $200 a month in support payments.

Justice Bora Laskin disagreed with the Supreme Court decision. He wrote a report that led to changes in family law across Canada. It is too late for Irene Murdoch. But millions of other Canadian women are now protected against such unfair decisions.

- **What can a wife do to protect herself if her husband beats her?**
- **Do you think it is ever all right for husbands or wives to hit each other? (Or for parents and children to hit each other?)**

27 Driving

Figure 27.1 The Caribou Trail, 1862 *Before there were cars and trucks, it wasn't always so easy to get around. In 1862 they even tried to use camels in British Columbia. But the experiment was a failure.*

When automobiles were first invented, not many people could afford to buy them. And since there were so few cars on the roads, there was no need for licences or traffic signs or even traffic laws.

Today, however, there are millions of cars on the roads in Canada. With so many cars, we need laws to help drivers move about safely and efficiently together.

Most of the laws about driving are made by the provinces. Laws about speed **limits** and road signs and so on are all explained in the provincial Highway Traffic Acts. These laws can vary slightly from province to province. For example, in some provinces it is the law that all drivers and passengers must wear seat belts. But in other provinces there is no such law.

Every province has laws about who can drive. In the early days, anyone who could reach the steering wheel and pedals was allowed to drive. But now it is against the law to drive without a licence. And in most provinces, a person has to be at least 16 before he or she is allowed to apply for even a learner's licence.

To get a learner's licence, you normally have to pass a test to prove you know the rules of the road. You also have to have your vision tested. And you have to pay a small fee. Even then, you cannot just go out on the roads alone to learn how to drive. You must always have a **qualified** driver beside you whenever you drive the car.

Once you feel **confident** about your driving abilities, you can take a driving test. If you pass this test, you will be given a licence that allows you to drive on your own. You must always carry this licence with you when you drive.

You have to prove you can drive well before you can get a driver's licence. Unfortunately, many people forget their good driving habits once they are on the road alone. Every day, thousands of drivers are stopped by the police for breaking the rules of the road. They may have been

One Canadian air regulation states that it is forbidden to enter a plane while it is in flight.

speeding. They may have been making a left turn when they shouldn't have. They may have gone through a red light.

All of these are summary offences. They are not considered major crimes. The police officers give the guilty drivers tickets that say what the offence was and how much the fine will be. In most cases, the drivers just pay the fine on the ticket without bothering to go to court. However, if they do think a ticket is unfair, the drivers can go to a special traffic court to explain their side to a judge.

Every time a driver is given a ticket, this is put on his or her driving record. In some provinces there is a point system so that drivers with too many tickets can have their licences taken away for a period of time. Drivers can also lose their licences if they commit a major crime like dangerous driving.

When you think of the words *crime* and *criminal*, you probably think first of someone stealing or murdering before you think of someone driving dangerously. But when you think about the number of people who are killed by dangerous or drunk drivers every year, you can understand why these drivers are called *criminals*.

Serious driving offences come under the Criminal Code of Canada. For example, under the Criminal Code, it is an offence for a driver to have care and control of a vehicle when **impaired**. What this means is that it is against the law for someone who is drunk or who has taken drugs to be driving a car.

The sturdy Cape Island fishing boat, designed by Ephraim Atkinson of Nova Scotia in 1905, is now used on both Canadian coasts.

Figure 27.2 Car crash *Car crashes are a constant hazard. This is one of the first in British Columbia. The cars have already been dragged to the side of the road and the mess swept up with a broom. Around when do you think this photograph was taken?*

Figure 27.3 A breath test taken at roadside *As everybody knows, drugs and driving do not mix. Here an officer asks a driver to blow into a machine that checks how much alcohol is in the blood. What should you do if one of your friends tries to drive and you know that this person has had too much to drink?*

In order to tell whether a person is drunk, the police are allowed by law to give a breath test. This test measures the amount of alcohol in the driver's bloodstream. It is against the law for someone to refuse to take a breath test.

If the test shows the driver has drunk too much, he or she can be arrested and taken to court. The penalty for impaired driving can be anything from a fine and licence **suspension** to a jail term. But many citizens are now asking for much harsher sentences, especially when an impaired driver has killed someone.

Being able to drive is a wonderful freedom. But because there are so many drivers on our roads, it is necessary to control their actions. As usual, rights and responsibilities go hand in hand. And these responsibilities are set out for us in the law.

The first subway system in Canada opened in Toronto in 1954.

THE FACTS

Remembering Facts

1. Which level of government makes most of the laws for driving?
2. What steps do you have to take in order to get a driver's licence?
3. What usually happens when a police officer catches a person breaking one of the rules of the road?
4. What driving offence is in the Criminal Code of Canada?
5. What can happen to an impaired driver?

Finding Facts

In most provinces, drivers have to have car insurance. In other words, they pay money to an insurance company every year. Then if a driver has an accident, the insurance company will pay some or all of the costs.

Find out the answers to as many of the following questions as possible. To do this, you could write to insurance companies and ask for information pamphlets. Or you could find a book on insurance in the library. Or you could invite an insurance salesperson to come and speak to your class.

1. What are the differences between the following kinds of insurance?
   (a) collision insurance
   (b) comprehensive insurance
   (c) liability insurance
2. What is a "deductible"?
3. Is there a difference in insurance costs for a 16-year-old male and a 16-year-old female?
4. What happens to your insurance costs if you get a ticket for going through a red light?
5. What happens to your insurance costs if you have an accident?

YOUR OPINIONS

Stating Opinions

How do you feel about learning to drive a car? Is it something you really want to do? Do you think it will be easy? Or does it make you nervous?

Write a few sentences that explain your opinions about learning to drive a car.

Discussing Opinions

In some European countries, drivers are sent to jail if they've had even one drink. Do you think this is a good solution to the problem of drunk drivers?

Discuss with your class what you think would be the best legal solutions to the problem of impaired driving.

NEW WORDS

Learning Words

In your notebook, write the title Vocabulary: Lesson 27. Then write down the following words in a list. Using the Glossary or a dictionary, write the meaning beside each word.

When you are finished, write a short note telling what you have learned in this lesson. Try to use all 5 of these words in your note.

confident **impaired** **limit**
qualified **suspension**

Examining Words

Adjectives in English sometimes change their form. For example, we might say a law is harsh. But if we are comparing 2 laws we would say one is harsh*er* than the other. It would also be possible to say one law is *more* harsh than the other.

When you add the letters *er* to an adjective or use the word *more* with it, you have what is called the *comparative form*. Use *er* or *more* to make the comparative form for each of the following adjectives:

tall dark handsome

AN ILLUSTRATION

One form most people fill out in their lives is an application for a driver's licence. Each province uses a different form. But the one in Figure 27.4 is typical. When you sign your name on such a form, what does your signature mean?

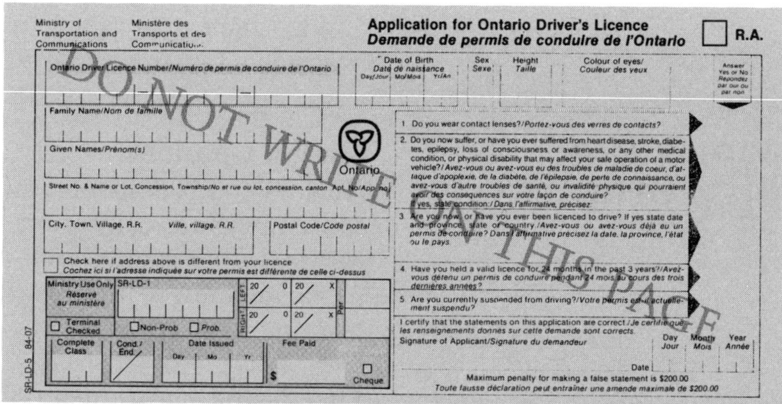

Ministry of Transportation and Communications / Ministère des Transports et des Communications

Application for Ontario Driver's Licence
Demande de permis de conduire de l'Ontario

R.A.

DO NOT WRITE ON THIS PAGE

Ontario Driver Licence Number/*Numéro de permis de conduire de l'Ontario*

Date of Birth / *Date de naissance* — Day/*Jour* Mo/*Mois* Yr/*An*

Sex / *Sexe*

Height / *Taille*

Colour of eyes/ *Couleur des yeux*

Answer Yes or No / *Répondez par oui ou par non*

Family Name/*Nom de famille*

Given Names/*Prénom(s)*

Ontario

Street No. & Name or Lot, Concession, Township/*No et rue ou lot, concession, canton* Apt. No/*App. no*

City, Town, Village, R.R. *Ville, village, R.R.*

Postal Code/*Code postal*

Check here if address above is different from your licence
Cochez ici si l'adresse indiquée sur votre permis est différente de celle ci-dessus

1. Do you wear contact lenses?/*Portez-vous des verres de contacts?*

2. Do you now suffer, or have you ever suffered from heart disease, stroke, diabetes, epilepsy, loss of consciousness or awareness, or any other medical condition, or physical disability that may affect your safe operation of a motor vehicle?/*Avez-vous ou avez-vous eu des troubles de maladie de coeur, d'attaque d'apoplexie, de la diabète, de l'épilepsie, de perte de connaissance, ou avez-vous d'autre troubles de santé, ou invalidité physique qui pourraient avoir des consequences sur votre façon de conduire?*
If yes, state condition:/*Dans l'affirmative, précisez:*

3. Are you now, or have you ever been licenced to drive? If yes state date and province, state or country./*Avez-vous ou avez-vous déjà eu un permis de conduire? Dans l'affirmative précisez la date, la province, l'état ou le pays.*

4. Have you held a valid licence for 24 months in the past 3 years?/*Avez-vous détenu un permis de conduire pendant 24 mois au cours des trois dernières années?*

5. Are you currently suspended from driving?/*Votre permis est-il actuellement suspendu?*

Ministry Use Only / *Réservé au ministère* — SR-LD-1

Terminal Checked

Non-Prob — *Prob.*

LEFT 20/ 0 20/ X — RIGHT 20/ 0 20/ X — Per

Complete Class — Cond./End. — Date Issued: Day Mo Yr — Fee Paid $ — Cheque

I certify that the statements on this application are correct./*Je certifie que les renseignements donnes sur cette demande sont corrects.*

Signature of Applicant/*Signature du demandeur*

Date — Day/*Jour* Month/*Mois* Year/*Année*

Maximum penalty for making a false statement is $200.00
Toute fausse déclaration peut entraîner une amende maximale de $200.00

SR-LD-5 84-07

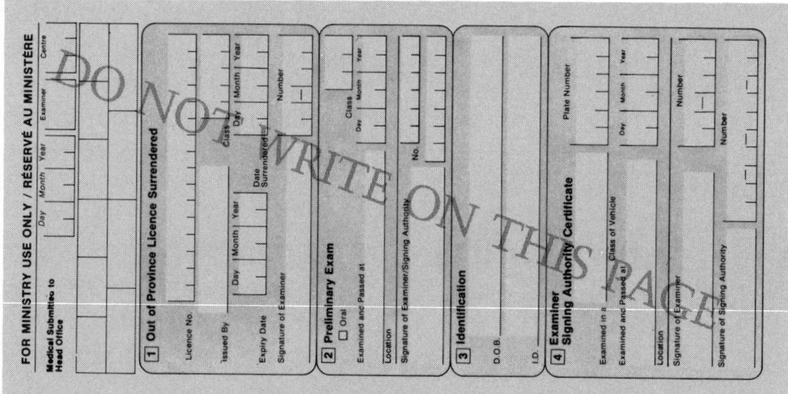

DO NOT WRITE ON THIS PAGE

FOR MINISTRY USE ONLY / RÉSERVÉ AU MINISTÈRE

Medical Submitted to Head Office — Day Month Year — Examiner — Centre

1 Out of Province Licence Surrendered — Licence No. — Issued By — Expiry Date — Signature of Examiner — Day Month Year — Class — Date Surrendered — Number

2 Preliminary Exam — Oral — Examined and Passed at — Location — Signature of Examiner/Signing Authority — Class — Day Month Year — No.

3 Identification — D.O.B. — I.D.

4 Examiner Signing Authority Certificate — Examined in a — Class of Vehicle — Examined and Passed at — Location — Signature of Examiner — Signature of Signing Authority — Plate Number — Day Month Year — Number — Number

Figure 27.4 *The front and back of an application form for a driver's licence*

James Fenwick Lansdowne

Figure 27.5 *Fen Lansdowne*

Claim to fame: He is world famous for his beautiful paintings of North American birds.

Born: 1937 in Hong Kong, of English parents

Career: When he was only 10 months old, James Fenwick Lansdowne came down with polio. The disease left him 75% paralyzed. Doctors said that Lansdowne would never walk or even sit up again. They were also sure that he would not live past the age of 5.

Lansdowne proved the doctors wrong. His mother took him to Canada when he was only 3. Four years later, he began a series of dangerous back operations. Lansdowne recovered so well that by the time he was 13 he could get around with just his crutches.

About the same time, Lansdowne became interested in painting birds. His pictures were both beautiful and accurate. People appreciated his work immediately. By the time he was 16, Lansdowne had earned $800 from selling his paintings.

In 1953, $800 was enough money to buy a car with special hand controls for the disabled. Lansdowne bought such a car and drove all over North America to study birds as they lived in the wild. Without the car, he never would have been able to paint so many different birds so well.

These days, Lansdowne is world famous. You can see his paintings on greeting cards and calendars. They are also hung in important museums and art galleries.

- **Does your library have any art books which contain some of Lansdowne's pictures?**
- **How do you think it must feel for disabled people to be able to drive their own cars?**

28 Drugs

What do a cup of coffee, an aspirin, and a marijuana cigarette have in common? If you said that they all contain **drugs**, you were right. Coffee contains a drug called caffeine. Aspirin contains a drug called ASA. Marijuana contains a drug called THC.

You might have been surprised to find that caffeine is a drug. Many of the substances you use every day contain drugs. In fact, a drug is any substance that people use to change the way their bodies or minds work. For example, people use anti-perspirants to stop their bodies from sweating. That means that anti-perspirants are legally drugs.

However, when most people talk about drugs they are probably talking about 1 of 2 things. First there are the medicines **prescribed** by doctors. Then there are substances people take in order to change their moods.

Most of the medicines that are prescribed by doctors are controlled by a federal law called the Food and Drugs Act. It controls how foods and cosmetics and medicines are made. And it also controls how people can buy these products.

At the end of the Food and Drugs Act are several schedules, or lists. One schedule lists drugs that are ''controlled''. These drugs can be very dangerous in large **doses**. But doctors find them useful in treating patients. Therefore, doctors are allowed to prescribe these drugs.

Another schedule in the Food and Drugs Act lists drugs that are ''restricted''. These are drugs that doctors are using for research. These drugs cannot even be prescribed by doctors.

The problem is that some people like to use these controlled and restricted drugs to change their moods. One example is LSD. The Food and Drugs Act says that LSD can only be used for research. But often this drug is sold illegally on the street.

There are 834 different flowering plants in the Arctic. But there are no climbing plants and no plants with thorns.

Figure 28.1 *Smugglers have many interesting ways to hide illegal goods. Here police have discovered dead pigs stuffed with bottles of whiskey. They were going to be smuggled across the British Columbia border into the United States. At the time, alcohol was prohibited, or illegal, in that country.*

There are other drugs such as marijuana and heroin and cocaine that some people use in order to change their moods. These drugs are controlled by another federal law called the Narcotic Control Act. This act is part of the Criminal Code.

Doctors are allowed to prescribe some of the drugs listed in the Narcotic Control Act. But they do not do this often. And usually it is a crime to have any of these drugs.

Both the Food and Drugs Act and the Narcotic Control Act describe 2 types of crime. The first of these crimes is **possession**. This means that people have a drug illegally. They can either be carrying the drug with them or it can be in their homes.

But possession can mean much more than this. For example, if several people are at a party where one of these drugs is being used illegally, then everyone in the room can be charged with possession. It does not matter who brought the drug to the party.

A person charged with possessing a restricted drug or a drug listed in the Narcotic Control Act faces very stiff penalties. First-time offenders can be fined up to $1000 and/or sent to jail for 6 months. After the first time, an offender can be fined up to $2000 and/or sent to jail for a year.

An even more serious crime is **trafficking**. The Food and Drugs Act and the Narcotic Control Act give slightly different definitions of trafficking. But in general, trafficking can mean illegally growing or making a drug. It can mean illegally selling or even giving away a drug. And it can mean illegally bringing a drug into or out of the country.

The famous baby food known as *Pablum* was created in 1930 by doctors working at the Hospital for Sick Children in Toronto.

Arthur Ganong of St. Stephen, New Brunswick, invented the chocolate bar in 1910.

A person can be sent to jail for up to 10 years for trafficking in either a controlled or a restricted drug. A person charged with trafficking in a drug listed in the Narcotic Control Act can be sent to jail for life.

Normally the police have to have a search warrant before they can search a place or a person for illegal goods. However, the law gives police officers much more freedom when they are searching for drugs.

In general, the police can search any place or person for drugs without having a search warrant. All the police officers need is a "reasonable belief" that drugs are there illegally. The only exception is that they must have a search warrant of some kind before they can search a private home and any person in it.

Figure 28.2 *For a time in 1917, alcohol was also illegal in Canada. Here police officers in Moncton, New Brunswick, dump kegs of alcohol into the sewers.*

THE FACTS

Remembering Facts

1. What are the 2 main laws in Canada that control drugs?
2. Read the following situations. Then answer the questions contained in them.
   (a) George's doctor gives him a prescription for amphetamines. Amphetamines are a controlled drug. Could George be charged with possession if the police catch him carrying the amphetamines?
   (b) Carol, Alice, Ted, and Bob are at a party. Bob brings some marijuana and starts to smoke it. He gives some to his friends. If the police came in, who would they charge? What would be the crime?
   (c) Two strangers ask Gail to carry a package for them in her suitcase when she flies home from a holiday. The police stop Gail and search her suitcase. They open the package and discover it contains heroin. What crime can Gail be charged with? What could be the penalty for this crime?
3. What special powers do the police have when they are searching for drugs?

Finding Facts

Alcohol is a drug. And each province has laws to control this drug. Find out the answers to the following questions for your province:

1. How old do people have to be before they are allowed to drink?
2. What is the penalty if you are caught drinking and you are not old enough?
3. What is the penalty for someone who serves alcohol to a teenager who is not old enough to drink?
4. Who is allowed to sell alcohol?
5. Are you allowed to make alcohol in your own home?

YOUR OPINIONS

Stating Opinions

A drug is any substance you take to change the way your body or mind works. Do you think we use too many drugs today? Explain your opinion in a few sentences.

Discussing Opinions

One reason the government makes drugs like heroin or cocaine illegal is that they are very dangerous to a person's health.

Cigarettes and pipe tobacco are perfectly legal. But they also contain a powerful drug called nicotine. And everyone knows that smoking is not good for your health. It even hurts the people around the smoker because they have to breathe the fumes.

There are almost no laws to control the use of cigarettes. Do you think that smoking should be more carefully controlled? Do you think it should be made illegal? What laws do you think should be passed to control smoking?

NEW WORDS

Learning Words

In your notebook, write the title Vocabulary: Lesson 28. Then write down the following words in a list. Using the Glossary or a dictionary, write the meaning beside each word.

When you are finished, write a short note telling what you have learned in this lesson. Try to use all 5 of these words in your note.

dose	**drug**	**possession**
prescribe	**trafficking**	

Examining Words

A *druggist* is someone who sells *drugs*. It is easy to tell this from the name.

But sometimes it is not so easy to tell what people do just from their names. Can you match each person on the left with the correct item from the list on the right? Use your dictionary to help you if necessary.

butcher	wine
vintner	rings
baker	meat
haberdasher	bread
jeweller	men's ties

AN ILLUSTRATION

When you drink wine or beer or liquor, the alcohol goes into your bloodstream. The more you drink, the longer it takes for this alcohol to disappear.

The chart in Figure 28.3 was prepared for a person weighing 56 kg. It shows how long that person must wait before he or she can safely drive a car after drinking. A person whose weight is less than 56 kg will have to wait even longer before driving.

According to Figure 28.3, does what kind of alcohol you drink make any difference?

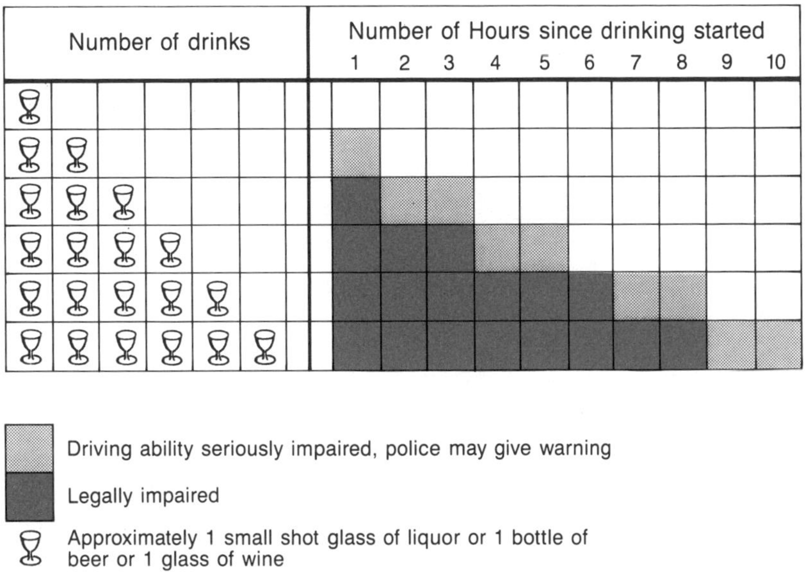

Number of drinks

Number of Hours since drinking started

1 2 3 4 5 6 7 8 9 10

Driving ability seriously impaired, police may give warning

Legally impaired

Approximately 1 small shot glass of liquor or 1 bottle of beer or 1 glass of wine

SOURCE: Adapted from *Road Worthy*, Ministry of Transportation and Communications, Ontario.

Figure 28.3 *The number of hours a 56 kg person should wait before driving a car after drinking*

Sergeant the Labrador

Figure 28.4 *Sergeant stands on guard in a Revenue Canada patrol car.*

Claim to fame: She has helped customs officials and police officers sniff out more than $15 million in illegal drugs.

Career: Sergeant was the first Labrador in Canada trained to sniff out drugs. Usually German shepherds are used for this purpose.

Sergeant began work with the Montreal police force in 1981. Her biggest find was $9.6 million of hashish behind some barn walls of a pig farm outside Montreal. She also found $1.6 million of heroin inside the cabin wall of a ship docked in Montreal.

Sergeant is frequently used by Canada Customs officials in Montreal. She jumps onto luggage as it is carried by conveyor belts from airplanes to the terminal. Her weight forces out enough air that she can sniff to see if there are drugs. If she smells any, she taps the suitcase with her nose to let the officers know.

Sergeant has been so successful that police forces across Canada are planning to switch to Labradors from German shepherds.

- **How did the Labrador dog get its name?**
- **Do you agree with the old saying that a dog is a person's best friend?**

Theft 29

There have been thieves in the world since the very beginning of history. When they have been caught, thieves have often been treated very harshly. For example, only 200 years ago in Britain a thief could be hanged for stealing a silver spoon. Even today in some countries a thief's hand will be chopped off as punishment for stealing.

In comparison, the Canadian laws for thieves seem mild. Even so, a thief can be sentenced to life imprisonment if he or she is found guilty. It all depends on the value of the **goods** stolen and the way the crime was committed.

Figure 29.1 *This picture was taken back in 1929 when police in Winnipeg discovered a safe that had been blown open. Do you think modern security methods are any better than those of 60 years ago?*

In Canada, the laws about theft are part of the Criminal Code. There are 2 main types of theft in the Criminal Code. The first type is **petty** theft. This is stealing property or goods that are worth less than $200. The second type is **grand** theft. This is stealing property or goods that are worth more than $200.

A common form of petty theft is shoplifting. Normally, shoplifters are charged with theft when they actually leave a store without paying for goods they have picked up. But they can also be charged in the store itself if someone catches them cutting off price tags or hiding the goods amongst their personal belongings.

If the store owners decide to press charges against a shoplifter, they will call the police. The police will put the shoplifter under arrest. Sometimes this means that the shoplifter will be taken to the police station, fingerprinted, and photographed. Usually the shoplifter will be allowed to go free until the date of the trial.

At the trial, if the judge decides the shoplifter is guilty, then the shoplifter can be given either a fine or a prison sentence or both. First-time offenders who plead guilty are often given a conditional discharge. In other words, they are allowed to go free without a criminal record as long as they obey the law and any special rules set by the judge.

Peter Easton, a famous pirate of 1600, kept his headquarters at Harbour Grace, Newfoundland.

On February 21, 1824, in Saint John, New Brunswick, an 18-year-old boy was hanged for stealing 25¢.

As always, the sentence depends on the nature of the crime. That is why, for example, that sentences for grand theft are usually harsher than sentences for petty theft. People who are convicted of grand theft may also be treated a little differently when they are first arrested. Before they are released or allowed to go home, they may be asked to ''post **bail**''.

Bail is like a security deposit. It allows people who have been charged with a crime to go free until the day of the trial. But it is also a way of making sure that they will appear in court when they are supposed to.

A judge will decide on how much money the person should post as bail in order to be released. Usually a friend will post bail by proving to the court that he or she has that amount of money in the bank. Then the friend will agree to pay that money to the court if the person charged does not appear on the trial day.

The more serious the crime, the more likely it is that a person will have to pay bail. That is why bail almost always has to be posted when a person is charged with **robbery**.

Robbery is a much more serious crime than theft. The law defines robbery as using violence in order to steal property or goods. In fact, the person doesn't actually have to use violence. If there is just the *threat* of violence, the person will be charged with robbery instead of theft.

"Out on bail for two weeks? — That hardly gives me time for enough bank jobs to pay my lawyer!"

Figure 29.2 *What comment is the cartoonist making about bail?*

Armed robbery is the most serious type of stealing. In armed robbery, the person uses a weapon such as a shotgun. It is quite common for people convicted of armed robbery to be sent to prison for life.

Often a robbery or theft will involve breaking and entering (also called break and enter). In breaking and entering the person goes into a privately owned building or area without the owner's permission. Usually the person will have to break a lock or window in order to get inside. But it is not necessary to actually *break* something in order to be charged with this crime.

Theft, robbery, and breaking and entering seem to be increasing. Some Canadians are beginning to demand harsher penalties for those who steal. We'll never go back to hanging or cutting off hands. But there is every chance that fines and jail sentences will be increased.

The first Canadian airmail flight was made June 24, 1918. A woman, Kathleen Stinson, was pilot for the second flight on July 9.

THE FACTS

Remembering Facts

1. What is the legal difference between petty theft and grand theft?
2. What happens to a person who is arrested for shoplifting?
3. Why do the courts ask some people to post bail?
4. What can happen to a person who is convicted of armed robbery?
5. What is breaking and entering?

Finding Facts

Shoplifting is a very common crime. It is so common, in fact, that most large stores now hire special detectives to watch their customers. And they may use other security systems, as well, such as closed-circuit television cameras or special tags on goods that set off an alarm if they are taken out of the store.

How much does shoplifting cost us? To find out, speak to the manager of a store near you and learn the answers to the following questions:

1. How much merchandise does the store lose through shoplifting each year?
2. Does the store use any security systems? If so, how much do these security systems cost?
3. Does the store pay for insurance against shoplifting? If so, how much does this cost?
4. How does the store pay for the costs of shoplifting, security systems, and insurance?

YOUR OPINIONS

Stating Opinions

If a person is charged and convicted of shoplifting, or robbery, or any other crime in the Criminal Code, he or she will have a criminal record. Often it is very difficult for a person with a criminal record to get a job.

Imagine you owned a store and needed to hire someone to help you out. Would *you* hire someone who had a criminal record? Explain your reasons in a few sentences.

Discussing Opinions

How do you think you would feel if you came home one night and found that your house had been robbed? Most victims of thieves say it is an awful experience. They never really feel safe again in their own homes.

That explains why there are so many new items available today to burglar-proof your home. Discuss with the class all the different ways you can try to protect your home against thieves. Decide which methods seem to be the least effective and which methods seem to be the most effective.

NEW WORDS

Learning Words

In your notebook, write the title Vocabulary: Lesson 29. Then write down the following words in a list. Using the Glossary or a dictionary, write the meaning beside each word.

When you are finished, write a short note telling what you have learned in this lesson. Try to use all 5 of these words in your note.

bail	**goods**	**grand**
petty	**robbery**	

Examining Words

You may have noticed that the plural of *thief* is *thieves*. This is not too surprising since the letters *f* and *v* sound very much the same. In fact, we make their sounds in almost exactly the same way except for one small difference.

Try this simple experiment. Put your fingers on your throat just over your vocal cords. Then say the words *fan* and *van*, emphasizing the letters *f* and *v* each time you say them. You should notice a vibration in your throat when you say one of these letters but not the other. Which letter is made with a vibration?

Does the close similarity between the way *f* and *v* sound help explain any spelling errors you make?

AN ILLUSTRATION

Break and enter is a serious offence. But in the end, very few of the criminals who do break and enter are convicted and sent to jail. The graph in Figure 29.3 gives an estimate of what happens to break and enter cases as they go through our system of justice. Do the figures in this graph shock you? Do you think anything can or should be done to improve this situation?

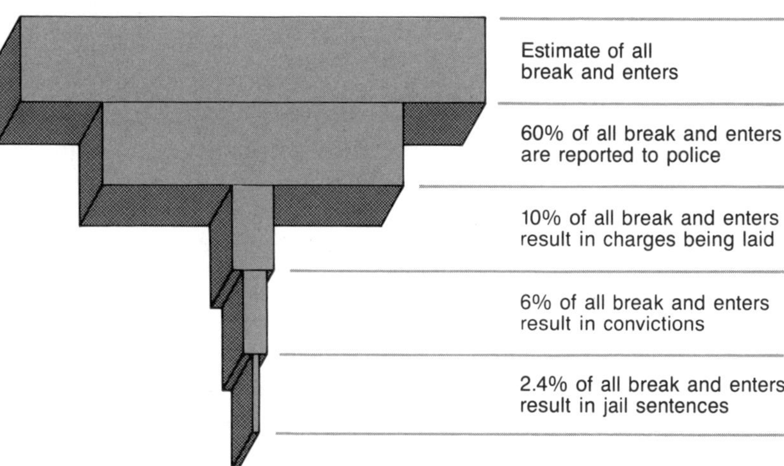

SOURCE: *The Criminal Law in Canadian Society*, August 1982, Government of Canada

Figure 29.3 *An estimate of what happens to break-and-enter cases in the judicial system*

Norman (Red) Ryan

Figure 29.4 *Red Ryan is shown with Father Kingsley, the chaplain who led the drive for Ryan's release.*

Claim to fame: He was Canada's most notorious criminal.

Born: 1895 in Toronto, the fourth of 8 brothers and sisters

Career: Red Ryan began his criminal life early. At the age of 12, he was convicted of stealing a bicycle. Other crimes followed, including burglary, shopbreaking, and shooting. Finally, he was sent to Kingston Penitentiary.

When World War I broke out, Ryan was released to serve in the army. But once he was in England, he began again to rob and steal. He deserted the army and stayed in England until returning to Toronto in 1921.

Within a few months, Ryan was arrested for robbery and murder and sent once again to Kingston. But he escaped and robbed several banks in Canada and the United States before being recaptured. This time, the judge sentenced him to Kingston for life.

But Ryan seemed to change completely. He became a model prisoner. He became religious and served as an altar boy. The prison chaplain set out to get his release. Many Canadians, including the prime minister, asked for his freedom. So in July of 1935, after serving only 11 years of his sentence, Ryan was set free.

Died: Ryan seemed to have reformed. But in reality, he led a double life after his release. He was killed in a shoot-out 10 months later while trying to rob a liquor store.

Canadians were shocked at his betrayal. For many years afterwards, very few prisoners were let out on parole.

- **A Canadian author wrote a book about Red Ryan called** *More Joy in Heaven*. **When was the book written? Who was the author?**
- **Should convicted murderers ever be allowed out on parole?**

Assault 30

Have you ever thrown a snowball at a passing car? Have you ever pushed roughly past a stranger to get off a bus? Have you ever tried to frighten a friend for a practical joke? People do these things all the time. But did you ever stop to think what might happen if something went wrong?

The snowball might startle the car driver. The driver could then lose control of the car and be involved in a serious accident. The stranger on the bus might not be holding on to the handrail tightly. When you push your way through, the stranger could fall and be hurt. Your practical joke might really scare your friend. Your friend could suffer a serious nervous shock.

Of course you wouldn't **intend** these things to happen. But they could happen, just the same. And if they did, you would be guilty in the eyes of the law. Because you intended to throw the snowball, push past the stranger, or frighten your friend, you would be responsible for the consequences of your actions. The car driver, the stranger, and your friend could all charge you with **assault**.

The legal meaning of assault is a threat of danger. The situation may not really be dangerous. The victim just has to have a good reason for believing there is danger.

For example, imagine someone pointing an unloaded gun at you. If you didn't know it was unloaded, you would probably be afraid that the person would shoot you. In the eyes of the law, you would have a good reason for being afraid. And therefore, in the eyes of the law, you would have been assaulted. As you can see, assault doesn't have to involve any physical contact. It can just mean frightening someone.

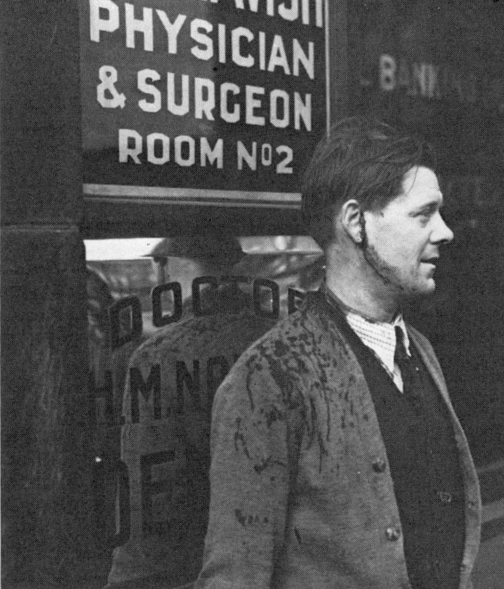

Figure 30.1 *A demonstrator clubbed by police in a 1938 demonstration of the unemployed goes for medical aid. Why do demonstrations become violent? Should the police ever use force against demonstrators?*

Four treasure hunters were killed in 1965 while searching for Captain Kidd's treasure, supposedly buried on Oak Island, Nova Scotia.

Of course, most people think of assault as something physical like hitting or beating. In legal terms, the actual physical contact is often called **battery**. In most situations, assault and battery go together. That is why you will often read or hear about people who have been charged with assault and battery.

Unfortunately, there are many times when people disagree with each other and start to fight. The law says that there are only 3 good reasons for attacking someone else.

The first reason is self defence. If someone attacked you first, the law would say that you had a right to defend yourself. However, the law says you should not use any more force than is absolutely necessary to protect yourself. For example, if you woke up to find someone robbing your house, the law would not necessarily excuse you if you shot and killed the robber.

The second defence for assault is coming to the aid of another party. For example, if you saw a friend being beaten, then the law would say it was all right if you joined in the fight to help him or her.

Finally, the law allows you to assault someone if he or she has consented to it. A wrestler, for example, expects to be assaulted. The wrestler would have no legal reason for complaining if he or she was hurt in a fight.

It is a fact that most assaults take place between people who know each other. In particular, there is a great deal of what police call "**domestic** violence". Parents assault their children. Husbands beat their wives. And sometimes wives even beat their husbands.

Recently Canadians have become more concerned about domestic violence. Children's aid groups have started to take children from homes where they have been **abused**. Other social agencies have set up homes for battered wives. And the police have started charging husbands with assault and battery when they have beaten their wives.

These are very sensitive issues. Often wives will not want to appear in court as witnesses against their husbands. In the same way, many women are afraid to tell the police when they have been raped.

These victims are afraid of what other people will say about them. And these victims often have nowhere else to go. It is important for our legal system to show that hurting someone else is not acceptable behaviour. But it will take some time before men and women and children all recognize that they do not have to suffer from violence.

The murder of the Canadian millionaire Sir Harry Oakes in the Bahamas in 1943 was never solved: there were too many suspects.

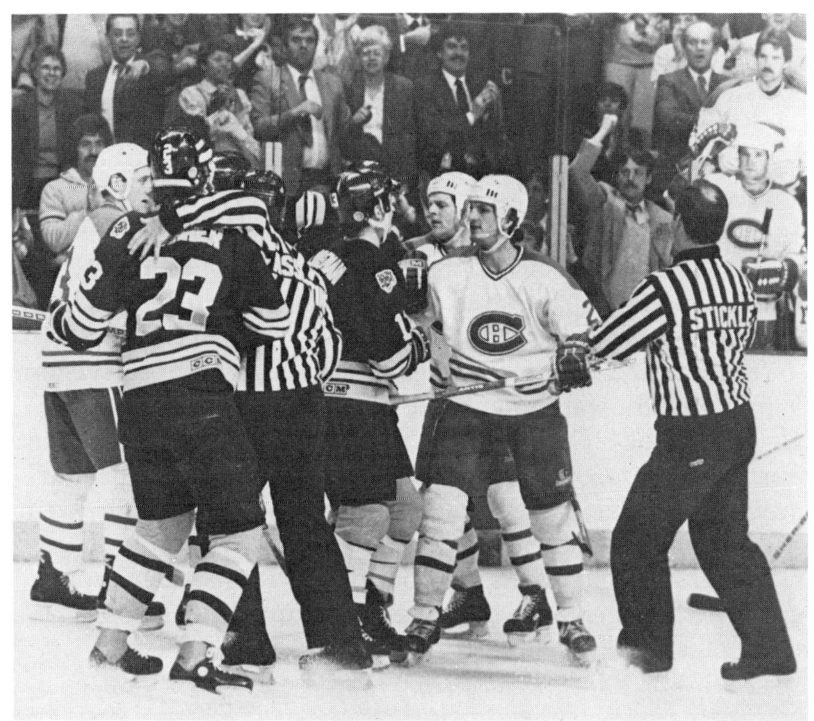

Figure 30.2 Hockey violence *Officials have been very worried about the amount of violence in organized sports. Should the police ignore violent fights between players, or should the players be charged with assault?*

THE FACTS

Remembering Facts

1. Read each of the following situations. For each one, could Pat be found guilty of assault?
   (a) Pat was outside playing in the snow with some friends. Pat threw a snowball at one of them but it missed and hit a passing car. The driver was startled and lost control. The car crashed into a light pole, causing serious damage.
   (b) Pat saw a friend being punched by a stranger. Pat's friend fell to the ground, but the stranger kept on hitting. Pat picked up a stick, ran over, and started to hit the stranger until the stranger let go of Pat's friend.
   (c) Pat was playing hockey. The puck came whizzing by, and Pat and a player from the other team both dashed towards it. Pat pushed hard against the other player and knocked the player off balance in order to reach the puck first.

2. Are you more likely to be assaulted by a stranger or by someone who knows you?
3. Why are some victims of assault afraid to complain to the police?

Finding Facts

People often argue that one reason there is so much violence in our society is that there is so much violence on television. The question is, just how much violence is there on television compared to real life?

Sometime in the next week, watch 2 hours of television. While you are watching, write down every example of assault, using a chart like the one in Table 30.1. Sometime during the same week, spend 2 hours watching the people around you. Every time you see an example of assault, write it down on the chart.

When you have finished your observations, share your chart with the rest of your class. How much violence is there on television compared with real life?

#	Date	Time	Violent Act
1.			
2.			

Table 30.1 *Observation chart for violence on television*

YOUR OPINIONS

Stating Opinions

Most people used to think it was all right if parents spanked their children. At the same time, it used to be considered all right for teachers to strap students who misbehaved.

Do you think that these were good practices? Explain your opinion in a few sentences.

Discussing Opinions

Of course the most serious kind of assault is murder. It used to be that people who were found guilty of murder were sentenced to death. This was called capital punishment.

In the recent past, however, many countries have abolished capital punishment. The maximum penalty allowed for people who have committed murder is life in prison.

Some people believe that capital punishment should be brought back. Discuss with your classmates whether or not you think murderers should be put to death.

NEW WORDS

Learning Words

In your notebook, write the title Vocabulary: Lesson 30. Then write down the following words in a list. Using the Glossary or a dictionary, write the meaning beside each word.

When you are finished, write a short note telling what you have learned in this lesson. Try to use all 5 of these words in your note.

abuse **assault** **battery**
domestic **intend**

Examining Words

To *batter* something means to strike it with heavy and repeated blows. Can you explain why *batter* is used in each of the following?

cake batter
battering ram
baseball batter

AN ILLUSTRATION

When people think of crime and criminals, they usually think of violent crimes like assault and murder. Take a moment to think about how many of the crimes that are committed involve violence. If you were asked to guess, what would you say?

Compare the pie charts in Figure 30.3. What do they tell you about violent crime in this country?

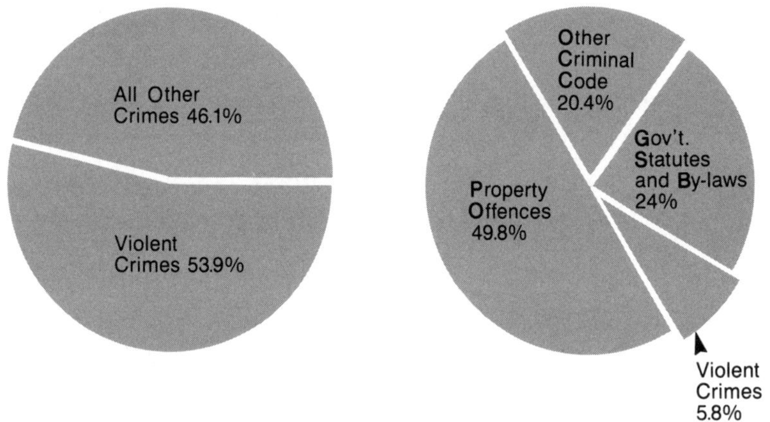

SOURCE: The Criminal Law in Canadian Society, August 1982, Government of Canada

(30.3.a.) *Public perception of how many crimes involve violence based on a Gallup survey, 1980*

(30.3.b.) *Offences known to police in 1980*

Figure 30.3 Charts comparing the public perception of the amount of violent crime with the actual amount of violent crime *Can you explain why people think there is much more violent crime than there actually is? Would you consider theft a violent crime?*

Barbara Turnbull

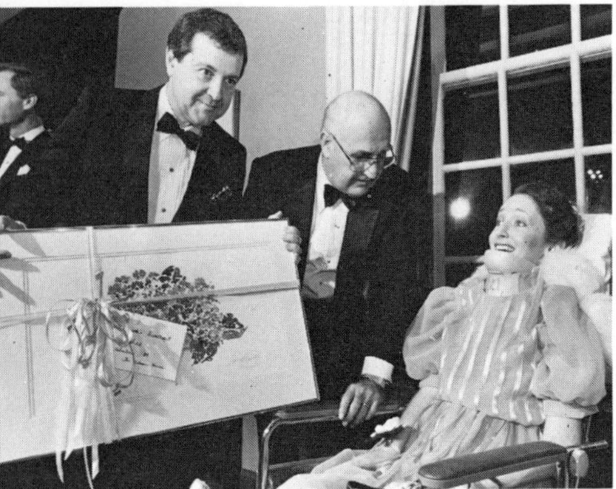

Figure 30.4 *Barbara Turnbull is being presented with an original painting during a party held in her honour.*

Claim to fame: She was left paralyzed after a milk-store robbery, but she has shown incredible courage in her fight for life.

Born: 1965 in Mississauga, Ontario, one of 4 daughters

Career: Barbara was an energetic and out-going teenager. She was a camp counsellor for 3 summers, and she also worked as a volunteer helping the elderly and disadvantaged.

Barbara worked part-time in a local milk store where she usually finished her shift at nine o'clock. But on September 23, 1983, she worked late for the first time.

That night, 18-year-old Barbara was shot through the neck by someone who tried to rob the store. The injury left her a quadriplegic — paralyzed from the neck down.

The doctors thought she might never be able to talk or even breathe on her own. But Barbara fought back. Within 9 weeks, she was breathing on her own and had spoken her first word. Everyone was amazed by her courage and cheerfulness as she slowly learned to live with her injuries.

Thousands of people gave donations to help Barbara. She was also given the highest possible awards by both the Ontario Criminal Injuries Compensation Board and the Workers' Compensation Board.

Of course, this money can never make up for Barbara's terrible loss. Three men were charged for armed robbery and attempted murder.

- **What changes have to be made to an ordinary home in order to accommodate someone in a wheelchair?**
- **Should stores be allowed to stay open for 24 hours?**

QUIZ 4

The following questions are based on the lessons in Chapter 4. **DO NOT WRITE YOUR ANSWERS IN THIS TEXTBOOK.** Instead, you should write the answers in your notebook or on a separate sheet of paper.

1. Write the letters from (a) to (j) on your paper. Then write a T if the statement is TRUE. Write an F if the statement is FALSE.

   (a) A contract is only legal if it is written down.
   (b) Your landlord has the right to walk into your apartment anytime he or she wants to.
   (c) All tenants are responsible for keeping their homes clean and in good repair.
   (d) Every province sets the lowest wage an employer is allowed to pay a full-time worker.
   (e) It is against the law to refuse to hire someone because of his or her race or religion.
   (f) Driving laws are exactly the same all across Canada.
   (g) Even if you give away an illegal drug you can be charged with trafficking.
   (h) The only legal reason for divorce is adultery.
   (i) Some tenants have to pay for the utilities when they rent an apartment.
   (j) You can be charged with assault even if you don't actually hit someone.

2. Match the item in the list on the left side with the correct description from the list on the right side. For each one, write the letter and the number together on your paper.

(a) contract	(1) a document that proves the owner is legally allowed to drive
(b) lease	(2) a legally binding contract between a man and a woman
(c) prescription	(3) a legally binding contract between a landlord and a tenant
(d) driver's licence	(4) a document from a doctor that allows the person named to buy special drugs
(e) marriage	(5) any legal agreement between two people or sides

3. Find the correct answer from the list given after each statement. Then write the whole statement on your paper.

(a) The person who rents property to someone is called a ______.
tenant
arbitrator
clerk
landlord

(b) ______ drugs can only be used for research and cannot even be prescribed by a doctor.
Controlled
Restricted
Prescribed
Narcotic

(c) In Canada you are not allowed to marry ______.
a ten-year-old child
a close relative
more than one person
any of the people listed

(d) In ______ a company refuses to let union members come in to work until an agreement is reached.
binding arbitration
a strike
collective bargaining
a lockout

(e) The legal term for shoplifting is ______.
grand theft
robbery
petty theft
break and enter

4. There are 8 blanks in the following paragraphs about Canada. They have been labelled from (a) to (h). Write down the 8 answers in a list on your paper. Then beside each answer write the letter of the blank where it belongs.

assault	bail
Criminal Code	criminal record
impaired	job
Narcotic Control Act	self defence

Most crimes in Canada are explained in the (a) ______. For example, it is a crime if you drive a car while you are (b) ______. It is a crime if you buy a drug listed in the (c) ______ without a doctor's prescription. It is also a crime if you (d) ______ another person unless it is in (e) ______.

Usually, people who have been charged with a crime are not kept in jail. Instead, they are allowed to post (f) ______ and go free until the trial.

If someone is convicted of a crime, he or she will have a (g) ______. This may cause trouble later when the person looks for a (h) ______.

UNIT THREE

Our Dual Heritage

Canada has a dual heritage. In other words, there are 2 major backgrounds to Canada: it was settled by both English-speaking people from Britain and French-speaking people from France. This explains why there are 2 official languages in Canada and why the government is run in both English and French.

Canada's dual heritage has sometimes been a problem. At times English and French Canadians have been so divided that it seemed as though the country might be torn apart. But our dual heritage has also been an advantage. It makes our lives much richer.

The symbol for Unit III is a fleur-de-lis. This was the ancient sign of the kings and queens of France.

CHAPTER FIVE

Uneasy Conquest

Today, Britain and France are friends. The British and French buy food and manufactured goods from each other. They travel freely from one country to the other. They even work on projects together. For example, the Concorde supersonic airplane was built jointly by the British and French governments.

But things have not always been this way. In fact, Britain and France have often been bitter enemies. It's not surprising, then, that there were troubles between the British and French settlers when they first came to North America. Even though it was a new land, the settlers brought old hatreds with them.

The lessons in this chapter tell the early history of the British and French in North America. This history is important. You can tell how important it is when you see that Quebec's motto is the saying *Je me souviens* — "I remember."

The Conquest of New France 31

What are your feelings about French Canada? What do you know about it? Have you ever visited Quebec? Can you speak any French?

Most English-speaking Canadians know a little about French Canada. They know that often in the past there has been trouble between English and French Canadians. But it is impossible to understand the feelings of French Canadians today unless you go right back in time to the late 1700s.

Figure 31.1 North America before 1760 *This map shows the colonies in North America before New France was conquered by Britain.*

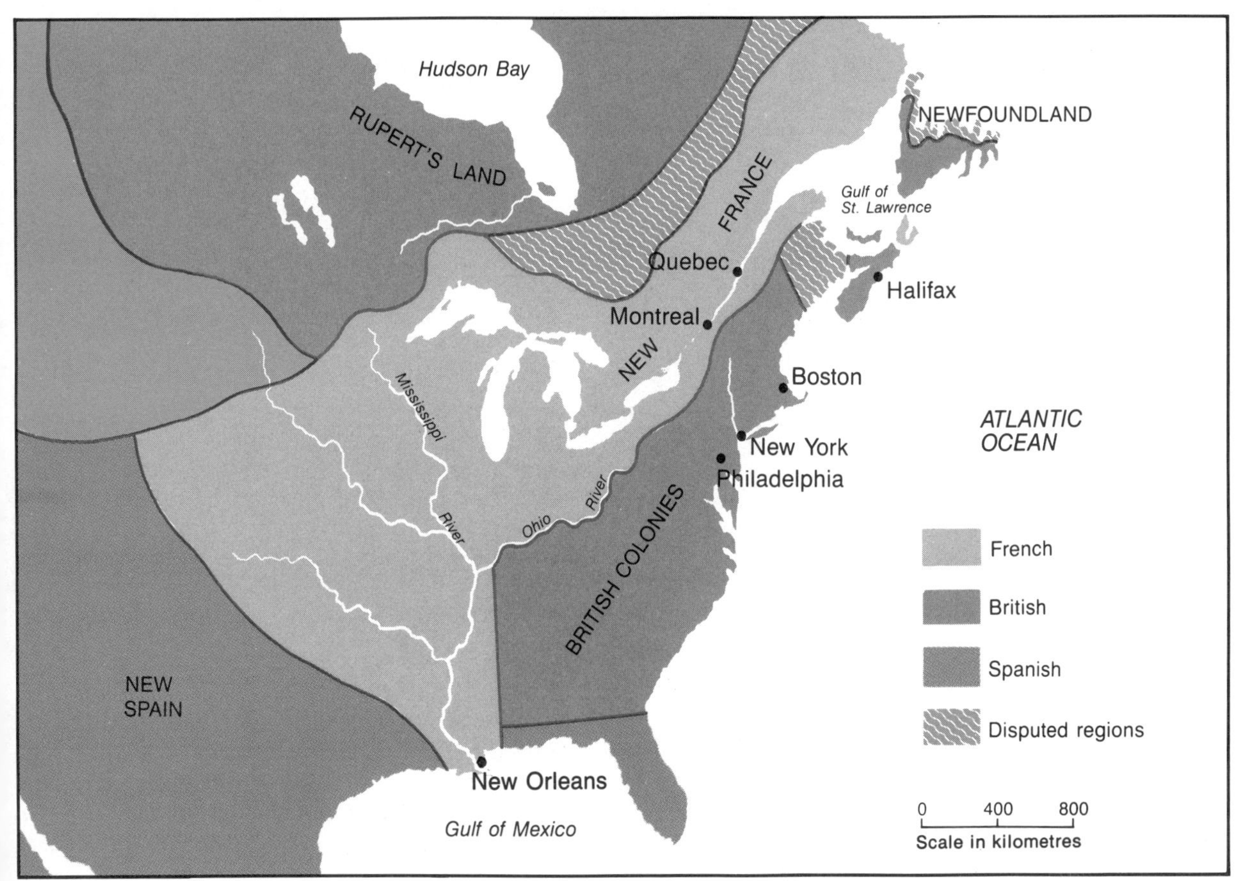

Figure 31.2 The Plains of Abraham — then and now *It is said that General Wolfe believed there was no way down the rocky cliffs until he saw 2 French Canadian women doing their washing in the river. He watched as they went back up to the city, and that was the route he used for his soldiers and guns. The drawing is an artist's idea of the battle on the Plains of Abraham. The photograph is of the Plains of Abraham as they are today. Do you think the Plains have changed very much from the way they were in Wolfe's day?*

By the late 1700s, there were nearly 3 million European settlers living in North America. The 2 biggest groups were from France and Britain.

The French settlers lived in 2 separate **colonies**. The first of these colonies was Acadia. It covered the area we now call New Brunswick and Nova Scotia. Most Acadians lived near the Bay of Fundy.

The second French colony was called New France. It covered a huge area right down to New Orleans. Almost all of the French colonists lived along the St. Lawrence River. Their settlements stretched in a thin line between Quebec, the capital city, and Montreal, the centre of the fur trade.

Settlers from Britain had started 13 new colonies. These colonies were located along the Atlantic coast of the United States. The British colonies grew much more quickly than the French colonies. This was partly because there was better weather. It was also because the British colonies had more help from the mother country.

It was true that these French and British colonies were thousands of kilometres away from Europe. But they were still controlled by their mother countries. For example, both France and Britain sent soldiers to defend their colonies.

This meant that the colonies could not escape what was happening in Europe. Every time France and Britain were at war, the colonies had to be at war too. In fact, France and Britain soon learned that they could hurt each other by attacking each other's colonies.

This was especially hard on the Acadians. The British settlers constantly attacked Acadia. For a time they would rule the colony. Then Britain and France would stop fighting in Europe, and Acadia would be given back to the French.

By 1755, most of Acadia belonged to Britain. Only a small part of Acadia on Cape Breton Island was still run by France. The Acadian people didn't really care too much. They were very tired of war. They just wanted to be left in peace to farm their lands.

But in 1755, trouble started once again between France and Britain. This time, the British were worried that the Acadians might help the French along the St. Lawrence. So the British forced the French-speaking Acadians into **exile**. Families and friends were split up. They were forced to leave their homes and go to live in the 13 English-speaking colonies.

In the meantime, the British decided to **capture** the rest of Acadia and New France once and for all. To do this, they sent soldiers commanded by General James Wolfe.

Figure 31.3 *In 1985, Gilles Rheaume walked all the way from Montreal to Quebec. He did it to protest against the monument to General Wolfe in Quebec city. M. Rheaume wants Quebec to separate from the rest of Canada and become a country on its own. Do you think many Quebeckers share his opinion today?*

Highland officers in General Wolfe's army were the first people to play golf in Canada.

Figure 31.4 *The memory of Wolfe's victory is still very much alive in the hearts of Quebeckers today. Can you explain the meaning of this cartoon?*

Wolfe reached Quebec in 1759. He and his soldiers spent all of August trying to capture the city. But Quebec sits high up above the St. Lawrence river on a rocky cliff. There seemed to be no way for Wolfe to get his soldiers and guns up the cliff.

Then one September morning, Wolfe found a way to attack the city from the rear. He was able to surprise the French general, Montcalm, on the Plains of Abraham behind the city. After a **fierce** battle in which both generals were killed, the smaller French army was forced to **surrender** to the British.

Wolfe's victory did not mean that Britain would control New France forever. The outcome depended partly on which country would send ships and soldiers first to Quebec. Therefore, the settlers had to wait for spring. Until then, the St. Lawrence would be frozen and no ships could reach Quebec.

As it turned out, France was too busy fighting in Europe to send help to its colonies. So the first ships down the St. Lawrence the next spring were British. This gave Britain control of New France. When Britain and France stopped fighting in 1763, it became official. North America was now ruled by Britain.

Naturally the French-speaking settlers were upset by this. They did not like being ruled by a foreign country. Their feelings about this were strong. In fact, their feelings were so strong that they affect life in Canada to this very day.

The first book to be printed in Canada appeared in 1764.

THE FACTS

Remembering Facts

1. Where did the first French settlers live in North America?
2. Where did the first British settlers live in North America?
3. Why did the colonies go to war whenever Britain and France went to war in Europe?
4. What happened to the Acadians?
5. How did New France become a British colony?

Finding Facts

Every year, thousands of Canadians visit Quebec City. It is one of the oldest and most beautiful cities in Canada. Read books or travel brochures about Quebec City to find out what are the best sights to see there. Write a description of 1 of these sights in your notebook.

Research hint: Many libraries keep travel brochures in vertical files. You could also write for information to the Ministry of Tourism in Quebec, or contact your local travel agent.

YOUR OPINIONS

Stating Opinions

Imagine that you were treated in the same way as the Acadians. Imagine that you were forced to leave your family and home. Imagine that you were forced to live in a strange country where a strange language was spoken.

How do you think you would feel about the people who had done this to you? Would you ever forgive them? Explain your opinion in a few sentences.

Discussing Opinions

The quarrels between Britain and France in Europe spilled over into North America. This caused many problems for the settlers, especially the Acadians.

In the future, human beings will probably start colonies in outer space. Do you think that quarrels between countries on earth will affect outer space colonies in the same way? Is there any way this could be prevented?

NEW WORDS

Learning Words

In your notebook, write the title Vocabulary: Lesson 31. Then write down the following words in a list. Using the Glossary or a dictionary, write the meaning beside each word.

When you are finished, write a short note telling what you have learned in this lesson. Try to use all 5 of these words in your note.

capture **colony** **exile**
fierce **surrender**

Examining Words

The word *exile* means ''living away from your home or country''. The letters *ex* at the beginning of the word mean ''out''.

Many other words begin with the letters *ex* meaning ''out''. Can you think of others? Explain why the letters *ex* suit the meanings of the words you have thought of.

AN ILLUSTRATION

Many of the settlements that were started in the areas controlled by France and the areas controlled by Britain are still with us today. Look at the map of North America in Figure 31.1. Then compare it with any map of Canada and the United States today.

Look closely at the towns and cities marked on these maps. Can you find 2 cities that exist today that were once controlled by the French? Can you find 2 cities that exist today that were once controlled by the British?

Marguerite Bourgeoys

Figure 31.5 *A stamp issued by Canada Post in honour of Marguerite Bourgeoys, 1620-1700.*

Claim to fame: She was the French Canadian pioneer who became Canada's first saint.

Born: 1620 at Troyes, France, the daughter of a candle maker

Career: When Marguerite Bourgeoys was a young girl, she refused to become a nun. But when she was 20 years old, she had a vision of the Virgin Mary. Bourgeoys suddenly felt changed. Everyone around her noticed this change, too. Bourgeoys decided that God was telling her to become a nun. So she became Sister Marguerite.

While working in France to help the poor and sick, Sister Marguerite heard stories about the New World. She felt that she could do some good there. So in 1653 she set sail for Montreal.

As soon as she arrived, Sister Marguerite set to work. She started the first stone church in Montreal (Notre Dame) which still stands today (even though it has changed a great deal).

Sister Marguerite also began several schools for girls. She began a new order of nuns to teach in these schools. And she also took care of the *filles du roi* — the orphan girls who were sent to Quebec as wives for the settlers.

Died: Sister Marguerite died in 1700 after praying to God to take her life instead of the life of a young nun who was near death. In 1982, Pope John Paul II declared her the first Canadian saint in the Roman Catholic church.

- **Who are nuns? How does someone become a nun?**
- **Many people in history have said they had a vision that changed them. What do you think these visions are?**

32 The Survival of French Culture

Figure 32.1 *This is a typical home built in New France 300 years ago. It is still in use today. How is it different from modern houses?*

How do you feel when you lose a game of cards? How do you feel when your favourite team losses the championship? If you're like most people, you feel sad, angry, and frustrated.

What happened to the French colonists in Canada was far worse than losing a game. When they were defeated by the British, it meant their lives had changed forever. The British **conquest** seemed like the greatest disaster in their lives. In fact, some French Canadians believe this to this very day.

The conquest also caused problems for the British. They wondered just what they should do with their new French-speaking colonists. How should they treat the French Canadians? How should they govern this new colony called Quebec?

At first, the British decided that they should try to **assimilate**, or absorb, the French Canadians. What the British wanted was for the French to be absorbed into an English-speaking population. They wanted the French way of life — their **culture** — to disappear. The trouble was that there were many more French-speaking settlers in the new colony than there were English-speaking settlers.

Of course, there were lots of English-speaking settlers in the Thirteen Colonies to the south. In fact, these colonies were getting crowded. And many of the settlers were moving farther west to find more land. Therefore the British government decided to force these English-speaking settlers to move north to Quebec instead.

The British government did this by passing the **Proclamation** of 1763. This proclamation said that the English-speaking settlers in the Thirteen Colonies were not allowed to move any farther west. Instead, they had to move north to Quebec if they wanted more land.

Louis Vincent, a Huron Indian, was the first Native Canadian to earn a college degree. He received a B.A. in 1781.

The purpose was to try to turn Quebec into an English-speaking colony. But it didn't work. The English-speaking colonists did not move north to Quebec. They did not want to live with people who had a different culture. And besides, most of the good land was already taken.

It didn't take long for the British government to realize that it had made a mistake. It was not going to be able to assimilate the French Canadians. Instead, the British government would have to **accommodate** them. Therefore, the British government decided to make a special law that would help the French Canadians to keep their culture.

This special law was the Quebec Act of 1774. The Quebec Act promised that the French Canadians could keep their language and their religion. It promised that the French would have a place in government. And it also said that the French Canadians could keep their old civil law for things like marrying and renting and owning land.

The British government had a good reason for wanting to keep the French happy. It was clear that the settlers in the Thirteen Colonies were thinking of rebellion. These settlers had ignored the Proclamation of 1763. And they had ignored many other British laws. They were going to try to break away from Britain.

Transportation by stagecoach between Kingston and York (now Toronto), Ontario, began on January 4, 1817.

Figure 32.2 Cross of Calvary Procession, 1908 *Even though they were sent into exile, many Acadians came back to New Brunswick and Nova Scotia. To this day there are still many people of Acadian descent living there. Religion has always been a strong part of Acadian culture. In this picture, an Acadian community raises a cross on a hill near the town of Caraquet. Find Caraquet on a map of Canada.*

Note: You can learn more about the American Revolution in Lesson 45.

The British government was afraid that the French Canadians might join in this rebellion. So the British government hoped the Quebec Act would help keep the French Canadians loyal to Britain.

As it turned out, the Thirteen Colonies did rebel in 1775. And they tried very hard to get Quebec to join their rebellion. But the French Canadians saw no reason to join. At least under the British they had their own language, law, and religion. They *would* be assimilated if they started a new country with the Thirteen Colonies. Besides, the English-speaking settlers in the Thirteen Colonies had been their enemies for 150 years.

So the French Canadians did not think it was worthwhile to join the rebellion. On the other hand, they did not help the British soldiers fight the rebels either. After all, they still resented the British for conquering them. Instead, the French Canadians just waited to see what would happen.

Note: You can learn more about the Loyalists in Lesson 46.

In the end, the Thirteen Colonies won the rebellion. They turned themselves into a new country — the United States of America. But thousands of settlers from the United States stayed loyal to Britain. Many of these Loyalists, as they were called, moved north to Quebec. And suddenly the British government had a colony with both French and English settlers. How could it accommodate them both?

Figure 32.3 *Citizens of an Acadian town celebrate August 15. The idea in this parade is to make the greatest noise possible.*

Figure 32.4 La Fête Nationale celebrations *The Monday nearest June 24 is a special holiday in Quebec. It used to be called* St. Jean Baptiste Day, *but it is now known as* La Fête Nationale. *The people celebrate with picnics, parades, and fireworks. What does "La Fête Nationale" mean in English?*

THE FACTS

Remembering Facts

1. How did the French feel about the British conquest?
2. Why was it impossible for the British to assimilate the French settlers?
3. What did the Quebec Act say?
4. Why did the British want to keep the French settlers happy?
5. Why didn't the French settlers join the rebellion in 1776?

Finding Facts

In 1776 there were nearly 100 000 French settlers in Quebec. In the next year about 10 000 English Loyalists from the Thirteen Colonies came to live in Quebec.

Find out how many people live in your city, town, or township. Is this number of people greater or smaller than the number of French settlers in Quebec in 1776? Is it greater or smaller than the number of English Loyalists who came to live in Quebec?

YOUR OPINIONS

Stating Opinions

Almost everybody has had the terrible experience of losing something important. What do you think would be the worst thing for you to lose? Explain your opinion in a few sentences.

Discussing Opinions

Imagine that Canada has been conquered by a foreign country. These foreigners speak a different language. Their religion is different. And they have a different system of law.

How would you feel about being conquered by these foreigners? Would you want them to try to assimilate you or to accommodate you?

NEW WORDS

Learning Words

In your notebook, write the title Vocabulary: Lesson 32. Then write down the following words in a list. Using the Glossary or a dictionary, write the meaning beside each word.

When you are finished, write a short note telling what you have learned in this lesson. Try to use all 5 of these words in your note.

accommodate	**assimilate**	**conquest**
culture	**proclamation**	

Examining Words

You can use the letters in the word *accommodate* to make the word *date*. You can also make the words *code, dot, tea,* and *tame*. How many words can you make in the same way using the letters in *assimilate*?

AN ILLUSTRATION

The Quebec Act gave Quebec a huge area of land. You can see this by looking at the map in Figure 32.5. Compare this map to a modern map of the same area. How many provinces and states would have been part of Quebec if the boundaries in the Quebec Act were still used today?

Figure 32.5 *Boundaries set by the Quebec Act, 1774*

Thayendanegea (Joseph Brant)

Figure 32.6 *Joseph Brant*

Claim to fame: He was a Mohawk statesman and chief who persuaded the Iroquois Confederacy to remain loyal to Britain during the American Revolution.

Born: 1743 in Cayahoga (now Akron, Ohio, in the United States)

Married: 1765 to Margaret, an Oneida Indian. They had 2 children before Margaret died in 1771.

In 1771 Brant married Margaret's sister, Susanna. She died soon afterwards, so they had no children.

In 1779 Brant married Catherine. They had 7 children. Brant accidentally killed one of the sons, Isaac. He was haunted by this accident until his death.

Career: When he was only 15, Brant fought for the British during their war against France. The British were so impressed with the boy that they decided to send him to school. He was so good at languages that they made him the official translator for the British Army.

During the American Revolution, Brant remained loyal to Britain and led bands of Indians against the Americans. After the war, Brant worked hard to stop the United States from taking more land and to keep the Indians together.

Brant bought a large estate near present-day Hamilton, Ontario. He lived there like a British nobleman, with 20 servants. But he never stopped fighting to improve the lives of his people.

Died: Brant died in 1807 near what is now Burlington, Ontario.

- **Three different Indian groups are mentioned in this biography — Mohawk, Iroquois, and Oneida. Where did they live?**
- **Would you like to have live-in servants?**

33 Rebellion in 1837

When over 10 000 Loyalists came from the United States to Quebec, the British government had a problem. It had promised the French Canadians that they could keep their own laws, religion, and language. But the Loyalists did not want to live in a French culture. They wanted a colony set up just like the ones they had come from.

The solution was the Constitution Act of 1791. This act divided the old colony of Quebec into 2 separate parts — one for the French and one for the English. The colony for the French was called Lower Canada. It covered most of the area we now call Quebec. The colony for the English was called Upper Canada. It covered most of the area we now call Ontario.

Upper and Lower Canada were given the same kind of government. At the top in each colony was the governor, who came from England. Each governor appointed a **council** from the important people in the colony. This council was supposed to give the governor advice about how the colony should be run.

Each colony also had a legislature. This legislature was something like our House of Commons in Ottawa. It was made up of representatives who were voted for by the people. And it was the job of these representatives to suggest laws for the colonies.

The trouble was that the governor and his council did not have to accept these laws. They could cancel any laws passed by the legislature. This meant that the ordinary people did not really have any say in how they were ruled.

The British government had hoped that this plan for 2 colonies would help keep both the French and the English settlers happy. But this did not happen. The new form of government actually caused trouble between the French and English in Lower Canada.

In 1685 there was a shortage of paper money in Canada. So the government authorized the use of playing cards instead.

Most of the representatives in the legislature in Lower Canada were French. But most of the members of the governor's council were English **merchants** and businessmen. The legislature would pass laws to protect the way of life of the French settlers. But then the governor's council would cancel these laws. Instead, they would pass laws that helped the English keep control of business in Lower Canada.

In Canada's early days, it was illegal to hang men's and women's undergarments on the same washing line.

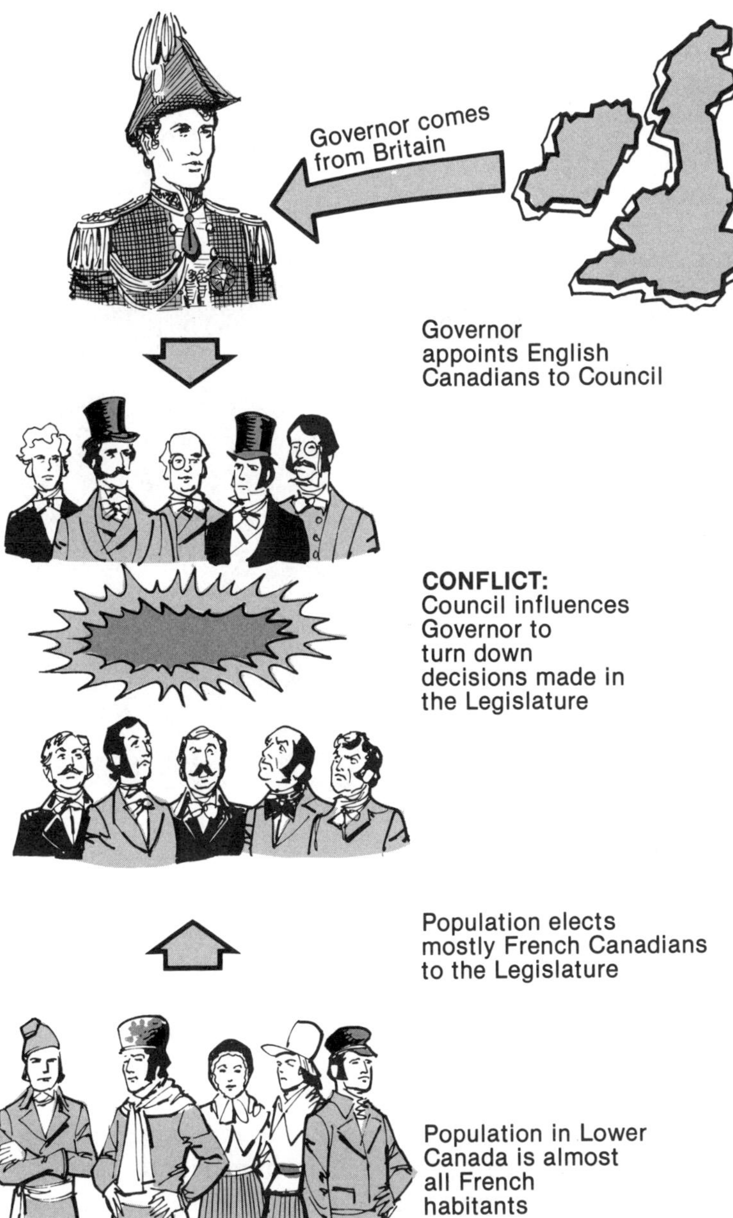

Figure 33.1 *The system of government in Lower Canada that led to rebellion in 1837*

Figure 33.2 St. Eustache then and now

(33.2.a.) *This drawing shows the scene at St. Eustache when the rebel* Patriotes *hid in a church. The British soldiers set fire to the church. The* Patriotes *then had a terrible choice. They could either die in the flames, or they could be shot to death as they leapt out the church windows. Do you think this incident would have any effect on how French Canadians feel about the British today?*

(33.2.b.) *These days, St. Eustache is a peaceful town outside of Montreal.*

The French leaders in the legislature soon demanded changes in the system of government. They formed a group called the *Patriotes*. The *Patriotes* said that the governor's council should be abolished. Some of them even thought that Lower Canada should follow the United States and break away from Britain.

The *Patriotes* sent a list of their demands to Britain. But the British government paid no attention. Finally, in 1837, tempers flared. On November 7, the *Patriotes* started a riot in Montreal. People threw rocks through windows. They **looted** stores. They set buildings on fire. The governor had to send British troops to stop the rioters.

One of the measures set by the Upper Canadian Parliament in 1825 was the price of bread.

Figure 33.3 Montebello *Louis Joseph Papineau was one of the leaders of the rebellion in Lower Canada. He owned a wonderful estate called Montebello (Beautiful Mountain). Montebello is now a well known tourist resort and convention centre. You can read more about Papineau in the biography at the end of this lesson.*

After the riot was over, soldiers were sent to several small towns outside of Montreal. They were supposed to arrest the leaders of the *Patriotes*. Some of the French settlers fought with the soldiers. But in a town called St. Eustache, many *Patriotes* were killed and injured. The leaders fled to the United States. For the time being, the rebellion was over.

It would be wrong to say that the problems in Lower Canada were caused completely by the differences between the French and the English. This was proved by the situation in Upper Canada.

In Upper Canada the members of the governor's council and the representatives in the legislature were all English. But at the same time there was **rebellion** in Lower Canada, there was also rebellion in Upper Canada. The Upper Canadian settlers were just as angry that their governor listened only to the council and not to the legislature. This proves that the rebellion in Lower Canada was about more than the French **versus** the English.

The trouble was that it was much easier for people to think of the situation as just a French versus English problem. The French settlers in Lower Canada could never forget that they had been conquered by Britain.

Note: You can learn more about the United States and the 1837 rebellions in Lesson 48.

THE FACTS

Remembering Facts

1. Why did the British government pass the Constitution Act?
2. Describe the system of government in Lower Canada?
3. Why did this system of government cause problems in Lower Canada?
4. Who were the *Patriotes*?
5. What happened in Lower Canada in 1837?

Finding Facts

The members of the governor's council in Upper Canada were called the Family Compact. Use other history books to find out what people called the governor's council in Lower Canada.

YOUR OPINIONS

Stating Opinions

Can you think of any situation in Canada today that you would fight for? In other words, is there any situation that makes you want to go out and fight a battle with the opposing side?

Explain your opinion in a few sentences.

Discussing Opinions

At the time of the rebellions in Upper and Lower Canada, the rich, educated people had power. On the other hand, the farmers and labourers had very little power.

Discuss with the rest of the class whether you think this situation was right. Should rich, educated people have more power than poor labourers? Should they have more right to say how the country should be run?

NEW WORDS

Learning Words

In your notebook, write the title Vocabulary: Lesson 33. Then write down the following words in a list. Using the Glossary or a dictionary, write the meaning beside each word.

When you are finished, write a short note telling what you have learned in this lesson. Try to use all 5 of these words in your note.

council **loot** **merchant**
rebellion **versus**

Examining Words

One of the last sentences in this lesson (p. 241) reads "*This proves that* the rebellion in Lower Canada was about more than the French versus the English." Instead of writing *This proves that*, we could have used the word *Therefore*. Or wc could have used the word *Consequently*. Or we could even have used the word *Evidently*.

Words like *therefore, consequently*, and *evidently* are called conjunctions. They join 2 ideas. And they help to show the relationships between ideas.

In each of the following, there are 2 conjunctions. Decide which you think fits the sentence best. Then write out the statements as you think they should be. Compare your answers with those of the rest of the class.

1. Dogs love to follow their owners around. (Therefore,/However,) cats are more independent.
2. A rabbit's foot is supposed to bring good luck. (Consequently,/Meanwhile,) I always carry one.
3. Teachers often talk about students. (Similarly,/Afterwards,) students often talk about teachers.

AN ILLUSTRATION

You may have wondered where the names Upper Canada and Lower Canada come from. The words *Upper* and *Lower* refer to where the provinces are in relation to the St. Lawrence River.

Upper Canada (now Ontario) is *up*stream. It is closer to the beginning of the St. Lawrence River. *Lower* Canada (now Quebec) is *down*stream. It is closer to the mouth of the St. Lawrence.

Look at a map of these provinces today. Then answer the following questions.

1. Is Kingston upstream or downstream from Montreal?
2. Is Quebec City upstream or downstream from Montreal?
3. Is Sept-Îles upstream or downstream from Kingston?
4. Is Trois Rivières upstream or downstream from Quebec City?

You may find it helpful in doing this exercise to draw a sketch map of the area around the St. Lawrence. Then add arrows pointing upstream and downstream.

Louis Joseph Papineau

Figure 33.4 *Louis Joseph Papineau in later years*

Claim to fame: He was a French Canadian patriot and leader.

Born: 1786 in Montreal, Lower Canada

Married: 1818 to Julie Brunneau. She was very ambitious and influenced him to stay in politics, even when he wanted to retire to his estate in the country.

They had 3 sons and 2 daughters. One of their grandsons was the French nationalist, Henri Bourassa (see the biography in Lesson 38).

Career: Papineau served in the War of 1812. In 1814 he was elected to the legislative assembly in Lower Canada. The very next year, he became the speaker. He soon had a great influence on other politicians and was seen as a leader of the French Canadian nationalists, or *Patriotes*.

Papineau wanted political changes. but he did not want to try new ways of government. Instead, he was quite conservative. He wanted to go back to the old ways and values of New France.

Papineau's ideas for change helped cause the rebellion in 1837. But Papineau did not fight in the rebellion himself. Instead, he ran to the United States, where he tried to get help from the Americans. The government of Lower Canada sent him into exile. This meant he was not allowed to return home. So he moved to Paris, France.

In 1844, the rebels were forgiven and allowed to return home. Papineau came back to his old home.

Died: He died in 1871 at his estate, Montebello.

Note: You can learn about the War of 1812 in Lesson 47.

- **In 1970, some Quebeckers who were members of a group called the FLQ were sent into exile. Why were they sent into exile?**
- **If you were forced to leave Canada, where would you choose to live?**

The Union of Upper and Lower Canada

34

The rebels lost their battles in 1837. But at least the British government now realized that there were serious problems. It decided to send someone to find out just what these problems were.

The man chosen by the British government to do this was Lord Durham. He was a **wealthy** English businessman. And he was a man who believed that all colonies should be given more control over their own affairs.

Lord Durham arrived at the city of Quebec in May, 1838. He was wearing a splendid uniform covered with decorations. The crowds cheered as he rode a magnificent white horse through the streets. All Canadians hoped that this man would finally solve their problems.

Lord Durham stayed in Upper and Lower Canada for only 5 months. But even in that short time, he had a big effect on the colonies. First of all, he showed the rebels that there was no hope of winning a fight. He made sure the rebel leaders who had gone to the United States would not start new fights from there. But he was also fair to the rebels who had been captured.

Then Lord Durham travelled back and forth across the 2 colonies. He wanted to find out what the people in the colonies were like. He wanted to learn how they lived. And he wanted to discover some solutions for how they should be governed.

Unfortunately, Lord Durham did not understand the French settlers. He was angered by how much they hated the British. He also thought that the French were lazy and badly educated.

Instead, Lord Durham **sided** with the English businessmen and merchants who controlled Lower Canada.

Figure 34.1 Lord Durham *At home in England, Lord Durham was known as Radical Jack. He believed that the people should have more say in how they were governed. This was considered very liberal at the time. Do these ideas seem liberal today?*

Figure 34.2 Life in a habitant home *This picture was painted in 1852 by Cornelius Krieghoff. (You can read more about him in the biography at the end of this lesson.) The woman is plaiting straw for a hat. At the same time she is watching the children and a pot on the stove while she talks to her husband. In what ways is life at home today different from the way it was in the 1850s?*

He spent most of his time talking with them. And he agreed with their ideas about how the colonies should grow.

When he returned home to England in September, Lord Durham immediately began writing a report. In his report he said that there were 2 main problems in the Canadian colonies.

He said that the first main problem was the French. Durham thought that the French settlers blocked progress in Canada. He thought that they should be assimilated by the English settlers. He wanted to see the French culture die out.

The second main problem that Durham found was the system of government. He felt that the legislatures did not have enough power. He agreed that the elected representatives should have more say in the laws that were made.

Durham's solution to these problems was to **unite** the 2 colonies. Then there would be only 1 governor and 1 legislature. And Durham said that the governor should not be allowed to **cancel** the laws that were passed by the elected representatives.

Black squirrels were considered a delicacy by early Canadians because their flavour was not too strong.

Durham knew that there were more French settlers than English settlers in the Canadas. This meant that in the beginning there would be more French representatives than English representatives in the legislature. But Durham also knew that this situation would soon change. He knew that

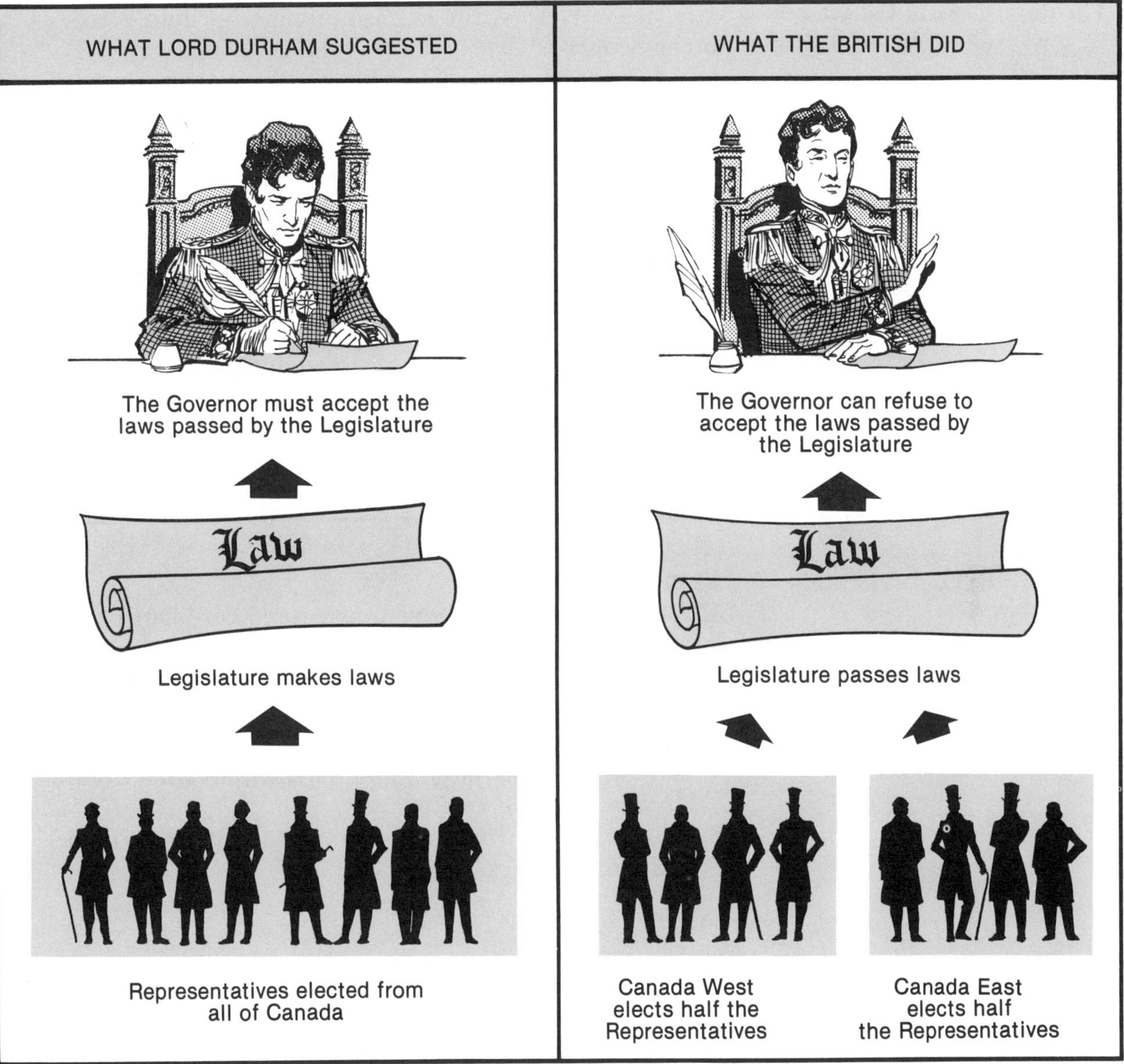

Figure 34.3 *The drawing on the left shows how Durham thought Canada should be governed. The drawing on the right shows the kind of government the British set up with the Act of Union in 1840. If you were an English Canadian living in Canada West at the time, which system do you think you would prefer?*

the English population would grow. And he was sure that the French settlers would soon be assimilated.

The British government was not as sure as Durham. Therefore, it only accepted part of his ideas. In 1840 it passed a new law called the Act of Union. As Durham had suggested, this law joined the 2 Canadas together. There was to be just 1 governor and 1 legislature.

However, the British government kept the old **division** between Upper and Lower Canada. Only now they were called the provinces of Canada West (Ontario) and Canada East (Quebec).

The Royal Bank of Canada used to be called the Merchant Bank of Halifax.

Canada West — the English province — didn't have as many people as Canada East — the French province. To be fair, Canada West shouldn't have had as many elected representatives as Canada East. But the British government gave both provinces exactly the same number of seats in the new legislature.

In this way, the British government made sure that the French would not outnumber the English in the new legislature. Naturally, this decision did not please the French in Lower Canada.

Also, the British government did not accept Durham's idea about the Governor not being allowed to cancel laws. In the Act of Union, the Governor still had the right to cancel laws passed by the Legislature.

THE FACTS

Remembering Facts

1. Why did the British government send Lord Durham to Canada?
2. What were the 2 main problems Lord Durham found in Upper and Lower Canada?
3. What was Lord Durham's solution to these problems?
4. How was the Act of Union different from what Lord Durham had suggested?
5. Why didn't the British government follow what Lord Durham had suggested?

Finding Facts

Where did the British government make the capital of the new colony of Canada?

YOUR OPINIONS

Stating Opinions

The British government paid Lord Durham to make his report. But the British government didn't pay attention to a lot of what Lord Durham said.

How would you feel if someone asked you for advice and then didn't follow it? Explain your opinion in a few sentences.

Discussing Opinions

Imagine that you are one of the French settlers in Lower Canada. Discuss with the rest of the class how you would feel about Lord Durham's report. How do you think you would feel about the Act of Union?

NEW WORDS

Learning Words

In your notebook, write the title Vocabulary: Lesson 34. Then write down the following words in a list. Using the Glossary or a dictionary, write the meaning beside each word.

When you are finished, write a short note telling what you have learned in this lesson. Try to use all 5 of these words in your note.

cancel	**division**	**side**
unite	**wealthy**	

Examining Words

The words *splendid* and *magnificent* mean the same thing. They both mean ''grand'' or ''gorgeous.''

When 2 words mean the same thing, they are called *synonymous*. See if you can find synonyms in this lesson for the following words.

caught disliked fights stopped

AN ILLUSTRATION

The biography for this lesson is about an artist called Cornelius Krieghoff. Krieghoff lived and worked in many different cities. After you read the biography, draw a map of the east half of North America. On it, label all the places where Krieghoff lived. Also label the city where many of Krieghoff's paintings are now kept. Give your map a suitable title.

Cornelius Krieghoff

Figure 34.4 *A self-portrait by Cornelius Krieghoff. What is a self-portrait?*

Claim to fame: His oil paintings show the lives of French settlers and Indians in Quebec in the 1800s.

Born: 1815 in Amsterdam, Holland, the son of a carpet-maker

Married: around 1840, to a French-Canadian woman called Louise Gauthier. She and their daughter Emilie appear in many of Krieghoff's paintings.

Career: After graduating from university Krieghoff spent a few years travelling around Europe. He paid his way by working as a painter and as a musician.

Then in 1837, the year of the rebellions in Canada, he sailed to New York. Krieghoff immediately joined the United States army. His job was to draw pictures of the battles his regiment was involved in.

In 1840, Krieghoff deserted the army and came to Canada with his wife. After staying for a while in Toronto and Montreal, he moved to Quebec city. There he began the series of Canadian paintings for which he is now famous. He painted the French settlers and Indians as they went about their daily lives, almost in the same way as photographers record how we live today.

Krieghoff painted nearly 1000 pictures of Canadian life before he left Quebec in 1867 to live with his daughter in Chicago.

Died: Since his death in 1872, Krieghoff's paintings of Canada have become very valuable. Many of them can be seen today in the Lord Beaverbrook Gallery in Fredericton, New Brunswick.

- **Who was Lord Beaverbrook?**
- **Which do you like best: photographs or oil paintings that show how people lived?**

Confederation 35

Naturally the French Canadians did not like Lord Durham's report. They were **insulted** when he called them lazy. And they were furious that he wanted to destroy their culture.

But the French Canadians did agree with one part of Lord Durham's report. Lord Durham had suggested that the governor should not be allowed to cancel laws passed by the legislature. In other words, he thought that the elected representatives should be responsible for what happened in the colony. He thought that Canada should have what is called **responsible** government.

The English Canadians in Canada West also agreed with this idea. But the British government did not want to give Canada responsible government. So in the beginning the French and the English in Canada had a reason to work together. It took them 9 years. But they finally won responsible government in 1849.

After they had won responsible government, there was not as much reason for the representatives from Canada West and Canada East to work together. The English and the French did agree on some things. But most of the time they disagreed. When the legislature voted on new laws, the English and French often voted against each other.

John A. Macdonald from Canada West and George Etienne Cartier from Canada East did run the government several times. But each time it broke down over something that one Canada wanted and the other Canada didn't want. Finally there was a **deadlock**. Nothing seemed to get done.

The main cause of the deadlock was the system of government the British government had set up in 1840. At that time, the settlers in Canada West had been happy that they had as many seats in the legislature as the settlers in Canada East. After all, Canada West was much smaller than Canada East.

Figure 35.1 *Throughout the 1850s and 1860s, thousands of immigrants came to settle in Canada. Most of them did not do this of their own free will. At home they faced unemployment and starvation. At least there was a chance for a better life in North America. What opinions did this cartoonist seem to have about immigrants to Canada?*

Canada's first covered skating rink opened in 1863 at Halifax, Nova Scotia.

But by 1851, the population in Canada West had grown much larger. Now there were more English than French. So the English in Canada West decided that the representation in the legislature was unfair. They began to demand "representation by population". They wanted more seats because they had more people.

George Brown was the leader of the English Canadians who wanted representation by population. He felt that if there were more seats for Canada West, then there would not be a deadlock. The French would not be able to pass any laws. And they would soon be assimilated as Lord Durham had said they would.

Of course the French people in Canada East did not want representation by population. They had accepted the equal seats when there were more French than English. Why should they change now?

Figure 35.2 *The Fathers of Confederation were photographed at the Charlottetown Conference in September 1864. John A. Macdonald and George Etienne Cartier are in the middle of the front row. What does the term "Father of Confederation" mean?*

But something had to be done. Between 1862 and 1864 there were actually 5 different governments that tried to run the colony. Not one of them managed to make it work.

The only solution was to have an entirely new system of government. So in 1864, George Brown made an important move. He promised that he would work with any other representative in the legislature in order to win a new system of government.

Macdonald and Cartier accepted Brown's offer. Together, they came up with the idea of a **federation** with all the British colonies in North America. In this new country, each of the old colonies would have its own separate provincial government. But there would also be a federal government for the whole country.

The English in Canada West liked this idea. Finally, they would be able to run the government the way they wanted to without having to worry about the French. And the French in Canada East were happy, too. If they became a separate province, they would be able to protect their language and their culture.

But the French also wanted to protect their culture in any federal government. So they agreed to accept Confederation only if it would be legal to speak French in the federal government of Canada. They also demanded that it be legal to speak French in all federal courts.

In 1867, the year of Confederation, rowers from St. John, New Brunswick, won the World's Championship.

Figure 35.3 *Quebec at the time of Confederation*

(35.3.a.) *Ice-boat sailing on the St. Lawrence, c. 1867*

(35.3.b.) *Women working in a copper mine in Quebec, 1867.*

In 1870, the Canadian government issued its first banknotes for 25¢, $1, and $2. The $5 bill came in 1912.

Macdonald, Cartier, and Brown went to Charlottetown in Prince Edward Island in 1864. As you learned in Lesson 1, they talked with the **maritime** colonies about becoming a single country. And the rest is history. Confederation took place on July 1, 1867. The new country of Canada came into being.

The deadlock between Canada West and Canada East had been solved. But the problems between the English and French had not gone away. Soon they would start again.

THE FACTS

Remembering Facts

1. What is responsible government?
2. What happened to the English and French in Canada after they had won responsible government?
3. What caused the deadlock in Canada?
4. What docs "representation by population" mean?
5. How did the leaders in Canada West and Canada East solve the deadlock?

Finding Facts

John A. Macdonald was the first prime minister of Canada. Who was the prime minister when you were born? Who was the prime minister when your school was first opened?

YOUR OPINIONS

Stating Opinions

Between 1862 and 1864 there was an election almost every year in the colony of Canada. Do you think it would be a good thing to elect the government every year? Or do you think this would cause problems? Explain your opinion in a few sentences.

Discussing Opinions

Divide the class into 2 groups. One of the groups should represent the people in Canada West. The other group should represent the people in Canada East. Then discuss whether it was fair for George Brown to ask for "representation by population".

Debate this question with the other group in the class.

NEW WORDS

Learning Words

In your notebook, write the title Vocabulary: Lesson 35. Then write down the following words in a list. Using the Glossary or a dictionary, write the meaning beside each word.

When you are finished, write a short note telling what you have learned in this lesson. Try to use all 5 of these words in your note.

deadlock	**federation**	**insult**
maritime	**responsible**	

Examining Words

George Etienne Cartier was named George in honour of the British king at the time. But most French people spell the name George with an *s* as in *Georges*.

How do French people usually spell the following names? If you do not already know the answers, ask a French teacher, or a friend who speaks French, or look in a French dictionary.

- your own name
- your favourite singer's name

AN ILLUSTRATION

Some people in Lower Canada did not like the idea of Confederation. They were worried that French Canadians would gradually be swamped by English Canadians as the new country grew. Look at the pie charts in Figure 35.4. Was this worry correct?

Find out the percent of seats Quebec has today in the House of Commons compared to the rest of the country. Draw a pie chart like the ones in Figure 35.4. How much change has there been since 1917?

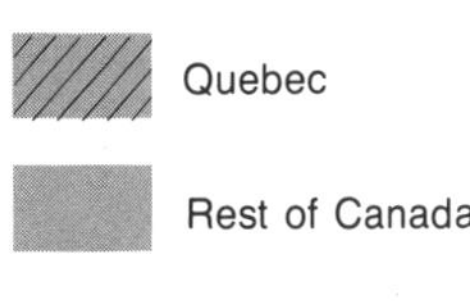

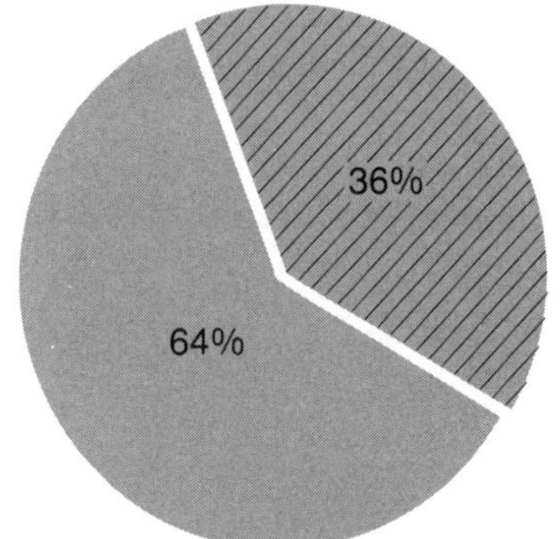

(35.4.a.) *Percent of seats in the House of Commons: 1867*

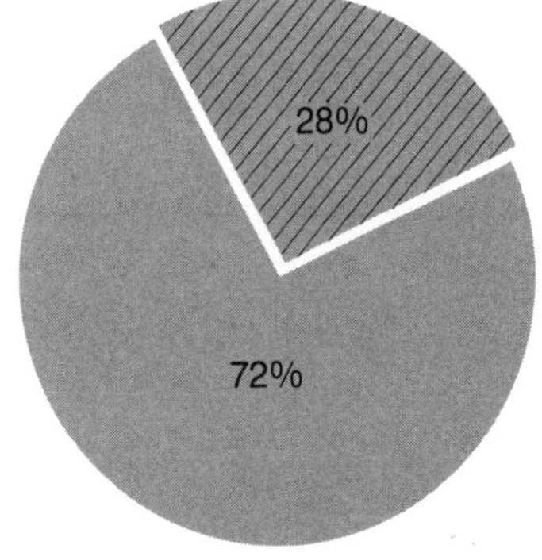

(35.4.b.) *Percent of seats in the House of Commons: 1917*

Fig. 35.4 *The percent of seats in the House of Commons held by Quebec as compared to the rest of Canada.*

Catherine Parr Traill

Figure 35.5 *Catherine Parr Traill*

Claim to fame: Her many books show what life was like in Upper Canada around the time of Confederation.

Born: 1802 in London, England. Her younger sister, Susanna Moodie, also became a famous early Canadian writer.

Married: 1832 to Lieutenant Thomas Traill, an officer in the British army

Career: When she was only 16, Traill published her first work, a short story for children. This was the first of several children's stories she wrote during her lifetime.

In 1832, Traill moved with her husband to Upper Canada. The journey was terrible. She almost died of cholera. But luckily she and her husband settled happily into pioneer life in Upper Canada.

Traill wrote many letters home to her family. And in 1835, these letters were put together and published as a book, *The Backwoods of Canada*. This popular book gave lots of good advice to British people who were thinking of moving to Canada. Twenty years later, Traill published a second book filled with more practical advice.

Traill's most important books gave descriptions of the different plants in Upper Canada. These were the first books of their kind. Traill's niece, Agnes Fitzgibbon, painted the pictures for these classic books.

Died: Traill kept writing almost until the day she died in 1899. Her books are still read by many students and historians.

- **What is cholera? How can it be cured?**
- **What advice would you give to a person from another country who was coming to live in Canada?**

The Riel Rebellions

36

For a time after Confederation, there were no problems between French and English Canadians. The young country was growing rapidly. In particular, settlers from Ontario started moving west in search of new land. Many of them moved to the Red River area (near Winnipeg, Manitoba, today).

When the Canadian settlers arrived, there were people already living in the Red River area. There were Indians. And there were people of mixed blood called **Métis**. They were half Indian and half European (usually French).

For a long time, the Red River land had been owned by the Hudson's Bay Company. But in 1869 Britain bought this land for a million and a half dollars. Then Britain gave the land to the Canadian government.

Figure 36.1 Surveyors on the Prairies, 1873 *In this photograph, Royal Engineers are hard at work. It was survey work like this that made the Métis afraid they were going to lose their homes and land. Have you ever seen surveyors at work?*

Figure 36.2 Buffalo bones for sale *In the 1880s and 1890s, settlers on the prairies would collect the bleached buffalo bones that were scattered everywhere. Among other things, these bones could be sold for fertilizer. They were often a settler's first way of making money.*

All of this was done without finding out how the Indians and Métis who lived there felt about it. No one bothered to ask them whether they would like to be part of Canada.

Naturally, the Indians and Métis were upset when the first Canadian settlers arrived. They were even more worried when Canadian surveyors started to map the area in 1869.

The Indians and Métis were worried about what would happen when the Red River area became part of Canada. They were worried that the Canadians might take their land. They were also afraid that they might lose their culture. The French-speaking Métis did not want to lose their language or their Roman Catholic schools.

They decided to force the Canadian government to talk to them. So the Indians and the Métis set up their own government. They chose Louis Riel, a French-speaking Métis, as their leader.

Some of the English Canadians who had come to the Red River area from Ontario did not like this. They had known Canada would soon take over the Red River area. And they had expected to take charge in the area when it became part of Canada. Therefore, these new settlers made trouble for Riel.

The leader of these English Canadian settlers was Thomas Scott. Thomas Scott led a fight against Riel. Scott lost the fight and was put in jail. But even after he was in jail, Scott made trouble for Riel. Finally, Riel lost his temper with Scott and had him put to death.

The first woman president of the YMCA was Reynell Andreychuck, a 30-year-old lawyer from Moose Jaw, Saskatchewan.

Figure 36.3 Asleep in the trenches, 1885 *This photograph was taken by one of the soldiers sent in 1885 to put down the Riel rebellion. These are government soldiers asleep in a trench near Batoche. Does anything about their clothing surprise you? Explain your answer.*

Suddenly the problem in the Red River area became very important in the rest of Canada. The English-speaking people in Ontario were furious over Scott's death. They were sure he had been killed just because he was a Canadian and a **Protestant**. The newspapers printed stories calling Riel a murderer and **traitor**.

The French-speaking people in Quebec were just the opposite. They sided with Riel and the Métis. They thought the Métis were being badly treated by the government just because they were French and Roman Catholic. Their newspapers printed stories saying that Riel was a hero and a protector of minority rights.

The Canadian government settled the problem by promising the Métis that they could keep their land, language, and religion. Riel was afraid he might be put to death himself, so he escaped to the United States.

But this was not the end of the Riel situation. Fifteen years later there was more trouble in the Northwest. This time the Indians and Métis living along the Saskatchewan River had been having troubles with the Canadian government. No one in Ottawa seemed to listen to their problems.

The Indians and Métis decided they needed Louis Riel once again. Riel returned and led a second rebellion. But this one was much more serious. There were several battles with Canadian troops. And people lost their lives in the fighting.

The fastest mammal in Canada is the pronghorn antelope from southern Alberta. It can reach speeds of 96 km/h.

The first non-Indian child born in western Canada was Reine Lajimonière in 1807.

Riel gave himself up and was taken to Regina for trial. He was defended by lawyers from Quebec. They wanted him to say he was insane. But Riel refused. He believed that what he had done was right. He said it was the only way the government would listen to the problems of the Indians and the Métis.

The English-speaking Protestant jury decided that Riel was sane. They said he was guilty of treason. Therefore, Riel was **condemned** to die.

The French in Quebec were outraged at the verdict. They asked the prime minister, John A. Macdonald, to **pardon** Riel. But Macdonald refused. There was too much pressure from English-speaking Canada to hang Riel.

Riel was hanged in November, 1885. This was a major turning point in French-English relations in Canada. The French suddenly felt very alone. Even today, more than 100 years later, Riel is still remembered. French Canadians often speak about him when they try to explain why they feel so separate from the rest of Canada.

Figure 36.4 A French poster in support of Riel *This poster reads "Louis Riel, Métis Leader, Executed on November 16, 1885, Political martyr! Guilty of having loved his oppressed countrymen, victim of Orange fanaticism to which the politicians sacrificed him without soul and without heart. Let true patriots remember him!!"*

The phrase about "Orange fanaticism" refers to people who were members of the Orange Order in Canada. Use an encyclopedia to find out about the Orange Order. What do its members stand for?

THE FACTS

Remembering Facts

1. How did the Indians and Métis feel about the Red River area becoming part of Canada?
2. Who was Thomas Scott?
3. How did the problem in the Red River cause bad feelings between people in Ontario and Quebec?
4. Why did Riel come back to Canada in 1885?
5. What happened to Riel after the second rebellion?

Finding Facts

Are there countries in the world today where citizens are openly fighting against their government? Check the international pages of the newspaper or listen to the international news on the radio or television to get information. Why are these people fighting their government? How long has the fighting been going on?

YOUR OPINIONS

Stating Opinions

Traitors are people who go against their own country. They might actually fight battles with guns. Or they might go against their country by spying and selling secrets to the enemy.

Do you think that traitors should be put to death? Explain your opinion in a few sentences.

Discussing Opinions

Imagine that you are looking out your window into your backyard when 3 strangers walk into the garden. They set up tripods and other equipment and begin to drive pegs into the ground and draw lines. You don't understand why they are there or what they are doing.

When you go out to find out what they are doing, they say they have orders to be there. How do you feel about the situation? What can you do about this?

NEW WORDS

Learning Words

In your notebook, write the title Vocabulary: Lesson 36. Then write down the following words in a list. Using the Glossary or a dictionary, write the meaning beside each word.

When you are finished, write a short note telling what you have learned in this lesson. Try to use all 5 of these words in your note.

condemn **Métis** **pardon**
Protestant **traitor**

Examining Words

The word *Métis* is a French word that is now used freely in the English language. Actually, there are many French words that we use in English.

As an example, think of cooking and food. When you go to a restaurant and order apple pie *à la mode*, you're asking for a scoop of ice cream on the pie. Read recipe books or restaurant menus to find at least one other French cooking term. Can you explain what it means?

The rebellion in 1885 might have turned out very differently except for the railway. Railway lines to the Red River area had just been completed. This meant that the Canadian government could send troops quickly to the trouble spots.

There have been many more kilometres of railway lines built since 1885. Find a map of Canada that shows all the main railway lines. Your task is to figure out how many kilometres of railway lines there are in Canada today.

To do this, you will need a thread or a piece of thin string. Lay the thread along the railway lines on the map. Then measure the length of thread it takes to cover all those lines. Check the scale on the map. This will help you figure out how many kilometres of railway lines there are in Canada today.

Compare answers with your classmates. Are there differences in your answers? If there are, can you explain where these differences came from?

Mistahimaskwa (Big Bear)

Figure 36.5 *Big Bear, standing second from the left, trades at Fort Pitt with a representative of the Hudson's Bay Company.*

Claim to fame: He was the Indian chief who fought against being put on a reserve.

Born: sometime around 1825 near Fort Carlton, Saskatchewan

Married: Big Bear had several wives and at least 4 sons.

Career: Big Bear was chief of a small band of Cree Indians who travelled across the prairies hunting buffalo.

Then settlers started moving out west. They asked all the Indian chiefs to sign treaties. These treaties said that the Indians would live on reserves instead of travelling across the prairies. In return, they would get food and medicine.

Big Bear realized these treaties would be bad for the Indians. Other chiefs signed the treaties and took their people to live on reserves. But Big Bear refused.

Then the last of the buffalo were killed off in 1882. Big Bear's people were starving. Big Bear signed a treaty so that his people would get food. But he was not satisfied. He kept asking for better conditions.

Other Indians soon realized that Big Bear had been right. They joined his band. Unfortunately, some of them wanted to use violence. Big Bear tried to stop them. But in 1885, several warriors killed 9 people at Frog Lake, Saskatchewan.

Died: Big Bear gave himself up to the government on July 2, 1885. He was sentenced to 2 years in jail. The time in jail broke his health and his spirit. He died in 1888.

- **What are Indian reserves? How are they run? What is the Indian reserve closest to where you live?**
- **Do you think it was fair to put Big Bear in jail?**

37 The Manitoba Schools Question

After the first rebellion in the Northwest, Canada had promised the Métis that their language and religion would be protected. Canada kept this promise when it passed the Manitoba Act in 1870.

The Manitoba Act made Manitoba a province of Canada. It also said that there would be separate schools for French-speaking Roman Catholics in the province. In this way, the French-speaking Roman Catholic children could be educated in their own language and about their own religion.

But in 1890, the government in Manitoba decided to close the separate schools in the province. The French-speaking Roman Catholics were furious. Naturally, the other French-speaking Roman Catholics in the rest of Canada were also angry.

Figure 37.1 Outside a 1-room school near Brandon, Manitoba, c. 1900 *What flag is being flown on the flagpole?*

At first, they took the issue to court. After a few years, the judges gave their answer. They said that it was quite legal for Manitoba to close the schools. After all, education was a provincial responsibility.

But then the judges were asked to decide whether the federal government could do something about the problem. One section in the BNA Act said that sometimes the federal government could **interfere** in education. It could interfere in order to protect minority rights. So, in 1895 the judges decided that the federal government could force Manitoba to bring back the separate schools if it wanted to.

The federal government then asked the Manitoba government to re-open the separate schools. But many Manitoban voters did not want this. So the Manitoba government refused. Now the federal government was in a **dilemma**.

There was a federal election in 1896. And the Manitoba Schools Question became the most important issue. Charles Tupper, the leader of the Conservatives, said he would force Manitoba to bring back the separate schools. If his party won the election, they would pass a law making Manitoba do this.

In 1981, 17-year-old Heather Peniuk of Winnipeg won a $5000 award for her research on the common cold.

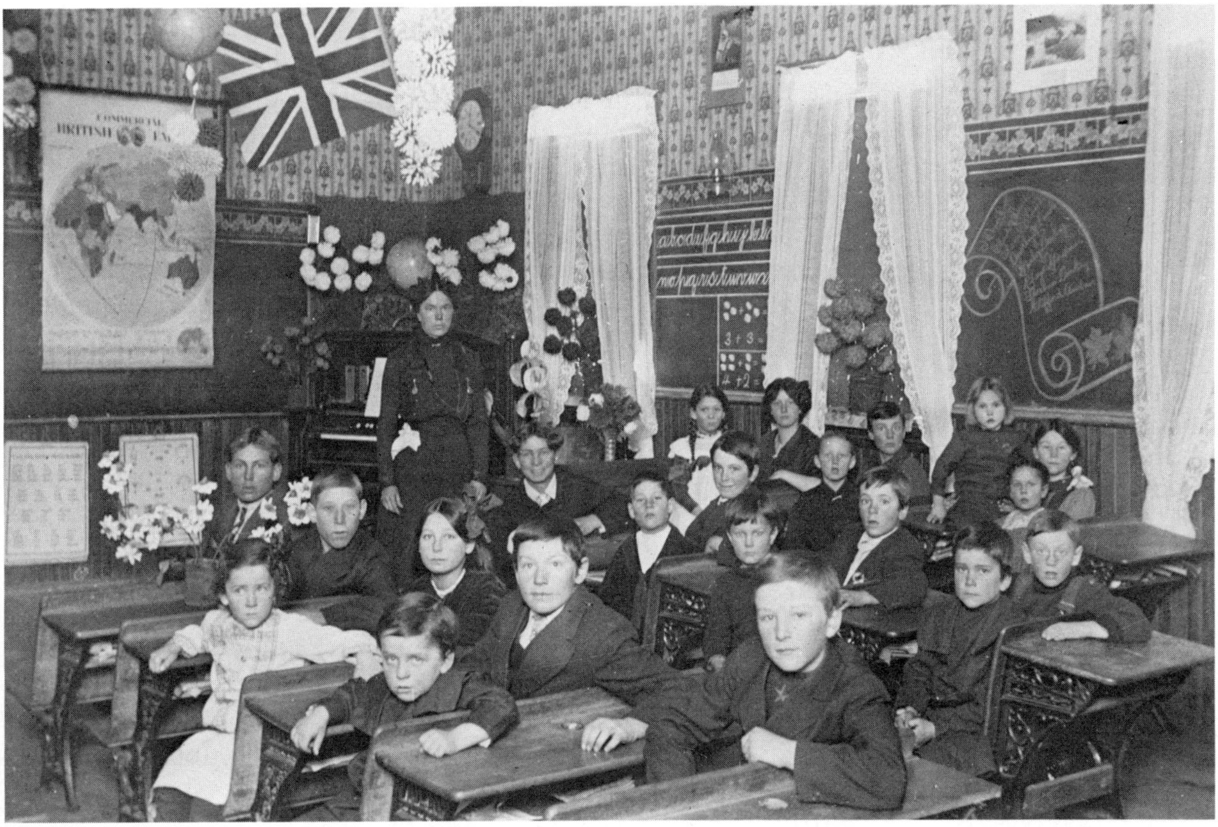

Figure 37.2 The interior of a 1-room school in Vulcan, Alberta, 1915 *How is this classroom different from the way yours is arranged? Which classroom would you prefer to be educated in?*

Figure 37.3 St. Mary's Academy Group, 1870 *These girls were being educated privately by nuns in a school near Ottawa. Based on the evidence in the photograph, what subjects do you think these girls studied?*

Many people were surprised at this. After all, Tupper was an English-speaking Protestant. They thought he would not care about separate schools for French-speaking Roman Catholics. But Tupper felt strongly about the BNA Act. Because the BNA Act said that minority rights should be protected, Tupper felt the federal government should use force.

Wilfrid Laurier, the leader of the Liberals, **disagreed** with using force. And this also surprised many Canadians. After all, Laurier was a French-speaking Roman Catholic himself. They expected he would want the separate schools in Manitoba.

And it was true. Laurier *did* want Manitoba to bring back the separate schools. But Laurier was also from Quebec. And he knew that Quebec was always fighting to protect its rights. So naturally Laurier wanted to protect the powers of the provinces. Since education was a provincial power, Laurier felt that the federal government should not interfere.

Instead, Laurier suggested using "sunny ways". What he meant was that he would try to get the 2 sides to agree. He promised that if he won the election he would not use force. Instead, he would try to talk the Manitoba government into bringing back the separate schools.

The first practical electric car in North America was shown in Toronto in 1893. Its top speed was 24 km/h.

Figure 37.4 The graduating class, Acadia University, 1884 *Clara Belle Marshall Raymond is sitting in the centre of this graduation group. She was the first woman to graduate from Acadia University, and one of the first ever to graduate from a Canadian university. How many women students do you think go to university today compared to the number of men?*

The election campaign was fierce. But in the end, Laurier and the Liberal party won. They were supported by both English-speaking and French-speaking people across Canada.

One of the first things that the new federal government did was to **settle** the Manitoba Schools Question. Leaders from both the federal government and the Manitoba government met together. They came up with a plan that allowed students in the regular schools to have classes in the French language and the Roman Catholic religion.

This was a **compromise**. Neither side got exactly what it wanted. But then, neither side lost completely. There have been several times in Canadian history when English Canadians and French Canadians have been against each other. The compromise solution to the Manitoba Schools Question shows that there are also times when both English Canadians and French Canadians can agree.

In 1870, Manitoba was basically bilingual. By 1876, it was multilingual, with 2 more major languages: German and Icelandic.

THE FACTS

Remembering Facts

1. How did Canada keep its promise to the Métis that their language and religion would be protected?
2. What did the government of Manitoba do in 1890?
3. How did Charles Tupper and the Conservatives want to solve the Manitoba Schools Question?
4. How did Wilfrid Laurier and the Liberals want to solve the Manitoba Schools Question?
5. How was the Manitoba Schools Question finally solved?

Finding Facts

Schools in the 1890s were very different from schools today. Read the encyclopedia or other books to find out what schools were like in the early days. Can you find out what rules the students had to follow? What were the school buildings and classrooms like? What were the teachers like? What subjects did the students learn?

YOUR OPINIONS

Stating Opinions

Do you think that religion should be taught in schools? Explain your opinion in a few sentences.

Discussing Opinions

Imagine that the students in a school with 1000 students have decided to have a dance. Four hundred of the students in the school want to have a disc jockey come in to play hit records. The other 600 want to have a live rock band.

The students' council has the right to decide about the dance. If you were on the students' council, would you suggest using force, or would you suggest a compromise? In most cases, do you think it is better for leaders to use force or to find a compromise?

NEW WORDS

Learning Words

In your notebook, write the title Vocabulary: Lesson 37. Then write down the following words in a list. Using the Glossary or a dictionary, write the meaning beside each word.

When you are finished, write a short note telling what you have learned in this lesson. Try to use all 5 of these words in your note.

compromise	**dilemma**	**disagree**
interfere	**settle**	

Examining Words

When we say someone has a *sunny* personality, we mean that he or she is cheerful and makes us feel happy in just the same way that warm sunshine can. So we compare the person to the sun.

Can you explain what we mean when we compare a person to each of the following animals?

a bear	a chicken	a fox
a lion	a rabbit	a snake

Many provinces have public schools, separate schools, *and* private schools. Draw a map of the area in which you live. On it mark all the schools in the area. Show whether these schools are public, separate, or private.

Henry Bibb

Figure 37.5 *Henry Bibb*

Claim to fame: He fought to stop segregated schools in Ontario.

Born: 1815 in Kentucky, U.S.A.

Married: Mary who ran her own school for children of all ethnic backgrounds.

Career: Henry Bibb was born the son of a mixed marriage. He was a slave. He ran away from his first masters 6 times. They sold him in 1839 to new masters from whom he finally escaped to Detroit.

Bibb led groups in Detroit to try to stop slavery. But it didn't seem to be working, so he moved across the Canadian border to Windsor. In Windsor, he started a Black newspaper, *Voice of the Fugitive*. He also started a charity group to help Black refugees.

Bibb was best known for his fight against the segregation of education. In 1850, Ontario had passed the Common Schools Act. This made it legal for communities to segregate the schools. In other words, there would be a school for the Blacks and a school for other children. Bibb criticized Blacks who accepted these separate schools.

Bibb raised a great deal of money to help the cause of Blacks in Ontario. But he was accused of keeping a lot of the money for his personal use. He also quarrelled in public with other Blacks over the education issue.

Died: Bibb's printing office was burned down in October, 1853. He died 9 months later, still convinced his office had been burned down on purpose.

- **Name a modern magazine or newspaper which is written for Blacks.**
- **What are some similarities between the Manitoba Schools Question and the problem of segregated schools in Ontario?**

QUIZ 5

The following questions are based on the lessons in Chapter 5. **DO NOT WRITE YOUR ANSWERS IN THIS TEXTBOOK.** Instead, you should write the answers in your notebook or on a separate sheet of paper.

1. There are 8 blanks in the following paragraphs. They have been labelled from (a) to (h). Write down the 8 answers in a list on your paper. Then beside each answer write the letter of the blank where it belongs.

Acadia	St. Lawrence	Quebec City
cliffs	British	Thirteen Colonies
New France	General Wolfe	

French settlers in North America lived in two main areas. One of these areas was in Nova Scotia. It was called (a) ______ by the French. The other colony was along the banks of the (b) ______ River. It was called (c) ______.

Settlers from Britain lived in the (d) ______ along the Atlantic coastline. In 1759, British soldiers led by (e) ______ attacked the French at (f) ______. After several weeks, the British found a way to bring soldiers and guns up the rocky (g) ______. So the British defeated Quebec, and New France became a (h) ______ colony.

2. Match the person in the list on the left side with the correct description from the list on the right side. For each one, write the letter and the number together on your paper.

(a) Lord Durham	(1)	the leader of new Canadian settlers against the Métis in Red River
(b) George Etienne Cartier	(2)	the prime minister who solved the Manitoba Schools Question
(c) *Patriotes*	(3)	the British Governor who wrote a report about the 1837 rebellions in Canada
(d) Wilfrid Laurier	(4)	French Canadians who rebelled in Lower Canada
(e) Métis	(5)	a French Canadian politician who was one of the fathers of Confederation
(f) Thomas Scott	(6)	people of mixed blood — half Indian and half European

3. Write the letters from (a) to (e) on your paper. Then write a T if the statement is TRUE. Write an F if the statement is FALSE.
   (a) The area that was called Lower Canada is now called Quebec.
   (b) The area that was called Canada East is now called Ontario.
   (c) The British were able to assimilate the French Canadians.
   (d) Lord Durham did not understand the French Canadians.
   (e) Canada East and Canada West had representation by population in the government they shared together.

4. Match the date in the list on the left side with the correct item from the list on the right side. For each one, write the letter and the number together on your paper.

(a) 1867	(1) rebellion in Upper and Lower Canada
(b) 1759	(2) the hanging of Louis Riel
(c) 1864	(3) Confederation
(d) 1837	(4) the conquest of Quebec city
(e) 1885	(5) the Charlottetown Conference

CHAPTER SIX

Uneasy Partnership

When World War I started in Europe, Britain and France were on the same side. But this did not help English and French Canadians to get along any better. In fact, it was just the opposite.

During World War I, there was a crisis that almost tore Canada apart. For the first time, there was serious talk of Quebec leaving Confederation.

After the war, English Canadians began to take the problems of the French Canadians more seriously. And in the past few years, much has been done to try to make the French feel more at home in their own country.

But the English and French in Canada are still not equal partners. And talk of separatism has not gone away. Today there are still powerful political groups that want to separate Quebec from the rest of Canada. This would have an enormous effect on the lives of all Canadians.

38 Conscription in World War I

Figure 38.1 A French recruiting poster from World War I *In this poster, the farmer says to his son "You understand me, my son, it's your duty." The son replies "I'm going." Only a few French Canadians who lived on farms actually volunteered to fight in the war. Why do you think this was so? Can you translate any of the other words and phrases in this poster?*

When Britain declared war on Germany in August, 1914, that meant that Canada was also at war. There was a chance that some Canadians might have resented this. But in fact, almost every Canadian was convinced that the war was right.

This was true for both English and French Canadians. The editors of the French newspaper *La Patrie* even said:

> There are no longer French Canadians and English Canadians. Only one race now exists, united by the closest bonds in a common cause.

And for a time this was the case. Canadians joined together to help the war effort. And thousands of young men from across the country **volunteered** to join the **military**.

However, by 1917 the French and English were once more at odds with each other. And once again the problem had to do with French language education. This time the problem was in Ontario. The Ontario government passed a law that said students could be taught in the French language only in the very early grades. The law also tried to stop any new French-language schools being built in the province.

Naturally the French Canadians in Ontario were furious with this legislation. And the French in Quebec supported their cause. Henri Bourassa, a leading French politician from Quebec, wrote that the English in Ontario were as dangerous as the Germans in Europe. He felt that the English were trying to destroy the French culture in Canada.

Just when the debate about the Ontario schools reached its peak, there was a **crisis** in the war effort. As World War I dragged on, thousands of soldiers were wounded or killed. Stories of the horrible conditions at the battlefront came back to Canada. And the newspaper pages were filled every day with long lists of the dead and missing.

It was not surprising that fewer and fewer men volunteered for the military. But the Canadian divisions in Europe desperately needed more troops. Men had to be found somehow.

English Canadians felt that they had sent enough young men overseas. They said that the French Canadians had not done their fair share in the war effort. And it was true that there had been very few volunteers from Quebec compared to the other provinces.

But there were many reasons for this. For one thing, the government had used poor judgement in trying to get French-speaking Quebeckers to volunteer. They sent English-speaking officers to try to persuade the young men to join. And those French Canadians who did **enlist** had a very hard time, because most of their commanders spoke only English.

Because the troops were so desperately needed, the prime minister, Robert Borden, decided that men would have to be forced to serve. At the beginning of the war, Borden had promised that there would be no **conscription**.

Note: You can read more about World War I in Lessons 57 and 58.

Figure 38.2 An anti-conscription parade, Montreal, 1917 *This parade was held on May 24, Victoria Day. Why do you think these French Canadians chose Victoria Day for their demonstration against conscription?*

Figure 38.3 Windsor Train Station in Montreal, 1918 *The sign has been put up to welcome the troops home from Europe. Listed on the sign are the names of battles in which thousands of Canadians died. How do you think French-speaking soldiers would feel about this sign?*

But in 1917, his government passed the Military Service Act. This law gave the government the power to force any single man between the ages of 18 and 60 to go overseas to fight.

Relations between the French and English were already bad enough because of the Ontario schools situation. The Military Service Act caused an explosion of emotions. There were angry riots and demonstrations across Quebec. French Canadians began to believe that their real enemy was the Canadian government in Ottawa, not the Germans in Europe.

Many English Canadians were also opposed to conscription. But they were angry with the French Canadians, not with the government. They said that if the French Canadians had done their duty, conscription would not have been necessary.

The results of the election held in December of 1917, showed just how divided the country had become. Quebec was set against the rest of English Canada. For the first time, there were no important French politicians in the Cabinet or the ruling party.

The situation was so bad that one member of the Quebec legislative assembly started a debate on whether Quebec should leave Confederation. Only 50 years after the provinces had joined together, there was now open talk of separation.

When the war suddenly ended in November, 1918, conscription had added only a few more soldiers. And most of these men never even fought. In the end, conscription had not been necessary. But the conscription debate had torn the whole country apart.

Raymond Burr, who played Perry Mason — the lawyer who never lost a case — was born in New Westminster, British Columbia, in 1917.

THE FACTS

Remembering Facts

1. How did French Canadians feel about Canada joining World War I when it first started?
2. What happened in Ontario that angered French Canadians?
3. What did the Military Service Act say?
4. Why did many English Canadians blame the French Canadians in Quebec for conscription?
5. What happened in the election of 1917?

Finding Facts

Are there countries in the world today that force people to join the military? Read newspaper stories about other countries to see whether they have conscription.

YOUR OPINIONS

Stating Opinions

If Britain declared war today on another country, do you think that Canada should also go to war? Explain your opinion in a few sentences.

Discussing Opinions

When researchers looked carefully at the people who had volunteered to fight in World War I, they found some interesting facts:

1. Not many English-speaking people who lived on farms enlisted in the army. Most Quebeckers lived on farms and not in cities.
2. Most of the English-speaking people who volunteered had just recently come to Canada from Britain. Or their parents or grandparents had come from Britain.
3. English Canadians who had been in Canada for many generations did not volunteer in great numbers.

Can you suggest reasons for these 3 facts? Discuss your explanations with your classmates.

NEW WORDS

Learning Words

In your notebook, write the title Vocabulary: Lesson 38. Then write down the following words in a list. Using the Glossary or a dictionary, write the meaning beside each word.

When you are finished, write a short note telling what you have learned in this lesson. Try to use all 5 of these words in your note.

conscription	**crisis**	**enlist**
military	**volunteer**	

Examining Words

A *battle front* is the place where the two enemy armies meet and fight. Does this help you explain what a *weather front* is?

AN ILLUSTRATION

In Lesson 34, you learned about Lord Durham, who was sent to study the problems in Canada after the rebellions in 1837. In his report, Lord Durham said that in Canada he found "two nations warring in the bosom of a single state." In other words, it was as though French and English Canadians belonged to 2 different countries that were always fighting.

Table 38.1 shows the Canadian election results for 1917 — 80 years after Lord Durham visited Canada. Look carefully at the table. Do you think the situation in 1917 was very different from Lord Durham's time? Explain your answer.

	Quebec	Canadian Provinces other than Quebec	Total all Canadian Provinces
Liberal Seats	62	20	82
Conservative Seats	3	150	153
Total Seats	65	170	235

SOURCE: Canadian Parliamentary Guide

Table 38.1 *The results of the 1917 federal election*

Henri Bourassa

Figure 38.4 *Henri Bourassa addressing a political rally*

Claim to fame: Bourassa was a leading French Canadian thinker and writer.

Born: 1868 in Montreal, Quebec, the grandson of Louis-Joseph Papineau and the son of a famous French Canadian writer

Married: 1905 to Josephine Papineau. They had 8 children.

Career: Even when he was very young, Bourassa was interested in politics. He was elected to Parliament for the first time in 1896. He resigned in 1899 because he disagreed with sending Canadian troops to fight in the Boer War.

The next year, however, Bourassa won the seat back in a by-election. Nobody opposed him in this election. He had become the chief spokesperson for French Canadians in Parliament.

In 1907, Bourassa resigned from the federal Parliament. He did this in order to run in the Quebec provincial elections. He served in the Assembly until 1912. Then he decided to leave government and spend his time writing about politics.

In 1910 he started *Le Devoir*, which is still an important French Canadian newspaper. Through the newspaper, Bourassa campaigned against conscription. He also wrote personal attacks against Wilfrid Laurier. This helped to defeat the Liberals in the 1911 elections.

Bourassa went back to the House of Commons from 1925 to 1932. Then he resigned both as MP and as editor of *Le Devoir*.

Died: Bourassa died in 1952 in Outremont, Quebec.

- **When was the Boer War? Who fought in this war?**
- **Do you think that newspaper writers can cause politicians to lose elections?**

39 The Return of War and Conscription

At the end of World War I in 1918, everyone had hoped there would be no more wars. But in 1939, World War II broke out, and Britain was at war with Germany again. Historians have said that really it was the same war being continued. The 20 years in between had been just like an intermission.

Note: You can learn more about World War II in Lessons 61 and 62.

However, there had been some changes in the past 20 years. For one thing, Canada was not automatically at war becausc Britain had declared war on Germany. This time, the Canadian government had the right to decide for itself whether it was going to declare war. And the Canadian government took a week after Britain's decision before it agreed to fight.

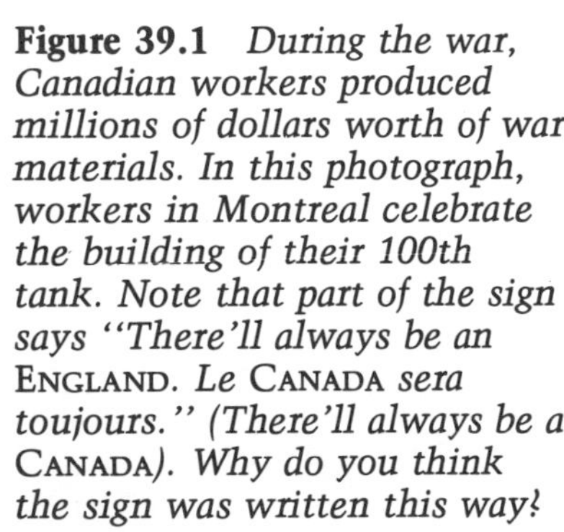

Figure 39.1 *During the war, Canadian workers produced millions of dollars worth of war materials. In this photograph, workers in Montreal celebrate the building of their 100th tank. Note that part of the sign says "There'll always be an* ENGLAND. *Le* CANADA *sera toujours." (There'll always be a* CANADA*). Why do you think the sign was written this way?*

Naturally as soon as Canada declared war, the question of conscription came up. The French Canadians had not forgotten how they had been **isolated** from the rest of Canada in 1917.

Just as in World War I, the French Canadians supported Canada's decision to fight in World War II. And the French Canadian leaders said that they would support conscription if soldiers were needed to protect Canada itself. But they also made it clear that they would not accept conscription just to send soldiers to Europe. They felt that only volunteers should be asked to die in a foreign country.

The prime minister at the time was Mackenzie King, leader of the Liberal Party. In the federal election in 1940, Mackenzie King promised that his party would never use conscription. Canadians across the country believed this promise. And the Liberals were re-elected.

But soon after the election, Germany **invaded** France. The British were forced out of Europe. There was real fear that Germany would try to invade England. The Canadian government now realized that it had to send many more men to help in the fight.

There was pressure on the government from many English Canadians to use conscription. But Mackenzie King had made a firm promise in the election that the Liberals would not force men to fight.

Foster Hewitt, who died in 1985, made the world's first hockey broadcast in 1923 from a telephone installed in the penalty box.

Figure 39.2 *The people in this photograph are promoting conscription. They are urging Canadians to vote yes to conscription. What do the letters OHMS stand for?*

Figure 39.3 *Louis St. Laurent eventually became Prime Minister of Canada. This photograph was taken on December 11, 1948. On that day, St. Laurent signed the agreement that said Newfoundland would join Canada.*

Instead, the government decided to have a special kind of conscription. It passed a law saying that men could be forced to join the armed forces. But these men would be trained to fight only at home. They would never be sent **overseas.**

This did not anger the French Canadians too much. And it kept the English quiet for a time. But as the war dragged on, there was new pressure for conscription to send men overseas. Finally Mackenzie King decided to ask the country to **release** his government from the promise not to bring in conscription.

In April, 1942, there was a **plebiscite**. Every voter was given the chance to say yes or no. When the ballots were counted, 80% of English Canadians said that the government could break its promise. But 71% of the voters in Quebec said no.

Mackenzie King was very worried when he saw the results. He remembered the terrible conscription crisis in World War I. And he was determined to avoid that kind of split between French and English Canada. After the plebiscite he said, "Not necessarily conscription, but conscription if necessary." Many English Canadians were angry that he did not act. But the French Canadians felt that he was taking their feelings into account.

By 1944, the whole problem became very serious. As in World War I, men were not volunteering fast enough to replace those being lost in the fighting. Mackenzie King searched desperately for another way to avoid conscription. But there seemed to be no other solution.

Fortunately, one of the federal Cabinet ministers from Quebec, Louis St. Laurent, decided to go along with limited conscription. When the Liberals introduced a law to allow conscription, St. Laurent was able to speak in favour of it. And he had earned enough respect in Quebec to win over the other French Canadian Members of Parliament.

In the end, the conscripted soldiers that were sent overseas were the men who had been trained to protect Canada. People in Quebec were not happy about conscription. But this time they did not feel that they had been completely ignored by English Canadians. They still had bitter feelings, but there were no big riots the way there had been in World War I.

Canadians had learned from the last conscription crisis. The country had to work out its problems, not by argument and rioting, but by talking and reaching a compromise.

After he died in 1938, Canadians were shocked to learn that the conservationist Grey Owl was not an Indian but an Englishman.

THE FACTS

Remembering Facts

1. What did Mackenzie King promise at the start of World War II?
2. What special kind of conscription did the government bring in?
3. What were the results of the plebiscite in 1942?
4. How did Mackenzie King feel about the plebiscite results?
5. Why did the people in Quebec feel better about conscription in 1944 than they did in 1917?

Finding Facts

What qualifications would you need to join the armed forces? What would you have to agree to if you joined the armed forces?

Contact your local recruiting office for the armed forces in order to find out the answers to these questions.

YOUR OPINIONS

Stating Opinions

In some countries, every student has to serve in the military for 2 years after leaving school. How would you feel about having to join the military? Explain your opinion in a few sentences.

Discussing Opinions

In most countries where there is military service, or conscription, only men are forced to join. However, in some other countries in the world, women fight alongside men. If Canada were to bring back conscription, do you think women should also be forced to join? Discuss your opinions with your classmates.

NEW WORDS

Learning Words

In your notebook, write the title Vocabulary: Lesson 39. Then write down the following words in a list. Using the Glossary or a dictionary, write the meaning beside each word.

When you are finished, write a short note telling what you have learned in this lesson. Try to use all 5 of these words in your note.

overseas	**invade**	**isolate**
plebiscite	**release**	

Examining Words

The prefix *inter* in the word *intermission* means "between". Can you think of another word that begins with *inter* meaning "between"?

AN ILLUSTRATION

The pie charts in Figure 39.4 show the results of the plebiscite on conscription. The results from Quebec were the highest *against* conscription. The results from Ontario were the highest *for* conscription. Compare these results with the pie chart for all of Canada. What does this tell you about how the other provinces in Canada voted on the conscription issue?

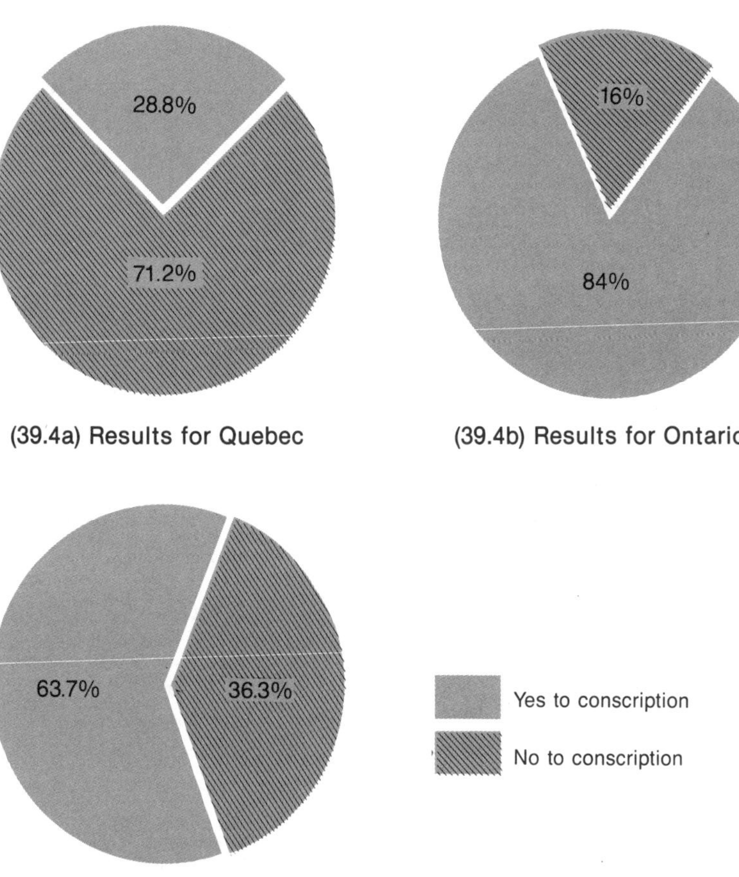

Figure 39.4 *Results of the plebiscite on conscription, April 27, 1942*

William Lyon Mackenzie King

Figure 39.5 *Prime Minister Mackenzie King takes his dog, Pat, for a stroll.*

Claim to fame: Mackenzie King kept Canada from being torn apart by the issue of conscription in World War II.

Born: 1874 in Berlin (now Kitchener), Ontario, the grandson of the famous Canadian rebel, William Lyon Mackenzie

Married: Mackenzie King never married. His mother was always the most important woman in his life. She died in 1917, but her memory haunted Mackenzie King for the rest of his life.

Career: Mackenzie King worked as a newspaper reporter and civil servant before he became an MP in 1908. He became leader of the Liberal Party in 1919. He first became prime minister when the Liberals won a majority in 1921. Except for a few months in 1926, Mackenzie King was prime minister until 1930, when his government was defeated by the Conservatives. But he came back into power in 1935. He stayed on as prime minister until he retired in 1948.

Mackenzie King was not a glamorous leader. But he was an excellent politician. His greatest achievement was during World War II when he kept English and French Canadians from breaking apart over conscription.

Died: Mackenzie King died in England, in 1950. After his death, Canadians made a shocking discovery. While Mackenzie King was prime minister, he had often gone to spiritualists. He used to talk to the dead about how to run the government!

- **How many years was Mackenzie King the prime minister?**
- **Do you think people would have voted for Mackenzie King if they had known that he went to spiritualists?**

40 Quebec under Duplessis

Figure 40.1 *Duplessis waving at his supporters*

Before the world wars, Quebec's economy had been mostly **agricultural**. In other words, the biggest business was farming. Most French Canadians in Quebec lived on farms in rural areas.

Also, the Roman Catholic church had always been very important in the culture of Quebec. The church ran the schools: the teachers were nuns and priests. The church even played a part in politics: bishops and priests often told the people how to vote.

But by 1936 this society was changing. Large numbers of Quebeckers were moving away from the farms to the cities. And the Roman Catholic church didn't seem to be as powerful as it had been in the early days. For this reason a new provincial party was formed. It was called the Union Nationale. Its first leader was Maurice Duplessis.

Duplessis promised to protect the old French culture of Quebec. He promised to help the farmers. He promised to work closely with the church. And he promised to keep the federal government in Ottawa out of Quebec's affairs.

The Union Nationale won the provincial election in 1936, and Duplessis became premier of Quebec. But as soon as Canada joined the war in 1939, Duplessis became worried for Quebec. He **predicted** that conscription would be used again. And he also predicted that the federal government would try to take over the province's powers during the war. So he decided to fight an election to give his party more strength.

But Duplessis and the Union Nationale lost the election in 1939. Instead, the people of Quebec believed the Liberals in Ottawa, who promised there would be no conscription. So they voted for the provincial Liberals.

As you read in the last lesson, Duplessis had been right. Quebeckers felt that they had been **betrayed** by the Liberals. Also, during the war, Ottawa had taken control of some provincial responsibilities. Quebeckers began to worry that the French culture would be destroyed.

In 1955, 3 Quebeckers and their 2 pet cats sailed on a raft across the Atlantic Ocean from Halifax to Falmouth, England.

In the elections in 1944, near the end of the war, the Union Nationale won the most seats. Duplessis became premier of Quebec again. And he never lost another election. He ruled Quebec until he died 15 years later, in 1959.

While Duplessis was in power, he kept many of his promises. He gave money to help farmers. He gave large grants of money to the church to support the schools. And he tried to keep groups that he thought were against Roman Catholics out of Quebec. These groups ranged from communists to Jehovah's Witnesses.

Duplessis also worked to keep control of Quebec away from Ottawa. For example, he refused to take grants of money from Ottawa for the schools. He said that if he took the money, then that would be allowing the federal government to interfere in education. And education was a provincial responsibility.

Instead of taking money from Ottawa, Duplessis worked to get **foreigners** to set up businesses in Quebec. He gave tax breaks to large American companies so that they would invest in Quebec. He also gave these companies huge pieces of land in northern Quebec. And he worked hard to put down labour unions and strikes.

Figure 40.2 *These children living in the slums of Montreal in the 1930s had nowhere else to play but the street.*

Actress Margot Kidder, who played Lois Lane in the *Superman* movies, was born in Yellowknife, Northwest Territories, in 1949.

In 1954, Canada's 16-year-old Marilyn Bell became the first person to swim across Lake Ontario.

Figure 40.3 *Meeting of a Canadian branch of the Ku Klux Klan. One group Duplessis worked hard to keep out of Quebec was the Ku Klux Klan. What are the beliefs of the Ku Klux Klan? Why would Duplessis not want them in Quebec?*

During the years that Duplessis was premier of Quebec, the province seemed to work well. But towards the end, people began to criticize Duplessis.

One thing these people said was that Duplessis was **corrupt**: he didn't run an honest government. To prove this, they used Duplessis' own words. At a public election rally in 1952, Duplessis actually said:

> I warned you in 1948 not to vote for the Liberal candidate. You didn't listen to me. Unfortunately your county did not receive the grants that would have made it happier. I hope that this was a good enough lesson for you.
>
> (Address to political rally in Verchères, 1952. Richard Jones, "Duplessis and the Union Nationale Administration," The Canadian Historical Association, Historical Booklet No. 35, 1983.)

In 1953, the Montreal Canadiens bought the entire Quebec Aces senior team in order to acquire 1 player — Jean Beliveau.

It was this kind of corruption that helped keep Duplessis in power for so long. But it was also this kind of corruption that helped cause the Union Nationale to lose the election in 1960.

THE FACTS

Remembering Facts

1. What was Quebec society like before the two world wars?
2. Why was the Union Nationale Party formed?
3. Why did Duplessis lose the election in 1939?
4. How long was Duplessis premier of Quebec?
5. Why did Duplessis refuse to accept money from the federal government in Ottawa?

Finding Facts

One thing Duplessis did to keep Quebec independent was to start a provincial income tax. He decided that Quebec workers would have to pay a certain amount to the provincial government. This amount would be equal to 15% of the workers' federal income tax.

Today everybody pays much more than 15% of their federal income tax to their province. How much do people in your province pay for provincial taxes? How much do people in the province closest to yours pay for provincial taxes?

YOUR OPINIONS

Stating Opinions

In 1944, only 2 out of 10 homes in rural areas of Quebec were able to get electricity. But Duplessis changed all that. By 1955 he had made sure that 9 out of 10 rural homes were able to get electricity.

What do you think it would have been like to live on a farm without electricity? Explain your feelings in a few sentences.

Discussing Opinions

Politicians often give special favours to people who have supported them. For example, think of a factory owner who donates several thousand dollars for some politician's election campaign.

If the politician wins, the politician will naturally be grateful. And he or she will want to find some way of paying the factory owner back. This could be by giving the factory owner a government contract or special licence.

This is called *patronage*. Duplessis's government was well known for its patronage. Jean Lesage, an opponent of Duplessis said, "everyone got something, even the voter who, on the eve of the election, received a load of gravel to spread on the mud in the entry to his farm."

Many people think that patronage is a corrupt practice. Others say that as long as your friends are qualified, there is no reason why you shouldn't help them. What are your opinions on patronage? Do you think it happens very often today? Is patronage fair? Are there ways that patronage can be stopped?

NEW WORDS

Learning Words

In your notebook, write the title Vocabulary: Lesson 40. Then write down the following words in a list. Using the Glossary or a dictionary, write the meaning beside each word.

When you are finished, write a short note telling what you have learned in this lesson. Try to use all 5 of these words in your note.

agriculture **betray** **corrupt**
foreigner **predict**

Examining Words

Look closely at the following sentence.

> The church ran the schools: the teachers were nuns and priests.

The punctuation mark between the 2 parts of this sentence — : — is called a colon. In this case, the colon has a special purpose. It tells us that the second part of the sentence will make the first part clearer. The fact that the teachers were nuns and priests explains the idea that the church ran the schools.

Find 1 other sentence in this lesson where a colon is used in the same way. Can you show how the second part of the sentence makes the first part clearer?

AN ILLUSTRATION

What does Table 40.1 tell you about agriculture in Quebec during the years Duplessis was premier?

	1941	1951	1961
Number of Farms	154 669	134 366	95 777
Population on Farms (as % of total pop.)	25.2%	19.5%	11.1%
Average Area of Farms (in hectares)	46.5 ha	50 ha	59.2 ha

SOURCE: 1971 Census of Canada

Table 40.1 *Quebec agricultural statistics*

Thérèse Casgrain

Figure 40.4 *Thérèse Casgrain was always ready to stand up for the causes she believed in.*

Claim to fame: She was a leading suffragist and defender of women's rights in Quebec.

Born: 1896 in Montreal

Married: in 1916 to Pierre François Casgrain, Speaker of the House of Commons. They had 2 sons and 2 daughters.

Career: Thérèse Casgrain joined the suffragist movement in Quebec in the 1920s. The Quebec premier at the time, Taschereau, had promised that he would never let women vote.

In 1929, Casgrain became president of a Quebec women's group. She worked tirelessly to get the vote: making speeches, sending petitions, even starting a short radio program on women's issues. She also fought for other rights for Quebec women, such as the right to become lawyers and accountants.

But Premier Taschereau kept his word. He stayed in office until 1936, when he was replaced by Duplessis. Duplessis was also against women's rights. So in the 1939 election, Casgrain led a campaign among women to support the opposition party. The opposition won. And in 1940, Quebec women were given the right to vote.

Casgrain spent many years afterwards in politics. She became head of the NDP in Quebec, but she never won a seat in Parliament. However, Casgrain was appointed to the Senate in 1970. She was the only one of the leading Canadian suffragists to be given such a position.

Died: 1981 at the age of 85.

- **When was the International Year of Women?**
- **What are your feelings about the fact that Quebec women were not allowed to vote or become lawyers or accountants until 1940?**

41 The Quiet Revolution

Figure 41.1 *"Le Bonhomme Carnaval" became another source of pride for Quebeckers. "Le Bonhomme" is the cheery snowman symbol of the Quebec winter carnival. For 1 week each year, tourists flood into Quebec City to enjoy contests, parades, fireworks, and fabulous ice sculptures. Does your nearest travel agent have any information about this year's Winter Carnival?*

Duplessis had worked hard to keep the old Quebec culture and society. And he had worked hard to keep the federal government out of Quebec's affairs. But in many ways, he had held French Canadians back. In 1960, French Canadians were still second-class citizens in their own province.

One major problem was the educational system. Duplessis had worked with the church to keep the old courses of study. So French students were taught subjects that were important to the church. These were subjects like religion, philosophy, and Latin. The students didn't learn **practical** subjects like math, science, or **business**.

This was very hard on the French students who wanted to get jobs in the modern business world. They didn't have the proper qualifications or knowledge.

In addition, the business world was run by English-speaking bosses. English Canadians had always owned most of the businesses in Montreal. And Duplessis didn't do much to change this.

In fact, Duplessis encouraged American businesses to come to Quebec. Many of them set up offices in cities like Montreal. But they ran their businesses completely in English. This made it difficult for the French Canadians to get good jobs. They had to learn English if they wanted to keep their jobs or get ahead.

Duplessis had even fought against unions. He sent in police to break up strikes. This made the English bosses happy. But it was hard on the French workers. Their wages were poor. And they did not have good working conditions.

By 1960, many Quebeckers were tired of this situation. They felt that keeping the old ways of Quebec was just keeping them back. Also, they wanted to get rid of the corruption in the Union Nationale government.

On June 22, 1960, the Liberal Party won the provincial election. And Jean Lesage became the new premier of Quebec. It was the beginning of a time we now call the Quiet **Revolution**.

First of all, the Lesage government wanted to change the way things were done in the province itself. It took over the electricity companies. Then it increased the minimum wage. It set up a special Quebec pension plan. And it made changes in education: it built new schools to train young people for jobs in business and **industry**.

Second, the Lesage government wanted to change the way Ottawa treated Quebec and French Canadians in the rest of Canada. At the time of the Quiet Revolution, the prime minister of Canada did not speak French. There were only a few French Canadians in the Cabinet. And most of the top civil servants were English.

When French Canadians from Quebec went to Ottawa, they found everything was done in English. They felt like foreigners in their own capital city. And they felt like foreigners wherever they travelled in the rest of the country. Lesage wanted to change all this.

In Kiluktoo Bay, Northwest Territories, the first 1.5 m are fresh water, but below that is salt water.

Figure 41.2 *The World's Fair was hosted by Montreal in 1967. Expo '67, as it was called, was a huge success. It attracted several million visitors from around the world. Later, the fair was made into a permanent exhibition known as Man and His World. Why was 1967 such an important year for Canadians?*

Figure 41.3 *Madame Benoit taught Canadians outside Quebec about the joys and good flavours of French-Canadian cooking. Does your family own any of her cookbooks?*

Lesage called an election in 1962. In that election the Liberal Party **slogan** was *maîtres chez nous*. In English that means "masters in our own house". Lesage asked the voters in Quebec to give him a big majority. He said he would use this majority to make sure that French Canadians were treated as equals by the rest of Canada.

Lesage won the majority he wanted. And he began to put pressure on the politicians in Ottawa to make changes. He said that the federal government should pay more attention to the provinces. The federal government should not just act on its own without talking to the provincial leaders first.

Lesage also wanted Quebec to have more control over its own economy. So he asked the federal government to let Quebec run its own pension plan and medical plan. He also asked for more money from the federal government. He demanded that Quebec be given a larger share of the income taxes collected in the province. Lesage made it very clear that the federal government would not have any say in how the money was to be spent.

Leaders in other provinces liked many of Lesage's ideas. But they were also amazed at his demands. He seemed to be asking for too many changes all at once. The revolution had started out quietly. But now it was very loud.

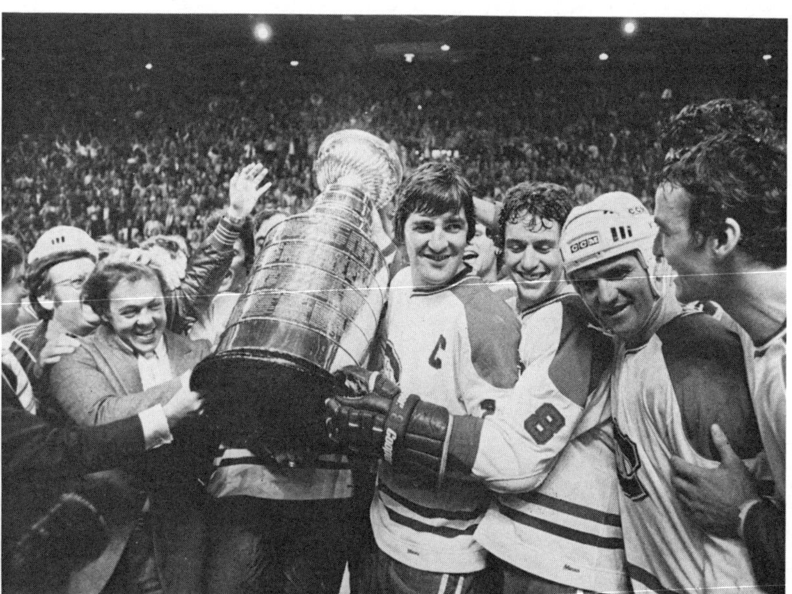

Figure 41.4 *During the Quiet Revolution, Quebeckers were justly proud of their hockey team. For 20 years, Hockey Night in Canada was dominated by the Montreal Canadiens. Between 1951 and 1970, Montreal reached the finals 15 times, winning the Stanley Cup in 10 of those contests. When was the last time the Montreal Canadiens won the Stanley Cup?*

THE FACTS

Remembering Facts

1. What courses did Quebec students take in the 1940s and 1950s?
2. Who owned most of the businesses in Quebec?
3. Explain 2 changes that Jean Lesage made in Quebec.
4. What was it like for French Canadians who travelled to other parts of Canada?
5. Explain 2 things that Jean Lesage demanded from the federal government.

Finding Facts

How easy would it be for a person who speaks only French to live in your community? Try to find out the answers to the following questions:

1. Is there a store in your community where at least 1 attendant speaks French?
2. Where is the nearest school for French-speaking students?
3. Is there a French-language radio or television station in the area?
4. Could someone buy French books, magazines, and newspapers in your community?
5. Do the police and other government agencies offer services in the French language?

YOUR OPINIONS

Stating Opinions

If someone gives you money, does that person have the right to tell you what to do with it? Explain your opinion in a few sentences.

Discussing Opinions

The courses that you are taking in school are probably not the same ones taken by your parents. In fact, every few years in every province of Canada the courses of study are changed.

Every time the education system is changed, there are many arguments about what courses would be best for the students. If you were giving the department of education some advice about changing the system, what would you say? Discuss your answers to the following questions with the rest of the class.

Are there any old courses that you think should be dropped?

Are there any new courses that you think should be taught?

Should there be any changes in the way students earn their diplomas?

NEW WORDS

Learning Words

In your notebook, write the title Vocabulary: Lesson 41. Then write down the following words in a list. Using the Glossary or a dictionary, write the meaning beside each word.

When you are finished, write a short note telling what you have learned in this lesson. Try to use all 5 of these words in your note.

business **industry** **practical**
revolution **slogan**

Examining Words

Maîtres chez nous is a slogan. In other words, it is a phrase used by members of a group. Slogans help keep group members working together. And they are an easy way to explain a group's goals to outsiders.

Advertisers also use slogans for their products. These are phrases or catchwords that stick easily in the customers' minds. For example, think of the slogans used these days to advertise hamburger chains.

Can you think of a slogan used to advertise another product? The product could be anything from a car muffler to a candy bar.

AN ILLUSTRATION

In 1964, a survey showed that 60% of the employees of certain firms in Montreal were Francophones. In other words, French was their first language or mother tongue. Only 40% were Anglophones: English was their mother tongue.

Figure 41.5 is based on the employees who earned more than $5000 a year in these firms. These were the managers and professionals. The figure doesn't show the factory workers who were paid by the hour.

What does Figure 41.5 tell you about the position of Francophones in Quebec? How does it relate to the slogan *maîtres chez nous*?

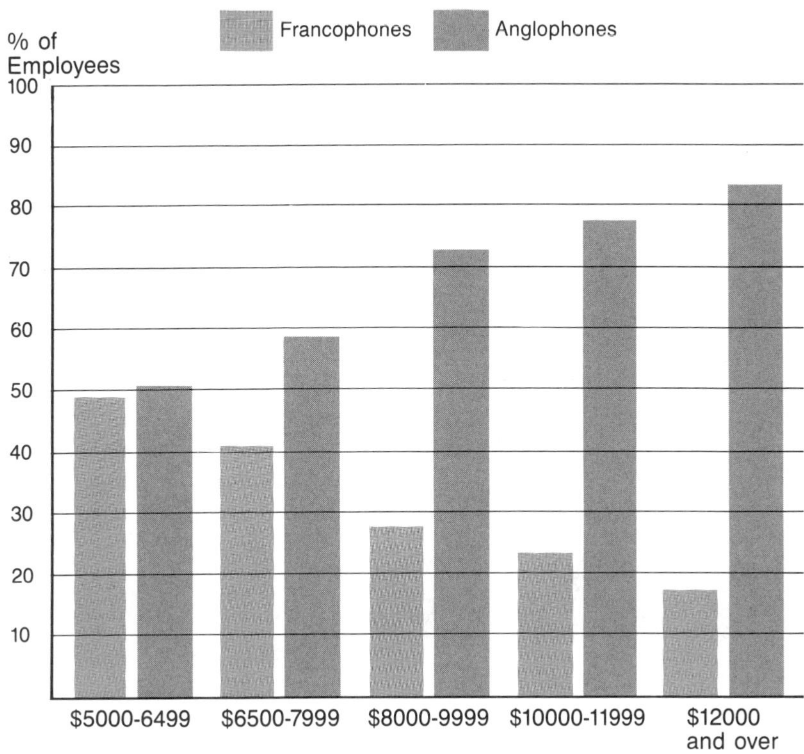

SOURCE: Morrison, "Large Manufacturing Firms" in *Report of the Royal Commission on Bilingualism and Biculturalism, Book III*

Figure 41.5 *Languages spoken by employees earning more than $5000 in 36 large manufacturing firms in Montreal, 1964*

Gabrielle Roy

Figure 41.6 *Gabrielle Roy*

Claim to fame: She was a French Canadian author who wrote many award-winning novels.

Born: 1909 in St. Boniface, Manitoba. She was the youngest of 11 brothers and sisters.

Married: in 1947 to Dr. Marcel Carbotte

Career: After finishing her own education, Gabrielle Roy taught school in a small village in Manitoba. She also acted in several award-winning plays. In 1937, she decided to go to Europe to study acting.

While she was in Europe, Roy realized that her real talent was as a writer. After only 2 years, she returned to Canada. This time, she settled in Quebec.

In Montreal, Roy worked as a journalist for several newspapers and magazines. In her spare time, she also wrote short stories.

Her first novel, *Bonheur d'Occasion*, was published in 1945. This book told a story about a very poor French Canadian family that lived in the slums in Montreal. It was translated into English as *The Tin Flute*. The book was an instant hit across Canada and in the United States, Britain, and Europe.

Roy wrote several more best-selling novels. She was awarded many prizes for these books. For example, she won France's most important prize for writing — the *Prix Goncourt*. In Canada, she won the Governor General's Award for literature 3 times.

Died: Gabrielle Roy died in Quebec City in 1983.

- **Where can students go in Canada to study acting?**
- **What would it be like to live in a family with 11 children?**

Bilingualism and Biculturalism 42

In 1962, Jean Lesage had won the election in Quebec under the slogan *maîtres chez-nous*. That same year, there was a federal election in Canada. The Liberal Party won. And Lester Pearson became the new prime minister.

Pearson came from a British background. He had lived most of his life in Ontario. And he could not speak more than a few words in French. For many French Canadians, Pearson stood for all that was wrong with the political system in Canada.

But Pearson was worried about the Quiet Revolution. He was **sympathetic** to the French. And he knew that things had to be changed if Canada was going to survive. So in 1963 he set up the Royal Commission on Bilingualism and Biculturalism.

This Royal Commission was called the "Bi and Bi" for short. It was led by two people, one English and one French. Their job was to find out how the French language and culture were treated across the country. They were supposed to **recommend** any changes that should be made.

The task was huge. The members of the Bi and Bi Commission went right across Canada collecting information. They spent hundreds of hours listening to reports from different people and groups.

The Commission published its first report in 1965. It said:

> Canada, without being fully conscious of the fact, is passing through the greatest crisis in its history.

The Commission members were not **exaggerating**. In 1963, the same year that the Bi and Bi Commission was set up, violence broke out in Quebec. A small group of **radicals** exploded bombs in public places. They stole guns and ammunition. They called themselves the *Front de*

Figure 42.1 *Hundreds of Quebeckers came to greet General de Gaulle, the President of France, when he visited Quebec in 1967. Here he is waving to enthusiastic crowds. Can you understand the message of the 2 signs being held up by the people in the crowd behind him?*

Canada's first gasoline-driven car was built in 1897 by George Foss, a bicycle repairman from Sherbrooke, Quebec.

Liberation du Québec — the FLQ. And their goal was for Quebec to separate from the rest of Canada.

The bombings continued in 1964. Students held violent demonstrations. When Queen Elizabeth II visited Montreal, there were riots in the streets. The French Canadians were angry. They did not want this British connection.

In 1967, another important visitor came to Montreal. It was the president of France, General de Gaulle. Huge crowds greeted him. Naturally, the French Canadians liked this connection with France. At the end of one speech, General de Gaulle cried out, "*Vive le Québec libre!*" — "Long life to a free Quebec!" The French Canadian crowd went wild with delight.

In 1970, the demonstrations, riots, and bombings turned more serious. A small group of FLQ members **kidnapped** James Cross, a British diplomat in Montreal. Then they kidnapped Pierre Laporte, a member of the Quebec government.

In order to help catch the kidnappers, the federal government used a law called the War Measures Act. This Act gives the government special powers to arrest anyone it wants to during an emergency such as war. By this Act,

Figure 42.2 *This is a map of Canada based on statistics from the 1961 Census of Canada. It shows the different divisions used by the people who took the census. Examine the map and its key carefully. What information does this map give? Did any of the information surprise you?*

SOURCE: Report of the Royal Commission on Bilingualism and Biculturalism

nearly 500 Canadians were arrested and held without charges. This angered many people across the country. And in the end, it did not work.

Soon after the Cross kidnapping, there was shocking news. Pierre Laporte's body had been found stuffed in the trunk of a car. James Cross was later found unharmed. But the FLQ had gone too far. French Canadians lost sympathy for them. Quebeckers now realized that they had to find a political solution to their problems.

Just as the FLQ violence was becoming extreme, the Bi and Bi Commission published its final report. This report showed how poorly the French had been treated in their own country and even in their own province. And the report made several recommendations to improve the situation.

First, the report said that Canada should be officially bilingual. Both English and French should be official languages for Parliament and for the courts. And the capital region of Ottawa-Hull should be made bilingual.

Second, the report said that more French Canadians should be hired by the government. And federal government workers should be able to help people in French as well as in English.

The original Stanley Cup, donated in 1892, was only 25 cm high. Base panels have since been added for winners' names.

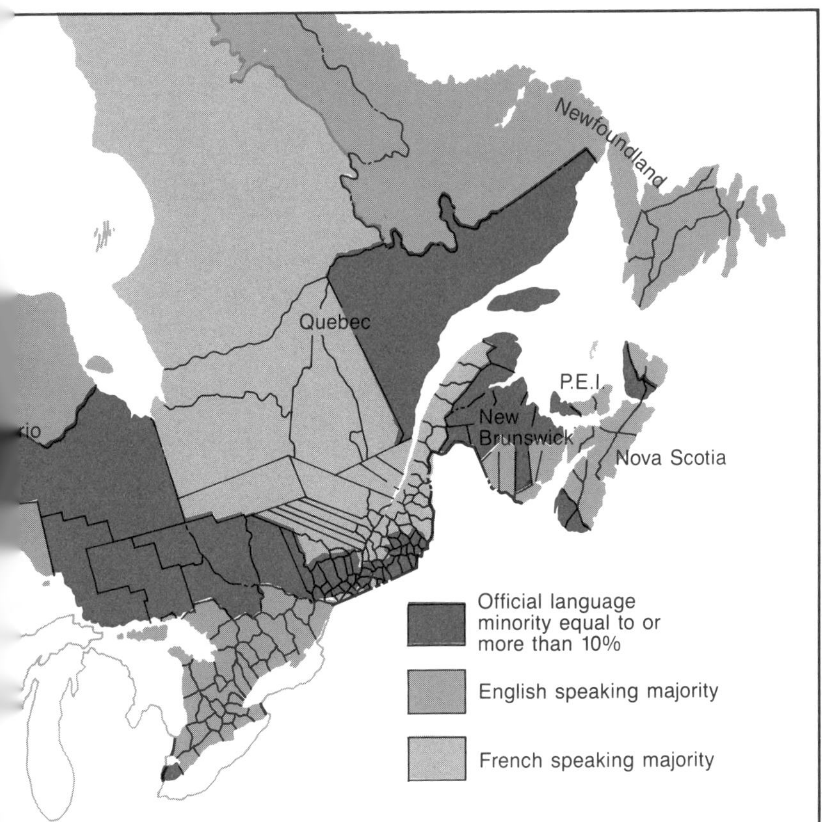

CBC Television's high school quiz show, *Reach for the Top*, started in 1961.

Figure 42.3 *Newspapers from around the world reported the story of the kidnapping of Pierre Laporte and James Cross. In what countries were these newspapers printed? On what date were they printed?*

Third, the report said that the provinces should make sure that every student could learn both languages. It also said that in provinces where there was a large minority of English or French, there should be schools and other government services in the minority language.

These were major recommendations. But changes had already begun. By 1970, a French Canadian — Pierre Trudeau — had become prime minister. And he brought with him many important French Canadian politicians from Quebec.

One of Trudeau's first actions was to declare Canada officially bilingual. The Quiet Revolution had moved to Ottawa.

THE FACTS

Remembering Facts

1. What was the job of the Royal Commission on Bilingualism and Biculturalism?
2. What did the Bi and Bi Commission say in its report in 1965?
3. What was the FLQ?
4. Why did most French Canadians finally lose sympathy for the FLQ?
5. What was 1 of the recommendations of the Bi and Bi Commission?

Finding Facts

Lester Pearson was sympathetic to the French Canadians. He tried to make things easier for them in their own country.

One thing Pearson did was to get a new flag for Canada. Read encyclopedias or other books to find the answers to the following questions about the flag.

1. When did Canada get its flag?
2. What did Canada use as its flag before this?
3. What was the first design that Pearson had for the flag?
4. How did the English Canadians feel about getting a new flag?
5. How did the French Canadians feel about getting a new flag?

YOUR OPINIONS

Stating Opinions

Pearson was the last Canadian prime minister who could not speak both French and English. When the Conservatives chose a new leader in 1983, they decided that they must choose someone who could speak both official languages.

Do you think that the prime minister of Canada should be able to speak both languages? Or do you think that this isn't necessary? Explain your opinion in a few sentences.

Discussing Opinions

When Trudeau made Canada bilingual, that meant that civil servants had to speak French. But most civil servants in Canada could speak only English.

How do you think the government should have handled this problem? What would you have done if you were a civil servant who spoke only English?

NEW WORDS

Learning Words

In your notebook, write the title Vocabulary: Lesson 42. Then write down the following words in a list. Using the Glossary or a dictionary, write the meaning beside each word.

When you are finished, write a short note telling what you have learned in this lesson. Try to use all 5 of these words in your note.

exaggerate	**kidnap**	**radical**
recommend	**sympathetic**	

Examining Words

The prefix *bi* means "two". *Bilingual* means "speaking 2 languages". *Bicultural* means "of 2 cultures".

There are several other words that begin with the prefix *bi*. Think of a word beginning with *bi* meaning "2 of something". Use a dictionary if you need help. Explain how the prefix *bi* fits your word.

AN ILLUSTRATION

Table 42.1 shows how many Canadians in each province were officially bilingual in 1981. In other words, it shows what percent of the people in each province could speak both French and English.

Draw an outline map of Canada showing the provinces. Then put the numbers from Table 42.1 in the correct places on your map. Which province has the highest percentage of bilingual people? Why do you think this is so? Which province has the smallest percentage of bilingual people? Why do you think this is so? What other information would you need in order to judge whether the Bi and Bi Commission had any effect on bilingualism in Canada?

Province	% Bilingual	Province	% Bilingual
British Columbia	5.7	Quebec	32.4
Alberta	6.4	New Brunswick	26.5
Saskatchewan	4.6	Nova Scotia	7.4
Manitoba	7.9	Prince Edward Island	8.1
Ontario	10.8	Newfoundland	2.3

SOURCE: 1981 Census of Canada

Table 42.1 *The percent of people in each Canadian province who are officially bilingual*

Antonine Maillet

Figure 42.4 *Antonine Maillet*

Claim to fame: She is an Acadian writer who has helped to keep the Acadian culture alive and make Acadians proud of their background.

Born: 1929 in Bouctouche, New Brunswick, one of 9 children

Career: Maillet went to elementary school in her home town. Then she went to a number of different schools and universities. Finally, she entered Laval University in Quebec, where she earned her Ph.D.

While she was still studying at university, Maillet became a nun. She joined the order of nuns who had taught her in high school. And for a time Maillet went back to her old high school to teach. Soon, however, she was sent to teach at the University of Moncton.

Maillet began to write seriously. She published some award-winning plays as well as some books. Soon she found she wanted to spend more time on writing and less on teaching. She decided she could no longer be a nun. And so she left the order.

Maillet's big success came several years later when she wrote *La Sagouine*. This was a funny but moving play about an Acadian washerwoman. It was seen by thousands of people in Canada, the United States, and Europe.

La Sagouine was so successful that Maillet was able to give up teaching altogether and concentrate on writing full-time. She has gone on to write several award-winning novels about the Acadian people.

- **Where do most Acadians live in Canada today?**
- **How do you think it would feel to come back to your old school as a teacher?**

43 The Parti Québécois

Figure 43.1 *René Lévesque, former leader of the Parti Québécois and Premier of Quebec, 1976-1985*

As you have seen, a lot was happening in Quebec in the 1960s. There was the Quiet Revolution: Jean Lesage and the Liberals changed the way Quebec was run. There was violence: a small group of radicals wanted to force Quebec to separate from the rest of Canada.

But during the 1960s there was also another movement in Quebec. Groups of politicians and writers and other concerned people began to talk about peaceful separation. They formed small political parties. The main **goal** of each party was for Quebec to separate from the rest of Canada.

In 1968, these groups decided that it would be better if they worked together. They joined to form the Parti Québécois. Their first leader was a news reporter called René Lévesque. And their main goal was for Quebec to leave Confederation and become a country on its own.

In the Quebec elections in 1973, the Parti Québécois won enough seats to become the official Opposition party. People across Canada began to feel a little uneasy.

Then an election was called in Quebec in 1976. The Parti Québécois decided to change its **strategy**. Lévesque promised that the Parti Québécois would not make Quebec separate right away if they won enough seats to form the government. Instead, he promised they would wait and hold a **referendum** on the question. In other words, every Quebecker would be given a chance to say whether Quebec should separate or not.

This was enough to satisfy most Quebeckers. They were tired of their old government. Its leaders had been corrupt. They wanted a change. And they hoped that the Parti Québécois would make a more honest government.

Many people in the rest of Canada didn't believe it would happen. But on November 15, 1976, the Parti Québécois won a large majority. The Parti Québécois — a party whose main goal was to separate Quebec from the rest of Canada — had won!

The Summer Olympics in Montreal in 1976 were the first Olympics ever to be held in Canada.

In the first few years, Lévesque concentrated on governing Quebec well. He wanted to prove that he could be an effective leader. And he wanted to show Quebeckers that he could run an honest government.

Lévesque also wanted to show he could make major changes for French Quebeckers. He didn't want just to protect the French culture. He wanted to make it even stronger.

As a result, the Parti Québécois passed several important laws. By law, French became the only official language in Quebec. By law, all businesses were forced to communicate in French. By law, most signs (such as those on stores and restaurants) had to be in French only. By law, only children of English parents who had been educated in Quebec were allowed to go to English schools. All others were forced to go to French schools.

Needless to say, these laws angered most English Quebeckers. Hundreds of English families moved out of the province. Many companies moved their head offices out of Montreal. On the other hand, most French Quebeckers were thrilled with the new laws. And many of them wanted more.

One of the great race car drivers in the world, Canada's Gilles Villeneuve, died in a car crash in Belgium in 1982.

Figure 43.2 *The Inuit schoolchildren in this photograph come from the James Bay area in northern Quebec. What lesson are they being taught? Do you think this photograph was taken before or after the Parti Québécois came to power? Explain your answer.*

Figure 43.3 A sign in rural Quebec, 1963 *Do you think that you would find signs like this one in Quebec today?*

It is always daytime in July in the Northwest Territories. The sun shines around the clock.

Meanwhile, everyone was waiting for the referendum to see whether Quebec would leave Confederation. By 1980, Lévesque could not hold back any longer. The members of his party said it was now or never. And so Lévesque said that there would be a referendum. Quebeckers would be given a chance to decide whether or not the province should separate.

The referendum asked every Quebecker a single question. It asked whether the voters would allow the Parti Québécois to start talks with the federal government about something called **sovereignty-association**.

Sovereignty-association was a new idea. The way Lévesque explained it, it meant that Quebec would be a country on its own, but that it would share certain things with Canada. For example, it would have the same money system. And it would have the same defence system. Lévesque didn't say that not one of the provincial leaders had agreed to this plan.

In the months before the referendum, politicians from across Canada visited Quebec. The campaign was fierce. Emotions ran high. All of Canada held its breath waiting for the results. Almost every Quebecker went out to vote. But when the votes were counted, the rest of Canada breathed a sigh of relief. Sixty percent of Quebeckers had said they did not want to separate.

Even so, Canada had to face the fact that 40% had said yes — Lévesque *should* go ahead and try for sovereignty-association. This was a large number of people. And something had to be done if Quebec was to stay in Confederation.

Figure 43.4 *The people in this photograph are demonstrating their separatist ideas. What flag are they waving?*

THE FACTS

Remembering Facts

1. What was the main goal of the Parti Québécois?
2. How did Lévesque change his strategy for the 1976 elections?
3. What did the referendum question ask?
4. What did Lévesque mean by "sovereignty-association"?
5. What were the results of the referendum?

Finding Facts

Politicians have a saying: nothing is ever certain. In other words, no matter what the situation is like one day, it can easily change the next.

In 1984, the Parti Québécois was still in charge of Quebec. Look in newspapers, magazines, or encyclopedia yearbooks to find the answers to the following questions.

1. Which party governs Quebec today?
2. Does this party want Quebec to separate from Canada?
3. Which party is the official Opposition in Quebec today?
4. Does this party want Quebec to separate from Canada?
5. Is there soon going to be a referendum about Quebec separating from Canada?

YOUR OPINIONS

Stating Opinions

Some students in Quebec who spoke English were forced by the new laws to switch to French-language schools. How would you feel if this happened to you? What would you do about it? Explain your opinion in a few sentences.

Discussing Opinions

Many people have talked about what would happen to Canada if Quebec decided to separate. They have also tried to decide whether it would be possible for Quebec to separate.

There is no doubt that Quebec *could* separate if the majority wanted to. But *if* Quebec separated, some important things would happen:

- Canada would lose a quarter of its population.
- The Maritimes would be cut off from the rest of Canada.
- Other countries like the United States or Russia might become interested in controlling Quebec.

Considering these points, do you think it would be serious if Quebec decided to leave Confederation? Can you think of any other reasons why Quebec should or should not separate?

NEW WORDS

Learning Words

In your notebook, write the title Vocabulary: Lesson 43. Then write down the following words in a list. Using the Glossary or a dictionary, write the meaning beside each word.

When you are finished, write a short note telling what you have learned in this lesson. Try to use all 5 of these words in your note.

association **goal** **referendum**
sovereignty **strategy**

Examining Words

Sovereignty-association was a new word made up by Lévesque and the Parti Québécois. People often come up with new ideas. And then they try to come up with words that will stand for these new ideas.

Do you have a word that you and your friends use but no one else knows what it means? Is there a word you think *should* be in the English language but isn't?

Working with another group of students, create a new word to explain a new idea. Then see whether the rest of your classmates think this is a good word.

AN ILLUSTRATION

Table 43.1 shows the results for the Quebec provincial elections of 1970, 1973, and 1976. How big a difference was made by Lévesque's promise of a referendum?

	1970	1973	1976
Liberals	72	102	26
Parti Québécois	7	6	71
Union Nationale	17	0	11
Creditiste	12	2	1
Others	0	0	1

SOURCE: Le Directeur général des élections du Québec

Table 43.1 *Results of Quebec provincial elections, 1970-76*

Monique Mercure

Figure 43.5 *Monique Mercure*

Claim to fame: She is an award-winning Quebec actress who acts in both French and English.

Born: 1930 in Montreal, Quebec, the oldest of 4 children

Married: 1949 to Pierre Mercure, an important Canadian composer. They had a girl and twin boys before their divorce in 1959. Eight years later, Pierre died in a car crash.

Career: When she was only 10 years old, Mercure started playing the cello. She was so good at this instrument that she won a scholarship to study music at L'Ecole Vincent d'Indy in Montreal.

It was at this time that she also became interested in acting. She had a few parts in amateur plays. Later, she studied drama in Paris, France.

After her husband's death, Mercure had to support herself and her children by working in a jewellery store. But by 1969 she had begun to earn her living from acting. The high point in her career came in 1977, when she won the award for Best Actress at the Cannes Film Festival.

Mercure acts in both French and English. Very often, she will act in the French version of a play in Quebec, and then act again in the English version elsewhere in Canada.

Mercure is not a separatist. But she is sad that there are so few bilingual people in English Canada. Therefore she approves of the laws passed by the Parti Québécois to protect the French language.

- **What is the Cannes Festival? Where is it held?**
- **If you had to study a second language besides English, which language would you study and why?**

44 The Constitution and Beyond

Figure 44.1 Jean Chrétien *Jean Chrétien was one of the key people who worked out the compromise on bringing the constitution home. Chrétien was popular with voters from across Canada. But when he ran for the leadership of the Liberal Party against John Turner in 1984, he lost. Pierre Trudeau, the last leader, was French. And the Liberal Party did not want to break the old tradition of alternating between French and English leaders. Do you think this is a good tradition?*

During the referendum campaign, the Canadian prime minister, Pierre Trudeau, travelled across Quebec making speeches. Trudeau was a Quebecker. But he was also a strong **federalist**. He desperately wanted Quebec to stay in Confederation.

In his speeches, Trudeau promised a new deal for Quebeckers if they voted no to separation. He promised that he would start new talks on the constitution.

As you learned in Lesson 2, the original constitution of Canada was the BNA Act. This act had been passed by the British government. And any changes to the BNA Act still had to be made by the British government, not by Canadians.

Many French Canadians disliked this **connection** with Britain. Therefore, they liked the idea of bringing the constitution home. They also hoped that Trudeau would make major changes in the way Canada was set up. They wanted more independence for Quebec in the new constitution.

As soon as the referendum was over, Trudeau kept his promise. He called all the provincial premiers together to talk about bringing the constitution home. But he did not suggest any big changes for Quebec. So the Quebec premier, René Lévesque, did not agree with Trudeau's plans.

Lévesque was not alone. Seven of the other premiers also said no to Trudeau's proposals. But Trudeau said that the talks had gone on long enough. Something had to be done. He decided that the federal government would act on its own. It would not wait for the provinces to agree on a new constitution.

The 8 provincial premiers who had said no were furious. They even took the federal government to court. But the

Figure 44.2 *These angry Manitoban voters in January, 1984, were protesting any increase in French-language rights in their province.*

Philip McGinnes of Huntingdon, Quebec, was the inventor of the starting gate for horse races.

Supreme Court judges said that the federal government was in the right. It could bring home the constitution on its own.

In November, 1981, all the premiers met for a last time to see if they could agree on a new constitution. The **breakthrough** came just before dawn on November 5. All the premiers except Lévesque were together. Finally, they agreed to a compromise plan. They were sure Lévesque would also agree.

When Lévesque came into the meeting room in the early morning, the other premiers told him about the compromise. To their surprise, he disagreed with it. He said they had betrayed Quebec. And he said he would never sign.

Some people said that Lévesque would never agree to any plan, because what he really wanted was for Quebec to separate. Others thought there was a chance Lévesque would agree. They thought Trudeau should wait and spend more time trying to reach a compromise for Quebec.

But Trudeau refused to do this. And in the end, Quebec did not sign the new constitution. When Queen Elizabeth came to Ottawa in April, 1982, to sign the Canada Act, there were no representatives from Quebec. Lévesque was not there.

This was very awkward. Trudeau had started the constitutional talks because of his promise to help Quebec. Yet he had succeeded only in making Quebec even more unhappy.

Figure 44.3 *Premier Richard Hatfield of New Brunswick listens intently to voters' complaints about bilingualism. Hatfield was responsible for making the province officially bilingual in 1977. Is Hatfield still the premier of New Brunswick?*

A total of 721 people were hanged in Canada before the death penalty was abolished in 1967.

Most English Canadians think that the constitution is now finished. But this is not true. By 1985, Quebec still had not signed the constitution. And the issue is sure to come up again.

In fact, there are still many tensions between the French and the English in Canada. For example, in 1983, the whole issue of French language rights came up again in the province of Manitoba. The provincial government tried to make Manitoba officially bilingual. But the opposition party disagreed. Tempers **flared**. Emotions ran high. The government came to a standstill. Some French-speaking Manitobans were even afraid to admit that they were French.

New Brunswick is officially bilingual. However, even there bilingualism is a problem. This frustration came out at special hearings held by the provincial government in 1984. Many English-speaking New Brunswickers resent the laws that make French official. But many French-speaking New Brunswickers feel that the law does not go far enough.

Figure 44.4 Aerial View of the Daniel Johnson Dam *This dam is part of the huge James Bay hydro project in Quebec. It is located in Manicouagan, Prime Minister Brian Mulroney's riding on the north shore of the St. Lawrence. The dam has become a symbol of Quebec's strength and the resources Quebec has to offer Canada. Who was Daniel Johnson, the politician for whom the dam was named?*

Added to this, many English-speaking Canadians from across the country are angered by the language laws in Quebec. They do not feel that other provinces should become officially bilingual as long as Quebec uses only French.

So you can see there is trouble on both sides. This will change only when all Canadians start to listen to each other. They need to try to understand each other's point of view. Only then will the English and the French become real **partners** in Canada.

In the 1980 federal elections in Quebec, it was Conservatives 1, Liberals 74. In 1984, it was Conservatives 58, Liberals 17.

THE FACTS

Remembering Facts

1. What did Prime Minister Trudeau promise Quebeckers if they voted no to separation?
2. Why did the provincial premiers take the federal government to court?
3. Why did René Lévesque not agree with Trudeau's plans for the constitution?
4. How many provinces accepted the new constitution in 1982?
5. What happened in Manitoba in 1983?

Finding Facts

In 1985, Quebec had still not accepted the new constitution; Quebec still had language laws that forced people to use French; and Manitoba and Ontario had still not become officially bilingual.

Have these situations changed? Read newspapers or other references to find out whether there have been any changes.

YOUR OPINIONS

Stating Opinions

Many people have said that the way to solve the problems between French and English Canadians would be for them to get to know each other better.

Perhaps you know some French Canadians. Or perhaps you come from a French Canadian family yourself. If so, do you think this helps you to understand how French Canadians feel about English Canadians?

Perhaps you don't know any French Canadians. If so, do you think you would change your mind about French Canadians if you had some as friends or as relatives?

Explain your opinions in a few sentences.

Discussing Opinions

Do you think that relations between English and French Canadians are better or worse today than they have been in the past? Do you think that there is a chance that Quebec will still separate? What can or should be done to help improve relations between the French and English in Canada?

Discuss your opinions on these questions with your classmates.

NEW WORDS

Learning Words

In your notebook, write the title Vocabulary: Lesson 44. Then write down the following words in a list. Using the Glossary or a dictionary, write the meaning beside each word.

When you are finished, write a short note telling what you have learned in this lesson. Try to use all 5 of these words in your note.

breakthrough	**connection**	**federalist**
flare	**partner**	

Examining Words

To *dis*like something is the opposite of liking it. The prefix *dis* means "no" or "the opposite". But this is not the case for every word that begins with the letters *dis*. It doesn't always mean "the opposite".

Can you tell which of the following words begin with the prefix *dis* meaning "the opposite"?

disagree	disinfect	disobey
display	district	disunite

AN ILLUSTRATION

Study the maps in Figure 44.5. Someone's "mother tongue" is the first language he or she learned as a child. What do these maps tell you about bilingualism in Canada? In which provinces is French *not* one of the top 3 mother tongues? How do these maps help explain the problems in Manitoba?

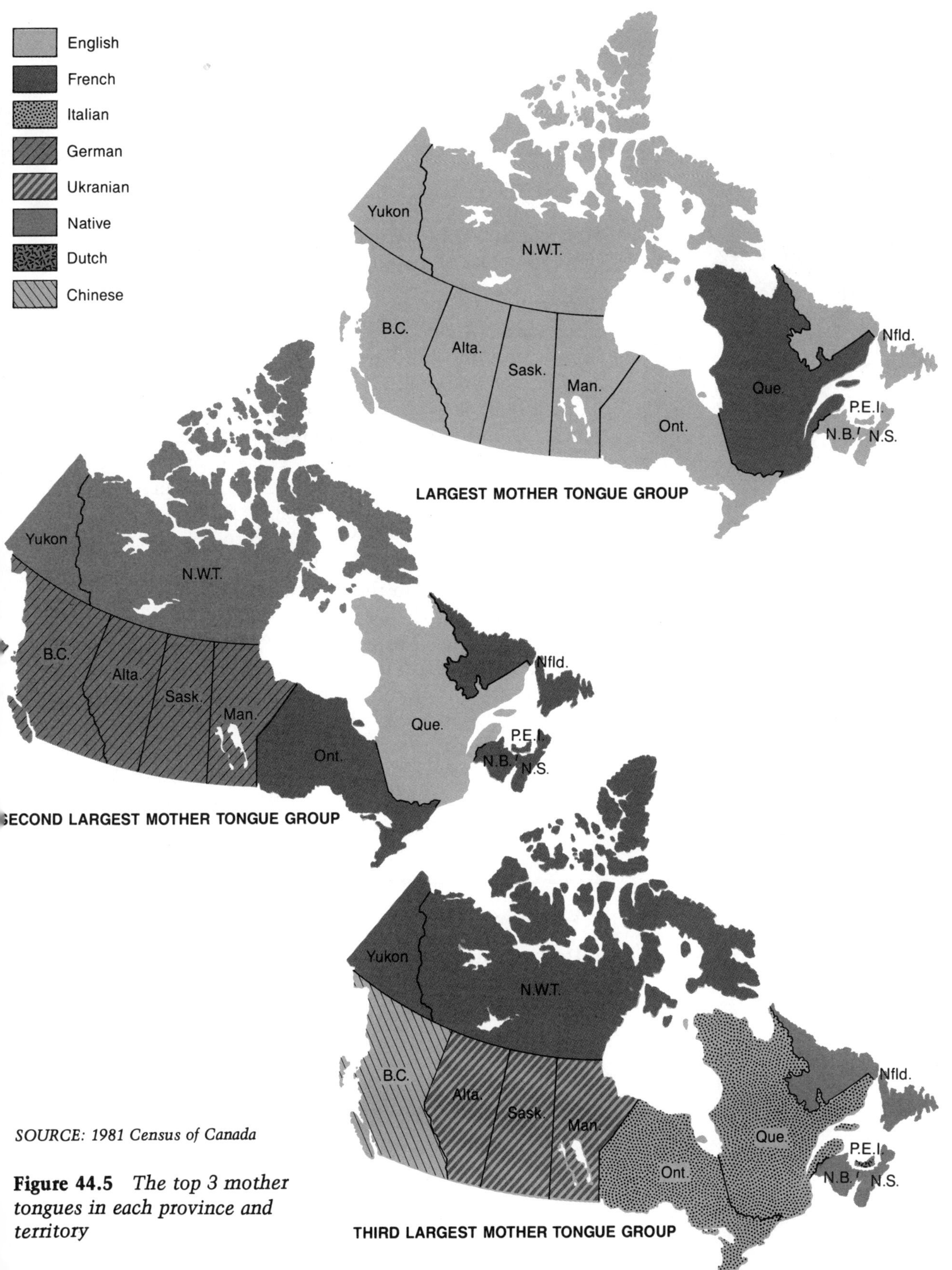

SOURCE: 1981 Census of Canada

Figure 44.5 *The top 3 mother tongues in each province and territory*

Brian Mulroney

Figure 44.6 *Brian Mulroney and his wife, Mila, greet supporters during the 1984 election campaign.*

Claim to fame: He is a prime minister who can relate to the problems of both French and English Canadians.

Born: 1939 in Baie Comeau, Quebec

Married: in 1973 to Mila Pivnicki. They have 1 daughter, Carolyn, and 3 sons, Benedict, Robert, and Nicolas.

Career: Brian Mulroney is the son of an English-speaking electrician of Irish background. Because his family lived in a small community in Quebec, Mulroney grew up speaking both French and English.

Mulroney went to St. Francis Xavier University in Nova Scotia. Then he came back to Quebec to study law. He worked as a lawyer for a while. Then he entered business and became president of the Iron Ore Company of Canada.

From the time he was a teenager, Mulroney was interested in politics. He never tried to win a seat in Parliament. But he did work for the Conservative Party and made many friends in the Party across the country.

Then in 1976, the Conservatives held a convention to pick a new leader. Mulroney entered the race but lost to Joe Clark. He tried again in 1983. And this time he won.

Mulroney automatically became leader of the Opposition, even though he was not an MP.

In the general election in 1984, Mulroney ran for a seat in his home province of Quebec. He won a huge victory in his own riding. And the Conservatives won 211 of the 282 seats across the country.

- **Where was Mulroney's *first* seat in Parliament?**
- **Do you think it is a good thing when 1 party wins almost all the seats in an election?**

QUIZ 6

The following questions are based on the lessons in Chapter 6. **DO NOT WRITE YOUR ANSWERS IN THIS TEXTBOOK.** Instead, you should write the answers in your notebook or on a separate sheet of paper.

1. There are 10 blanks in the following paragraphs about Canada. They have been labelled from (a) to (j). Write down the 10 answers in a list on your paper. Then beside each answer write the letter of the blank where it belongs.

plebiscite	Mackenzie King	1914
Quebec	riots	1939
conscription	soldiers	
overseas	officers	

During both World War I and World War II there was a conscription crisis in Canada. World War I started in the year (a) ______. At first there were lots of volunteers. But after a while the army needed more (b) ______ than were volunteering.

English Canadians blamed the French in (c) ______. They thought that not enough French-speaking men had volunteered. But this was partly because the army was run by English-speaking (d) ______. When the prime minister decided men would be forced to serve, there were (e) ______ in Quebec. By the end of the war, Canada was deeply divided.

World War II started in (f) ______. The prime minister at the time was (g) ______. He promised that there would be no (h) ______. But after a while, the same thing happened as in World War I. More soldiers were needed.

The government held a (i) ______ to see if Canadians would let it break its promise. The majority of English Canadians said yes, but most French Canadians said no. Therefore the prime minister didn't send conscripted soldiers (j) ______ to Europe until much later.

2. Write the letters from (a) to (e) on your paper. Then write a T if the statement is TRUE. Write an F if the statement is FALSE.

(a) Before the world wars the biggest business in Quebec was farming.

(b) Duplessis refused to take grants of money from Ottawa to pay for the schools in Quebec.

(c) Duplessis worked hard to put French Canadians in charge of businesses in Quebec.

(d) Most French students in Quebec did not study math or science or business while Duplessis was the premier.

(e) Duplessis was always an honest politician.

3. Match the item in the list on the left side with the correct description from the list on the right side. For each one, write the letter and the number together on your paper.

(a) Jean Lesage	(1) the premier of Quebec who led the Union Nationale in the 40s and 50s
(b) René Lévesque	(2) the prime minister from Quebec who brought the constitution home from Britain
(c) Pierre Trudeau	(3) the prime minister who set up the Bi and Bi commission
(d) Maurice Duplessis	(4) the leader of the Liberal Party in Quebec in the 1960s
(e) Lester Pearson	(5) the separatist leader of the Parti Québécois

4. Match the item in the list on the left side with the correct description from the list on the right side. For each one, write the letter and the number together on your paper.

(a) Parti Québécois	(1) the slogan of the Liberal Party in Quebec during the Quiet Revolution
(b) FLQ	(2) the Quebec party that wanted to separate Quebec from the rest of Canada
(c) Bi and Bi	(3) the Quebec party that wanted to keep the old culture of Quebec
(d) *Maîtres chez-nous*	(4) the Royal Commission that studied the status of the French culture and language in Canada
(e) Union Nationale	(5) the group that used violence to try to make Quebec separate from the rest of Canada

UNIT FOUR

Our Shared Border

When you look at the *political* map of North America on page 322, you can see the border cutting right across the middle from west to east. Canada is on the north and the United States is on the south. And you can see that they are 2 completely separate countries.

But then look at the *physical* map of North America on page 322. You will see that the lines go up and down the continent. The lakes, rivers, mountains, and prairies tend to run from north to south.

The difference between the political and physical maps of North America helps to explain the special relationship between Canada and the United States. Canadians and Americans living across the border from each other often have more in common than they do with their fellow citizens on the other side of the continent. We are separate countries, but we are also tied closely together.

The symbol for this unit is Uncle Sam's hat. Uncle Sam is always pictured as an old man wearing patriotic clothes. He is a cartoon character who is a common symbol of the United States. His hat is made from the stars and stripes of the American flag.

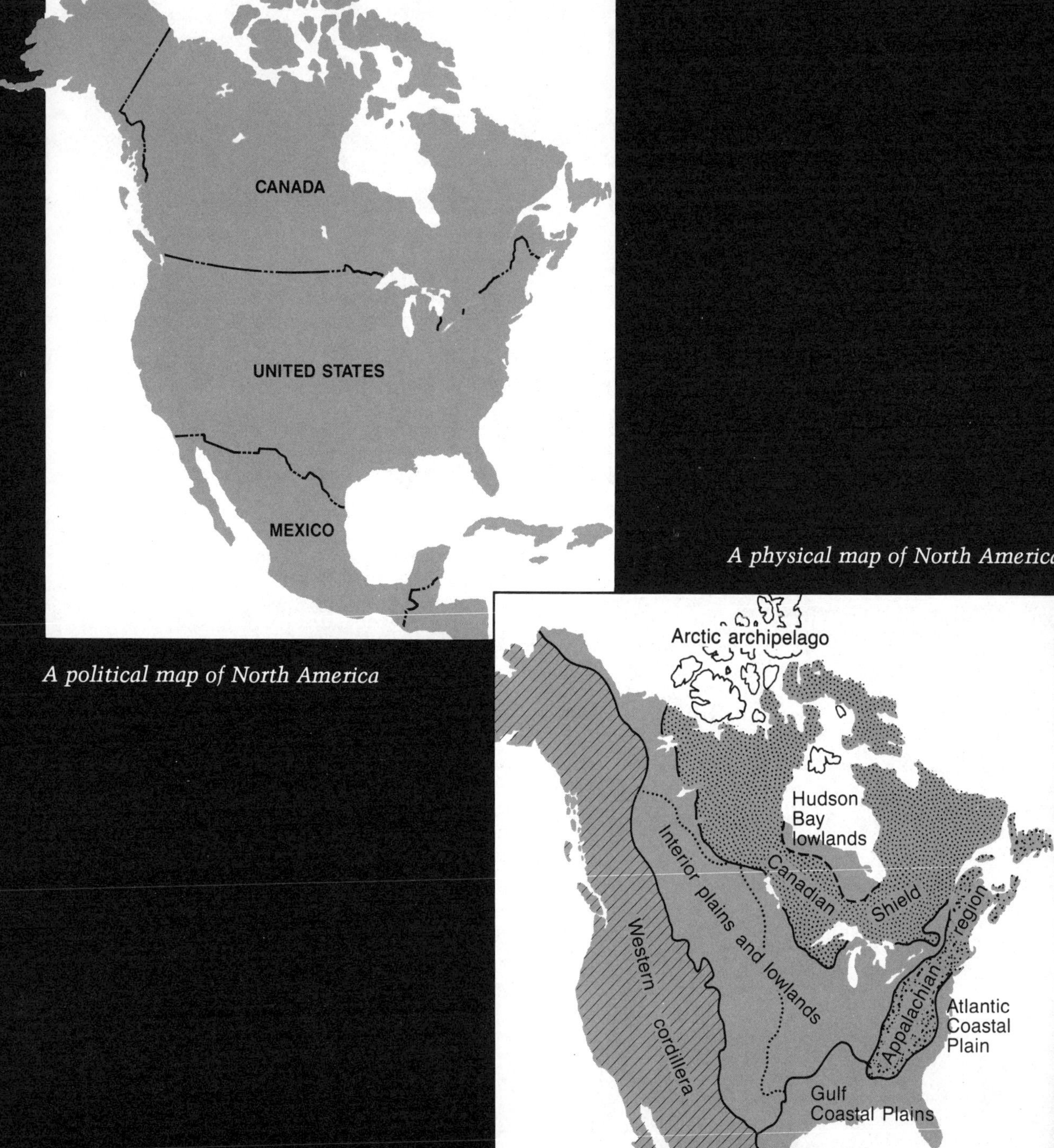

A political map of North America

A physical map of North America

CHAPTER SEVEN

Defending the Border

Can you imagine Canada and the United States going to war against each other? Most people laugh at this question and say, "Of course not!"

Today, the border between Canada and the United States is the longest undefended border in the world. It stretches right across the North American continent. And we don't have any soldiers stationed along the border in case of attack. People travel freely back and forth across this border every minute of every day.

But the fact is that Canadians and Americans were once bitter enemies. The following lessons will tell you how we turned from enemies into friends.

Who is the child in this cartoon from the 1870s? Who does Mother Britannia stand for? Who does Uncle Sam stand for? What point is the cartoonist trying to make?

45 The American Revolution

Figure 45.1 *The Americans launched a double attack on Canada. As this map shows, General Arnold travelled up the Kennebec and Chaudière Rivers to Quebec. Meanwhile, another general, Montgomery, took the easier route up through Lake Champlain to Montreal. Trace the journeys taken by these generals on a modern map of central North America.*

By 1763, most of North America belonged to Britain. Along the Atlantic coast, there were the Thirteen Colonies that had always been British. And now Britain had also taken over the old French colonies in Quebec and Nova Scotia. It seemed possible that North America might one day become 1 huge country.

At first Britain tried to assimilate the French colonists. The British wanted the French to become just like the settlers in the Thirteen Colonies. But as you learned in Lesson 32, this did not work.

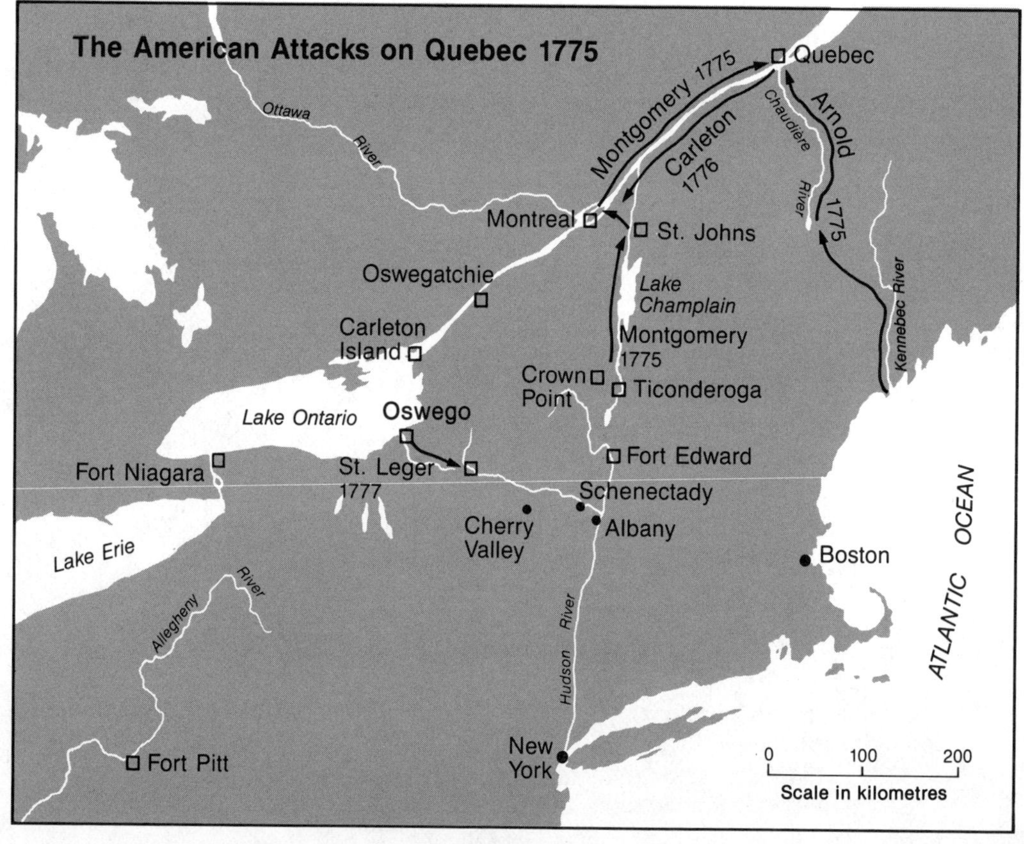

So the British gave up and decided to accommodate the French instead. In 1774, the British Parliament passed the Quebec Act. As you may remember, this Act allowed the French to keep their religion and many of their old customs and laws. The Act also gave much more land to Quebec.

The Quebec Act was supposed to make the French Canadians happy. But all it did was to make the settlers in the Thirteen Colonies very angry. They were against the Roman Catholic religion. And they were **furious** that Quebec was given so much land.

This was not the only complaint of the settlers in the Thirteen Colonies. Many of them had been born and raised in North America. They didn't like being governed from across the ocean by the British Parliament. And they didn't like paying taxes to Britain.

The leaders of the Thirteen Colonies met in Philadelphia in 1775. They wanted to discuss the idea of breaking away from Britain completely. They had also invited leaders from Quebec to join them. But the Quebeckers decided to be **neutral**. They did not want to support either the British or the Americans.

Then there was a **clash** between a small group of British soldiers and some American volunteers. Only 1 shot was fired. But it was enough to start the American Revolution.

The Americans decided that their first step should be to invade Quebec. This would destroy the British **base** in the north. So it would be harder for the British to fight the Americans.

Late in 1775, the Americans sent an army to capture Montreal. There were no British troops in the city, because they had been sent south to fight the Americans in Boston. And the French Canadian citizens didn't really try to fight back. So the American soldiers just walked in and took over.

Then the Americans decided that they should capture the capital of the colony, Quebec City. This was where the governor of Quebec was living. And there were some British soldiers there as well.

On New Year's Eve of 1775, the Americans started their main attack. But the British soldiers fought bravely. And the weather was against the Americans. There was a wild blizzard. Snow blinded the troops. Four hundred American soldiers were captured. The attack was a complete failure.

Even back in Montreal, the Americans were having trouble. They had laughed at the French Canadians for their different religion and customs. Naturally, this made the French Canadians angry. And the Americans paid for things

Figure 45.2 Tecumseh *Chief Tecumseh fought on the side of the British during the American Revolution. Without Tecumseh, the British would have lost the war on the western frontier. Find out more about Chief Tecumseh.*

Note: You can read more about the invasion of Quebec in Lesson 32.

If you stand on the tip of Cape Spear, Newfoundland, you are the first (or last!) person in North America.

Figure 45.3 *Withstanding the attack of Arnold's men at the second barrier*

like food with paper money that was worthless. So the Quebeckers felt cheated.

In the beginning, the Americans had been sure that the Canadians would want to join the revolution against Britain. But instead, the Canadians began to hate these invaders from the Thirteen Colonies.

In the spring of 1776, Britain sent ships and soldiers down the St. Lawrence to free the Quebeckers. The Americans did not have enough troops to face an attack. So they retreated quickly to the Thirteen Colonies.

This was not the end of the American Revolution. All the rest of the fighting took place in the Thirteen Colonies. Some Nova Scotians did try to join the Americans in 1776. But this small **uprising** was easily put down by the British troops.

The real effect of the American Revolution came afterwards when Britain and the Thirteen Colonies stopped fighting. You will learn more about this in the next lesson.

Canada Dry ginger ale was invented by John McLaughlin, brother of Sam, whose carriage business became General Motors of Canada.

Figure 45.4 *Today there are fine roads and highways across North America. But in 1776, there were no such roads. Travellers had to rely on rivers and lakes or hike through the wilderness. The route taken by Arnold was extremely difficult. This drawing shows some of his soldiers pushing a boat along through a shallow, muddy stream on their journey to Quebec.*

THE FACTS

Remembering Facts

1. Why were settlers in the Thirteen Colonies angry with Britain?
2. What side were the French Canadians on at the beginning of the American Revolution?
3. Why did soldiers from the Thirteen Colonies invade Quebec?
4. What happened when the soldiers from the Thirteen Colonies tried to capture Quebec City?
5. Why didn't the settlers in Montreal like the invaders from the Thirteen Colonies?

Finding Facts

These days, money from the United States is not worthless. In fact, there's a good chance 1 United States dollar is worth more today than 1 Canadian dollar.

For the next 5 weekdays, find the answers to the following questions. Sometimes this information will be printed in your newspaper. If not, you can get this information from a bank or from a neighbourhood store.

1. How much would it cost for a Canadian to buy 1 United States dollar?
2. How much would a person from the United States be given in Canadian dollars for 1 United States dollar?

YOUR OPINIONS

Stating Opinions

How would you react if someone laughed at your religion? Explain your feelings in a few sentences.

Discussing Opinions

Do you think it would be a good idea to attack a city during a snowstorm? Or do you think it would be a bad idea? Discuss reasons why a commander might or might not decide to attack a city in bad weather.

NEW WORDS

Learning Words

In your notebook, write the title Vocabulary: Lesson 45. Then write down the following words in a list. Using the Glossary or a dictionary, write the meaning beside each word.

When you are finished, write a short note telling what you have learned in this lesson. Try to use all 5 of these words in your note.

base	**clash**	**furious**
neutral	**uprising**	

Examining Words

New Year's Eve is the special name we give to every December 31. Do you know the special names we give to the following days in the year?

January 1	November 11
July 1	December 25
October 31	December 26

AN ILLUSTRATION

Find a road map of central North America. How would you travel by car from Boston to Quebec? Use the scale on the map to figure out how far the journey would be in kilometres. If you had to go on foot from Boston to Quebec, how long do you think the journey would take?

Ann Mallard

Figure 45.5 *Mallard house still stands today. It is an important tourist attraction in Saint John.*

Claim to fame: She remained loyal to Britain during the American Revolution.

Born: 1758 probably in the Thirteen Colonies

Married: Thomas Mallard, a lieutenant in the British militia. They had 2 daughters, Nancy and Margaret.

Career: Little is known of Ann Mallard's early life. All that is certain is that she married Thomas Mallard, who served on British sailing ships. When the American Revolution started, the Mallards refused to join. They remained loyal to Britain. As a result, their house in New York was taken from them and their belongings destroyed. So Ann and Thomas decided to travel north.

The Mallards arrived in Saint John, New Brunswick, with almost nothing but the clothes on their backs. But they were given a piece of land by the government.

Ann and Thomas decided to set up an inn called Mallard House. They built a large building, 2 1/2 storeys high. Downstairs was a tavern and dining room. Upstairs were bedrooms and a large room for meetings.

Mallard House became the finest inn in Saint John. The first legislature of New Brunswick met in Mallard House in the large meeting room. The first play ever to be acted in New Brunswick was also shown there.

Died: Thomas died in 1803. Ann continued to run Mallard House on her own, until she herself died in 1807.

- **Look for travel books or magazines or articles about New Brunswick. Is Mallard House mentioned in them?**
- **Would you like to run an inn for a living?**

46 The First Border

The American Revolution was ended by a peace treaty signed in 1783. In this treaty, the British agreed that the Thirteen Colonies would no longer be governed by Britain. Instead, they would become an independent country called the United States of America.

The peace treaty also said where the boundaries between the United States and the rest of British North America would be. At first the Americans asked Britain to give them all of Quebec and Nova Scotia. In other words, they wanted North America all to themselves.

This was a strange **request**. After all, Quebec and Nova Scotia had stayed loyal to Britain. And Britain still controlled all of the land in the west around the Great Lakes.

But one of the British **negotiators** thought that it might not be such a bad idea. The people in Britain were tired of war. And they were also angry that the Thirteen Colonies had turned against them. They thought that the other colonies might do the same thing one day.

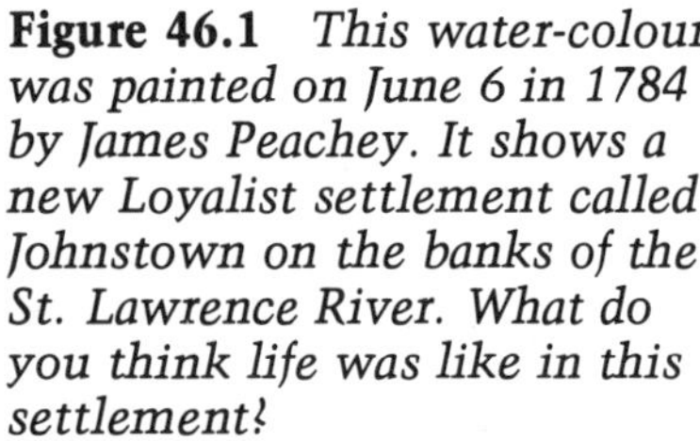

Figure 46.1 *This water-colour was painted on June 6 in 1784 by James Peachey. It shows a new Loyalist settlement called Johnstown on the banks of the St. Lawrence River. What do you think life was like in this settlement?*

However, the British government refused to leave. And the negotiators sat down to work out a new border. In the end, they decided on the line shown on the map in Figure 46.2

As you can see, all the land between the Great Lakes and the Ohio River became part of the United States. This was land that had first been given to Quebec in the Quebec Act of 1774. And now it was given to the Americans.

The people in Quebec were very upset about losing this land. It was valuable fur-trading land. And it had still been controlled by the British at the end of the Revolution. It just didn't seem fair that Britain would give it away.

The first Canadian rock group to become an international success was The Guess Who with their 1969 hit *American Woman*.

Note: A map of the boundaries under the Quebec Act is in Lesson 32, Figure 32.5.

HUDSON BAY TERRITORY
QUEBEC
Quebec
Montreal
St. Lawrence River
NOVA SCOTIA
Lake Superior
Lake Michigan
Lake Huron
Lake Ontario
Lake Erie
NORTHWEST TERRITORY
Ohio River
Mississippi River
UNITED STATES OF AMERICA
ATLANTIC OCEAN

North America After the American Revolution

0 200 400
Scale in kilometres

Figure 46.2 The boundaries of North America after the American Revolution *When the negotiators drew the boundaries, they used a map that had been drawn in 1755. It turned out that parts of this older map were wrong. This later caused trouble between Canada and the United States. Compare this map with a modern map of Canada. Look carefully at the northwest section. Where is the map wrong?*

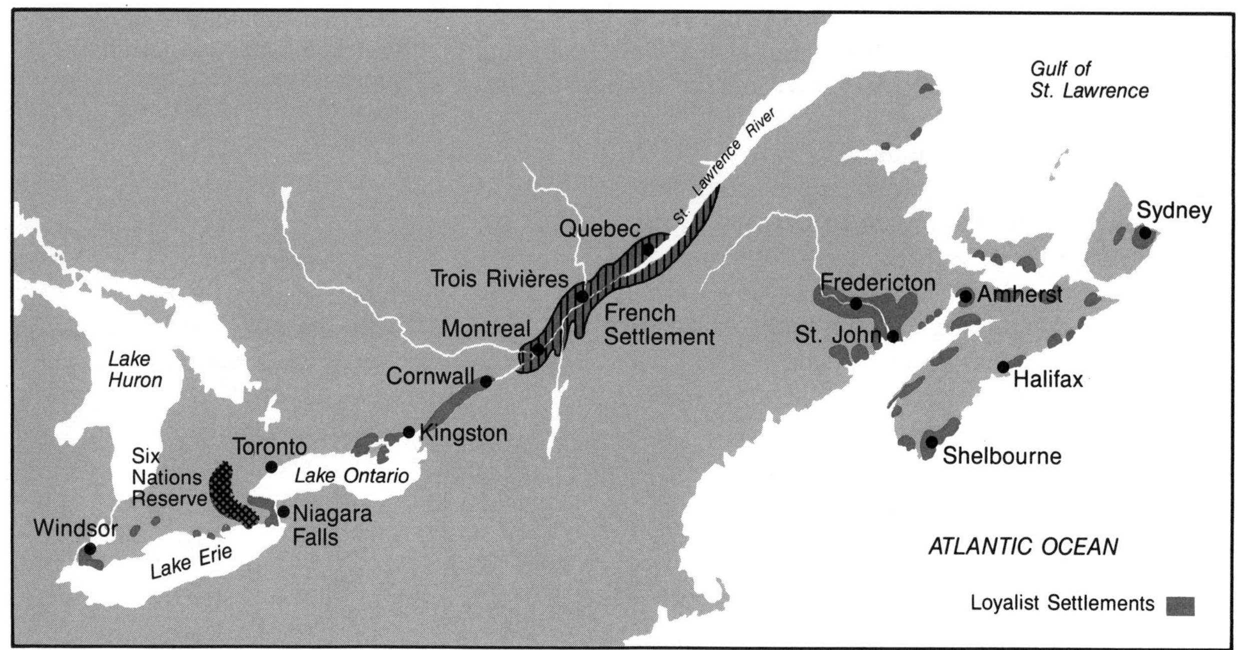

Figure 46.3 *This map shows many of the new Loyalist settlements. Compare it with a modern map of Canada. How many of these settlements still exist today?*

The people in Nova Scotia were also upset by parts of the treaty. In those days, a country would usually claim the waters for about 5 km out from the coast. In other words, they would say they owned that water. And only the people from that country would be allowed to catch fish in that water. But the Americans demanded the right to fish in Nova Scotia's waters too.

In the end, Britain said that the Americans could fish right up to the shores of Nova Scotia. They also said that the Americans could take their fish on shore in Nova Scotia to dry and **cure** before taking them home. Unfortunately, this agreement caused problems for Nova Scotia in the years that followed.

You can see that the treaty ending the American Revolution had major **consequences** for the future of Canada. But there was an ever bigger consequence of the American Revolution. This was the coming of the Loyalists.

It would be wrong to say that all the settlers in the Thirteen Colonies agreed with the American Revolution. In fact, many of these settlers were against the Revolution. They didn't want to break away from Britain.

These people were called Loyalists. And when the United States became independent, many of them left their homes. Some were forced to leave by their neighbours. Others simply did not want to give up their ties with Britain.

The *St. Roch*, the first ship to sail the Northwest Passage in both directions, is now on display at Vancouver Marine Museum.

Whatever their reasons, the Loyalists had to move somewhere. And many of them poured into British North America. No one had seen anything like it. In just a few short years, nearly 30 000 Loyalists moved to the colony of Nova Scotia. And at the same time, another 6000 moved into Quebec.

These settlers were like a new wave of **pioneers**. Most of them had to leave all of their money and possessions behind in the United States. So they couldn't afford to settle in the old cities like Halifax or Quebec. Instead, they moved to new land that had to be cleared of trees before it could be farmed.

This new land was usually quite far away from the older towns and cities. The Loyalist settlers felt isolated. It took them many days to travel to the capital cities to speak to government officials. So the British leaders decided to solve this problem by dividing the colonies.

By 1784, Nova Scotia had been broken into 3 separate parts: Nova Scotia, New Brunswick, and Cape Breton. The same thing happened a little later in Quebec. By 1791, Quebec was divided into 2 parts: Upper Canada (now Ontario) and Lower Canada (now Quebec).

The American Revolution had changed the whole map of North America.

Canadian Guy Lombardo, the world-famous band leader, also won the International Gold Cup for speed-boat racing.

Note: You can read more about the effects of the Loyalists in Lesson 33.

THE FACTS

Remembering Facts

1. How was the American Revolution ended?
2. What upset the people in Quebec about the treaty?
3. What upset the people in Nova Scotia about the treaty?
4. Why did the Loyalists move to British North America?
5. How did the coming of the Loyalists change the map of British North America?

Finding Facts

It was very important for the Americans in 1783 to be able to dry and cure their fish on the Nova Scotia coast. What does it mean "to dry and cure" fish? Why was this done? Is it still done today?

Read an encyclopedia or other book to find the answers to these questions.

YOUR OPINIONS

Stating Opinions

Britain could have given all of North America to the United States in 1783. Do you think this would have been a good idea? Or do you think it would have been a bad idea?

Explain your opinion in a few sentences.

Discussing Opinions

Try to imagine what it would be like if 30 000 people suddenly came to live in your area. What problems would this cause? What preparations would you have to make for them? How would you and your neighbours feel about these people? How would your own lives be changed?

Discuss these questions with a small group of your classmates. Then all the groups should share their opinions.

NEW WORDS

Learning Words

In your notebook, write the title Vocabulary: Lesson 46. Then write down the following words in a list. Using the Glossary or a dictionary, write the meaning beside each word.

When you are finished, write a short note telling what you have learned in this lesson. Try to use all 5 of these words in your note.

consequence	**cure**	**negotiator**
pioneer	**request**	

Examining Words

To *unite* people is to make them join together and feel like 1 person. The letters *uni* at the beginning of the word come from the Latin word for *one*.

Do you know a word beginning with the letters *uni* to fit each of the following definitions?

(a) something you wear to make you look the same as all the other people in your group
(b) a group of workers who join together to get better wages and working conditions
(c) a make-believe animal that looks like a horse with one horn on its forehead

AN ILLUSTRATION

There was trouble between Canada and the United States over the Nova Scotia boundary right up to modern times. Both sides wanted control of the area around Georges Bank, a rich fishing ground. Finally, Canada and the United States took their problem to the World Court.

In October, 1984, the Court made its decision. The results are shown in Figure 46.4. Study the map carefully. Does the boundary seem fair?

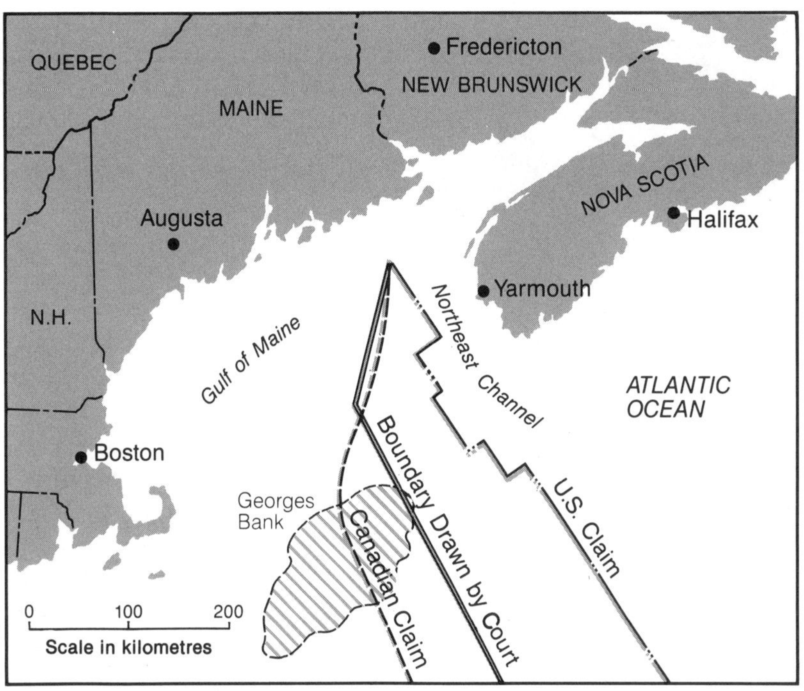

Figure 46.4 *The final decision for the Canadian-American boundary in the Gulf of Maine*

Elizabeth Simcoe

Figure 46.5 *Elizabeth Simcoe in later life*

Claim to fame: Her diary and her paintings tell us what life was like in British North America in the 1790s.

Born: 1762 in England. Her father had died 7 months before. Her mother died giving birth to Elizabeth.

Married: 1782 to Colonel John Graves Simcoe, a British army officer who had been wounded in the American Revolution. She was only 20 and he was 30. They had 7 children.

Career: Elizabeth was raised by an aunt and uncle who lived on a large estate. And she lived a life of luxury. But she was not lazy. She learned to speak many foreign languages. She learned to paint. And she liked going for long hikes. John Simcoe admired her energy. He knew she would make the perfect wife to take to Canada.

The chance came in 1791 when John was appointed as the first governor of Upper Canada. The Simcoes travelled to Quebec and then on to Kingston and Niagara and York.

Sometimes life was very hard. Elizabeth spent months living in tents in the bitter cold. She faced storms and mosquitoes. But she also fell in love with the beautiful country and the people who lived there.

Elizabeth described everything that happened in her diary. She also made many paintings of the world around her. These were later published.

Died: The Simcoes returned to England after 6 years. Elizabeth was very sad to leave. She lived until she was 84. She never forgot the beauties of her beloved Canada.

- **Look in other books to find examples of Elizabeth Simcoe's paintings.**
- **How would you feel if you were told that you had to live in a tent during the winter?**

The War of 1812

47

After the American Revolution, the population in the United States grew quickly. The older areas near the ocean were already crowded. As a result, many Americans started to move westwards across the Ohio River.

These Americans wanted to start new settlements. But there was a problem. Indians had lived and hunted on this land for hundreds of years. They still did business with the British fur traders. And they did not want the Americans to come in and take over.

The Indians decided to fight back. They refused to obey the Americans. And they attacked many of the new settlements. The Indians had received their guns from the British fur traders. So the Americans believed that the British were **encouraging** the Indians to fight.

There was also trouble between the Americans and the British out at sea. In Europe, Britain and France were at war again. This time, the United States was on the side of France. American merchants sold food and supplies to the French.

Of course Britain didn't want anyone to help France. So the British began to stop American ships. They made sure that the American supplies could not reach France.

The Americans had never liked the **treaty** that ended the American Revolution. And now these new troubles in the West and at sea made them even angrier with the British. So in June, 1812, the United States **declared** war on Britain. In reality, that meant that the United States had declared war on the colonies in British North America.

The Americans had chosen their time wisely. The British were too busy fighting France to think much about problems in North America. There were only a few hundred British soldiers in the colonies. The Americans were sure they would be able to get the British out of North America forever.

Canadian comics Wayne and Shuster appeared more than any other performers on Ed Sullivan's television show — 65 times.

Street lights were put up in Montreal for the first time in 1815.

The Americans attacked Upper Canada first. There were many settlers in Upper Canada who had come from the United States. And the Americans thought that these settlers would be glad to overthrow the British. So the Americans expected a quick **victory**.

In fact, 2 members of the Upper Canadian legislature did join the Americans. However, most Upper Canadians did not openly help the Americans. On the other hand, they did not do much to fight against the Americans, either.

Most Upper Canadians expected that the Americans would win the war. After all, there were only 500 000 people living in the northern colonies compared to 7 500 000 Americans in the United States. But the British commander, General Brock, was determined to save the colonies.

Figure 47.1 *Each year, tourists to the Niagara Falls area can watch re-enactments like these of famous battles in the War of 1812.*

Brock had only a few hundred British soldiers to command. But he used them very cleverly. And he was helped by a large group of Indians led by Chief Tecumseh, who had earlier helped the British against the Americans during the American Revolution.

First, Brock captured Detroit while Tecumseh captured Fort Dearborn. Then Brock returned quickly to the Niagara Peninsula. The Americans were getting ready to cross the river and invade Upper Canada. But in a battle at Queenston Heights, Brock was able to defeat them.

Brock died in the fighting at Queenston Heights. But his death was not a total loss. Brock had become a hero. His victories had made the Upper Canadians feel proud. Now they became more active in the fight against the United States.

The war see-sawed back and forth for 2 years. The Americans burned the towns of York (now Toronto) and Newark (now Niagara-on-the-Lake). In 1814 the fighting stopped in Europe. So the British were able to send over more troops. And these soldiers burned the American city of Washington in **revenge**.

In the Maritime colonies the battle was fought at sea. British and American ships tried to capture each other. But just as in the Canadas, neither side really seemed to be winning.

The first Stanley Cup hockey game was played in 1894.

Figure 47.2 *This medal was awarded to soldiers 35 years after the Battle of the Chateauguay. On the back or obverse of the medal is a picture of Victoria Regina. She was the queen of England at the time the medals were given out. When did Victoria become queen? How long did she reign? What annual holiday is named after her?*

Niagara Falls, Ontario, is known as the honeymoon capital of the world.

After 2 years, everyone was tired of war. So with no clear winner on either side, the battles came to a stop in 1814. Britain and the United States signed a peace treaty.

The treaty said that the Americans were not allowed to fish in the waters close to the shore in Nova Scotia. But apart from this, the treaty didn't really make any big changes. Probably the most important thing it did was to prove that British North America was here to stay.

THE FACTS

Remembering Facts

1. Why did the United States declare war on Britain?
2. Why was 1812 a good time for the United States to declare war?
3. Who was General Brock?
4. Who was Chief Tecumseh?
5. Who won the War of 1812?

Finding Facts

There were several famous battles during the war of 1812. They were fought at places like

Lundy's Lane,
Moraviantown,
Crysler's Farm, and
Chateauguay.

Choose one of these places. Use an encyclopedia or other book to find out *when* the battle was fought at this place, *what* happened, and *who* won. On a modern map of Canada, find where this place was and what modern cities are near it.

YOUR OPINIONS

Stating Opinions

The names of towns sometimes change. For example, "York" became "Toronto" and "Newark" became "Niagara-on-the-Lake".

Do you think your town or city or area should have a new name? Explain your opinion in a few sentences.

Discussing Opinions

The Indians traded their furs with the British for guns and ammunition. The British didn't tell the Indians to fight, but they did let them buy the weapons. Therefore the Americans felt that the British were partly responsible for the Indian attacks.

Do you think that it was fair to blame the British? Do you think that today if one country sells weapons to another country then the first country is to blame for how the weapons are used?

Discuss your opinions on these questions with your classmates.

NEW WORDS

Learning Words

In your notebook, write the title Vocabulary: Lesson 47. Then write down the following words in a list. Using the Glossary or a dictionary, write the meaning beside each word.

When you are finished, write a short note telling what you have learned in this lesson. Try to use all 5 of these words in your note.

declare	**encourage**	**revenge**
treaty	**victory**	

Examining Words

To see-saw means to go up and down or back and forth. A see-saw is also a ride in a children's playground. Children sit at each end of a board and move up and down. The name *see-saw* really suits this ride.

Can you think of another ride that has a really suitable name? Explain how the name suits the ride.

AN ILLUSTRATION

Soldiers at the time of the War of 1812 often wore very colourful uniforms. Find and copy a picture of a soldier's uniform from earlier times. State what regiment this uniform came from. Explain whether this uniform involves any special symbols or colours.

Laura Secord

Figure 47.3 *A woodcut print of Laura Secord*

Claim to fame: She was a heroine in the War of 1812.

Born: 1775 in Massachussetts, United States

Married: She was married sometime around 1797 to James Secord, a merchant of Queenston, Upper Canada. They had 6 daughters and 1 son.

Career: Early in the war of 1812, Laura Secord's husband was wounded while fighting the Americans. Laura Secord saved his life by carrying him from the battlefield herself.

Later, in June of 1813, Laura Secord was in Niagara. She overheard some American officers talking. They said that United States soldiers were going to make a surprise attack on the British soldiers at Beaver Dams.

Laura Secord walked more than 30 km through enemy territory to warn the British. With the information she provided, a group of Indians and some British soldiers were able to ambush the large American force and capture them. But in the official reports, no mention was made of Laura Secord's great courage.

Laura Secord and her husband lived in poverty after the war. When he died in 1841, she ran a school in her small cottage. Many people asked the government to help her because of her heroic actions in the war. But she was never officially rewarded until she was 85.

Died: Laura Secord died in 1868. After her death, many legends grew up around her. One of these was the story that she led a cow through the woods on her way to warn the British.

- **What is the story of Laura Secord and the cow?**
- **Why do you think the senior officer did not mention Laura Secord in his official report?**

Uneasy Peace 48

The War of 1812 was over. But the settlers in British North America could not forget what had happened. They were afraid that war might start again at any moment. And so they decided it was time to improve their defences.

For example, there had always been British soldiers **stationed** in Quebec City. But there wasn't a permanent fort for them. So in 1820 the British government started building a strong fort, or **citadel**.

Another improvement in defences was the Rideau Canal. It was built between 1826 and 1832. Its main purpose was to connect Montreal with Kingston. This provided a safe **route** between the 2 cities. It would be useful for transporting soldiers and supplies in case there was a new war with the United States.

The Quebec Citadel and the Rideau Canal were never used in a war with the Americans. And today they are mainly tourist attractions. But when the citadel and the canal were built, people honestly believed that they would soon be used in war with the United States.

Figure 48.1 *Quebec City was the site for the 1985 meeting between Prime Minister Brian Mulroney and President Ronald Reagan of the United States. In this photograph, the president and his wife have just arrived. The main talks were held at the Citadel in Quebec. Once built to protect Canadians against Americans, the Citadel was now the site for friendly talks.*

Figure 48.2 *After the 1840s, large numbers of people from both Canada and the United States began to settle the West. At first most settlers ignored the exact border between the 2 countries. This photograph is of Fort Whoop-Up. Fort Whoop-Up was actually on Canadian territory. But several times American traders took control. Which side controlled the fort when this photograph was taken? How do you know?*

British North Americans had good reason to believe that there might be another war. In fact, as early as 1838 there was armed conflict between the Canadian provinces and the United States.

Note: You can learn more about the 1837 rebellions in Lesson 33.

This trouble was a direct result of the rebellions of 1837. Many of the *Patriotes* from Lower Canada (now Quebec) fled across the United States border when they were defeated. The same thing happened with the rebels led by William Lyon Mackenzie in Upper Canada (now Ontario).

The Americans in the towns and cities along the border with Canada strongly supported the rebels. They formed groups such as the Patriot Societies and Hunters' Lodges. The only purpose of these groups was to invade Canada and set the colony "free".

Hundreds of Americans and Canadian rebels bought weapons and practised for war. And small groups of these soldiers made **raids** across the border. In most cases they would rob and murder a few Canadians and set fire to some buildings. Then they would slip back across the border to the United States.

The British soldiers on the Canadian side didn't have any trouble stopping these raids. But the raids still made the Canadians uneasy. They were angry that the United States government did not seem to be doing anything to stop the raiders. And they became worried that there might be an official war.

The Robertson square-slotted screw was invented by Peter Robertson of Milton, Ontario. It is almost never used outside Canada.

Fortunately, the leaders in both Canada and the United States remained calm. After a few months the raids across the border into Canada died away. And the Canadians were able to relax. But there was soon new trouble in the East.

Figure 48.3 *This photograph was taken in the early 1860s. It shows the Royal Engineers cutting wood along the 49th parallel near the Moodie River. What is the 49th parallel? Why is it important in Canadian-American relations?*

For some time there had been a disagreement about the border between New Brunswick and Maine. This land had many valuable forests. And naturally the settlers in both countries wanted the rights to the **timber**.

In 1839 the "Aroostook War" broke out. It was not a war in the usual sense of the word. No one was killed. There were no soldiers involved. Instead, groups of lumberjacks from either side of the border fought and tried to interrupt each other's work.

The situation was explosive. But once again, the leaders on both sides remained calm. And in 1842 they signed a treaty that settled the boundary between New Brunswick and Maine.

The same sort of situation arose just 2 years later. But this time it involved the boundary between Oregon and British North America in the far West. Once again there was fear of war. And once again the leaders were able to work out their differences peacefully. The problem of the Oregon border was settled in a treaty in 1846.

It was clear that the 2 groups in North America could solve their differences peacefully. There was no need to go to war every time there was a dispute. The 2 countries could live peacefully side by side.

Yellowknife, Northwest Territories, got its name from the native tribe of Indians who used knives with copper blades.

THE FACTS

Remembering Facts

1. Why did the British improve the defences of Canada after the War of 1812?
2. What events led to trouble with the United States in 1838?
3. What were the Patriot Societies and Hunters' Lodges?
4. What was the cause of the "Aroostook War"?
5. What was the cause of trouble with the United States in 1844?

Finding Facts

During the 1840s, many Americans settled Oregon and the land to the north along the Fraser River. They demanded that this land be taken over by the United States government. Read in other books about the Oregon boundary dispute. Then answer the following questions:

1. Who had owned the land in Oregon and near the Fraser River in the first place?
2. Which side had the slogan "Fifty-four Forty or Fight"? What did this slogan mean?
3. What was the final decision about the boundary in Oregon?
4. Draw a map showing the final boundary as well as the boundaries each side had hoped to win.

YOUR OPINIONS

Stating Opinions

Would you like to visit the Quebec Citadel or travel down the Rideau Canal? Explain your opinion in a few sentences.

Discussing Opinions

The peace treaty that ended the War of 1812 said that the boundary just south of Montreal should run along the 45th parallel. So the Americans immediately started building a huge fort right on the border at Rouse's Point in New York.

But when experts came to survey the boundary in 1818, they discovered that the Americans had made a mistake. The fort was a kilometre too far to the north. It was on Canadian land!

The Americans had already spent $100 000 on the fort. But of course they stopped construction. Then in a treaty in 1842, the British negotiators agreed to move the border slightly so that the fort would be on American land.

Do you think it was fair that the border was changed? Divide the class into 2 groups: one group should take the side of the Americans, and the other group should take the side of the British. Think of reasons your side would give for either changing the border or keeping it the same.

NEW WORDS

Learning Words

In your notebook, write the title Vocabulary: Lesson 48. Then write down the following words in a list. Using the Glossary or a dictionary, write the meaning beside each word.

When you are finished, write a short note telling what you have learned in this lesson. Try to use all 5 of these words in your note.

citadel	**raid**	**route**
station	**timber**	

Examining Words

When the word *practise* is spelled with an *s*, it means "to do something". For example, you might practise slapshots in hockey. Or you might practise playing the piano.

But when the word *practice* is spelled with a *c*, it describes the exercise itself. For example, you might have to go to hockey practice 3 times a week. Or your piano teacher might think you need more practice before taking the exam.

Should *practise* or *practice* be used in the following sentences? **(DO NOT WRITE YOUR ANSWERS IN THIS BOOK.)**

1. Sam promised to get to band practi_e on time.
2. I practi_e skating for 2 hours every day.
3. The team will practi_e today after school.
4. Practi_e makes perfect.

AN ILLUSTRATION

By 1846 the border running between the Atlantic and the Pacific coasts had been decided on. Draw a map showing the full boundary between Canada and the United States. Mark the following items on this map:

- your own town (or the one nearest you),
- the capital city of your province,
- the capital city of Canada,
- the 45th parallel
- the 49th parallel

James Douglas

Figure 48.4 *James Douglas*

Claim to fame: He was the "Father of British Columbia".

Born: 1803 in the West Indies. His father was a Scottish merchant who sold sugar. His mother was a Creole woman.

Married: in 1828 to Amelia Conolly. She was a Métis. They had 13 children, but only 6 of them lived past childhood.

Career: James Douglas went to school in Scotland. He learned to speak excellent French. Then, when he was just 16, he joined a fur trading company and was sent to Canada.

In 1825, Douglas travelled to Fort Vancouver. At first he was an accountant for the Hudson's Bay Company. But by 1839, he became the head of Fort Vancouver.

At the time, many Americans were moving into the area. Douglas became worried that they might try to make the Pacific coast part of the United States. So in 1843, he set up a new fort where the city of Victoria is today.

The crisis came in 1858. Gold was discovered on the Fraser River. Thousands of Americans poured into the region. Many of them wanted to make a new state.

But Douglas took charge. He forced the newcomers to follow British laws. And he saved the region as a British colony. As a reward, the British government made Douglas the first governor of British Columbia.

As governor, Douglas set up many new cities. But he became unpopular for his high-handed ways. He was forced to resign in 1864.

Died: Douglas lived in Victoria until his death in 1877.

- **What do accountants do?**
- **How different do you think Canada would be today if British Columbia had joined the United States?**

Confederation 49

When the United States first became a country, **slavery** was legal. Black people were bought and sold. The Black slaves had no say in who would own them. And they were forced to do whatever their masters wanted.

But by 1861, slavery had been abolished in many states. Eighteen states in the North had passed laws saying that slavery was not legal. The slaves in these northern states were allowed to go free.

Slavery was still legal in the Southern part of the country. But the slave owners were afraid this might not last. They were afraid that the Northerners would soon force them to give up their slaves. So in 1861, the leaders from the Southern states met together. They decided that they should leave the United States and start a country of their own.

The Americans in the North said that they would not let this happen. In 1861, soldiers from the South attacked soldiers from the North. This was the start of the American Civil War.

At first, you might think that the American Civil War was only an American problem. You might think that the colonies in British North America would not be affected by it. But in fact, the American Civil War turned out to be one of the major causes of Confederation.

The Civil War was still going on in 1864. As you know, that was the year that leaders from the colonies met in Charlottetown to discuss Confederation. They gave reasons why they thought Confederation would be a good idea. And one of the strongest **arguments** was safety from the United States.

The Fathers of Confederation were worried about what might happen when the American Civil War was over. They knew that the North would win, and then the United States would have a huge army with nothing to do. The leaders from the Canadas and the Maritimes were afraid that the Americans might decide to use this army to conquer the British colonies.

Figure 49.1 *These British soldiers are firing at Fenian raiders on Eccles' Hill in the Eastern Townships, 1866. How accurate were their weapons compared with today's rifles?*

Many believe that Josiah Henson, a former slave who fled to Canada, was the model for Uncle Tom in the book *Uncle Tom's Cabin*.

Figure 49.2 *Life was not always dangerous or unpleasant for the British soldiers who fought the Fenians. Here, several officers are seen in camp entertaining visitors, 1866. Why do you think there are boards lying on the ground in this scene?*

The leaders had good reason to believe that the United States would attack. Britain had seemed to side with the South during the Civil War. Britain had even sold warships to the South. And this made many Northerners angry with the British. This meant they were also angry with the British colonies.

Soon after the Charlottetown **conference**, a small group of soldiers from the Southern states sneaked up to Canada East (now Quebec). One night these soldiers slipped across the border from Canada East into Vermont. They attacked a small village called St. Albans. Then they escaped back to safety in Canada East.

The Southern soldiers were taken to court in Canada. But they were allowed to go free. The Americans in the Northern states were furious. Many of them said that it was time to start the war with Britain. It was time to clear Britain out of North America for good.

This was exactly what the leaders from the Canadas and the Maritimes had been afraid of when they talked about safety from the United States. Now it seemed even more important to join together. If they were one country, the colonies could share their defences.

Fredericton is called the Poets' Corner of Canada. Two famous poets from there are Bliss Carmen and Charles G.D. Roberts.

Figure 49.3 Thomas D'Arcy McGee's funeral procession in Montreal, 1868 *Thomas D'Arcy McGee was a brilliant politician and one of the Fathers of Confederation. His career was cut tragically short when he was killed by a Fenian assassin. Above right is a photograph of D'Arcy McGee. Who was the man who murdered McGee? What happened to him?*

In the end, the United States did not declare war. But even after the Civil War ended in 1865, there was still danger of attack. This came from a group of Americans who called themselves the **Fenians**.

The Fenians were Americans who had an Irish background. The Irish and the British had a long history of trouble. The Fenians were still **loyal** to Ireland. So they hoped to hurt Britain and to help Ireland by capturing British North America.

There was no real chance of the Fenians winning. But in one raid in 1866, over 1500 Fenians marched across the border from the United States. Several colonists from Upper Canada were killed and many others were wounded.

Jumbo, "King of the Elephants", was killed in 1885 by a Grand Trunk freight train in St. Thomas, Ontario.

The Bruce Nature Trail, opened in 1967, runs 700 km along the Niagara escarpment. It is maintained completely by volunteers.

The Fenian attacks were soon stopped by United States officials. But as long as they could be attacked like this from across the border, the colonists in British North America were afraid for their safety.

Fear of the United States was not the only reason for Confederation. But it was an important one. And in this sense, the United States was partly responsible for the Confederation of Canada.

THE FACTS

Remembering Facts

1. What did Americans in the Northern states think about slavcry?
2. Why did the leaders in the Southern states decide to leave the United States and form their own country?
3. What were the leaders in British North America afraid would happen at the end of the American Civil War?
4. What happened at St. Albans?
5. Who were the Fenians?

Finding Facts

Before the Civil War, many slaves in the United States escaped to Canada. They did this through the Underground Railroad. Use an encyclopedia or other book to find out about the Underground Railroad. How did it work? What routes did it follow? Who were some of the people who escaped to Canada on the Underground Railroad?

YOUR OPINIONS

Stating Opinions

Slavery has gone on for many centuries. In fact, there are still some countries in the world today where slavery is practised.

What do you think it would be like to be a slave? Explain your opinion in a few sentences.

Discussing Opinions

In a civil war, people living in the same country go to war against each other. Sometimes friends find themselves on opposite sides. Sometimes even families are split: brothers and sisters or parents and children end up fighting on different sides.

Do you think there could ever be a civil war in Canada? If so, what do you think this war would be about? Which side would you be on? Do you think any members of your family or any of your friends would be on the other side?

NEW WORDS

Learning Words

In your notebook, write the title Vocabulary: Lesson 49. Then write down the following words in a list. Using the Glossary or a dictionary, write the meaning beside each word.

When you are finished, write a short note telling what you have learned in this lesson. Try to use all 5 of these words in your note.

argument **conference** **Fenian**
loyal **slavery**

Examining Words

People who wanted to abolish slavery were called *abolitionists*. In other words, they supported or were interested in abolition.

The letters *ist* at the end of a word mean "a person who is interested in this subject". A Loyal*ist* is a person who is interested in being loyal. In the same way, an artist is a person who is interested in art.

Using this information, explain what each of the following words mean.

balloonist tourist terrorist
machinist guitarist typist

AN ILLUSTRATION

At the time of Confederation there were only about 3 million people in Canada. Table 49.1 lists Canada's population figures for 1871 and every 10 years afterwards. When was the biggest growth in population? When was the smallest growth?

Use the information in Table 49.1 to make a graph like the one in Figure 49.4. Then compare these 2 graphs. In what way do they look similar? In what way do they look different? How are the scales different on these 2 graphs?

Year	Population	Year	Population
1871	3 689 257	1931	10 376 786
1881	4 324 810	1941	11 506 655
1891	4 833 239	1951	14 009 429
1901	5 371 315	1961	18 238 247
1911	7 206 643	1971	21 568 311
1921	8 787 949	1981	24 083 500

SOURCE: Census of Canada 1941, 1971, 1981

Table 49.1 *Growth of Canadian population*

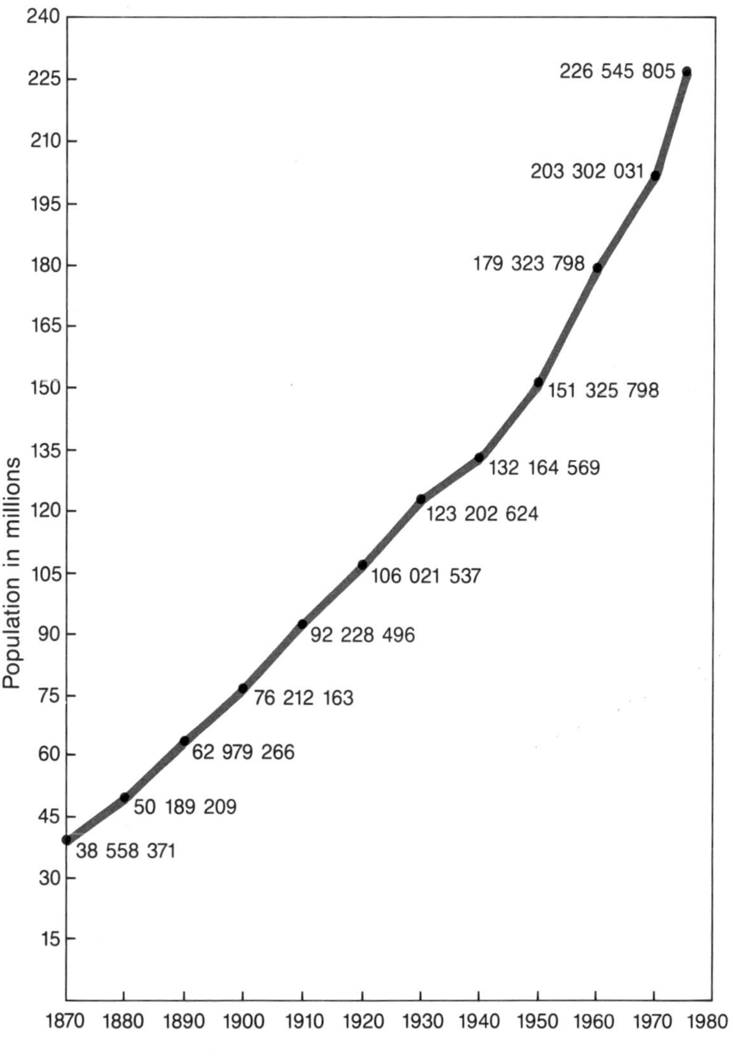

SOURCE: United States Bureau of the Census

Figure 49.4 *Population growth in the United States since 1870*

Mary Ann Shadd

Figure 49.5 *Mary Ann Shadd*

Claim to fame: She moved to Canada to help educate the people who had escaped from slavery.

Born: 1823 in Wilmington, Delaware

Career: Shadd's father was a Black agent in the Underground Railway. He hid and fed slaves who had escaped from their owners in the South.

Shadd herself was trained by Quakers to be a teacher. For a while she taught slaves in Delaware. Then, in 1851, she moved to the Windsor area in Canada.

Shadd set up a school for the children of slaves who had escaped to Canada. She was against segregation; her school was for all children.

Shadd fought constantly for Black rights. One time, American slave hunters grabbed a young slave who had reached safety in Chatham. Shadd dragged the boy from the slave hunters. Then she gave a speech to the townspeople. It stirred them up so much that the slave hunters fled for their lives.

Shadd set up the first Black newspaper in Canada — *The Provincial Freeman*. Her paper gave news about Blacks who had just arrived in the area. Shadd also wrote editorials urging escaped slaves to think of Canada as their permanent home.

But Shadd herself did not stay in Canada. In 1861, she returned to the United States to help in the Civil War.

Died: Shadd died in Washington, D.C., in 1893.

- **Who are Quakers? What are their beliefs?**
- **Do you think you will always live in Canada? Or do you think that you might go one day to live in another country?**

50 The Final Land Claims

Confederation was an important step for Canada. The new Canadian government was given complete control over *domestic* affairs. In other words, the Canadian government controlled what happened inside Canada. Britain would have no say in the day-to-day running of the country.

But Canada was not totally on its own. Canada was still not allowed to control its *foreign* affairs. Any problem that involved another country was still looked after by Britain.

This meant that Canadians could not deal directly with the United States. They still had to go through Britain. As you will see, this was not always a good thing for Canada.

In 1871, the British and the Americans decided to meet in Washington. They wanted to discuss some of the problems between them. And they wanted to solve these problems in a treaty.

Most of the problems they discussed involved Canada. For example, there was a problem with trade. It involved something called **reciprocity**.

When someone sells goods in a foreign country, he or she normally has to pay **customs** duties. Customs duties are a kind of tax. It is money the government charges based on how much the goods are worth.

Reciprocity is a special agreement between 2 countries. The 2 countries agree to lower the amount they will charge each other for selling certain products. Sometimes they agree to wipe out customs duties completely.

From 1854 to 1866, Canada had had reciprocity with the United States. Figure 50.1 shows how this reciprocity had really helped Canadian farmers and manufacturers. But the United States had cancelled this reciprocity in 1866. And now Canada wanted it back.

The Americans did not want reciprocity. It had not been such a good thing for American farmers and manufacturers. But the Americans *did* want to be given more fishing rights in the waters off Nova Scotia. The Canadians hoped that they would be able to trade the fishing rights for reciprocity.

Note: You can learn more about customs duties and trade with the United States in Lesson 53.

RECIPROCITY (*Free Trade*)

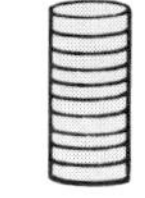

Canadian apples
cost $5.00 a basket

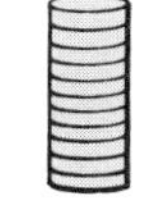

American apples
cost $5.50 a basket

Result:
Many Americans will buy Canadian apples. Canadian farmers can grow and sell more apples.

CUSTOMS DUTIES (*Tariffs*)

Canadian apples
cost $5.00 a basket
plus $2.00 customs
duty = $7.00

American apples
cost $5.50 a basket

Result:
Americans will not buy as many Canadian apples. Canadian farmers can not grow and sell as many apples as they would like.

Note: The prices are only samples.

Figure 50.1 *How reciprocity helped Canadian farmers and manufacturers*

The other main problems had to do with the border between Vancouver Island and the main shoreline. There were important islands there. And both the British and the Americans wanted the island of San Juan.

The British government sent negotiators to Washington to discuss the treaty. The British knew that Canadians were very concerned. So they said one of the negotiators could be a Canadian. This was the prime minister, John A. Macdonald.

The trouble was that there were 4 other negotiators. Macdonald was only one of 5. The other 4 negotiators all came from Britain. And Macdonald was very disappointed with their attitude. As he said in a letter home:

> They seem to have only one thing on their minds — that is, to go home to England with a treaty in their pockets settling everything, no matter at what cost to Canada.

In the end, most Canadians were disappointed with the Treaty of Washington. The Americans refused to have reciprocity with Canada. But the British still let them have the fishing rights. The Americans agreed to pay money for these rights. The amount would be worked out later by **arbitration**.

A Canadian rum-runner was sunk by the United States Coast Guard in the Gulf of Mexico on March 22, 1929.

Figure 50.2 *United States artillery forces on the island of San Juan, 1859-60*

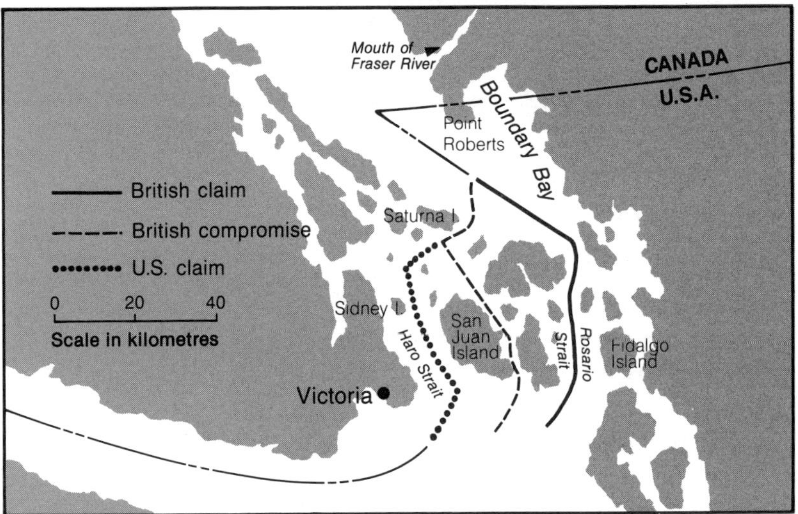

Figure 50.3 *The settlement of the San Juan boundary dispute*

The treaty also said that the border problem should be sent to arbitration. This meant that someone else would act as **referee**. And both sides agreed to accept the referee's ruling.

The Kaiser of Germany was asked to decide on the border dispute. In the end, he took the side of the Americans. The island of San Juan went to the United States, not to Canada.

Several years later, Canada lost another important border **dispute** in the north. The boundary between Alaska and Canada had never been very clear. But it suddenly became important in 1898 when gold was discovered in the Yukon. Canada wanted the seaport of Skagway to be part of the Yukon, not part of Alaska.

In 1890, Eugene Sayre Topping purchased a gold mine in British Columbia for $12.50.

The British and the Americans set up a commission to decide on the boundary. There were 6 members on the

Figure 50.4 The gold escort *This photograph was taken during the gold rush. These men had the dangerous job of protecting huge shipments of gold.*

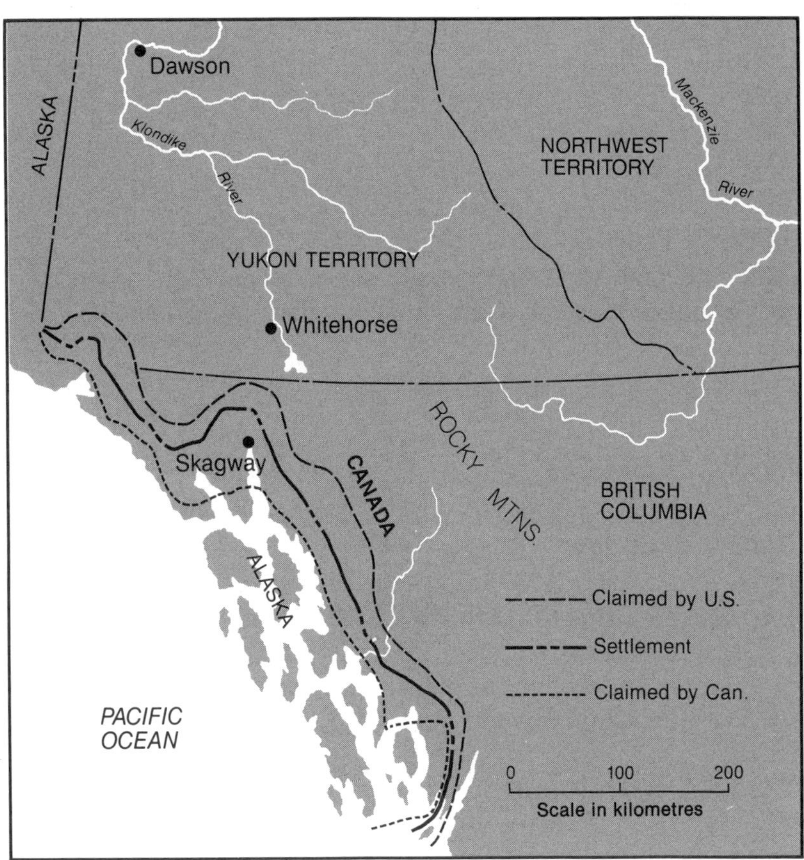

Figure 50.5 *The settlement of the Alaskan boundary dispute*

commission. Three were American, 2 were Canadian, and 1 was British.

The Americans and Canadians refused to compromise. But the British member gave in to pressure from the Americans. The British member said that Skagway would be part of Alaska.

Canadian Ted Rogers invented the "batteryless" radio in 1924. This allowed radios to run on ordinary household current.

Gold was discovered in creeks running into the Quesnel River, British Columbia, on August 21, 1860.

Needless to say, Canadians were furious. They felt they had been let down by Britain. They felt that it was time Canada took care of its own foreign affairs: the United States should deal with Canadians, not with officials from Britain. This happened just a few years later.

THE FACTS

Remembering Facts

1. Who controlled foreign affairs for Canada after Confederation?
2. What did Canada want from the conference in Washington?
3. What happened in the dispute over the island of San Juan?
4. What was the border dispute between Canada and the United States in 1898?
5. Why did Canada lose the border dispute in Alaska?

Finding Facts

The gold rush of 1898 is one of the most interesting periods in Canadian history. Read encyclopedias and other textbooks to find out more about what life was like for the people who came to the Yukon to find gold. Work with 2 or 3 other students to prepare a report on the gold rush of 1898.

YOUR OPINIONS

Stating Opinions

In the gold rush of 1898, hundreds of people gave up their lives in the cities to travel to the Yukon in search of gold.

Imagine that there was the same kind of gold rush today. Do you think you would leave everything behind and go off in search of gold? Explain your opinion in a few sentences.

Discussing Opinions

The Treaty of Washington said that several matters should be left to arbitration. In other words, the countries agreed that someone else should make the final decision.

Sometimes unions and employers cannot agree, so they take their case to arbitrators. They ask these people to decide what should happen.

Do you think arbitration is a good thing? Or do you think there are problems with it? Discuss your opinions with the other students in your class.

NEW WORDS

Learning Words

In your notebook, write the title Vocabulary: Lesson 50. Then write down the following words in a list. Using the Glossary or a dictionary, write the meaning beside each word.

When you are finished, write a short note telling what you have learned in this lesson. Try to use all 5 of these words in your note.

arbitration **customs** **dispute**
reciprocity **referee**

Examining Words

Domestic affairs have to do with the things that happen *inside* your own country. How is this related in meaning to the term *domestic animals* referring to cats and dogs?

AN ILLUSTRATION

The graph in Figure 50.6 shows Canada's income from 1980 to 1984. How much did Canada earn from customs duties in each of those years? Where did the rest of Canada's money come from?

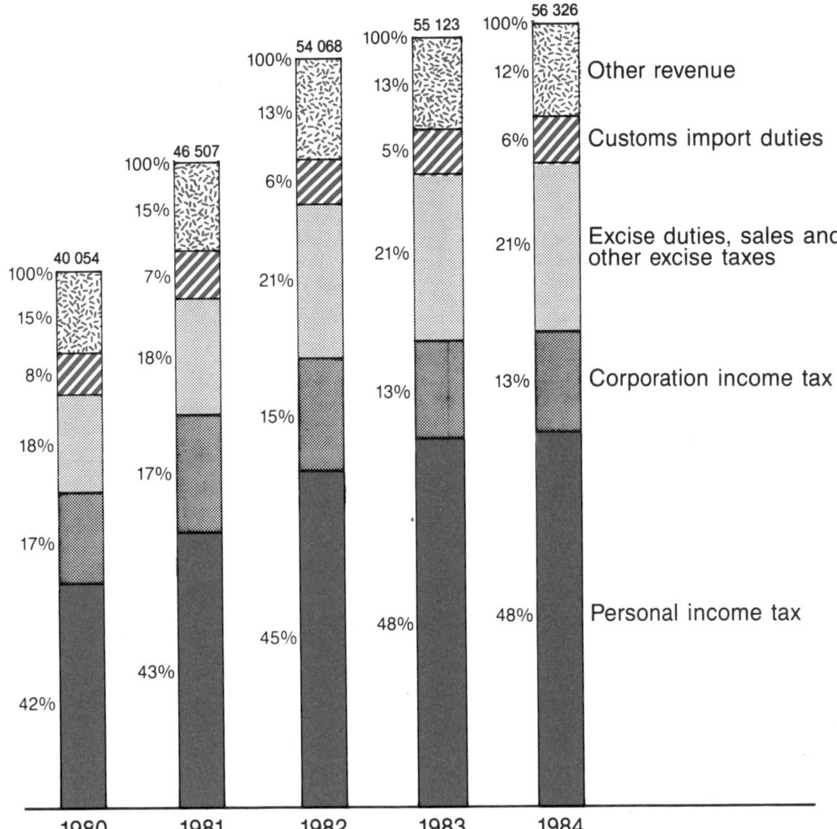

SOURCE: Government of Canada, Public Accounts 1983-84

Figure 50.6 *Canada's income (in millions of dollars) from 1980 to 1984*

Joe Boyle

Figure 50.7 *Joe Boyle*

Claim to fame: He was the "King of the Klondike".

Born: 1867 in Toronto, Ontario

Married: 1887 (after a 3-day romance) to a divorcee who had 1 child. They had 3 more before Joe left her in 1896.

Career: Boyle's adventures began when he was 17. Without telling anyone, he signed up as a sailor on an American ship.

After 3 years of adventures at sea, Joe settled in New York. There he met and married his wife. He went into business for himself and soon had earned a small fortune.

Tired of marriage, Boyle left all his money to his wife and children. With only a few cents in his pocket, he made the long and dangerous journey to the Yukon.

Boyle arrived just as gold was found in the Klondike. Somehow he persuaded the government to let him stake a huge claim. Nobody believed it was possible. But Boyle managed to haul in 2 huge machines for mining the gold.

Boyle made a fortune in the fields. And he soon owned many businesses in Dawson City, including the telephone and power companies. For 18 years he was the "King of the Klondike". There was no problem he could not solve.

When World War I broke out in 1914, Boyle went to Europe. He helped organize the war effort and made daring rescues of prisoners. He became a hero. He had a passionate romance with Queen Marie of Rumania. But after the war, he was forced to leave her country.

Died: Boyle retired to England. He died, penniless, in 1923.

- **Find a place where gold is mined in Canada today.**
- **Do you think it is a good thing for a single person to own services like the telephone or electric companies?**

Deep Waters 51

It's easy to mark a border on land. You can put up a fence, and it will stay there. You can dig a hole on one side, and it won't affect the other.

But a border on water is quite different. It's much harder to mark. And things that happen on one side often affect the other. An oil slick from a ship on one side of the border can easily cross over to the other side. A dam built on one side can cut off the water from the other.

A large part of the border between Canada and the United States is on water. It follows the path of the St. Lawrence River and the Great Lakes. And it crosses important rivers in the west like the Red, the Kootenay, and the Okanagan.

Figure 51.1 *This photograph was taken in 1906. A steamboat filled with tourists plunges down the Lachine Rapids near Quebec. The ride was thrilling for tourists. But the rapids made shipping impossible. Would you enjoy a ride like this?*

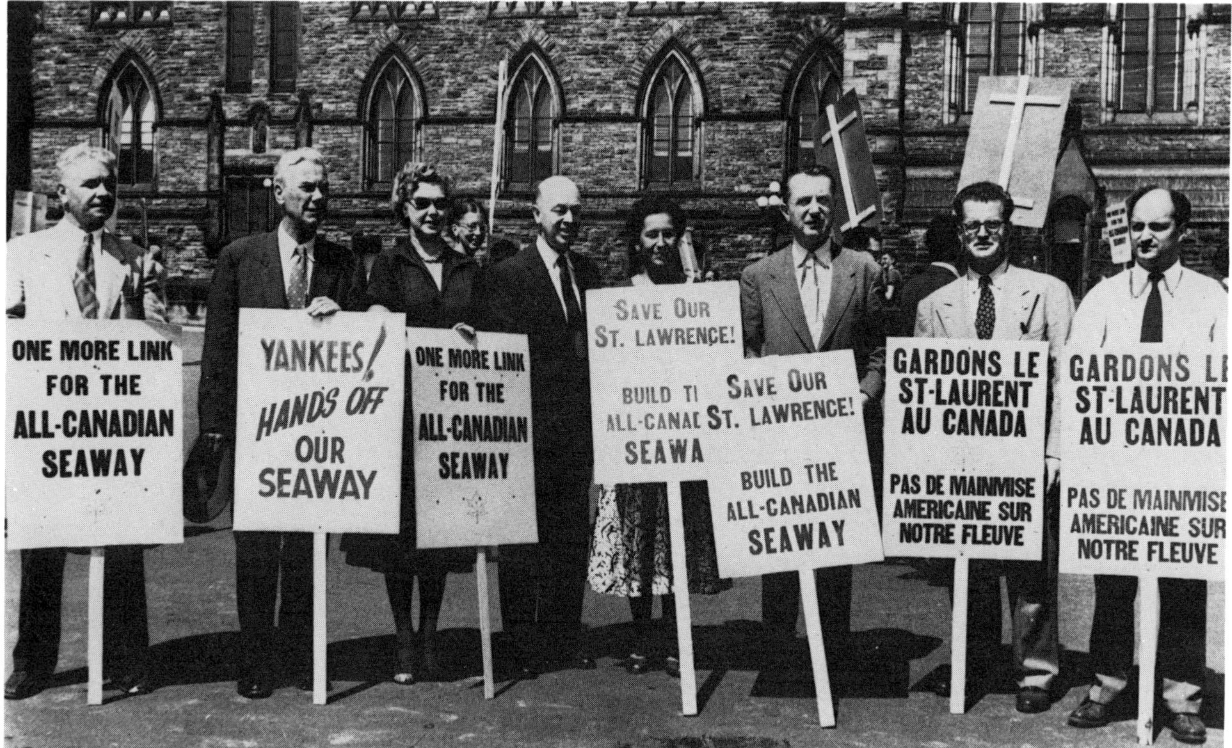

Figure 51.2 *In 1954, Canadians demonstrated for an all-Canadian Seaway. Why did the government reject this idea?*

Special problems can develop when 2 countries share so much water. Canadians and Americans realized this very early. They wanted to settle any problems peacefully. And so in 1909 they agreed to set up the International Joint Commission (or IJC for short).

The IJC is supposed to make decisions about projects affecting the boundary waters. These are all the lakes and rivers near the border. For example, the IJC will decide whether a company can build a power dam on a river that crosses the border.

The IJC has 6 members: 3 from Canada and 3 from the United States. These members are supposed to give **impartial** judgements. In other words, they aren't supposed to give just the feelings of their own country. They try to find the best solution for everyone involved.

You might think this would be impossible. But the IJC has listened to more than 100 different cases since it first met. The Canadian and American members have voted against each other in only 3 of these cases. In all the rest of the cases, they managed to find a compromise.

One of the biggest cases the IJC was ever involved in was the St. Lawrence Seaway. This is the system of rivers and lakes that starts at the Atlantic Ocean and goes all the way to the tip of Lake Superior.

In 1900, 3 Americans tried unsuccessfully to blow up the Welland Canal.

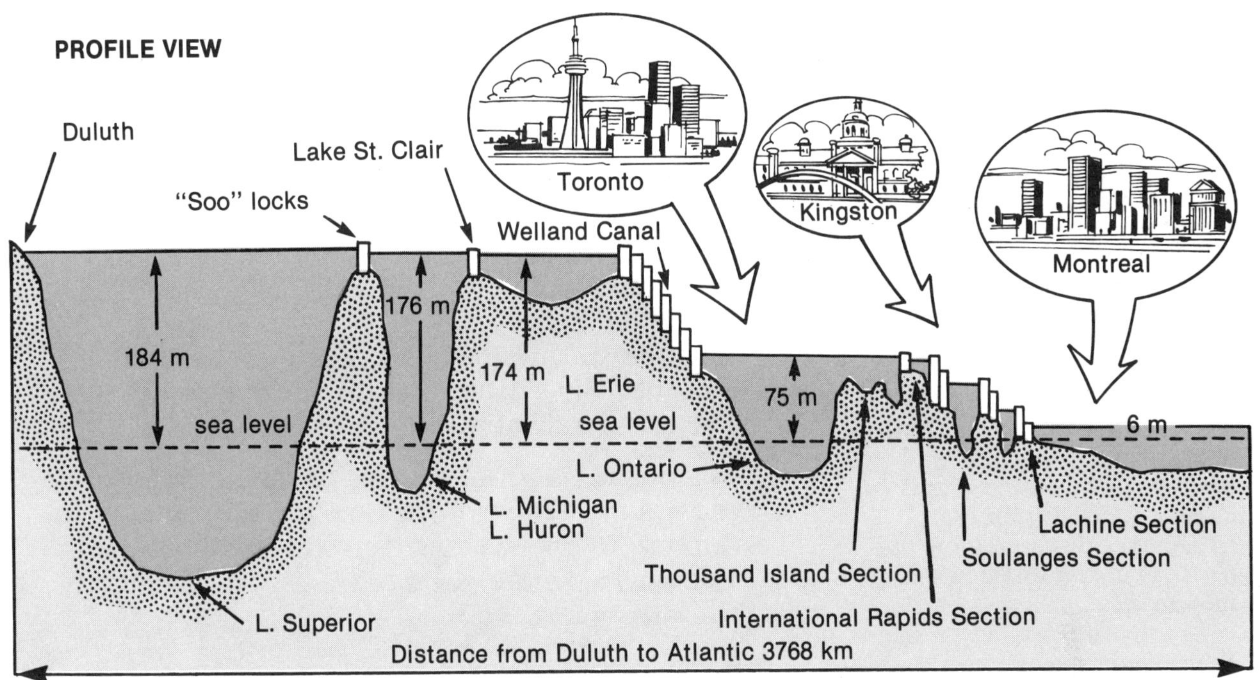

Figure 51.3 A profile of the St. Lawrence Seaway *Ships have to pay a toll each time they pass through a set of locks. This helps pay part of the cost of building and maintaining the Seaway.*

Major cities along the Seaway are Toronto, Kingston, and Montreal. According to this profile, which city is the highest above sea level?

The St. Lawrence system has always been extremely important. In the early days before Confederation, the St. Lawrence system was used by fur traders. By the 1900s the fur trade had gone. But ships still travelled from Montreal carrying manufactured goods to the West. And on the way back they carried western wheat and minerals.

The trouble was that the old St. Lawrence system was not one long smooth trip. There were rapids and waterfalls and shallow waters along the way. The worst of these **obstacles** were Niagara Falls and the Lachine Rapids to the west of Montreal. Of course, these obstacles made travelling very difficult.

By 1842, several canals and locks had been built to help improve travel. But a passenger still had to take 6 separate steamships, a train, and several stagecoaches in order to make the trip from Windsor to Montreal.

For a long time, Canadians and Americans realized that the St. Lawrence system had to be improved. They shared a dream that ocean ships would one day be able to travel all the way from Europe right up to the tip of Lake Superior.

But the trouble was that the Canadian and American governments could not seem to get together. They tried on 8 different occasions between 1914 and 1942. But each time, one side or the other was not ready to start the project. Finally in 1954, the 2 countries agreed to work together.

Thousand Islands salad dressing was created by an American chef to honour the beauty of Canada's Thousand Islands in the St. Lawrence.

Figure 51.4 *You didn't have to pack a single thing when your house was moved to make room for the Seaway. Plants could even be left on the windowsill. Estimate how tall the tires are on this house-moving machine.*

The project was **massive**. Huge areas of land had to be flooded. Highways were re-routed. Over 9000 homes were picked up by giant machines and moved to new locations. Nine-metre-deep canals were dug out of heavy clay and rock. One of these canals was over 100 km long.

In the beginning, many people wondered whether it would be possible to build the Seaway. It was one of the largest engineering projects in the world. But the Seaway was finished in just 5 years. It was officially opened in June, 1959.

Today, the St. Lawrence Seaway is a symbol of the special relationship between Canada and the United States. As the **plaque** marking the opening of the Seaway says:

> THIS STONE BEARS WITNESS TO THE COMMON PURPOSE OF TWO NATIONS WHOSE FRONTIERS ARE THE FRONTIERS OF FRIENDSHIP, WHOSE WAYS ARE THE WAYS OF FREEDOM, AND WHOSE WORKS ARE THE WORKS OF PEACE.

THE FACTS

Remembering Facts

1. Why did Canada and the United States decide to set up the IJC?
2. How does the IJC work?
3. Why did Canadians and Americans want to build the Seaway?
4. Prove that building the Seaway was a big job.
5. When was the Seaway finished?

Finding Facts

One of the most important cases the IJC ever studied was called the Garrison Water Diversion Project. This was a plan to change the direction of a river near the Canada-United States border.

Read other books or encyclopedia articles to answer the following questions about the Garrison Project:

1. Where was this project located?
2. Who wanted this project to go ahead?
3. Why did they want this project completed?
4. Who was against this project? Why?
5. What happened to the project?

YOUR OPINIONS

Stating Opinions

Many people in Ontario and Quebec and New York state had to move when the Seaway was built. Their lands were flooded by the new Lake St. Lawrence.

The people who had to move were given a choice. They could take the money that their houses were worth. Or they could have their old homes actually picked up and moved to a new location.

If you were in that situation, what would you do? Would you take the money? Or would you want your home moved? Explain your opinion in a few sentences.

Discussing Opinions

The Canadian and American governments had trouble getting together to build the Seaway. The problem was that not everyone in Canada and the United States wanted the Seaway built.

There was a split between the East and the West in both countries. The business people in Montreal and Buffalo and Albany *didn't* want the Seaway built. But the farmers on the prairies and the business people in Chicago and the Lakehead *did* want the Seaway built.

Can you think of any reason why the people in the East would feel differently from the people in the West?

NEW WORDS

Learning Words

In your notebook, write the title Vocabulary: Lesson 51. Then write down the following words in a list. Using the Glossary or a dictionary, write the meaning beside each word.

When you are finished, write a short note telling what you have learned in this lesson. Try to use all 5 of these words in your note.

commission	**impartial**	**massive**
obstacle	**plaque**	

Examining Words

You may have heard the saying "Still waters run deep". Can you explain what this saying means?

AN ILLUSTRATION

Read an encyclopedia or other book to find out how locks work. Then draw a series of pictures to show how a ship passes through a lock.

William Hamilton Merritt

Figure 51.5 *William Hamilton Merritt*

Claim to fame: He was responsible for the building of the first Welland Canal.

Born: 1793 in Bedford, New York State

Married: 1815 to Catherine Rodman. They had 6 children.

Career: Merritt's parents took him to live in St. Catharines in Upper Canada when he was a young boy. In 1812, war broke out with the United States. Merritt joined the Canadian militia. He was captured in the fighting at Detroit. He was kept prisoner until the fighting ended.

Merritt returned to St. Catharines at the end of the war. He set up a number of small businesses such as a chain of stores, a distillery, and sawmills.

Merritt needed water to power his sawmills. At first he thought of just digging a small canal from the Welland River to his own sawmills. But then he had a better idea. He would build a canal to link Lake Erie to Lake Ontario. It would be useful for transporting food and other goods as well as for powering his sawmills.

Merritt set up the Welland Canal Company in 1824. Using investments from other businessmen, he started work on the canal. The digging went quickly. In 1829, the first 2 ships sailed through.

The Welland Canal was a huge success. As a result, the government bought it from Merritt's company in 1843.

Died: Merritt spent the last 30 years of his life in politics. He died in 1862 while still in office.

- **How is water used to make sawmills run?**
- **Would you like to work as a sailor?**

QUIZ 7

The following questions are based on the lessons in Chapter 7. **DO NOT WRITE YOUR ANSWERS IN THIS TEXTBOOK.** Instead, you should write the answers in your notebook or on a separate sheet of paper.

1. There are 5 blanks in the following paragraphs. They have been labelled from (a) to (e). Write down the 5 answers in a list on your paper. Then beside each answer write the letter of the blank where it belongs.

   New Brunswick and P.E.I. — Loyalists
   Upper and Lower Canada — United States
   American Revolution

   Americans attacked British North America several times. The first time was during the (a) ______. This war changed the map of North America. The (b) ______ became a separate country. Then thousands of (c) ______ travelled north to live in British North America. They started 2 new Maritime colonies: (d) ______. And Quebec was cut in half to make (e) ______.

2. Match the item in the list on the left side with the correct description from the list on the right side. For each one, write the letter and the number together on your paper.

(a) Fenians	(1) a piece of land once wanted by both Canada and the United States
(b) IJC	(2) a defence route for soldiers travelling from Kingston to Montreal
(c) Tecumseh	(3) Irish-Americans who wanted to capture Canada in order to free Ireland
(d) Island of San Juan	(4) a group of 3 Canadians and 3 Americans who discuss problems with boundary waters
(e) Rideau Canal	(5) the Indian chief who helped the British fight the War of 1812

3. Write the letters from (a) to (e) on your paper. Then write a T if the statement is TRUE. Write an F if the statement is FALSE.
   (a) The American Civil War did not affect British North America at all.
   (b) The boundary between Maine and New Brunswick was important because of the timber.
   (c) Canada was pleased with the boundary decided on between the Yukon and Alaska.
   (d) Only Nova Scotians have ever been allowed to fish in the waters near the Nova Scotia shoreline.
   (e) The St. Lawrence Seaway was one of the largest engineering projects in the whole world.

4. Match the date in the list on the left side with the correct event from the list on the right side. For each one, write the letter and the number together on your paper.

(a) 1959	(1) General Brock fights the Americans at Queenston Heights
(b) 1812	(2) the Americans attack Quebec
(c) 1861	(3) the Treaty of Washington is signed
(d) 1775	(4) the St. Lawrence Seaway is completed
(e) 1871	(5) the fighting starts in the American Civil War

CHAPTER EIGHT

Issues Across the Border

Prime Minister Pierre Trudeau once told American reporters that living beside the United States is like sleeping with an elephant: "No matter how friendly or even-tempered is the beast, one is affected by its every twitch and grunt."

What Trudeau meant was that the United States is a giant in comparison with Canada. It has 10 times as many people; it is much richer; and it is much more powerful.

Everything that the United States does has an effect on Canada. As you will learn, this is true for every area of our lives — from the air we breathe to the television we watch.

52 Acid Rain

In 1966, a Canadian scientist named Dr. Harold Harvey tried an experiment. He released 4000 young salmon into a northern Ontario lake. He wanted to see how well they would grow.

The next spring, Dr. Harvey returned to check on the salmon. He dragged nets through the water for many days. But he didn't catch a single salmon. In fact, there were almost no fish in the lake at all. And even these fish were small and **deformed**.

He didn't know it then. But after a lot of research Dr. Harvey discovered that the fish had disappeared because of acid rain.

Figure 52.1 *Air pollution like this can cause acid rain many hundreds of kilometres away. But the situation is not so easy to clean up. Why won't the government just force industries to stop polluting?*

Acid rain is caused by the **polluted** smoke that pours into the air every day. The smoke comes from sources like mining **smelters** that make copper. It comes from power-generating stations that burn coal. And it comes from car and truck engines that burn fuel oil.

The smoke is full of sulphur and nitrogen. These **emissions** combine with moisture in the atmosphere. They form an acid. So when it rains, the drops of water can be very acidic.

It's easier to understand the problems this can cause if you think of an everyday acid like vinegar. Just try to image what it would be like if the skies rained vinegar instead of water. To say the least, it would be most unpleasant.

But the fact is that some rainfalls in North America have been almost as acidic as vinegar. And when acid rain falls, the effects are more than unpleasant. Acid rain can kill.

Research has now shown that hundreds of lakes in the world are dead because of acid rain. Fish no longer live in them. And even plants have difficulty growing. Naturally this has a terrible effect on the tourist industry.

But this isn't the only problem. Scientists have now found out that acid rain **stunts** the growth of forests and crops. They know that it damages buildings and statues. And they are worried about how it affects our health.

It is clear that something must be done about acid rain. Unfortunately, this is not so easy to do. For one thing, it would cost billions of dollars to reduce the emissions from smelters, power stations, and cars.

The environmental group Greenpeace was founded in Vancouver in the early 1970s to protect whales.

Figure 52.2 *This diagram shows how acid rain is formed. Does it always fall as rain? In the spring, lakes can suffer an acid rain "shock". Can you explain why this would happen at this time of year?*

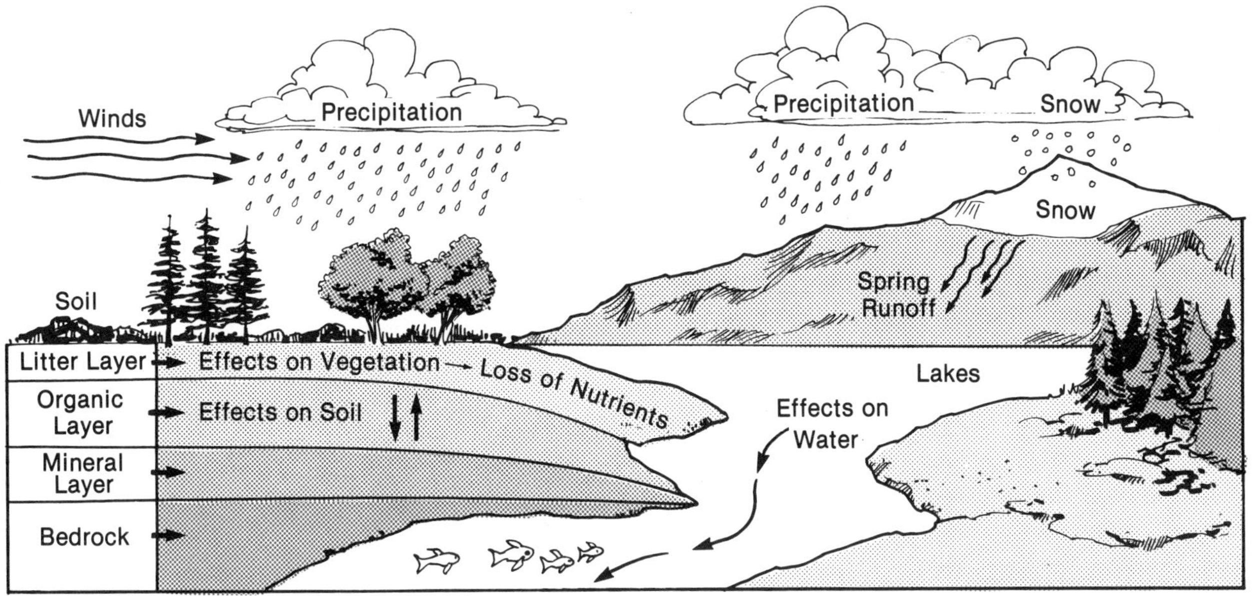

To fight pollution, world-famous Carl Klauck of Holland Landing, Ontario, feeds sewage to worms. The worms turn it into rich plant soil.

But there is an even greater problem than the cost. This comes from the fact that pollution isn't affected by political boundaries.

For example, polluted smoke from the United States is carried by winds across the Canadian border. And the acid rain from this American pollution kills Canadian lakes and harms Canadian crops. The worst problem is in the East. Power stations in states like Ohio and Indiana produce a lot of the pollution that causes acid rain in Ontario and Quebec.

The trouble is that Canadians cannot pass laws to make the major American polluters clean up the air. We have to rely on the Americans to pass these laws. But the Americans don't seem to be very interested in doing this.

Many other countries in the world have the same problem with acid rain. In 1984, representatives from 9 European countries met in Ottawa to discuss acid rain. But the United States refused to send an official representative. The Canadians and Europeans signed an agreement to reduce sulphur and nitrogen emissions by 30%. But the United States refused to do anything.

The problem is not all one-sided. In the past, Canadian politicians have not acted quickly. They have been reluctant to stop Canada's companies from polluting the air. The second-largest polluter in Ontario — Ontario Hydro — is actually owned by the provincial government.

Figure 52.3 *Our lakes and rivers suffer from more than acid rain. Oil spills have a devastating effect on ducks and other water birds as well as on the quality of water.*

Naturally the American politicians do not want to force their own companies to spend billions of dollars to reduce the emissions. This is especially true when acid rain seems to be a problem only in Canada.

But scientists have now shown that acid rain is killing many lakes in the United States. If enough Americans become worried about acid rain, then they may force their government to do something about the problem.

In 1985, Prime Minister Brian Mulroney and President Ronald Reagan agreed to set up a committee to study acid rain. This is just a small step. But it does show that the Americans understand how concerned Canadians are. Hopefully this concern will lead to action.

Nova Scotia's Abraham Gesner (1875-1926) was the inventor of kerosene.

THE FACTS

Remembering Facts

1. What is acid rain?
2. Describe 2 things acid rain can do.
3. Why won't companies just go ahead on their own to clean up the emissions that cause acid rain?
4. Why can't the Canadian government force all the companies that cause acid rain to cut back on their pollution?
5. What effect does acid rain have on Canada's relationship with the United States?

Finding Facts

The acid rain situation will probably have changed since this lesson was written. To find out what is happening right now, write a letter to one of the people or companies involved.

For example, you could write to the Minister for the Environment in Ottawa to ask what has been done about acid rain. Or you could write to one of the big companies that causes this pollution. Or you could write to one of the citizens' groups that is trying to solve pollution problems. Or you could write to politicians in the United States — even to the president.

It will be best if every person in your class can find a different person or company to write to. Then you can share and compare the information you receive.

YOUR OPINIONS

Stating Opinions

Acid rain is a serious problem. But it isn't the only problem we face. In your opinion, what is the biggest problem we face in the world today? Explain your opinion in a few sentences.

Discussing Opinions

Many groups of people are involved in the acid rain problem. There are the companies who are causing the pollution. There are the resort owners who are losing customers because there are no fish to catch. There are the politicians who have the power to force companies to reduce the pollution. And there are the taxpayers who will have to pay at least part of the cost of cleaning up acid rain.

Divide your class into 4 groups. Each group should represent 1 of the groups described above. Discuss how the group you represent probably feels about the acid rain situation. If possible, do some research to get more information. Then discuss the acid rain problem with the other groups in the class. In the discussion, you should give the point of view of the group you represent.

NEW WORDS

Learning Words

In your notebook, write the title Vocabulary: Lesson 52. Then write down the following words in a list. Using the Glossary or a dictionary, write the meaning beside each word.

When you are finished, write a short note telling what you have learned in this lesson. Try to use all 5 of these words in your note.

deform **emission** **pollute**
smelter **stunt**

Examining Words

Can you explain what the following sayings mean?

- It's raining cats and dogs.
- It never rains but it pours.
- Save it for a rainy day.

Do you know any other sayings that have to do with the weather?

AN ILLUSTRATION

Figure 52.4 shows the PH scale. As you can see, items range from acidic through neutral to basic. What level is human blood on this scale? What level is tomato juice? How acidic is vinegar?

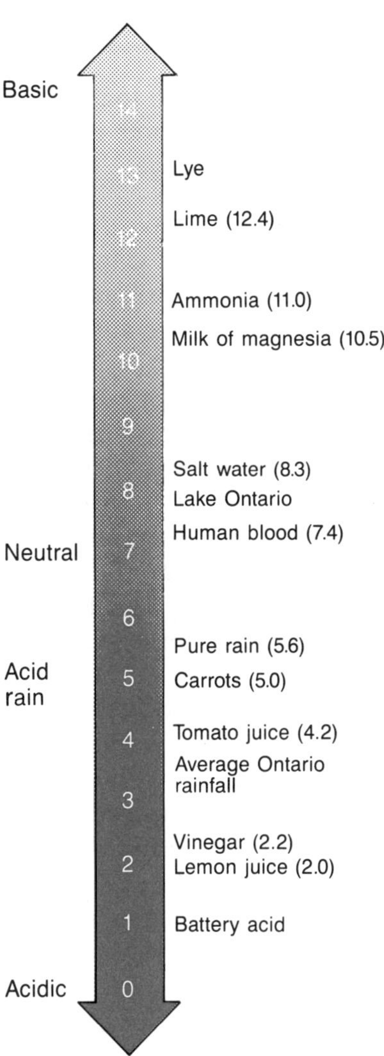

Figure 52.4 *The PH scale*

David Suzuki

Figure 52.5 *David Suzuki on location for his CBC television series,* A PLANET FOR THE TAKING.

Claim to fame: He is a popular scientist and TV host.

Born: 1936 in Vancouver. He has a twin sister.

Married: 1958 to Joane Sunahara. They had 3 children before their divorce in 1965. Then in 1972 he married Tara Cullis. They have 2 children.

Career: During World War II, Suzuki was kept prisoner in a special camp for Canadians of Japanese origins. His parents had been born in Canada; David couldn't even speak Japanese. But the authorities still treated them like enemies.

This taught Suzuki that he would always have to try harder if he was going to succeed. He decided to become a scientist. He would sometimes spend 15 hours at a time working in the lab. But the hard work paid off. Other scientists were impressed by his experiments in genetics. And soon he was given many scholarships and awards.

For a while, Suzuki worked in the United States. In his free time, he joined the civil rights movement to fight for rights for Blacks. Then he came home to be a professor at the University of British Columbia.

Suzuki still works as a scientist. But he is best known for his television shows like *The Nature of Things*. These shows are always good fun. At the same time, they give correct information about scientific discoveries.

Suzuki believes that ordinary people should have more say in what scientists are doing. That is why he continues to work on television as well as in the lab.

- **Watch a science show on television. Explain to the class 1 thing that you have learned from this show.**
- **How do you think Suzuki felt as a young boy in the camp?**

Trade 53

How many of the things in your home were made in some other country besides Canada? Maybe you haven't thought about it much. But chances are that your china, your radio, or even the tile on your bathroom floor came from somewhere else in the world.

All of these items came to Canada through something called foreign **trade**. Trade, as you know, involves exchanging one thing for another. For example, someone might trade a record album for a friend's old headphones. Or a hockey team might trade 3 junior players for a superstar right-winger from another team.

Foreign trade is trade that goes on between 2 countries. In Canada's case, we have extra supplies of products like wheat and lumber. We sell these and other goods to countries that need them. This is known as **exporting** goods.

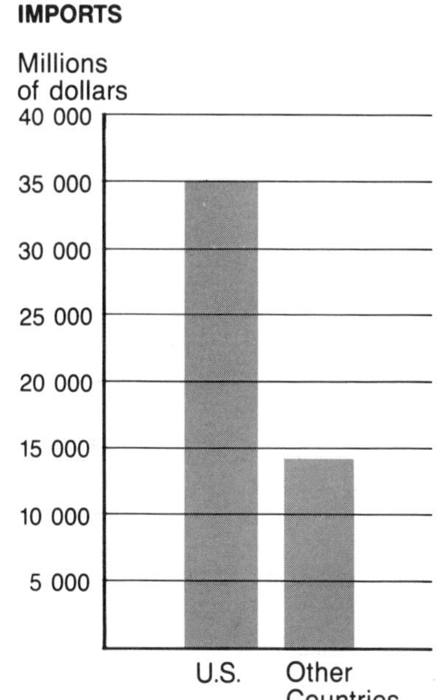

SOURCE: Canada Year Book 1985

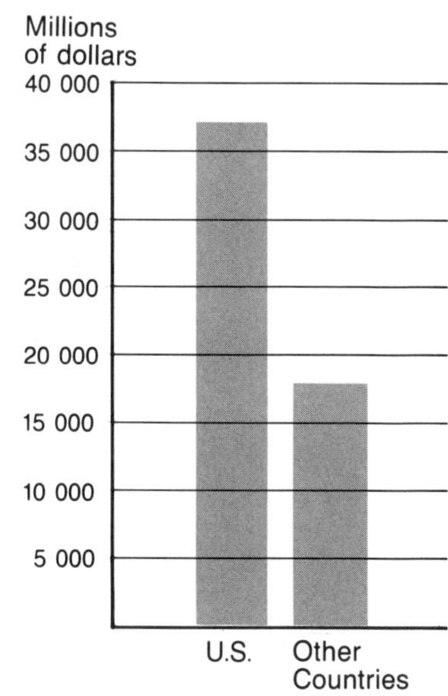

Figure 53.1 Canadian Trade, 1983 *The chart shows clearly that the United States is Canada's biggest trading partner. Find out what some of the "other countries" are.*

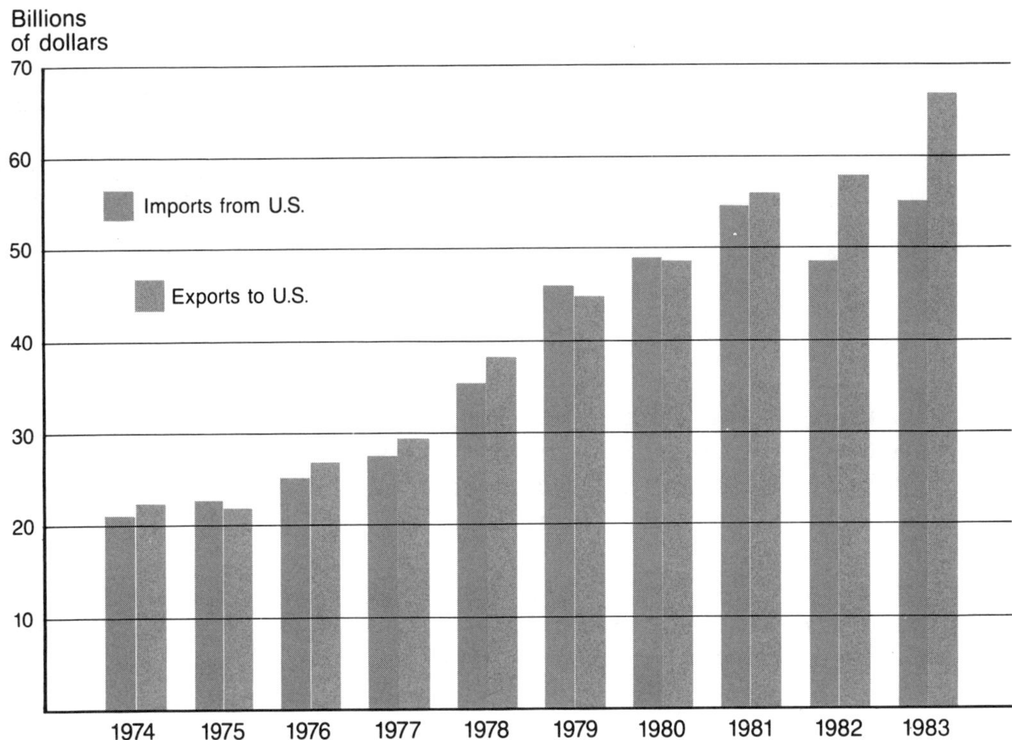

SOURCE: Canada Year Book 1980-81, 1985

Figure 53.2 *This chart compares the dollar value of goods that have been traded between Canada and the United States. Generally this trade has been quite balanced: Canada has imported about as much as it has exported. In what year was trade* most *balanced between the 2 countries? In what year was trade* least *balanced?*

In 1931, the notorious gangster Al Capone said, "I don't even know what street Canada is on."

In turn, other countries have extra supplies of products that Canadians want, like fresh vegetables and precious stones. We buy these and other goods from these countries and bring them into Canada. This is known as **importing** goods.

Canada depends a great deal on foreign trade. In fact, Canada trades goods with dozens of countries around the world. But if you look at Figure 53.1, you'll see that the United States is our biggest trading partner. In fact, it has about 70% of our trade in both exports and imports.

This probably isn't surprising. After all, Canada and the United States are side by side on the same continent. That means it is easy to transport the goods back and forth.

Also, the United States is a huge and wealthy country. It has 10 times as many people as Canada. And these people can afford to buy our goods. They make an excellent **market**, as it is called, for goods from Canada.

This trade with the United States seems to be very good for Canada. This can be seen in Figure 53.2. In general, Canadians sell more goods to Americans than we buy from them. In other words, the **balance** of trade is favourable. We receive more money than we spend.

But this favourable trade balance can be misleading. It doesn't tell the whole story. For there are 2 main problems in our trade relations with the United States.

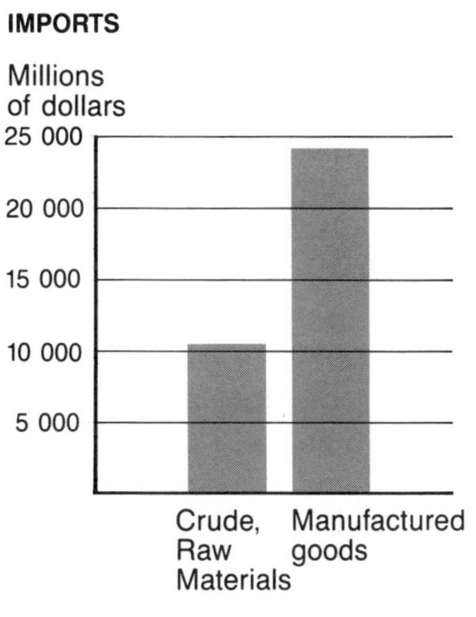

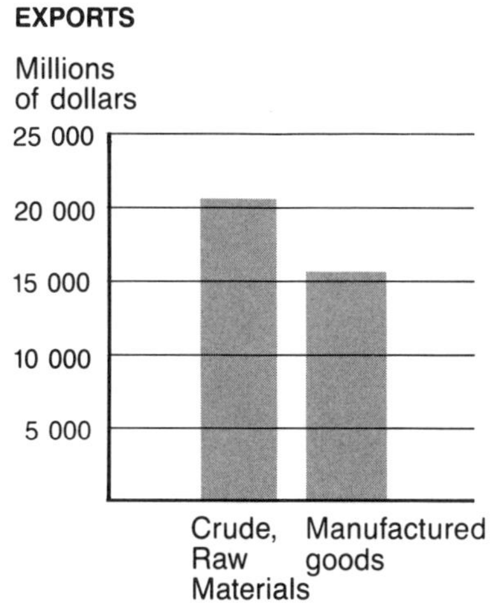

SOURCE: Canada Year Book 1980-81

Figure 53.3 Kinds of goods traded *This chart shows the different kinds of goods traded by Canada and the United States based on 1978 figures.*

The first problem involves the *kinds* of goods that we are trading. Figure 53.3 shows that well over half of the goods we export to the United States are raw or crude materials. That is, they are products like raw hides and wood chips and aluminum. These products will be used in the United States to make manufactured goods like leather jackets and furniture and saucepans.

On the other hand, about 70% of the goods we import from the United States are finished products. That is, we import many manufactured goods like leather jackets and furniture and saucepans.

Many people feel it would be better for Canada if we didn't export so many raw or crude materials. They say it would be better if we kept these materials in Canada for Canadians to turn into manufactured goods. This would give more jobs to Canadians that are right now being taken by Americans.

A second problem is that we depend so much on the United States for our trade. As long as the United States is friendly, this is fine. But if there are problems, there is a chance Canadians will really suffer.

This happened in the early 1970s. Many Americans were out of work. And the United States was importing more goods than it was exporting. To make the situation better, American President Richard Nixon decided to put a special 10% customs duty on all imported goods.

This meant that Americans had to pay 10% more to buy Canadian goods. Naturally they did not like paying so much extra. And so they didn't buy as many Canadian products. As a result, several thousand Canadians found themselves out of work.

Note: You can learn more about how customs duties work in Lesson 50.

Figure 53.4 *The president of the United States, Richard Nixon, visited Canada in April, 1972. He is on the left in this photograph. On the right is Canada's prime minister at the time. What was his name?*

In other words, because Canadians export so many goods to the United States, even the smallest changes in the rules of trade will have a big effect on Canada. This is why the Canadian government has been trying since the late 1970s to find new markets. It can be dangerous for Canada to be so dependent on just 1 other country.

THE FACTS

Remembering Facts

1. What country is Canada's biggest trading partner?
2. Why is the United States an excellent market for Canada?
3. What is the first problem in our trade relations with the United States?
4. What is the second problem in our trade relations with the United States?
5. How has the Canadian government been trying to solve these problems?

Finding Facts

Make a list of 15 different items in your own home that say where they were made. Try to get a variety of items: lamps, knives, shoes, and so on.

Then make a chart that shows how many of these items are from Canada, how many of these items are from the United States, and how many are from other countries.

Compare your chart with the charts of other students in the class. Add up the 3 different categories for all the members in your class. Were you surprised at the results?

YOUR OPINIONS

Stating Opinions

You are shopping in a store for a jacket and you find 2 that you like. One of them was made in Canada and the other was made in a foreign country. Would you buy the Canadian jacket even if it cost a little more? Explain your opinion in a few sentences.

Discussing Opinions

Imagine that you and your classmates are a group of politicians. You are trying to decide on some rules for foreign trade. To do this, you need to answer the following questions:

1. Are there any countries that Canada should not trade with, even if those countries want to buy Canadian goods?
2. Are there any products that Canada should not sell, even if other countries want them?
3. When it comes to foreign trade, should Canada treat all countries the same way? Or should it treat some countries differently from others?

Discuss your own opinions on these questions with the other students in your class.

NEW WORDS

Learning Words

In your notebook, write the title Vocabulary: Lesson 53. Then write down the following words in a list. Using the Glossary or a dictionary, write the meaning beside each word.

When you are finished, write a short note telling what you have learned in this lesson. Try to use all 5 of these words in your note.

balance **export** **import**
market **trade**

Examining Words

The words *export*, *import*, and *transport* have all been used in this lesson. The suffix *port* comes from the Latin word

that means "to carry". Many other words use the letters *port* meaning "to carry". The definitions of 5 of these words follow. What are the words?

- someone who carries luggage
- a place where airplanes land
- a word describing something that is easy to carry
- a city where ships unload their cargoes
- the act of carrying your canoe from one lake to another

AN ILLUSTRATION

More than goods and products can be traded between countries. They can also trade services, ideas, and even people. Each year, many people migrate across the Canada-United States border to live in the other country.

Figure 53.5 shows the pattern of immigration between our two countries over a 20-year period. At one time, Canada was extremely worried about the number of professional Canadians who decided to move to the United States. This was called the "brain drain". Study Figure 53.5 closely. When do you think the brain drain happened?

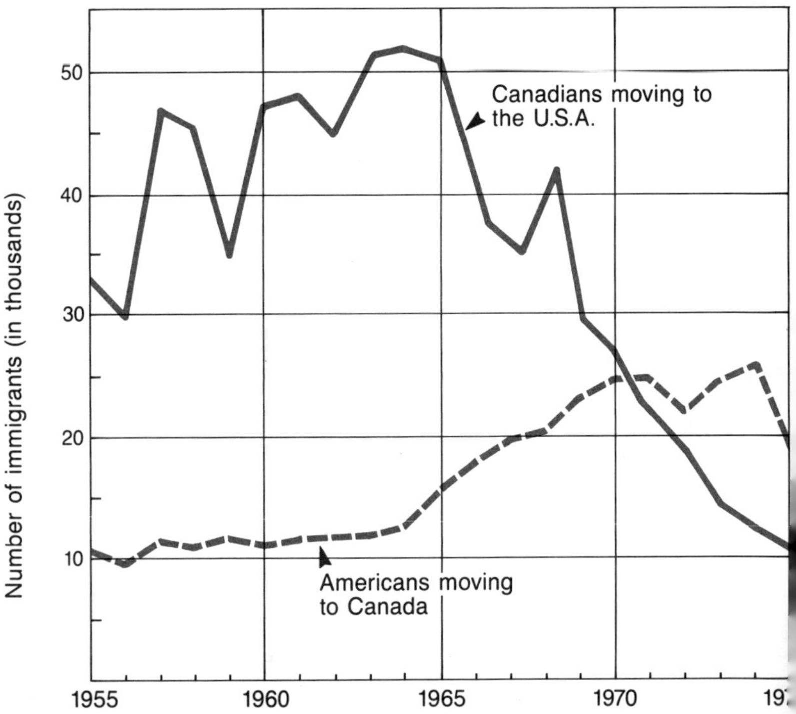

SOURCE: (U.S. immigrants to Canada), Canada Year Book
SOURCE: (Canadian immigrants to U.S.), United States Department of Justice, Immigration and Naturalization Service

Figure 53.5 *Migration across the Canada-United States border*

Elizabeth Arden

Figure 53.6 *Elizabeth Arden plants a maple tree in 1954 to dedicate a park near her home town of Woodbridge.*

Claim to fame: She began and ran a famous cosmetics company.

Born: 1884 in Woodbridge, Ontario, where she was christened Florence Nightingale Graham. Her father was a farmer. Her mother died when Florence was only 5.

Married: 1915 to Thomas Jenkins Lewis, an American citizen, who worked for her company until their divorce in 1934. In 1942 she was re-married, this time to a Russian prince, Michael Evlanoff, whom she divorced in 1944.

Career: Florence left school before she was 18, in order to become a nurse. But she soon grew tired of nursing. She then held a number of small jobs. She worked for a bank, a manufacturer, a real estate firm, and then a dentist.

In 1908, she moved to New York to join her brother. She began work in a cosmetics firm where she learned how to give facial treatments.

In 1910, she opened her own beauty salon under the name Elizabeth Arden. She developed her own line of beauty products which she sold through branch companies around the world. By 1929, Elizabeth Arden was famous and very, very rich.

When she was not travelling around the world to supervise her companies, Elizabeth Arden used to buy race-horses, using the name Mrs. Elizabeth N. Graham. She also spent time working for charities, gardening, and collecting art.

Died: She died in New York in 1966.

- **Who was the first Florence Nightingale?**
- **What is your opinion of cosmetics? Do you think they are important or not?**

54 Investment

In 1980, some Canadians invented a new board game. They didn't have enough money to start producing and selling the game. So they turned to their friends for help. They asked each friend to give them $1000.

In business terms, they were asking their friends to make an **investment**. The money would be **capital** to help print and manufacture the board game. In return for their capital investment, the friends would be given **shares**. That meant that they were part owners of the board game.

If the board game was successful, then it would make a **profit**. There would be money left over after it had been sold. And the friends would get a share of this left-over money.

Of course, if the board game didn't sell, then these friends would lose their investments. They wouldn't get any money back. And they would have lost their $1000.

It was a big gamble. The inventors wouldn't even let their own mothers risk the money. They were sorry for that later, because in the end, the gamble paid off.

The board game was *Trivial Pursuit*. The Canadians who invented it became billionaires. And after just the first year of sales, their friends got much more than $1000 as their share of the profits.

The whole business world is based on gambles like this. People invest money in different ideas or companies. This capital helps get things started. Or they buy shares or stocks in a company that has already been started. In both cases they are gambling that the company will do well.

The people who invest in companies can also have a say in how the companies are run. Of course, this depends on how many shares they own. If investors have only a few shares, then their opinions don't count for much. But if investors own more than half the shares, they have a controlling interest. In other words, they make the final decisions about what the company should do and how it should be run.

There are 5 stock exchanges in Canada: Vancouver, Calgary, Winnipeg, Toronto, and Montreal.

You don't have to be a friend in order to invest money in a company. In fact, you don't even have to be from the same country. There is a lot of foreign investment in Canada. People and businesses from other countries buy shares in Canadian companies.

If you look at Figure 54.1, you can see that most of the foreign investment in Canada today comes from the United States. Americans invest billions of dollars every year in our companies and industries.

Sometimes American companies decide to set up their own branches in Canada. For example, instead of investing money in a Canadian shoe factory, an American shoe company might decide to expand into Canada. It would set up a **branch** plant that would be controlled by the parent company in the United States.

In many ways, this American investment has been a good thing for Canada. It has given us the money we need to start new companies. It has helped increase our standard of living. We can afford to buy more cars, more houses, more appliances, and so on.

But this American investment may also be a bad thing for Canada. One problem is that there is too much American money. Many of our largest companies are actually controlled by Americans. Either they are American branch plants, or Americans own more than half of the shares.

The average savings account in Canadian banks in 1984 contained about $3400.

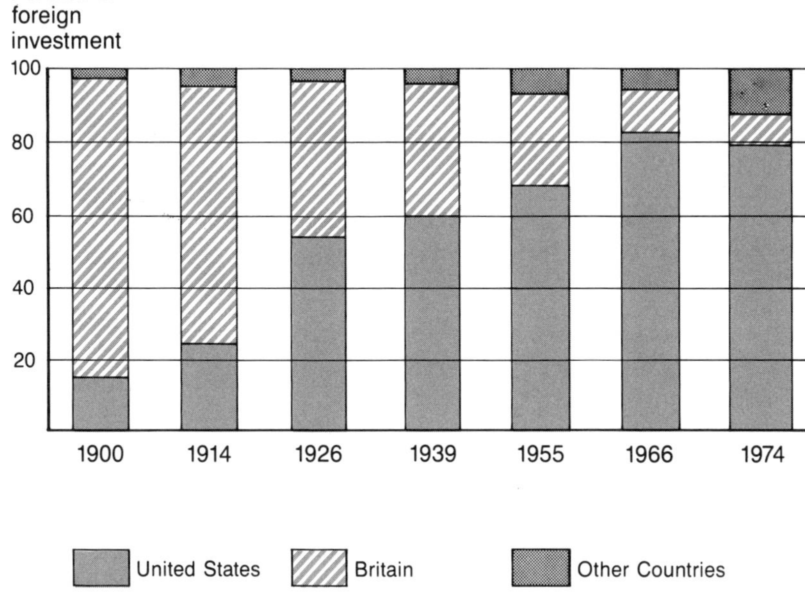

SOURCE: Statistics Canada

Figure 54.1 Foreign investment in Canada *During this century, more and more investment in Canada has come from the United States. Why do you think the percent of investment by Britain has gone down? Find out what some of the "other countries" that have foreign investment in Canada are.*

Figure 54.2 *These two historical cartoons represent a common theme in Canadian politics. What are the cartoonists saying about American investment and trade with Canada? Do you think this is still a problem today?*

UNCLE SAM—"I CAN ALMOST HEAR THEM SINGING 'THE STAR SPANGLED BANNER' IN OTTAWA, BE GOSH."

This is especially a problem in certain industries in Canada. Sometimes the Americans control almost all the companies involved in an industry. For example, Americans control almost all of our automotive industry. They also control much of our food industry.

This American control can be dangerous. First, it means that money is being taken out of Canada. Many of the American investors take their profits back into the United States. This money could have been used to create more jobs in Canada.

A power failure in Queenston, Ontario, left 30 million Canadians and Americans in the dark for up to 11 hours on Nov. 9, 1965.

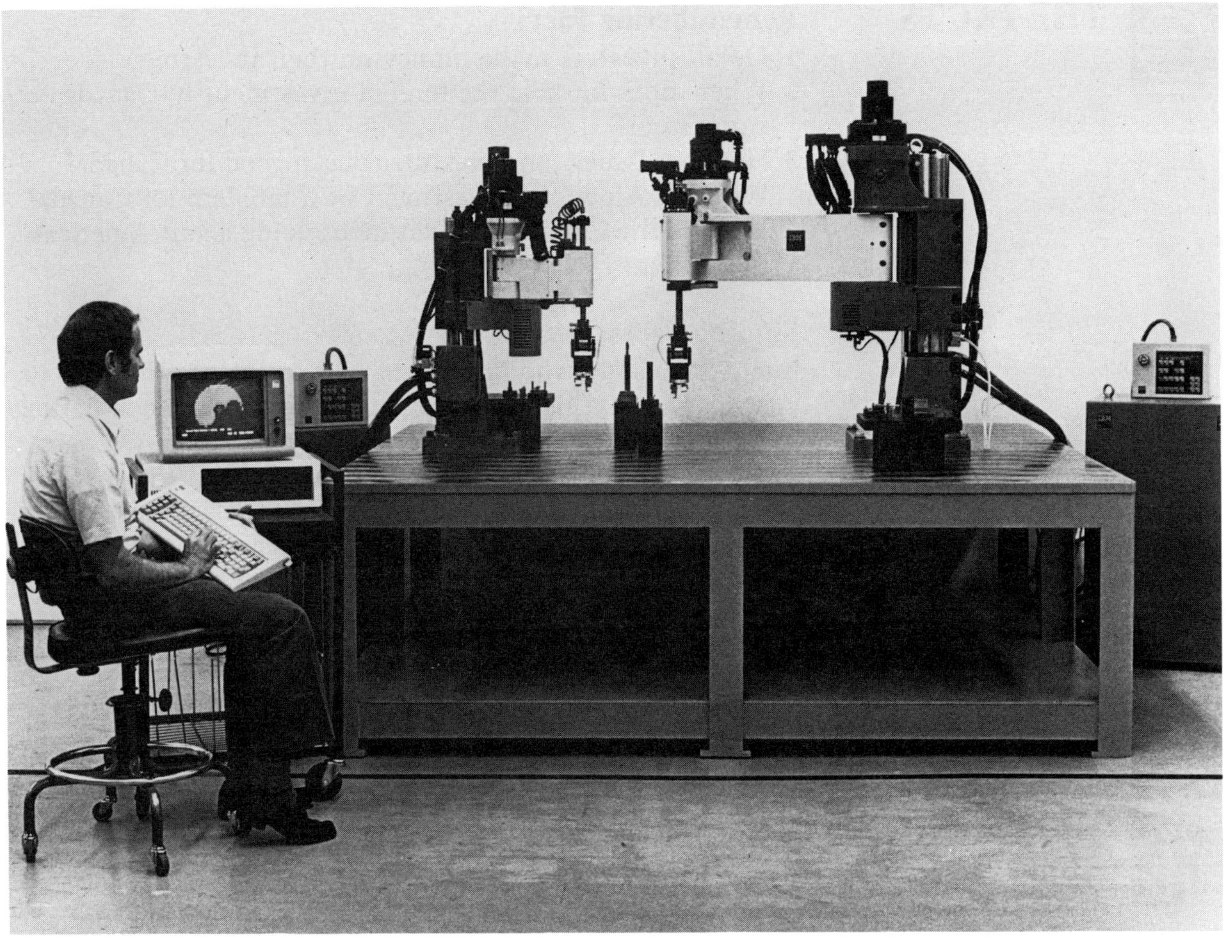

Second, if there is a problem between Canada and the United States, the American-controlled companies will side with the United States. The Americans could also put tremendous pressure on Canadian politicians to force them to give in to the American side.

In the 1970s and early 1980s, the Liberal government tried to change this situation. For example, it started Petro-Canada so that Canadians could buy control of the oil industry. It also set up a board called the Foreign Investment Review Agency (FIRA). FIRA's job was to stop any foreign investments that it did not think would be good for Canada.

The trouble was that these programs cost the taxpayers a lot of money. In 1984, the Conservatives formed the government. They abolished FIRA immediately. And there is always talk of selling Petro-Canada. It is clear that there is a big difference between the Liberal and the Conservative governments on this issue. Only time will tell which side is right.

Figure 54.3 *An engineer tests a new robot arm controlled by a computer. Research and development are critical in the communications industry. However, they require the investment of huge amounts of money. Do you think the government should help pay for this sort of research?*

Georges-Antoine Belcourt was the owner of Canada's first car, in 1866. He also caused Canada's first traffic accident.

THE FACTS

Remembering Facts

1. Do all investors make money on their investments?
2. Where does most of the foreign investment in Canada come from?
3. How has American investment been good for Canada?
4. Why can American investment be a problem for Canada?
5. What is the Canadian government doing about American investment in Canada?

Finding Facts

Invite somebody who knows about investments to speak to your class. Ask this expert to explain what the stock listings in the newspaper mean. Find out how a person buys shares or stocks. Be sure to ask about service charges. In other words, how much does it cost to buy and sell them?

Choose 2 companies from the ones listed in the newspaper. Every day, keep a record of how your companies are doing. If you had bought shares in the company, would you have made money at the end of the week? Every time you read a newspaper, check to see how your companies are doing in the stock market. It can take years for the value of a stock to change very much.

YOUR OPINIONS

Stating Opinions

Some people say that a problem with Canadians is that they aren't willing to take a chance. They'd rather save their money in a bank than risk it on investing in a new company.

What about you? If you'd been given a chance, would you have invested $1000 in the board game described at the beginning of this lesson? Explain your opinion in a few sentences.

Discussing Opinions

In the 1980s, many Canadian companies had financial trouble. Massey-Ferguson almost collapsed. DeHavilland Aircraft lost millions of dollars. Maislin Trucking could no longer operate.

In these cases and others, the federal government lent millions of dollars to help keep the companies going. Some people said that this was a waste. They felt the government should not interfere in business. They felt it was unfair to show favouritism for large companies and not help small ones. Others were happy that the government was trying to support Canadian industries. They felt this would keep jobs in Canada.

Should the government step in when a Canadian company is in financial trouble? Discuss your opinions with the class.

NEW WORDS

Learning Words

In your notebook, write the title Vocabulary: Lesson 54. Then write down the following words in a list. Using the Glossary or a dictionary, write the meaning beside each word.

When you are finished, write a short note telling what you have learned in this lesson. Try to use all 5 of these words in your note.

branch	**capital**	**investment**
profit	**share**	

Examining Words

People talk about investment in terms of millions and billions of dollars. Sometimes, you can even hear them talk about trillions of dollars.

Just how much are a million, a billion, and a trillion? Interview 5 people to find out what they think these amounts mean. Then check the meanings in 2 separate dictionaries. Share your results with the class.

AN ILLUSTRATION

The Canadian mint decided in the 1980s to issue a new coin worth $1. Some people disliked the first design that the mint put out. Imagine that you have been asked to re-design the $1 coin. Make a drawing of both the front (head) and back (tail) of your coin. Indicate exactly what size your coin would be and how much it would weigh.

R.S. McLaughlin

Figure 54.4 *Sam McLaughlin in an old car at the Canadian National Exhibition, n.d.*

Claim to fame: He was the father of Canada's automotive industry.

Born: 1871 in Enniskillen, Ontario, near Oshawa

Married: 1898 to Adelaide Louise Mowbray. They had 5 daughters.

Career: When he was just 16, McLaughlin started work in his father's carriage factory. This factory made wooden carriages and sleighs that were famous across Canada.

In 1905, young Sam bought one of the new "horseless carriages" — a car. From the moment he stepped on the gas, he realized that the car was the way of the future.

Sam went to the United States to find out about building cars. Then he came back home to design his own model. His father agreed to build 100 of the new cars.

But the chief engineer got sick. Sam had to call in Will Durant — the maker of the Buick in the United States. Together they worked out a deal. Soon the McLaughlin-Buick automobile was being sold across Canada.

Durant owned General Motors. In 1918, the McLaughlins sold their company outright to General Motors. But they continued as the heads of General Motors of Canada.

Sam made millions of dollars as head of General Motors of Canada. But he also gave away millions. He paid for wings in hospitals. He paid for a planetarium in Toronto. He paid for a new college at York University. He even set up a special fund so that doctors could study with the world's best scientists.

Died: McLaughlin died at the age of 100 in 1972.

- **Many makes of cars have been named for people. Find out how one of these cars got its name:** *Mercedes Benz, Ford,* **or** *Rolls Royce.*
- **If you had a million dollars to give away, how would you do it?**

Defence 55

There are about 82 000 men and women serving in the Canadian Armed Forces. Our government spends millions of dollars each year on **defence**. But who is our enemy? Who are we afraid will attack us?

If you ask most Canadians these questions, they will answer, "The Soviet Union." But, of course, no one seriously believes that the Soviet Union would attack Canada on its own. Instead, they expect the Soviet Union would attack the United States. Then Canada would be involved in the fighting automatically.

There was a time when the United States was Canada's worst enemy. But now we are military **allies**: we are friends who agree to fight on the same side.

This change in our relationship really happened because of the two world wars. Canadians and Americans fought on the same side in World War I. Then, during World War II, we signed an official agreement to help each other in case of attack.

Note: You can learn more about World Wars I and II in Chapter 9.

After the war, Canada and the United States continued to cooperate. We agreed to use many of the same weapons. And our soldiers sometimes trained together. In the late 1940s, our government also let the Americans build and operate **radar** stations in northern Canada.

This was done because the United States and the Soviet Union had become bitter enemies. During World War II, these countries had also fought on the same side. But there were many problems between them.

Simply put, the United States and the Soviet Union did not trust each other. After the war, they accused each other of wanting to control the whole world.

Americans were worried that the Soviets might attack them by flying over the North Pole and Canada. Naturally this situation would be very dangerous for Canada. It became even more dangerous in the early 1950s. Both the United States and the Soviet Union developed powerful new **nuclear missiles**. Some of these were called ICBMs — **I**nter**c**ontinental **B**allistic **M**issiles.

The first defensive hockey player to win the NHL scoring championship was Canada's Bobby Orr.

Canadian Wilbur Franks, "father of the space suit", invented the first pressurized flying suit in 1941.

The very first ICBMs could fly from the Soviet Union to the United States in 30 minutes. This didn't give much time for the Canadian and American military forces to react. It was clear that we needed to develop a better air defence system.

The answer was NORAD — the **Nor**th American **A**ir **D**efence system. In 1958, the Canadian and American governments agreed to link all of their air defence plans. The headquarters of NORAD was built deep inside a huge mountain near Colorado Springs.

Figure 55.1 *The entrance to* NORAD *underground headquarters in Colorado.*

Inside the mountain are 11 buildings. These buildings contain computers and communication equipment. They link all the NORAD bases. If North America is ever attacked, the defence will be controlled from inside the safety of the mountain.

The head of NORAD is an American. And the next in command is a Canadian. Each is in charge when the other one is away. In a war situation, the heads of Canada and the United States have the final say on what weapons will be used.

Many Canadians have worried about this close military relationship with the United States. Canadians do not always feel the same way about the world situation as Americans do.

In fact, there have been some problems between Canadians and Americans over NORAD forces. This was very clear in the Cuban Missile Crisis in 1962. The Soviet Union was trying to set up nuclear missiles in Cuba. These were aimed at the United States.

The president of the United States, John Kennedy, was furious. He demanded that the Soviets take away the missiles immediately. Kennedy asked the Canadians to get their NORAD forces ready for war. But he had not given the Canadians any advance information. So the Canadian prime

Alexander Graham Bell invented more than the telephone. The first recorded flight in Canada was made in a kite he designed.

Figure 55.2 Canada is linked to American actions around the world.

(55.2.a.) *Sometimes Canadians disagree with American actions. These demonstrators were photographed resting near a statue of John A. Macdonald. What do their signs say they are protesting against? Where is Vietnam? When were the Americans fighting in Vietnam?*

(55.2.b.) *Sometimes Canadians support American actions. Here, Governor- General Ed Schreyer accepts a valentine sent by Americans in appreciation for Canada's role in helping American embassy employees to escape from Iran. When did this event take place?*

Canadian-born Dr. James A. Naismith invented basketball in 1891 so that his students could get exercise indoors during winter.

minister, John Diefenbaker, held back. He did not do anything until after the crisis was over.

This incident made both Americans and Canadians angry. The Americans thought Canada had backed out of its agreement. The Canadians thought the Americans were asking them to go to war without giving them any background information.

After the Cuban Missile Crisis, Canada became more independent of the United States in NORAD. But the fact is that United States security depends on Canada. Americans need to use Canadian airspace and Canadian communications.

Note: You can learn more about nuclear weapons in Lesson 65.

Canadians may want to remain neutral. We may not want to be involved in a war. But it would be impossible for us to avoid the consequences of a nuclear war. We are tied to the United States no matter how we feel.

Figure 55.3 *The American space program is an important part of its defence system. This is a photograph of the emblem for the 1984 Shuttle space flight. It features the names of the astronauts on board. One of them was a Canadian. Can you tell which one? You can read more about him in the last biography in this book.*

THE FACTS

Remembering Facts

1. Why was NORAD set up?
2. Where are the headquarters of NORAD?
3. Who has the final say on what NORAD forces will do?
4. What was the Cuban Missile Crisis?
5. How did the Cuban Missile Crisis cause problems between Canada and the United States?

Finding Facts

Many of the Soviet Union's missiles are based in the Kamchatka Peninsula. They are aimed at important targets in the United States, including Los Angeles, Washington, and New York.

Find Kamchatka on a globe. Then take a piece of string. Place one end on the Kamchatka Peninsula. Then run the string across the top of the globe to the target cities in the United States.

What Canadian cities would Soviet missiles fly near if they were launched at these American cities?

YOUR OPINIONS

Stating Opinions

Do you think there will be a nuclear war between the United States and the Soviet Union in your lifetime? Explain your opinion in a few sentences.

Discussing Opinions

In 1936, President Roosevelt of the United States said:

> The people of the United States will not stand idly by if domination of Canadian soil is threatened by any other empire.
>
> (in a speech at Queen's University, 1938)

In other words, he said that the United States would send in soldiers to protect Canada if another country tried to attack us. The United States would protect Canadian freedom.

But imagine a slightly different situation. Imagine that Canadians decide to support the Soviet Union. Imagine that the Canadian government allows Soviet soldiers to set up bases in the far North. How do you think the Americans would react in this situation?

NEW WORDS

Learning Words

In your notebook, write the title Vocabulary: Lesson 55. Then write down the following words in a list. Using the Glossary or a dictionary, write the meaning beside each word.

When you are finished, write a short note telling what you have learned in this lesson. Try to use all 5 of these words in your note.

ally	**defence**	**missile**
nuclear	**radar**	

Examining Words

ICBM and NORAD are short forms. They have been made by using letters from longer words.

Do you know any other common short forms made by using letters from longer words? Do you know what the letters stand for? Start by thinking of your favourite radio station.

The map in Figure 55.4 shows how far the Soviet missiles being set up on Cuba could have reached. What major Canadian cities would have been in danger from these missiles?

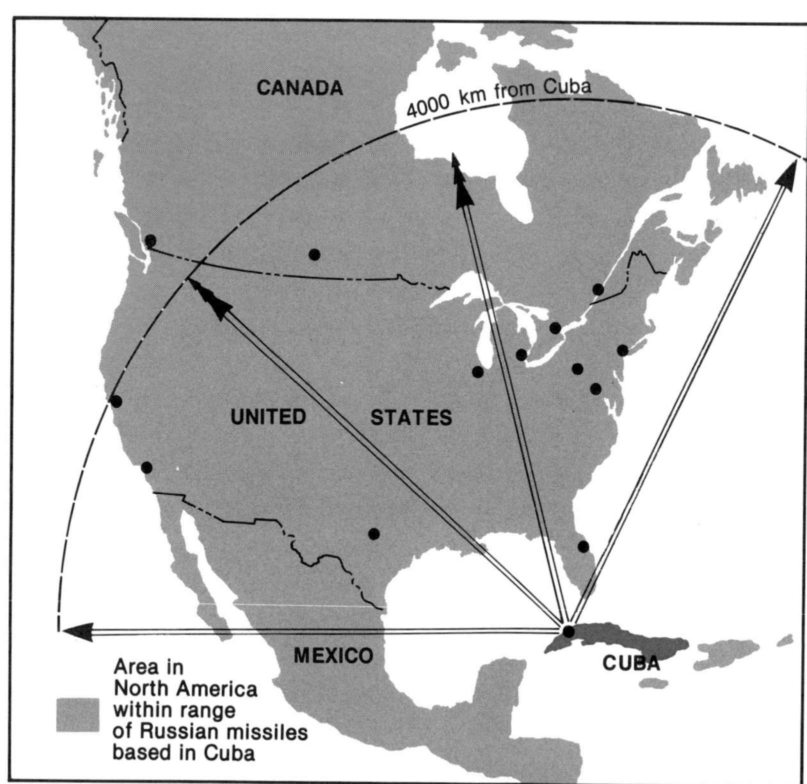

Figure 55.4 *The potential range of Soviet missiles in Cuba*

Ken Taylor

Figure 55.5 *Ken Taylor receiving his award as Officer of the Order of Canada from then Governor General Ed Schreyer*

Claim to fame: He was the Canadian Ambassador in Iran who saved 6 Americans from being taken hostage.

Born: 1934 in Calgary, Alberta

Married: 1960 to Pat Lee, a scientist and science professor. They have 1 son, Douglas.

Career: Ken Taylor joined the Canadian Department of External Affairs in 1959. His job was to represent Canada in different countries around the world. He and his wife lived in such far-off places as Guatemala and Pakistan.

In 1977, Taylor was made the Canadian Ambassador in Iran. Two years after the Taylors moved to Iran, there was a revolution led by the Ayatollah Khomeini. During this revolution, the U.S. Embassy was taken over by the Iranians. The Iranians took all the Americans hostage.

However, 6 Americans managed to escape. Taylor made the decision to hide these Americans, even though it was very dangerous. The Canadians would have also been taken hostage if the Iranians had ever found out.

The 6 Americans lived secretly with the Taylors and other Canadians. Meanwhile, Taylor arranged to shut down the Canadian embassy so that they could all leave safely. In early 1980, the Americans were smuggled out of Iran using false Canadian passports.

Taylor became an instant hero both in Canada and in the United States. He served as Consul General in New York before taking a job with an American company in 1984.

- **Does Canada have an embassy in Iran now?**
- **Diplomats often work in exciting countries. But they also sometimes face danger. Would you like to be a diplomat?**

56 Culture

Figure 56.1 *It has been said that a country's history is the sum total of its biographies. In other words, individual people make the country what it is. Francess Halpenny, shown in this photograph, is general editor of the* Dictionary of Canadian Biography. *This is a multi-million dollar project supported by the Canada Council. The dictionary tells the stories of the thousands of individual Canadians who have helped to shape our country. Are any of the volumes of the* Dictionary of Canadian Biography *in your library?*

There's no real difference between Canadians and Americans.

How does this statement make you feel? If you're like many Canadians, you will react strongly. You will argue that the statement is wrong. But how would you go about proving it?

When you first think about our culture, you will see that there are many American influences. English-speaking Canadians tend to watch American television programs and films. They read American books and magazines. And they listen to American records.

Part of the problem is our geography. Almost all of the Canadian population lives within 300 km of the American border. And this makes it very easy for us to share American culture.

Another part of the problem is our **attitude** to our own **artists**. Who are your favourite movie stars? Who are your favourite singers? Who are your favourite actors?

There is a good chance that most of your favourites are from the United States. In the past, we Canadians have been slow to praise our own artists. We have waited until they have become famous in the United States. This happened, for example, to Margot Kidder, Christopher Plummer, Lorne Greene, and Kate Nelligan.

An explanation for this is that the United States is so much larger than Canada. It has 10 times as many people. And that means that there is much more money to be spent on entertainment there.

Advertisers on television, for example, want to reach large audiences. They pay for their **commercial** time based on how many people are watching. The more people who are watching, the more the advertisers will pay.

Money from these advertisements is used to produce new programs. If a television series doesn't have many viewers, then it will not earn much money. It will be harder to produce good episodes. And in the end, it might be cancelled.

The Canadian government **recognized** the problem as early as 1928. That year, it set up a commission to study radio broadcasting in Canada. As a result, CBC radio (Canadian Broadcasting Corporation) was created.

If you've ever listened to CBC radio, you will know that there are no regular commercials. This is because the government pays for all the programs. We, the people of Canada, own the CBC. And it was set up by the government to help unite us, to help us learn about our world, and to help us understand one another.

In 1968, the government went one step further to protect our culture. It set up the CRTC (Canadian Radio-television and Telecommunications Commission).

The CRTC is a group of men and women appointed by the government. They set rules that all Canadian television and radio stations have to obey. Some of these rules state that a certain amount of the broadcast time has to have Canadian content.

The government took an even bigger step in 1975. Before this time, Canadian companies that advertised in American magazines like *Time* and *Reader's Digest* could get a tax break. They were allowed to deduct the advertising costs. But then the government took away this right.

Many people were angry about this law. The Americans were furious. But the Canadian government held firm. It wanted the advertising money to go to Canadian magazines.

More than 40% of Canadian homes have at least 2 television sets. Another 20% have 4 or more radios.

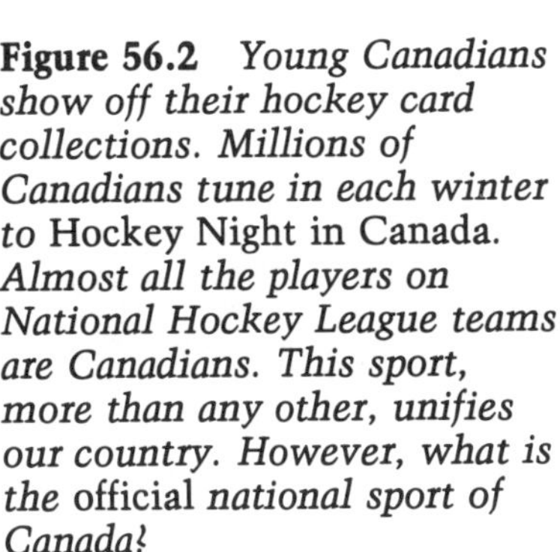

Figure 56.2 *Young Canadians show off their hockey card collections. Millions of Canadians tune in each winter to* Hockey Night in Canada. *Almost all the players on National Hockey League teams are Canadians. This sport, more than any other, unifies our country. However, what is the official national sport of Canada?*

American writer Ernest Hemingway worked for a Canadian newspaper. In 1923, he told a friend Canada was a "dreadful country."

The Canadian government has also interfered in sports. For example, the World Football League wanted to start teams in Canada. It was mostly an American league. The government refused to let them do this. They thought that such a move would end up with the Canadian Football League losing fans and money.

But government money and laws can't save Canadian culture by themselves. Canadians have to want this to happen.

There is one very important way in which Canadians seem to feel differently from Americans about culture. It has to do with our attitudes to the different backgrounds of the people who come to our country.

The United States has often been called a melting pot. In other words, the people who come to live there are expected to give up their old culture. They are expected to forget their old languages and customs.

In Canada, on the other hand, we support **multiculturalism**. The people who come here are encouraged to keep their old culture. We take pride in the number of people from different ethnic groups who have chosen Canada as their home.

Figure 56.3 *The Native people of Canada are also struggling to protect their culture. This photograph was taken in 1973 in Edmonton. Canadian Indians were demonstrating in support of American Indians. Where is Wounded Knee? What happened there?*

More than laws, it is different attitudes like this that help to keep our cultures separate. Many people have said that Canada may one day become part of the United States. And certainly we are tied to the United States in terms of our economy and defence. But how would you feel about becoming an American?

Percy Faith, an internationally famous conductor and arranger, was born in Canada and got his start with CBC radio.

YEAR AWARDED	AWARD CATEGORY	GENIE AWARD WINNERS	OSCAR AWARD WINNERS
1982	Actor	Nick Mancuso, *Ticket to Heaven*	Henry Fonda, *On Golden Pond*
	Actress	Margot Kidder, *Heartaches*	Katharine Hepburn, *On Golden Pond*
	Picture	*Ticket to Heaven*	*Chariots of Fire*
1983	Actor	Donald Sutherland, *Threshold*	Ben Kingsley, *Ghandi*
	Actress	Rae Dawn Chong, *Quest For Fire*	Meryl Streep, *Sophie's Choice*
	Picture	*The Grey Fox*	*Ghandi*
1984	Actor	Eric Fryer, *The Terry Fox Story*	Robert Duvall, *Tender Mercies*
	Actress	Martha Henry, *The Wars*	Shirley MacLaine, *Terms of Endearment*
	Picture	*The Terry Fox Story*	*Terms of Endearment*
1985	Actor	Gabriel Arcand, *The Crime of Ovide Plouffe*	F. Murray Abraham, *Amadeus*
	Actress	Louise Marleau, *La Femme de l'Hotel*	Sally Field, *Places in the Heart*
	Picture	*Bay Boy*	*Amadeus*

Table 56.1 *Genie Awards are given in Canada each year for outstanding Canadian actors and Canadian films. The Oscars are the annual film awards given in Hollywood. These are recent winners of film awards in Canada and the United States. How many names and films do you recognize on this list? What conclusions can you draw from this?*

CBC Radio boasts 5 million regular listeners in Canada.

THE FACTS

Remembering Facts

1. How does our geography make it easy for us to share the American culture?
2. Why are large audiences important for television programs?
3. Why did the government set up the CBC?
4. What sort of rules does the CRTC make?
5. Explain another way the government has tried to support Canadian culture besides the CBC and CRTC.

Finding Facts

Working with the students in your class, try to name 5 Canadians from each of the following groups.

actors	athletes	dancers
singers	painters	writers

Make up a list of these people. Then find out more about a person on the list. When and where was this person born? What is this person most famous for? Did this person ever live or work in the United States?

YOUR OPINIONS

Stating Opinions

Would you rather go on vacation in the United States or in another part of Canada? Explain your opinion in a few sentences.

Discussing Opinions

Some provinces will only use textbooks written by Canadians in their schools. Other provinces don't care whether the textbooks are Canadian or American or even British.

How many of your textbooks are written by Canadians? Do you think it matters whether your textbooks are written and published by Canadians or not?

NEW WORDS

Learning Words

In your notebook, write the title Vocabulary: Lesson 56. Then write down the following words in a list. Using the Glossary or a dictionary, write the meaning beside each word.

When you are finished, write a short note telling what you have learned in this lesson. Try to use all 5 of these words in your note.

artist	**attitude**	**commercial**
multiculturalism	**recognize**	

Examining Words

Canadian English is sometimes different from American English. The following are common words and phrases in some parts of the United States. What words and phrases would you use instead?

Put those groceries in a *sack* for me, please.
If you *flake school* once more, you will be suspended.
Turn on the *spigot* so I can fill the kettle.
They named the baby *from* her mother.
The poor boy is sick *on* his stomach.

AN ILLUSTRATION

The cartoon in Figure 56.4 was drawn in 1976. Study it carefully. Then answer the following questions:

1. Who are the two people in the cartoon? Whom do they represent? How do you know?
2. What are the titles of the books in the cartoon? What comment is the cartoonist making about Canadian culture? Explain how you came to this conclusion.
3. Do you think this cartoon is a fair comment on the state of Canadian culture today?

Figure 56.4 *A cartoonist's view of the Canadian cultural experience. Examine this cartoon carefully.*

Maureen Forrester

Figure 56.5 *Maureen Forrester*

Claim to fame: She is a world-famous singer.

Born: 1931 in Montreal, Quebec

Married: 1954 to a violinist, Eugene Kash. They had 5 children before they separated in 1974.

Career: Forrester left school when she was just 13. She didn't have her first real music lesson until she was 17. She joined a church choir and sang some classical music. But at the time, she was more interested in singing with dance bands.

Then, when she was 21, she heard a singer called Bernard Diament. She was impressed by his voice and asked him to teach her. He agreed. After 6 months of hard work, he decided she had the talent for a world career in classical music.

He was right. The critics loved her rich, velvety voice. She was soon well known across Canada. Then she went on to conquer audiences in Europe and the United States. Today, after more than 30 years of singing, she has millions of fans throughout the world.

Forrester does more than just sing. She has also helped to organize important groups in Canada. In 1984, she was appointed for 5 years as chairman of the Canada Council. This is an independent organization paid for by the government. Its job is to give grant money to support Canadian artists and arts groups across the country.

- **Find the titles of 2 of Maureen Forrester's recordings.**
- **In your opinion, what is the best kind of music to listen to?**

QUIZ 8

The following questions are based on the lessons in Chapter 8. **DO NOT WRITE YOUR ANSWERS IN THIS TEXTBOOK.** Instead, you should write the answers in your notebook or on a separate sheet of paper.

1. There are 5 blanks in the following paragraphs about Canada. They have been labelled from (a) to (e). Write down the 8 answers in a list on your paper. Then beside each answer write the letter of the blank where it belongs.

   fish　　　emissions
   health　　forests
   smoke

   Acid rain is caused by polluted (a) ______. It is full of sulphur and nitrogen. These (b) ______ combine with moisture in the atmosphere to make acid rain. Acid rain can be very harmful. It kills the (c) ______ in lakes. It stunts the growth of (d) ______. It may even hurt our own (e) ______.

2. Match the item in the list on the left side with the correct description from the list on the right side. For each one, write the letter and the number together on your paper.

(a) CRTC	(1) the radio and television network that is owned by all Canadians
(b) ICBM	(2) the defence system Canada shares with the United States
(c) CBC	(3) the special group of men and women who make the rules for Canadian radio and television stations
(d) NORAD	(4) a powerful missile that can cross long distances from one continent to another

3. Write the letters from (a) to (e) on your paper. Then write a T if the statement is TRUE. Write an F if the statement is FALSE.

   (a) If someone owns more than half of a company's shares, then that person says how the company is run.
   (b) Only a few companies in Canada are controlled by Americans.

(c) Canada and the United States are military allies.
(d) The United States does not care what happens in Canadian air space.
(e) Almost all Canadians live within 300 km of the American border.

4. There are 5 blanks in the following paragraphs about trade and investment between Canada and the United States. They have been labelled from (a) to (e). Write down the 5 answers in a list on your paper. Then beside each answer write the letter of the blank where it belongs.

   jobs　　import
   tax　　70%
   export

   Canada and the United States are big trading partners. In fact, (a) ______ of our foreign trade is with the United States. This can be a problem if the United States suddenly decides to put a higher (b) ______ on goods from Canada. We (c) ______ many raw materials to the United States. In turn, we (d) ______ many manufactured goods. Some Canadians feel that we lose (e) ______ because of this.

UNIT FIVE

Our Place in the World

Not so long ago, it took 3 *weeks* to travel from North America to Europe. Now the supersonic Concorde can whisk you there in just over 3 *hours*. In the same way, news of events on the other side of the world used to take weeks or even months to reach us. Now television satellites beam the news into our homes almost instantly.

The world has become a very small place. Canadians now visit dozens of other countries around the globe. We trade goods with some of these countries. We send aid to others. And sometimes we even try to change the way other countries are behaving.

All of this is part of Canada's foreign policy. It is part of the plan our government has for dealing with other countries in the world.

Of course Canadian foreign policy didn't spring up overnight. It has been shaped over many years by many world events. And our foreign policy won't always remain the same. It is constantly changing to fit the new events that occur every day on this planet.

The symbol for this unit is a globe. The globes pictured here show how the world has "shrunk" because of improvements in transportation.

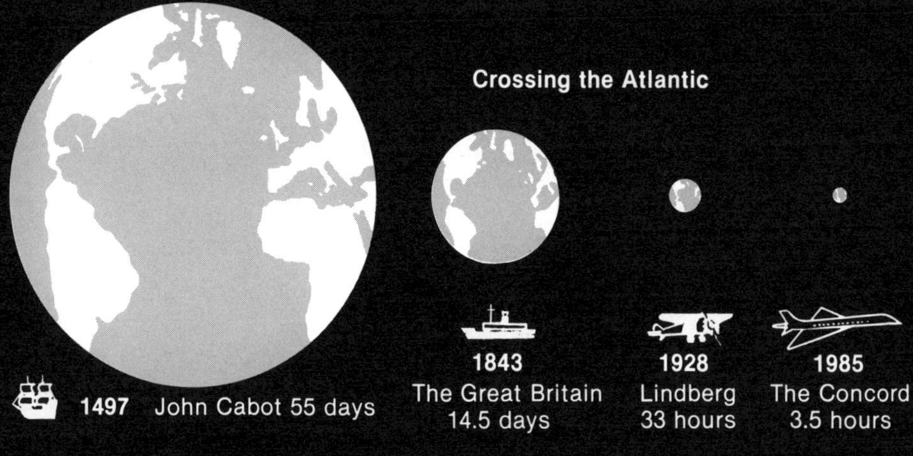

CHAPTER NINE

Canada's Century

The great Canadian prime minister, Wilfrid Laurier, once said that the twentieth century would belong to Canada. What he meant was that Canada would become an important world power.

Perhaps Laurier was too optimistic. As it has turned out, Canada is not one of the important world powers such as the United States and the Soviet Union. On the other hand, Canada does have power. It can still sometimes influence the way other countries in the world behave.

The lessons in this chapter tell the story of how Canada developed this power. They tell the story of how Canada changed from being a colony of Britain to being a power in its own right.

Canadians at War

57

In 1914, Archduke Franz Ferdinand of the Austro-Hungarian Empire was visiting a town in the country we now call Yugoslavia. A stranger stepped out of the crowd. He leaned into the Archduke's car. Then he shot both the Archduke and his wife.

You have probably never heard of the Archduke. And this is not surprising. Many Canadians and Britons living in 1914 had not heard of him either. Nevertheless, the **assassination** of the Archduke sparked what came to be known as the Great War — World War I.

The events that led from the assassination to the war were complicated. However, they were not the real cause. Europeans had been expecting a war for several years. And the assassination of the Archduke gave them a good excuse to start the fighting.

Figure 57.1 *A Canadian battalion goes "over the top", charging out of the trenches towards the enemy. What weapons do the soldiers carry with them?*

Figure 57.2 Voting at the front *Home seemed awfully far away when you were on the front lines. But it seemed a lot closer when there was a chance to vote in an election. These soldiers were voting in a Canadian federal election.*

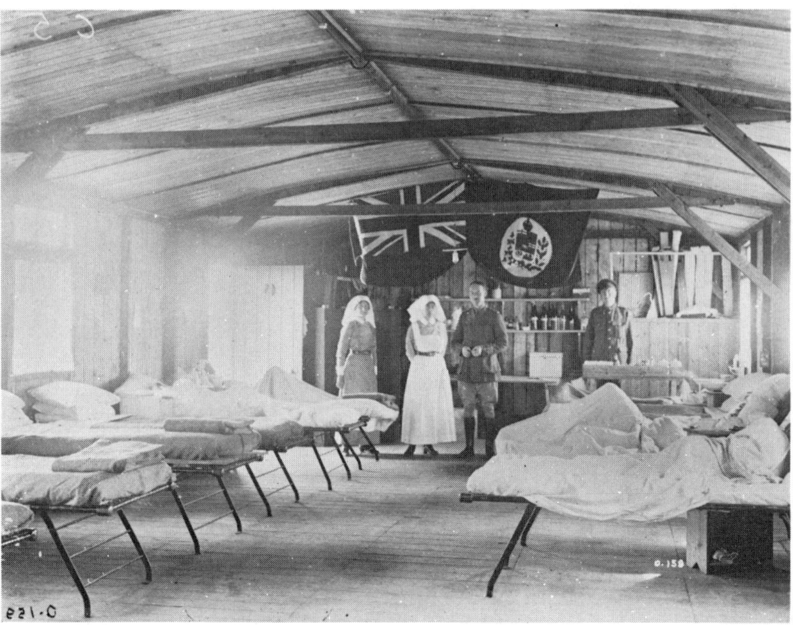

Figure 57.3 A casualty clearing station, 1916 *Hospitals were set up as close to the battlefront as possible in order to take care of the wounded. How is this station different from a modern hospital?*

The war was very much like a gang fight. Britain, France, Russia, and Italy were on one side. Germany and the Austro-Hungarian Empire were on the other.

As soon as Britain declared war on Germany, Canada was committed to join the British side. Most Europeans didn't expect that a colony like Canada could make much of a difference in the fighting. The Canadian army only had 3110 members. And Canada didn't own very many weapons or ships.

But the Europeans were wrong. Thousands of young Canadians volunteered immediately. And less than 2 months after war had been declared, Canada had already sent 30 000 soldiers overseas.

Most of the Canadians who volunteered immediately believed that the fighting would soon be over. In fact, most people expected the war would last for only a year.

No one imagined that the war would last for 4 years. And no one was prepared for how horrible it would be. By the time World War I came to an end, more than 30 million people had either died or been wounded.

When the Canadian troops reached the battlefront, they found the opposing armies facing each other in 2 long lines. These lines stretched for hundreds of kilometres across France and the Netherlands.

Canadian poet John McRae, author of "In Flanders Fields", died of pneumonia in 1918.

Figure 57.4 The Dumbells *The Dumbells were a group of entertainers who gave performances to the troops in World War I. They all came from the 3rd Canadian Division serving in France. This photograph shows the entire company in the closing number from their show. Why would such entertainers be important in wartime?*

The enemy lines were only a few metres apart. They were separated by rolls of barbed wire and land mines. The land in between was called "no man's land".

The soldiers on both sides lived in mud ditches called **trenches**. They dug these trenches themselves. And they stood, sat, ate, and slept in them. Life in the trenches was cold, wet, and miserable. The soldiers could never escape the mud. They were never dry. Lice and rats added to the misery.

In order to fight, the soldiers in the trenches would crawl "over the top" into no man's land. The enemy would shoot at them with machine guns and rifles. If enough soldiers made it across, the enemy soldiers would be chased out of their trenches and forced back.

If only a few soldiers made it across no man's land, the **advance** would fail. They would have to **retreat** back to their own trenches. Those who had been shot down in no man's land would lie there in agony and wait for death. Sometimes thousands of soldiers would fall there and die in the mud.

Throughout most of the 4 years of World War I, the lines of trenches changed very little. Many thousands of soldiers were **sacrificed** trying to push the enemy back just a few metres.

The Canadian soldiers had been kept together in the same fighting units. And they soon proved themselves to be extremely brave. Their first major test was at Ypres, a very old town in Belgium. One mild April evening there was a

More than 2800 Canadian nurses died in the fighting in World War I. 

The first sub-Atlantic cable was laid between Trinity Bay, Newfoundland, and Valentin, Ireland, in 1858.

gentle breeze. The Germans decided to use chlorine gas for the very first time.

No one on the Canadians' side was prepared for this. The clouds of greenish smoke blinded and choked the troops. Soldiers on either side of the Canadian division fled in pain. But the Canadians held firm. They defended their trenches courageously. And the Germans were unable to break through the line.

The Canadian soldiers proved their bravery again and again throughout the war at places like Somme and Passchendaele and Vimy Ridge. But the cost in lives was terrible. In all, more than 60 000 young Canadians were killed in the fighting.

THE FACTS

Remembering Facts

1. What side did Canada fight on in World War I?
2. How long did World War I last?
3. What was "no man's land"?
4. What was life like for the soldiers in the trenches?
5. How good were the Canadians at fighting in World War I?

Finding Facts

The Canadians were involved in many battles in World War I. The most important ones were

Ypres,
The Somme,
Passchendaele, and
Vimy Ridge.

Use an encyclopedia or other books to find out more about 1 of these battles. Draw a map showing where the battle happened. Explain why the battle was important. Tell who won the battle.

YOUR OPINIONS

Stating Opinions

To start a battle, the soldiers would go "over the top" of the trenches. Many times they knew for sure they would die. But they still went when their officers told them to.

Do you think *you* would have gone "over the top", even when you knew for sure you would die? Explain your opinion in a few sentences.

Discussing Opinions

In some ways, World War I began because many people *wanted* to have a war. Do you think that some people today *want* to have a war? Do you think there ever are any good reasons for declaring war?

NEW WORDS

Learning Words

In your notebook, write the title Vocabulary: Lesson 57. Then write down the following words in a list. Using the Glossary or a dictionary, write the meaning beside each word.

When you are finished, write a short note telling what you have learned in this lesson. Try to use all 5 of these words in your note.

advance **assassination** **retreat**
sacrifice **trench**

Examining Words

The expression "no man's land" came out of World War I. Two other expressions that came out of this war are "trench coat" and "shell shock". Can you explain what these 2 expressions mean? Can you explain how they are related to World War I?

AN ILLUSTRATION

Table 57.1 lists the enlistment and casualty rates for 1917. How does this table help to explain why the Canadian government voted for conscription? What does it tell you about what life was like on the front lines?

MONTH	ENLISTMENTS	CASUALTIES
January	9 194	4 396
February	6 809	1 250
March	6 640	6 161
April	5 530	13 477
May	6 407	13 457
June	6 348	7 931
July	3 882	7 906
August	3 117	13 232
September	3 588	10 990
October	4 884	5 929
November	4 019	30 741
December	3 921	7 476

SOURCE: Hux and Jarman, *Canada: A Growing Concern Globe/Modern Curriculum Press*

Table 57.1 *The number of enlistments compared with the number of casualties in 1917*

Wilfred May

Figure 57.5 *May standing by his plane*

Claim to fame: He was an air ace in World War I.

Born: 1896 in Carberry, Manitoba.

Career: May joined the Canadian army in 1916. He fought in the trenches before joining the Royal Flying Corps.

On his first flight, May's guns jammed. The legendary Red Baron (who had already shot down 80 planes) started to attack May. But another Canadian, Roy Brown, saw what was happening. He saved May by shooting down the Baron.

May shot down 18 planes before the war ended in 1918. He returned home to Canada. For a time, he did stunt flying. For example, he flew the mayor of Edmonton 3 m above the baseball diamond. This way, the mayor could make the opening pitch of the season from the air.

May also opened an airline company with his wartime friend, Vic Horner. They made the first winter flight into the North in January, 1929. They flew through a terrible blizzard to bring a vaccine to Fort Vermillion.

May also helped the RCMP track down Albert Johnson, the man they called the Mad Trapper of Rat River. Johnson was killed by the Mounties. But in the fighting, one of the officers was badly wounded. May saved the officer's life by flying him to hospital.

Died: May stopped flying in 1935 when he lost an eye. But he worked with airline companies and the RCAF until he died in 1952.

- **Who was the Red Baron? How did he get his name?**
- **Would you like to learn how to fly an airplane?**

Canadians on the Home Front

58

The war was a terrible experience for the young Canadians who served in the army overseas. But it was also very hard on those left at home. From the moment the war started, the whole country became involved.

The first thing that was needed was food. In Europe, many of the young farmers who should have been ploughing fields were now carrying rifles. And much of the **precious** farmland that should have been sown with seed had been turned into a battleground. Somehow the millions of soldiers had to be fed.

Canadians went to work immediately. People from every part of the country pitched in. Farmers worked many extra hours to grow larger crops of wheat. City dwellers volunteered time to work on the farms and help harvest the crops. Ordinary people grew their own vegetables instead of buying them. And Canadians everywhere tried to cut down the amount of food they ate.

All this effort paid off. Canadians were able to send many tonnes of wheat overseas. They also exported cheese and pork and beef to help feed the millions of soldiers.

The soldiers fighting overseas also needed weapons. They needed rifles and **ammunition**. The problem was that before the war there were not many Canadian factories. And only a few of these factories specialized in making weapons.

Almost as soon as war was declared, owners started to change the factories that already existed. Steel companies that used to make construction materials now started to make shell cases. Companies that had made explosives for mining now started to make bullets.

In addition, many new factories were built. Many new businesses were started to help manufacture all the weapons and trucks and aircraft and other equipment that the soldiers used.

Figure 58.1 *Home was not safe from disaster during World War I either. In 1916, the Parliament buildings caught fire in Ottawa. Flames had broken out in the reading room and spread quickly through the entire building. This photograph was taken the morning after the fire. What famous picture was burned during this fire? (Hint: check the Maple Leaf Facts in Lesson 1.)*

Note: You can learn more about the war at home in Lesson 38.

Figure 58.2 *Victory Loan parades were a common sight during World War I. Pictured here is the Canadian Aeroplane Victory Loan float from a parade in 1917. What is the message of this float?*

In fact, the war was a golden opportunity for people in business. There was a big demand for their products. Luckily, most manufacturers were happy just to make a fair profit. But some manufacturers decided to use the situation for their own good. They charged unfairly high prices because the soldiers needed this equipment so desperately.

The manufacturers who charged unfair prices were called "war **profiteers**". They only thought about themselves. They didn't care about the quality of their products. And they didn't care about other Canadians such as the soldiers at the front.

The worst example of profiteering in World War I was the Ross rifle. This was the rifle made in Canada for Canadian soldiers. The trouble was that it heated up too quickly. If a soldier had to fire the rifle rapidly, it would jam. Sometimes the rifle would backfire and actually kill the Canadian soldier who was trying to use it.

The profiteering also hurt Canadians at home. Some business people started charging high prices for **essential** goods like food and clothing. Many ordinary people had a hard time making ends meet.

Of course the war was also costing the government a lot of money. And so the government had to think up ways to get this money from Canadians.

From the beginning, the government sold Victory Bonds. Canadians were asked to buy these bonds from the government. It was just like giving the government a loan. Canadians would be given interest for their money. And they could get their money back at the end of the war.

The world's first radio station was Montreal's XWA, which began broadcasting in 1919. Today the station is known as CFCF.

Figure 58.3 *By the end of World War I, more than 30 000 women were working in munitions factories. Many thousands of others took on jobs usually thought of as men's work. These women were photographed in 1917 threading set-screw holes at the Russell Motor Car Co. Are their working conditions different from what you would expect to find in a factory today?*

Figure 58.4 *Even before the war started, women were beginning to break away from their traditional roles. This is a photograph of Lucille Mulhall, the 1912 champion woman bucking-horse rider of the world. Would a woman be considered unusual these days for riding bucking horses?*

Millions of dollars were raised through the Victory Bonds. But still it was not enough. So in 1917 the government decided to introduce income tax. This was meant to be a **temporary** measure. No one expected that income taxes would last for long. But they are still with us today.

Another permanent effect of World War I had to do with the role of women. Women began to break out of their traditional roles as housewives. They were needed to work in the new factories. They were needed to work as doctors and lawyers. And they were needed to work as bankers and civil servants.

As women took more and more jobs outside the home, there was new pressure to give them the right to vote. By the end of World War I, the government had taken the first steps to give all women the right to vote.

World War I made many changes in the Canadian lifestyle. And as you will learn in the next lesson, it also changed the way other countries in the world thought about Canada.

In 1889, writer Sara Duncan of Brantford, Ontario, scandalized the country by travelling around the world without a chaperone.

THE FACTS

Remembering Facts

1. Why was it difficult to feed the soldiers in World War I?
2. How did Canadians help to solve the food problem?
3. Why were so many new factories built?
4. How did the government raise money to pay for the war?
5. How did the war change the role of women?

Finding Facts

During World War I, there was another terrible disaster at home — the Halifax explosion. Read other books or encyclopedias to learn more about the disaster. Then answer the following questions.

1. When did the explosion occur?
2. How did it happen?
3. What were the results of the explosion?

Canadian author Hugh MacLennan wrote a novel about the Halifax explosion. What is his novel called?

YOUR OPINIONS

Stating Opinions

Which would you prefer — working on a farm to harvest crops or working in a factory making weapons? Explain your opinion in a few sentences.

Discussing Opinions

Most business is based on something called *supply and demand*. For example, imagine that a store has several copies of a record for sale. If only a few people want to buy the record, then the store will probably have to lower the price in order to get rid of the extra copies. On the other hand, if many people want to buy the record, then the store can charge a higher price and still be sure of selling all the copies.

This idea of supply and demand explains why there were profiteers in World War I. Because the soldiers needed certain supplies very badly, the manufacturers could charge very high prices for them.

Many Canadians in World War I were angry about this situation. They thought the government should pass a law to control prices. Do you think this law would have been fair to the manufacturers? What would the government have needed to do to put this law into action?

NEW WORDS

Learning Words

In your notebook, write the title Vocabulary: Lesson 58. Then write down the following words in a list. Using the

Glossary or a dictionary, write the meaning beside each word.

When you are finished, write a short note telling what you have learned in this lesson. Try to use all 5 of these words in your note.

ammunition	**essential**	**precious**
profiteer	**temporary**	

Examining Words

A "golden opportunity" is a good thing. It is an excellent chance to do well. Do you know any other common phrases about gold? Why do you think gold is used and not some other substance like silver or steel?

AN ILLUSTRATION

Figure 58.5 shows the annual average price of wheat from 1912 to 1920. Like today's cost-of-living index, this graph is based on an index of 100. The average price of wheat between 1909 and 1913 is taken as a starting point. The amount of wheat you could buy for $100 in 1909 cost $188 in 1916. What happened to the price of wheat during the war years? How do you explain this change?

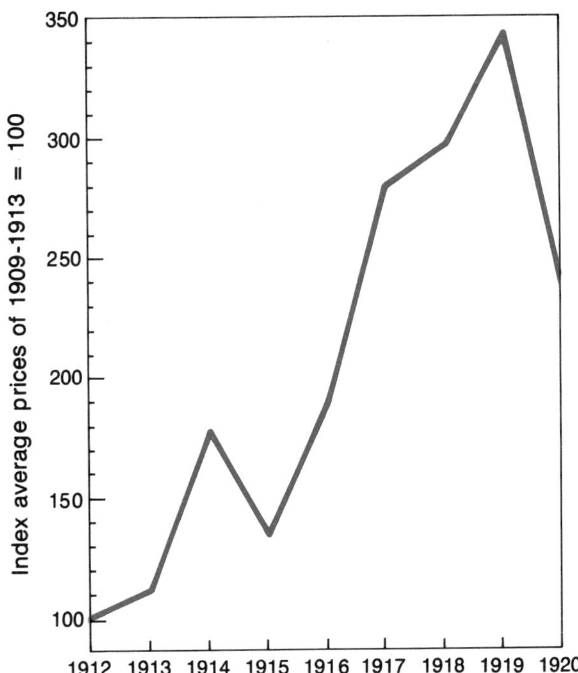

SOURCE: Canada Year Book 1920

Figure 58.5 *The average price of wheat, 1912-1920*

E. Cora Hind

Figure 58.6 *E. Cora Hind examining wheat in the field*

Claim to fame: She was a journalist who became world famous for her annual estimates of the Canadian wheat crop.

Born: 1861 in Toronto. She was orphaned at an early age.

Career: In 1882, Cora Hind moved to Winnipeg. She wanted to become a journalist. But this was considered a man's profession. So instead, she taught herself to type and became the first typist in western Canada.

By 1893, Hind had opened her own company. She hired typists to do secretarial work for other firms. This gave her a chance to try journalism again.

Eventually, she was hired by *The Winnipeg Free Press* as agricultural editor. Her most important job was to give estimates about how much wheat would be grown each year. To do this, she travelled for weeks across the prairies, talking to farmers and checking on the young crop.

Hind's estimates were always incredibly accurate. Her most famous estimate came in 1904 when the Americans said there would be very poor crops in Canada. Hind disagreed. She said there would be good crops. They laughed at her. But she was right. From then on, everyone listened to Hind.

Hind worked day and night to improve agriculture in Canada. She was given many awards. And when she was 74, *The Winnipeg Free Press* sent her on a trip around the world. The trip lasted 2 years. She later wrote a book about her travels.

Died: E. Cora Hind died in Winnipeg in 1942.

- **Look at the names of the journalists in your newspaper. How many are men? How many are women?**
- **Would you enjoy travelling for 2 whole years without a break?**

The Return of Peace 59

World War I ended on November 11, 1918, at 11:00: the eleventh hour of the eleventh day of the eleventh month. Britain and its allies had won.

More than 600 000 Canadians had fought to win this victory. But more than 1 in 10, or about 60 000, would never return: they had died on the battlefield. Thousands of others were wounded: many were permanently disabled.

This was a huge sacrifice for such a small country as Canada. Before the war, other countries in the world had not thought much about Canada. To them, it was just a part of Britain. But now there was new **respect** for Canada because of the sacrifice it had made.

Figure 59.1 *A family poses in front of their home to celebrate the return of troops from World War I. What flags are hanging from the windows?*

Figure 59.2 *Unfortunately, troops returning from Europe also brought with them a deadly flu virus. Thousands died from this virus in the first year after the war. Face masks like these were a common sight. Can you explain why people would wear them?*

This new respect was clear in the Treaty of Versailles. This was the peace treaty that ended the war. Each country sent teams to work out what the treaty should say. Before, Canada would just have been part of the British team. But now, Canada was allowed to send its own separate team.

Another proof that Canada was now accepted as a country in its own right — and not just as a British colony — came with the **League** of Nations. This was a group mainly of European countries. Their goal was to prevent any more world wars.

Canada became a separate member of the League of Nations. It was recognized as an equal partner with other countries. Canadian representatives went to meetings of the League. At these meetings they voted on different ways to keep peace.

For a while, there was peace and **prosperity** for all the countries who had been on the winning side. This was the time known as the "Roaring Twenties".

During the war, many new factories had been built to make weapons. Now these factories were changed to make products for the home. For the first time, people could buy appliances like electric ovens and toasters, washing machines and vacuum cleaners.

During the war, manufacturers had built fighter aircraft and tanks. Now they made products for peacetime transportation. Aircraft were built to take the mail across Canada. Electric streetcars were built to transport people in large cities. And thousands of people were soon able to buy their first cars.

The 2000 metal workers who joined the Winnipeg General Strike in 1919 were fighting for a minimum hourly wage of 85¢.

Canadians also had more time for **leisure** activities. This was the golden era of Hollywood. People flocked to movie

Figure 59.3 *Many families were extremely poor during the 1920s. In this photograph, young girls scramble under railway cars to gather fallen coal. For some families, this was their only source of heat. What dangers would these girls have faced in trying to gather coal in the railway yards?*

theatres each week. They might see a comedy starring Charlie Chaplin, who played a funny little tramp. Or they might see a romantic adventure starring Mary Pickford. She was the Canadian actress who was called "America's Sweetheart".

It was also the golden age of sports. Western and Eastern football teams competed in the Grey Cup for the first time in 1921. *Hockey Night in Canada* had its first broadcast on the radio in 1923. Canadians shone in worldwide sports as well. In the 1928 Olympic games in Holland, the Canadian athletes won a total of 15 medals.

On the surface, life seemed to be full of fun and excitement. Crazy dances such as the Charleston were all the rage. Young girls called "flappers" dressed in daring short skirts. People sang songs like "Happy Days Are Here Again."

But the Roaring Twenties had a darker side. Not everyone could afford the new electric appliances and cars. Not everyone could afford to go to the movies and dances. In fact, many workers in Canada were very poor.

The problem went back to the war. During the war, prices had doubled. But factory workers did not get big raises. When the soldiers came back at the end of the war, there were not enough jobs to go around. So that meant the employers could still keep the wages low.

In 1919, Alcock and Brown won £10 000 for being the first to fly across the Atlantic from Newfoundland to England.

Figure 59.4 *This photograph was taken during the Winnipeg strike of 1919. The billboard is an advertisement for Sweet Clover bacon and pork sausage. What do you think the strikers might have felt about this advertisement?*

Many workers tried to **protest** against this situation. On May 15, 1919, they called a general strike in Winnipeg. More than 22 000 workers went on strike. Some people called them communists. They thought these workers wanted to destroy the government. The strike was ended on June 21, when 2 demonstrators were shot and killed by police.

In 1920, critics hated the first exhibition of work by Canada's now world-famous painters, the Group of Seven.

There were strikes like this in other countries. But many people tried to ignore these protcsts. They wanted to forget about war and hardship. They wanted to have a good time. They didn't suspect that another world disaster was waiting just around the corner.

THE FACTS

Remembering Facts

1. How did the war change the attitude of other countries to Canada?
2. What happened to the factories that had made weapons for war?
3. What did life *seem* to be like in the "Roaring Twenties"?
4. Why were wages so low after the war?
5. What did Canadian workers do to fight their low wages?

Finding Facts

The role of women changed after the war. Before, women had been expected to stay at home. Now women were making headlines in many different fields.

Choose 1 of the following women. Find out who she was and what she did that made her famous.

- Ethel Catherwood
- Marie Dressler
- Henrietta Muir Edwards
- Emily Carr
- Ada MacKenzie

YOUR OPINIONS

Stating Opinions

It's hard to imagine life without electric appliances. If you could have only 1 electric appliance in your home, which would you keep? Explain your opinion in a few sentences.

Discussing Opinions

Very few strikes end with killing as happened in the Winnipeg general strike. But even today you will often read in the paper about violence on picket lines.

Is there ever any justifiable reason for strikers to become violent? Is there ever any justifiable reason for the police to become violent in controlling picket lines? How can picket line violence be stopped?

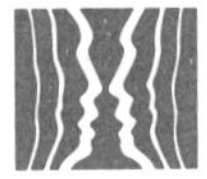

NEW WORDS

Learning Words

In your notebook, write the title Vocabulary: Lesson 59. Then write down the following words in a list. Using the Glossary or a dictionary, write the meaning beside each word.

When you are finished, write a short note telling what you have learned in this lesson. Try to use all 5 of these words in your note.

league **leisure** **prosperity**
protest **respect**

Examining Words

Famous or important people are sometimes given labels. For example, Mary Pickford was known as "America's Sweetheart".

Do you know any modern entertainers, athletes, or politicians who have been given labels?

AN ILLUSTRATION

During the 1920s the painters in Canada's famous Group of Seven began working together. Look in art books to find examples of the work of at least 3 different painters in this group. Write down the name of the painter you like most. Also write down the name of one of this painter's pictures and the place where it is hanging.

Fanny (Bobbie) Rosenfeld

Figure 59.5 *Fanny Rosenfeld at the 1928 Olympics, standing on the far right with other members of the women's relay team after winning the gold medal*

Claim to fame: She was one of Canada's greatest woman athletes.

Born: 1905 in Russia

Career: The Rosenfelds came to Ontario when Bobbie was still very young. As a girl, Bobbie was always active in sports.

One day Rosenfeld was playing in a softball tournament near her home town of Barrie. A track and field event was being run at the same time. At the last moment, Rosenfeld decided to enter the 100-yard* dash. She won the race. Then she discovered that one of the runners she had beaten was the Canadian champion — Rosa Grosse.

Rosenfeld moved to Toronto in 1922. She spent every spare minute at sports. It didn't matter what the sport was. It could be hockey, basketball, tennis, track and field. She won in them all.

In 1925, Rosenfeld entered the Ontario Ladies' Track and Field Championships. She won 4 firsts and 2 seconds. In 1928, Rosenfeld was a member of Canada's first women's track and field team at the Amsterdam Olympics. The team was outstanding and won gold and silver medals.

Unfortunately, just after the Olympics, Rosenfeld suffered a severe attack of arthritis. She was on crutches for more than a year. And she could no longer compete actively in sports. In 1949, Rosenfeld was one of the first athletes to be named to Canada's Sports Hall of Fame.

Died: Rosenfeld worked as a sports columnist until 3 years before her death in 1969.

- **Anne Ottenbrite, Sylvie Bernier, Lori Fung, and Carling Bassett are outstanding Canadian athletes. Find out more about 1 of these women.**
- **Should boys and girls be allowed to play on the same sports teams?**

*A yard is slightly less than a metre.

The Depression 60

One thing that really was "roaring" in the twenties was the stock market in the United States. After 1921, prices for stocks kept rising higher and higher. **Investors** made money quickly and easily.

One way investors made money was to buy stocks "on margin". That meant they did not actually pay the full price of the stocks they bought.

For example, an investor might buy $100 worth of stocks from a stockbroker. But the investor would only have to pay the **broker** $10 right away. The investor would just promise to pay the other $90 to the broker whenever the broker asked for it.

Usually brokers would not ask for this money. They would wait for the price of the stocks to go up. For example, the $100 worth of stocks might soon be worth $150.

The investor would then sell the stocks for $150. He or she would then pay the broker the $90 that was owed. And the investor would keep the rest as profit.

Figure 60.1 Members of a woman's club in Montreal making clothes for families without work, 1930s *Many charitable groups like this were operating in the Depression. How do these women seem to be feeling about what they are doing?*

Figure 60.2 The "On-to-Ottawa Trek" *Unemployed workers who were living in relief camps in the Vancouver area finally rebelled in 1935. One thousand of them jumped onto box cars to travel to Ottawa in an effort to get government action. They were stopped at Regina, where they rioted for a full day. Eventually the government closed the relief camps.*

This system was fine as long as the prices of stocks were going higher. But in September of 1929, prices began to fall. Brokers began to ask for the money that was owed to them.

Many investors did not have this money. They had depended on the stock prices to go up. So the investors had to sell their stocks. Suddenly, everyone was trying to sell stocks. And nobody wanted to buy. On October 29, "Black Tuesday", the stock market crashed.

The stock market crash was in the United States. But it had a big effect on many other countries in the world. Canada was very badly hurt by the crash.

The problem was that the Americans could no longer afford to buy goods from other countries. That meant that Canadian manufacturers had fewer people to buy their products. They had to lay off many workers. And the ones who weren't laid off had their wages cut.

The factories no longer needed as many raw materials. So workers like miners and lumberjacks were laid off. People who had lost their jobs couldn't afford to buy as much food. So fishermen and farmers couldn't make as much money as they had.

The whole situation was like a row of dominoes. The stock market crash was like the first domino. When it fell, all the rest followed.

The people who had lost their jobs were desperate. Today we have unemployment insurance and welfare. But there were no services like that during the Depression.

Thousands of men started "riding the rails". They would jump onto freight trains and travel from one city to the next looking for work. But there were almost no jobs.

Arctic terns fly 32 000 km each year just so that they can spend their winters in the Antarctic.

Figure 60.3 *Farmers were hit especially hard in the Depression. Here, a forlorn farmer watches as the wind tears away his land. To the left is a farmer and his family who have had to abandon their farm and move to the city. What chances do you think the farmer had of making a living in the city?*

The government set up **relief** camps for some of these men. But the conditions were horrible. The men had to work 8 hours a day at hard labour such as building roads. In return they were given clothes, **lodging**, and 20¢ a day.

The real problem was that there was nothing to do in the camps after work. But the men were not allowed to leave the camps. They were not even allowed to vote.

It was true that the relief camps were terrible. But the people who suffered the most in the Depression were the wheat farmers on the prairies. It was hard enough for them to sell their crops. And then there was a natural disaster to add to their problems.

Canada's most popular historic site is Signal Hill, Newfoundland, where Marconi made the first trans-Atlantic radio broadcast in 1925.

Figure 60.4 *Life was not all misery during the Depression. Here, crowds breathlessly watch Houdini, the famous escape artist. He is hanging head down in a strait-jacket 9 m above Carlton Street in Winnipeg just before his escape. Can you find where he is in the photograph?*

From 1933 to 1938 there was almost no rain on the prairies. The topsoil was like dust. And strong winds blew it away in swirling clouds. Only a little of the seed that was planted could grow in these conditions. And then to add to the misery, swarms of grasshoppers ate all the wheat they could find.

Life was a struggle. There was no money for shoes. Clothing was often made out of burlap flour bags. People lived on the gophers they could catch in the wild. Many prairie farmers couldn't keep up their **mortgage** payments. In the end, more than a quarter of them lost their farms.

The Depression lasted 10 long, hard years. Canadian voters became angry about the situation. First they elected the Conservatives. Then they elected the Liberals. But no government seemed able to make a difference.

In fact, the government had little real control. The Depression had started because of events in the United States. It only came to an end because of events in Europe.

In 1984, Canadian chefs won the World Culinary Olympics with their mousseline of pike and duck stuffed with wild mushrooms.

THE FACTS

Remembering Facts

1. What did it mean to buy stocks "on margin"?
2. Why was it a problem when stock prices began to fall in 1929?
3. How did the American stock market crash affect Canada?
4. What was life like in the relief camps?
5. Why did prairie farmers suffer the most during the Depression?

Finding Facts

Today, investors are not allowed to buy stocks on margin. They have to pay most of the cost of their shares immediately.

However, credit cards use a modern form of margin payment. Find out the answers to the following questions about credit and credit cards:

1. What is credit?
2. Who can get a credit card?
3. How do credit cards work?
4. What is a credit limit?
5. What are the dangers of credit cards?

To answer these questions, read pamphlets put out by the credit companies. Or speak to a bank manager. Or invite a financial expert to talk to your class about credit.

YOUR OPINIONS

Stating Opinions

In the 1930s, most people were ashamed to accept welfare. Do you think this attitude was sensible? Or do you think this attitude was silly? Explain your opinion in a few sentences.

Discussing Opinions

Many manufacturers had to lay off employees during the Depression. They would lay off single men and females before they would lay off married men. They did this because they felt that the married men needed the jobs more.

Today, most manufacturers lay people off according to how long they have worked for them. "Last hired, first fired" is the policy.

Which system do you think is best?

NEW WORDS

Learning Words

In your notebook, write the title Vocabulary: Lesson 60. Then write down the following words in a list. Using the Glossary or a dictionary, write the meaning beside each word.

When you are finished, write a short note telling what you have learned in this lesson. Try to use all 5 of these words in your note.

broker	**investor**	**lodging**
mortgage	**relief**	

Examining Words

The word *domino* is spelled without an *e* on the end. But the dictionary says that the plural of *domino* can be written either *dominos* or *dominoes*. Which way do you think looks best?

How do you spell the plural form of the following words that end in *o*? Check your spellings with a dictionary to make sure they are acceptable.

bravo	hello
potato	tomato

AN ILLUSTRATION

The graph in Figure 60.5 shows the employment rates in Canada from 1926 to 1934. The coloured line shows the annual average. The black line shows the employment rate over the 12 months of each year. Can you explain why the black line moves up and down in the way it does? When was the time of highest employment? When was the time of lowest employment?

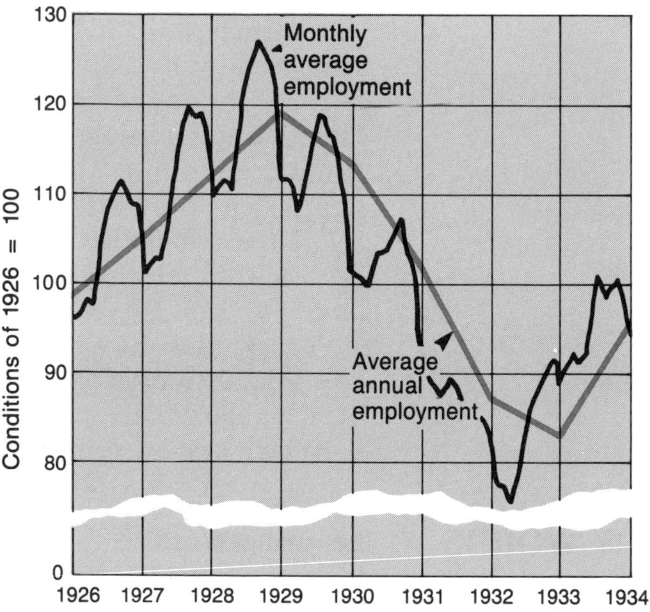

SOURCE: Canada Year Book 1934-35

Figure 60.5 *Employment rates, 1926-34*

Hanka Romanchych Kowalchuck

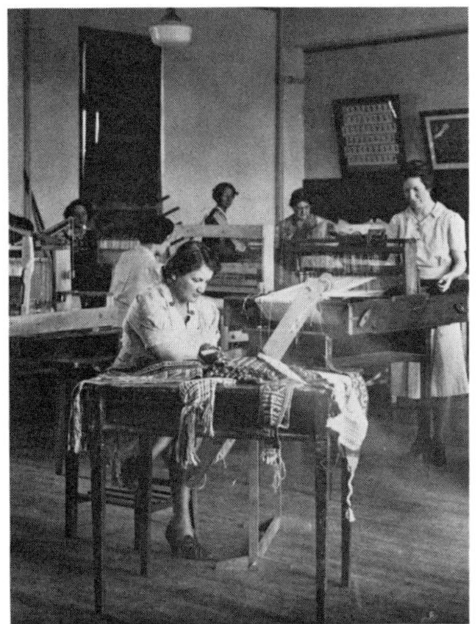

Figure 60.6 *Hanka Romanchych Kowalchuck is sitting in the middle foreground conducting a weaving class.*

Claim to fame: She helped families during the Depression.

Born: 1907 in Dauphin, Manitoba

Career: After attending high school in Manitoba, Kowalchuck started at university. But 2 years later, her father forced her to drop out. He had decided that university was a waste for a girl. If he had let her go on, she would have been the first Ukrainian girl to graduate from university in Canada.

Instead, Kowalchuck went to work for the government of Alberta. Her job was to help community groups. When the Depression came, she worked 10 to 18 hours every day to help families in distress.

For example, Kowalchuck organized groups of women to do crafts such as weaving and painting. Then she sold their work to big stores like Macy's in New York City. The women earned enough to pay for such things as food and farm machinery.

Kowalchuck also worked for women across the world. In 1934, she went to a meeting of Ukrainian women in Poland. In 1936, she was asked by the League of Nations to speak about the status of women in Canada.

When World War II started, Kowalchuck threw herself into the war effort. She travelled from coast to coast 27 times in order to help sell bonds. Afterwards, she worked for Canadian women's groups. She was a major supporter of International Women's Year in 1975.

Died: Kowalchuck died peacefully in October, 1984.

- **Hanka Kowalchuck also opened a museum of Ukrainian arts and crafts. Find a picture of some of these crafts.**
- **How have our attitudes toward women and education changed?**

61 World War Returns

Life in Canada was hard during the Depression. But it was even harder for the people in Europe. The trench warfare in World War I had destroyed many farms and small towns. It took a lot of time and effort and money for the people to rebuild.

The German people were in the worst situation. This was partly caused by the Treaty of Versailles that had ended World War I. This treaty forced Germany to pay billions of dollars for the damage caused in the fighting.

It was terribly difficult for the German people to pay so much. Even worse, with all this money leaving the country, there wasn't enough extra money to create new jobs. By 1932, nearly 6 million Germans were out of work.

The Treaty of Versailles had hurt Germany in other ways. It took large sections of land away from Germany. And it forced the Germans to reduce their army to only a few thousand soldiers.

Figure 61.1 *In this photograph, Hitler is being saluted by his officers. The symbol on their armbands is a swastika. How do most people react to the swastika today?*

The Germans felt that they had been **humiliated** by the rest of the world. They blamed their government for causing the situation. So they were ready to accept new ideas and leaders.

The Nazis were a new political party led by Adolf Hitler. But they were more like an army than a political party. They dressed in brown-shirted uniforms. They marched to patriotic songs. They held mass **rallies**. They flew their own flag with the symbol of the swastika.

Many Germans were attracted to Nazi ideas. The Nazis said that the Germans were better than any other people. They said that the Germans were the master race.

Hitler gained control of Germany in 1933. He became an **absolute dictator**. Anyone who opposed him was put in jail or a concentration camp. He blamed many of Germany's troubles on the Jewish people. So he started a campaign to imprison and murder them. Hitler simply ignored all human rights.

Hitler also ignored the Treaty of Versailles. He built up the German army. And he started to take back the lands that Germany had lost because of the treaty.

Most Europeans did not want another war. But when Hitler marched into Poland on August 31, 1939, they could no longer ignore the situation. On September 3, Britain and France declared war on Germany.

When Britain declared war in 1914, Canada had automatically been at war, too. But things had changed since then. In 1931, the British Parliament had passed a law

Canadian ski champ Steve Podborski was the first non-European to win the World Cup in downhill skiing.

Figure 61.2 *Left to right in this photograph, you can see Prime Minister Mackenzie King of Canada, President Roosevelt of the United States, and Prime Minister Churchill of Britain. They met together in Quebec in 1943 to discuss the war effort.*

The National Film Board of Canada's award-winning films are seen by 500 million people each year in 134 countries.

called the Statute of Westminster. This law said that Canada was completely in charge of its own affairs. Britain could no longer speak for Canada.

The Canadian Parliament was not in session when Britain declared war. But Prime Minister Mackenzie King wanted all the MPs to vote about entering the war. So the MPs were quickly called back to Ottawa. They officially voted to enter the war 1 week after Britain, on September 10.

At first, Canada concentrated on sending supplies to Britain. Dozens of ships would leave together from Halifax. These **convoys**, as they were called, carried the weapons and food and clothing that were needed so badly overseas.

Throughout the war, the Germans attacked these convoys. It was the job of the Canadian Navy and Air Force to see that the convoys made it safely across the Atlantic. Luckily, they succeeded. If they had failed, Britain might have lost the war.

Even so, it did seem for a while that Britain and its allies might lose. By June of 1940, Hitler's troops controlled all of Europe. Even France had been conquered. Italy had sided with Germany. Only Britain stood against the German forces in Europe.

Figure 61.3 RCAF *pilots race to their Hawker "Hurricane" aircraft in France, c. 1940. What is the symbol on these planes?*

There was real fear that Hitler would invade Britain. German planes dropped bombs night after night on British cities. But by 1941 Hitler turned his attention to attacking Russia.

Russia and Japan had been enemies for a long time. So Japan was pleased that Hitler was keeping the Russians busy. In fact, Japan took advantage of this to attack the United States. The Americans came into the war on the side of Britain and Canada. And at the same time, Britain and Canada declared war on the Japanese. It had truly become a *world* war.

The breakthrough came in 1944. On D-day, June 6, British, Canadian, and American troops crossed the English Channel and invaded France. The Canadian troops fought through Belgium and the Netherlands towards Berlin, the capital of Germany. Other Canadians landed in Italy and slowly worked their way northwards.

It took nearly a year of hard fighting. But on May 8, 1945, the Germans surrendered. The war in Europe was over.

During World War II, Canadians tried to make an iceberg large enough to serve as a refuelling stop for planes crossing the Atlantic.

Figure 61.4 *These soldiers from the Canadian army were passing through a village in France. The fresh eggs they are cooking must have been a welcome break from their regular rations. Why would food such as eggs be scarce during war time?*

THE FACTS

Remembering Facts

1. Why was the Depression so terrible in Germany?
2. Who were the Nazis?
3. Why didn't Canada declare war at the same time as Britain?
4. Why was the name *world* war so suitable for this war?
5. Where did Canadian soldiers fight in Europe?

Finding Facts

When people talk about World War II, certain place names often rise in the conversation. Choose one of the following place names. Locate this place on a map. Find out why this place was important in World War II.

- Dieppe
- Dunkirk
- Hiroshima
- Pearl Harbour
- Warsaw

YOUR OPINIONS

Stating Opinions

Some people enjoy wearing a uniform. Others hate it. How do you feel about uniforms? Express your opinion in a few sentences.

Discussing Opinions

The treaty at the end of World War I punished Germany. The Germans were forced to pay huge sums of money. They lost land and most of their army.

At the end of World War II, the United States started something called the Marshall Plan. The Americans poured billions of dollars back into Germany to help rebuild the towns and cities, factories, and farms.

Which approach do you think was best? Which approach do you think was fairest? Discuss your opinions with your classmates.

NEW WORDS

Learning Words

In your notebook, write the title Vocabulary: Lesson 61. Then write down the following words in a list. Using the Glossary or a dictionary, write the meaning beside each word.

When you are finished, write a short note telling what you have learned in this lesson. Try to use all 5 of these words in your note.

absolute	**convoy**	**dictator**
humiliate	**rally**	

Examining Words

When people talk about "brown shirts", they often mean Hitler and the type of government he ran. The brown shirt came to represent these political ideas.

Colours and clothing often go together to represent different occupations. Try to match the item of clothing on the left with the correct occupation from the list on the right.

black belt	a cardinal in the Roman Catholic church
blue collar	a special fighter in the U.S. army
green beret	an office manager or executive
red hat	a manual labourer
white collar	an expert in judo

Find out why these items of clothing are related to these occupations.

AN ILLUSTRATION

The map in Figure 61.5 shows the Canadian air and naval bases on the east coast. Why do you think there was a Canadian base in Reykjavik? Why did the convoy routes go so far north?

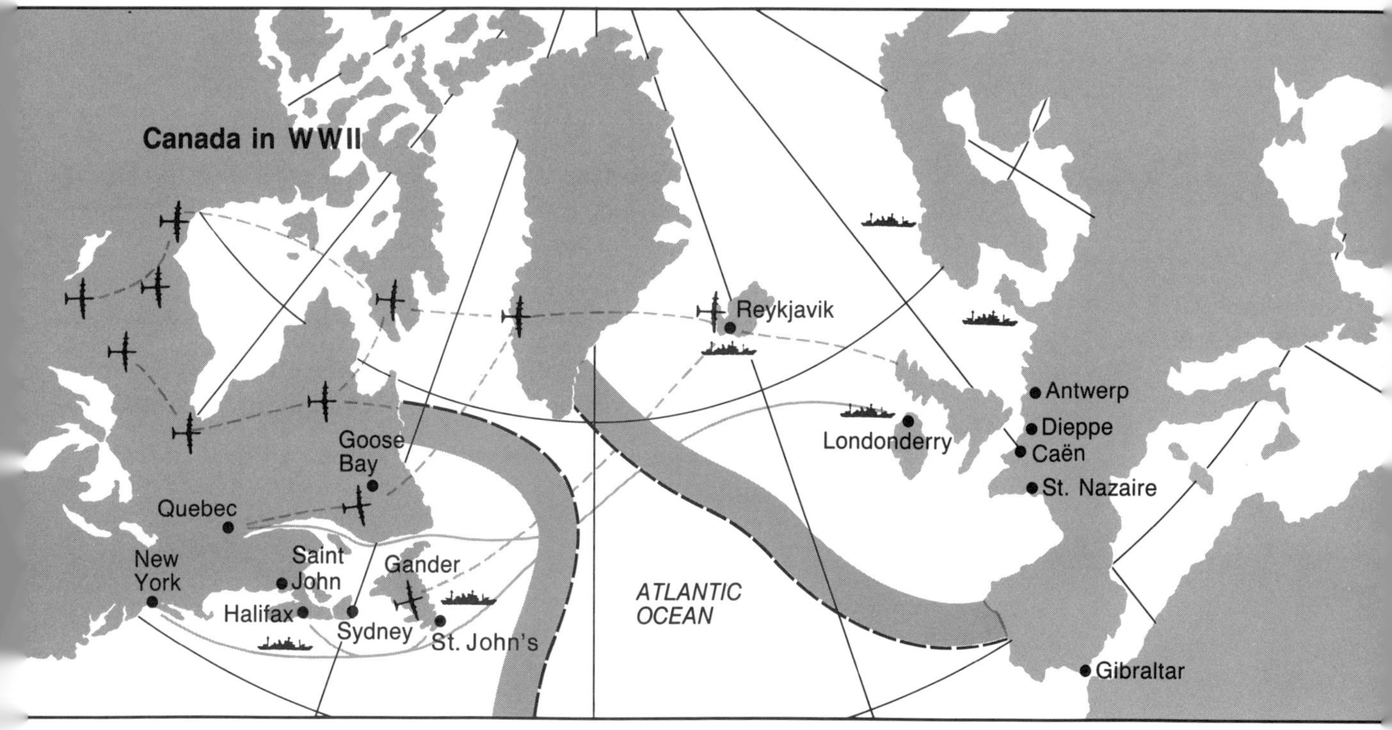

Figure 61.5 *The Battle of the North Atlantic*

John Meisel

Figure 61.6 *John Meisel (on the left) speaking to reporters*

Claim to fame: Canada gave him a home in World War II and he has given Canada much in return.

Born: 1923 in Vienna, Austria. His parents were Czechoslovakian.

Career: John Meisel started high school in Czechoslovakia. In 1937, his parents sent him to a boarding school in England. He contracted a bone infection. At the time, the only hope for a cure was surgery. After several operations, John was sent home to recover.

In 1939, the Meisel family moved to Casablanca. This city was run by France. John went to school when he was well enough. But he still had to have more surgery.

The Germans gained control of Casablanca in 1940. They would not give the Meisels permission to leave. But the Meisels managed to get false passports. They escaped first to Haiti and then, in 1942, to Canada.

John's fortunes improved once he reached Canada. He had one last operation. Then his infection was finally cured thanks to penicillin.

John went to university in Toronto and later in London, England. Since then, he has taught in universities in Canada, the United States, and Britain.

John has done much to serve Canada, his adopted country. He has served on many royal commissions. He has acted as an adviser to the federal government. And he has written several books about Canadian politics.

- **On a globe or map of the world, trace all the places John lived, starting from Vienna and stopping in Toronto.**
- **What do you think it would be like to go to boarding school?**

World War II at Home

62

Just as in World War I, Canadians put all their energy into the war effort. But they had also learned some lessons from the first war. So the situation on the home front was slightly different this time.

Once again, Canada produced large amounts of food for the soldiers overseas. But so much was sent that it was almost impossible to buy certain kinds of food at home. Storekeepers were allowed to sell canned milk only to people with very young babies. And there was a shortage of butter and meat.

To make sure that everyone shared the burden, the government started something called **rationing**. Each week, customers were allowed to purchase a set quantity of staples like butter and meat. To control this, every man, woman, and child was given a ration book. This book contained coupons. Customers had to give the storekeeper their coupons in order to buy their share of the rationed food.

Note: You can learn more about the war at home in Lesson 39.

Figure 62.1 *Factories and farms, as well as the army, navy, and police forces needed workers to replace the men who had gone to war. This is one of the many posters issued by the government to encourage women to go to work for their country. Can you identify each of the professions in the photograph?*

Figure 62.2 *In this photograph, a letter carrier is delivering ration books to a family early in the war. Later, people were given tokens such as the one shown.*

Of course, some people tried to get around these regulations. But the government paid many ordinary citizens to watch what happened in the stores. If a storekeeper broke the ration law, both the storekeeper and the customer were fined.

Householders tried to cut back on waste. Paper was kept separate for recycling. All bottles were returned for refilling. Tin cans and aluminum foil were carefully set aside to be melted down for scrap metal.

Every so often, the government would put on drives to get more scrap metal. Old lamps, irons, and alarm clocks could be used by the factories to make war supplies. Instead of making kettles and toasters and washing machines, the factories made guns and field radios and ammunition.

Manufacturers also produced airplanes as fast as they could. Before the war, there were only a few thousand people serving in the Royal Canadian Air Force (RCAF). But by 1943, there were more than 200 000.

Naturally, the new RCAF pilots and crews had to be trained. The government set up training camps across Canada. These were used for British and Allied pilots as well as for Canadians.

There was another training camp near Oshawa, Ontario. This camp was kept secret. Most people didn't know that "Camp X" existed until long after the war was over.

Canadian Norman Breakey revolutionized house painting when he invented the paint roller in 1940.

Figure 62.3 *The living conditions in the Japanese internment camps were overcrowded and primitive. The family in this photograph has been forced to live in a single room. What do the expressions on the family members' faces tell you about life in the camp?*

Figure 62.4 *Even children helped out in the war effort. In this photograph, young girls from Halifax are collecting scrap paper. What could scrap paper be used for?*

Camp X was run by a Canadian called William Stephenson. His specialty was **espionage**, or spying. He was in charge of the program to train spies for the Allies. They were taught how to collect secret information and how to disrupt enemy activities.

These spies were very important to the war effort. In fact, every country involved in the war used spies to gather information about the enemy. This meant that some people suspected anyone with a foreign accent or name of being a spy.

This **suspicion** was at its worst in Canada when Japan entered the war. At the time, there were about 23 000 Japanese living in British Columbia. Over half of these people had been born in Canada. Many could speak only English. They were loyal Canadian citizens.

In World War II, C.D. Howe convinced more than 200 experts to work for the government for a salary of $1 per year.

During World War II, Canadian children had to read black and white comics because the import of coloured comics was restricted.

But the government ignored these facts. It said that the Japanese Canadians were dangerous. They could be spies. So the government **interned** them. They were forced to live in prison camps. And all their possessions were auctioned off.

It wasn't until 1949 that all the rules against the Japanese were lifted. And it wasn't until 1984 that the government even said it "regretted" what had been done.

This was a tragic episode in Canadian history. It was just one of many tragic things done in World War II.

The most inhuman act was the **Holocaust**. While he was in power, Hitler systematically murdered millions of people. Six million of these people were murdered just because they were Jewish. Others were murdered because they were Gypsies. Still others were murdered because they disagreed with Hitler's ideas.

Another tragic act was the one that ended the war. The Americans dropped atomic bombs on 2 Japanese cities: Hiroshima and Nagasaki. The death and destruction were worse than anything the world had ever seen. But this seemed better than letting the war drag on with many more people losing their lives.

When World War II ended, there was much rejoicing in Canada. But there was also a sense of shock at the horrible waste of human lives and terrible amount of human suffering.

THE FACTS

Remembering Facts

1. How did food rationing work in Canada in World War II?
2. Why did people collect tin cans and aluminum foil?
3. What kind of training camps operated in Canada?
4. What happened to Japanese Canadians during the war?
5. What was the Holocaust?

Finding Facts

Interview someone who was living in Canada during World War II. This person could be a relative or a neighbour or perhaps someone who lives in a nearby retirement home.

Ask the person what it was like to be in Canada during the war. How is life today different from life during World War II? What are the person's strongest memories? How did he or she feel about incidents such as the internment of the Japanese or the Holocaust or the bombing of Hiroshima?

YOUR OPINIONS

Stating Opinions

Ian Fleming, the author of the James Bond spy stories, was trained at Camp X in Canada. In his books he shows the glamourous and adventurous side of spying. But spying can also be very dull as well as very dangerous.

Would you like to become a spy? Write a few sentences to explain your opinion.

Discussing Opinions

During World War II, many women wanted to join the army. But the government did not want to allow women to sign up. Finally, the government gave in to pressure and set up some women's units.

By the end of the war, more than 45 000 women had volunteered. But only a small number of these were actually sent overseas. And most of them were nurses.

Even by the early 1980s, women were not allowed to serve in *active* combat in the Canadian Armed Forces. In other words, they are not involved in the actual fighting. But women do serve in active combat in other parts of the world. Do you think women in the Canadian Forces should be allowed to join active combat?

NEW WORDS

Learning Words

In your notebook, write the title Vocabulary: Lesson 62. Then write down the following words in a list. Using the Glossary or a dictionary, write the meaning beside each word.

When you are finished, write a short note telling what you have learned in this lesson. Try to use all 5 of these words in your note.

espionage **Holocaust** **intern**
ration **suspicion**

Examining Words

It's usually easy to tell when people have learned English as a second language. Their accent gives them away. But if you stop to think about it, Canadians have accents too.

American border officers used to test whether people were Canadians by asking them to read the following paragraph. What words do you think would give a Canadian away?

> I have taken the wrong route. I am not juvenile or hostile. I live in a house with a roof. I am now out and about.

AN ILLUSTRATION

During World War II, the Americans built the Alaska Highway, an oil pipeline, and many air fields on Canadian territory. Canada gave part of the money for these projects in order to have a say in what happened. These projects are shown on the map in Figure 62.5. Can you explain why the Americans poured so much money into Canada? How does this relate to driving out the Japanese Canadians from British Columbia?

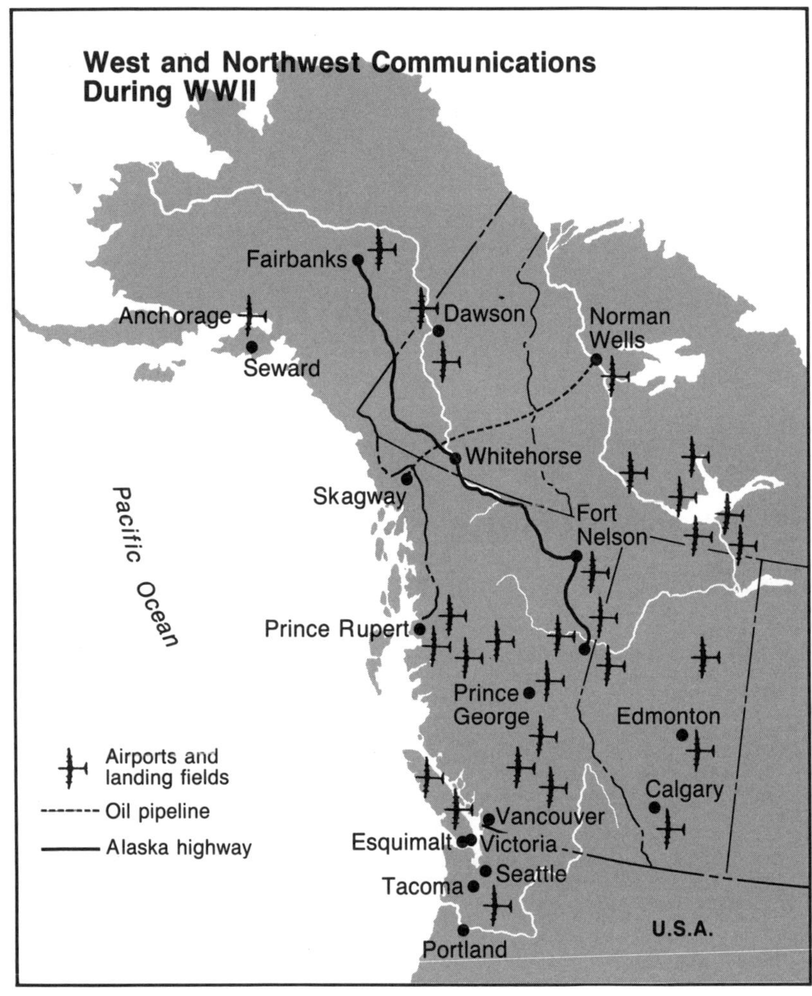

Figure 62.5 *The Battle of the Pacific Coast*

Joy Kogawa

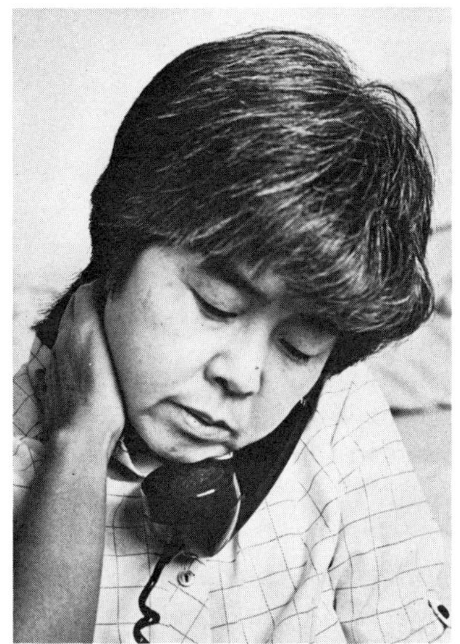

Figure 62.6 *Joy Kogawa*

Claim to fame: She is a Japanese-Canadian writer who was forced to live in an internment camp in World War II.

Born: 1935 in Vancouver, British Columbia

Career: Joy Kogawa's father was an Anglican minister. The family lived in a comfortable Vancouver home with every modern appliance. But when Joy was just 6 years old, Canada declared war on Japan. The government then decided that all Japanese Canadians should be forced to leave the coast of British Columbia.

First, the family was sent to an internment camp in the interior of British Columbia. The Kogawas had to live in a shack with walls made of newspaper.

When the war was over, the family was given the choice of moving either to Japan or to Alberta. (The government refused to let them return to British Columbia.) They chose Alberta. There they lived in a 1-room shack with no plumbing, no electricity, and no heating.

But Joy was determined to make things better. She graduated from the University of Alberta in 1954. She has worked as a writer ever since. Her third book of poetry was published in 1978. Her first novel, *Obasan*, came out in 1981. This book about life in the internment camps has won many awards both in Canada and the United States.

- **Is there a copy of *Obasan* in your library?**
- **Why do you think the government was worried about the Japanese living near the coast?**

63 The Cold War

Figure 63.1 *Igor Gouzenko was given a new name and life in Canada. He died peacefully in 1982 without his new identity ever being uncovered. In this photograph taken in 1966, he appeared in a hood for a television interview to talk about a book he had written. Why do you think he was so careful about revealing his face?*

Canada Park in Israel is a patch of once-rocky ground now planted with 5 million trees paid for by Canadian Jews.

It was 1 month after the atomic bomb had been dropped on Hiroshima, 1 month after the end of World War II. It was an ordinary day at the Soviet Embassy in Ottawa. Nobody noticed as a young clerk walked out the main door carrying a briefcase.

The clerk's name was Igor Gouzenko. Inside his briefcase he carried top-secret papers. He took them straight to Canadian officials and asked for **asylum**. He wanted to be made a Canadian citizen in exchange for the information in the papers.

Gouzenko's papers showed that the Soviet Union had a spy ring in Canada. It involved scientists, military officers, and even a Member of Parliament.

Many people could not believe that the spy ring existed. After all, the Soviet Union and Canada had been allies with Britain and the United States. They had all fought on the same side in the war.

But, the Soviets and the other Allies had never really trusted each other completely. This was mainly because they believed in different systems of government.

The Soviet system of government is based on communism. This is a kind of government in which the state owns all property. For example, individuals are not allowed to own their own stores or farms. Instead, all property and businesses are run by the government. The profits go to help all the citizens instead of just a few of them.

Communism does not allow any political opposition. No one is allowed to **criticize** the government. Those who do complain can be put in jail. In the Soviet system, citizens have very little personal freedom. They cannot leave the country when they want to. They cannot freely choose what jobs they will have. Even writers, dancers, and singers have to follow the government's wishes in what they create or perform.

This system is quite opposite to the system of government in countries such as ours. Canada, Britain, and the United States are democracies. In democracies, citizens can own their own property and businesses. If they make a lot of money, they are allowed to keep it. But of course if they lose money, the government will usually not help them out.

Also, democratic countries allow opposition. As you know, there are even opposition parties built right into the system of government. Individual citizens are allowed to criticize the government. They are free to leave the country if they wish to. They can choose their own jobs. They have individual freedom.

This difference in systems caused trouble among the Allies at the end of World War II. As you can see from the map in Figure 63.2, the Soviets **occupied** most of Eastern Europe. The other Allies occupied the countries in Western Europe.

As you might expect, the 2 sides disagreed on how to treat the countries they occupied. The countries in Western Europe were allowed to have free and democratic elections. But the Soviets kept their soldiers in Eastern Europe. They forced these countries to elect communist governments.

The world's first bent elevator is in the Peace Tower in Ottawa. It rises at an angle for 30 m before going straight up.

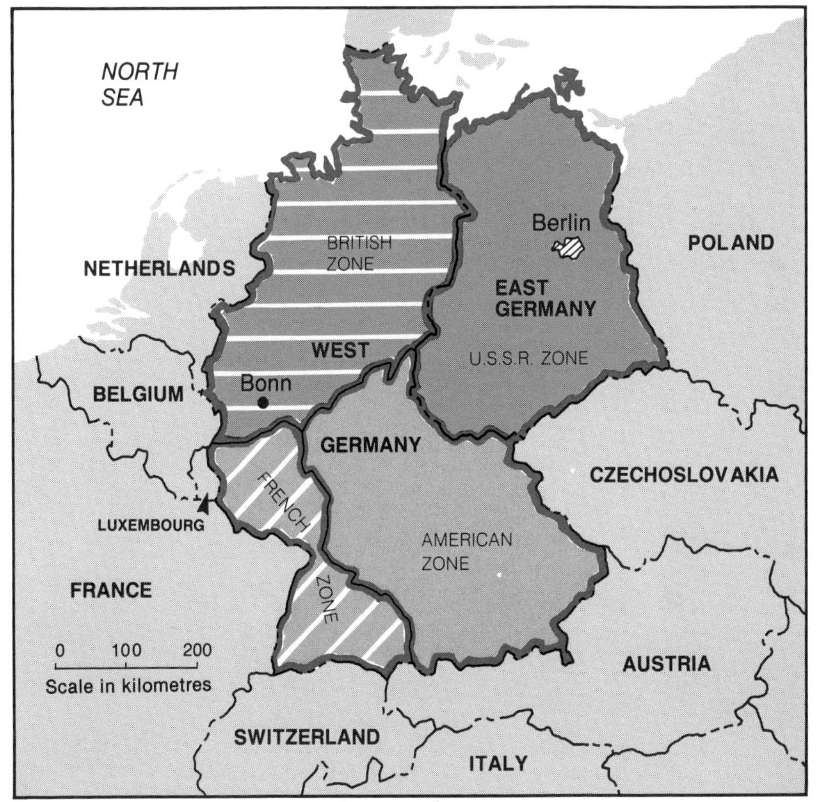

Figure 63.2 The occupation of Germany at the end of World War II *This map shows how the Allies divided control of Germany after it had surrendered. The Allies also divided Berlin, the capital of Germany. To this very day, Berlin is still divided into East and West Berlin. Which side is communist? Which side is democratic?*

The first Canadian Olympic gold medal for skiing was won by Anne Heggtveit of Ottawa in 1960.

Soon after the war, people began to talk about the "Iron Curtain." What they meant was that there was a barrier between the Soviet-controlled countries in Eastern Europe and the democracies in Western Europe. The Soviets did not want Western ideas influencing the countries they controlled.

In the beginning, the Iron Curtain was not a real barrier you could see and touch. But in time, the Soviets started to build a real barrier. Today, Eastern and Western Europe are separated by barbed-wire fences and mine fields. The Soviets are very careful about who is allowed to cross this barrier.

The Iron Curtain was a sign of what we call the "Cold War". In a cold war, 2 sides fight each other. But they don't use guns and bombs as they would in a hot war. Instead, they spy on each other. They try to make trouble for each other. And they build up weapons to protect themselves from each other in case of attack.

Figure 63.3 *This photograph is of the Brandenberg Gate in West Berlin looking towards East Berlin. What signs of the Cold War are there in this photograph?*

This Cold War worried the democratic countries. So in 1949, Canada, Britain, and the United States started an organization called NATO. This stands for the **N**orth **A**tlantic **T**reaty **O**rganization. NATO was meant to stop the Soviets from taking over more countries. All the countries who were members promised to help each other in case they were attacked.

NATO is still an important organization today. Every NATO member is expected to contribute weapons and soldiers. Most of these soldiers are stationed in West Germany. If the Soviets attack Europe, then these soldiers will be used to push the Soviet forces back.

The Soviets were worried about NATO. They thought that NATO forces might attack first and try to **overthrow** the Soviet system. So in 1955 the Soviets set up a similar group called the Warsaw **Pact**. Like NATO, the Warsaw Pact is still an important organization today. The countries in the Pact have all agreed to help each other in case they are attacked.

NATO and Warsaw Pact forces have never actually fought each other. But they are both prepared for an attack at any moment.

Harlequin Books romance novels were started in Winnipeg in 1949. They are now published in 80 countries in 15 languages.

Figure 63.4 *Many Canadian troops are stationed in West Germany, most of them at Lahr. It is important that their weapons and equipment be in top condition. In this photograph, a corporal in the Canadian Armed Forces tests communications equipment.*

THE FACTS

Remembering Facts

1. Who was Igor Gouzenko?
2. What is the Soviet system of government like?
3. How is life in the Soviet Union different from life in democracies like Canada?
4. Why is Europe divided into Western Europe and Eastern Europe?
5. What is a "cold" war?

Finding Facts

It is hard for people to get in or out of the Soviet Union. But today, there is some contact between Canada and the Soviet Union. This is mostly through entertainers and athletes.

Find out what the connection is between Canada and the Soviet Union for one of the following:

Mikhail Baryshnikov	The Canadian Brass
Glenn Gould	Karen Kain
Team Canada	

YOUR OPINIONS

Stating Opinions

The Soviet Union is a huge country. There is some spectacular scenery to see. There are also several beautiful cities and towns. Would you like to go to the Soviet Union sometime on a visit? Explain your opinion in a few sentences.

Discussing Opinions

In a democracy, the citizens are said to be free. What does "free" mean? Would you agree that we are free in Canada? Is there any way in which we are *not* free?

NEW WORDS

Learning Words

In your notebook, write the title Vocabulary: Lesson 63. Then write down the following words in a list. Using the Glossary or a dictionary, write the meaning beside each word.

When you are finished, write a short note telling what you have learned in this lesson. Try to use all 5 of these words in your note.

asylum	**criticize**	**occupy**
overthrow	**pact**	

Examining Words

There are many common expressions in English that use the word *cold*. The following expressions all relate to parts of the body. Can you explain what each one means?

cold blood	cold feet
cold heart	cold shoulder

What are some other expressions that use the word *cold*?

AN ILLUSTRATION

Trace an outline map of the world. On it, mark in one colour the members of NATO. Mark in another colour the members of the Warsaw Pact. The members of these 2 organizations as of 1985 are listed in Table 63.1.

WARSAW PACT COUNTRIES	NATO COUNTRIES	
Bulgaria	Belgium	Netherlands
Czechoslovakia	Canada	Norway
East Germany	Denmark	Portugal
Hungary	France	Spain
Poland	Greece	Turkey
Romania	Iceland	United Kingdom
USSR	Italy	United States
	Luxembourg	West Germany

Table 63.1 *Members of the Warsaw Pact and NATO*

Josef Skvorecky

Figure 63.5 *Joseph Skvorecky*

Claim to fame: He is a Czech-Canadian writer.

Born: 1924 in Nachod, Bohemia (now Czechoslovakia)

Married: 1958 to Salivarova (Zdena) Zdenka

Career: During World War II, Josef Skvorecky worked in a factory. But later he went to university. He graduated with a Ph.D. in philosophy from Prague University in 1951. He then worked as an editor of a world literature magazine.

However, in 1958, Skvorecky wrote a novel called *The Cowards*. It was about life in Czechoslovakia under the Communists. The Communist government was very angry with the things Skvorecky had written. Skvorecky and all the people involved in publishing his novel lost their jobs.

Skvorecky went into hiding for years. He was an enemy to the Communists. He kept writing about freedom. And his books were passed around secretly.

In 1969, Skvorecky left Czechoslovakia for Canada. He took a job as a professor at the University of Toronto. Since then he has written constantly. He has produced 10 novels, 15 collections of short stories, translations, film scripts, and articles. Skvorecky and his wife also run a mail-order publishing house. They print books by Czech writers who are enemies of the Communists. Then they smuggle the books into Czechoslovakia.

Skvorecky's work is important. A sign of this was his nomination for the Nobel Prize for Literature in 1982.

- **What are Nobel prizes? How did they come to be?**
- **Do you think it is right that some books and films are banned in Canada?**

Canada as Peacemaker

64

How often have you seen a soldier carrying a rifle? How often have you seen a tank driving down a street? It's quite possible you've never seen these things except on television.

This is because Canada is a very **peaceable** nation. Our soldiers have fought courageously when they had to. But generally speaking, Canadians are not **warlike** people.

In fact, Canada has a **reputation** in the world as a peacemaker. This reputation goes back to the days when Canada first became a member of the League of Nations.

As you might remember from Lesson 59, the League of Nations was formed after World War I. Its purpose was to prevent any more wars. But obviously the League failed. It did not stop World War II.

One problem was that the League had no power: it had no army of its own. So it could not *force* countries to keep the peace.

By the end of World War II, many countries in the world were determined to try again. In 1945, representatives from 51 countries met in San Francisco. They all agreed to form a new organization for peace. It was to be called the United Nations, or the UN for short.

Canada was one of the key members in setting up the UN. Canadian representatives worked hard to make sure that the UN would be an effective organization.

Canada realized that the League of Nations had failed because it had no army. Therefore Canada argued that the UN should set up its own army using soldiers and money from all the member countries.

The idea was that this army would act as a permanent peacekeeping force. It could be sent at a moment's notice to trouble spots anywhere in the world. It could keep the peace until the 2 sides worked their problems out.

Unfortunately, the other UN members did not agree to do this. They did not want to set up a permanent army. But just 5 years later, a peacekeeping force became necessary.

Figure 64.1 *Soldier of the 1st Battalion of the Royal Canadian Regiment awaits medical aid after a night patrol in Korea, 1952. Find Korea on the map in Figure 64.2.*

Farley Mowat's books about Canada have been translated into more than 20 languages.

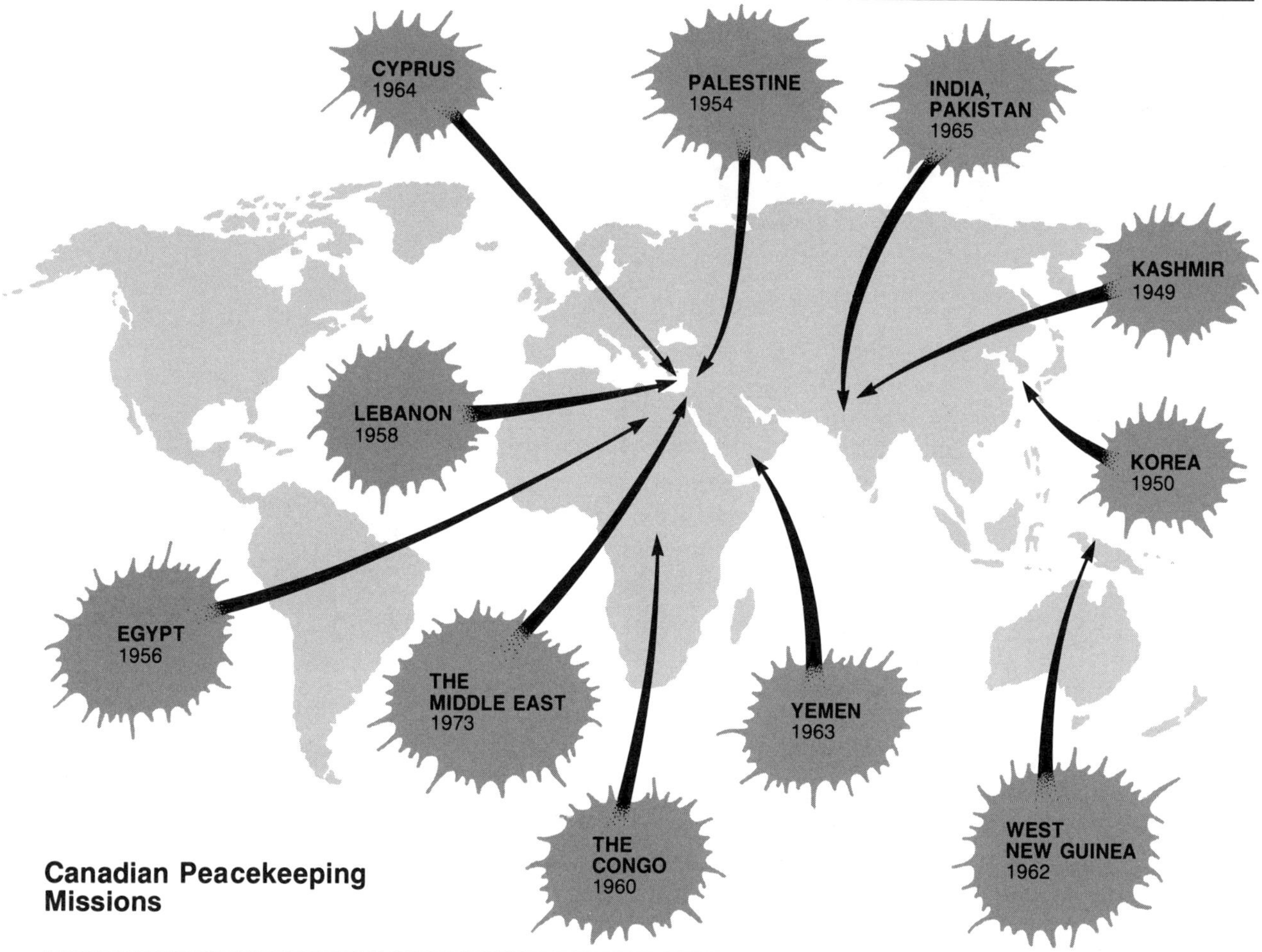

CYPRUS 1964

PALESTINE 1954

INDIA, PAKISTAN 1965

KASHMIR 1949

LEBANON 1958

KOREA 1950

EGYPT 1956

THE MIDDLE EAST 1973

YEMEN 1963

THE CONGO 1960

WEST NEW GUINEA 1962

Canadian Peacekeeping Missions

Figure 64.2 *This map shows the major areas in the world where Canada has helped the United Nations to keep the peace. The dates show when Canadian soldiers and observers were first sent to each trouble spot. Find out more about Canada's peace-keeping role in one of these areas. Why was there trouble? How long did Canadians serve there?*

In 1982, Karen Baldwin became the first Canadian ever to be crowned "Miss Universe".

The trouble spot was Korea. Korea is a peninsula very close to Japan. At the end of World War II, Korea had been divided into 2 parts: the North and the South. North Korea was friendly with the Soviets. South Korea was friendly with the United States.

In June, 1950, North Korea attacked South Korea. Most people believed that the Soviet Union was behind this attack. The United States went to the UN and asked for help.

The UN agreed to send an army to help bring back peace. More than 30 countries gave soldiers, weapons, and money to this army. Canada made the third-largest **contribution**. Only the United States and Britain gave more.

The situation was very dangerous. Several hundred Canadians were either killed or injured while serving in Korea. Finally the 2 sides agreed to stop fighting in 1953.

Figure 64.3 *A soldier of the Royal Canadian Regiment on outpost duty on top of a building in the divided city of Nicosia, Cyprus, 1970.*

The soldiers in the UN army went back to their own countries. But soon they were needed again in other parts of the world. Canada has often contributed generously to these forces. The map in Figure 64.2 shows all the far-off places where Canadian soldiers have been sent to keep the peace.

Probably Canada's most important contribution was during the Suez crisis in 1956. The Suez is a canal that runs through Egypt. It joins the Red Sea and the Mediterranean Sea. Before the canal was built, ships had to travel all the way around Africa to get from the Mediterranean Sea to the Indian Ocean and Red Sea. Once the canal was built, it cut several thousand kilometres off the journey.

Before 1956, the Suez canal was run by Britain. But then Egypt decided to take it over. It wanted to run the canal on its own. War broke out. Soon France, Britain, Egypt, and Israel were all involved in the fighting.

The situation was highly explosive. The whole world could have been drawn into the war. But the Canadian representative at the UN, Lester Pearson, worked out a compromise. The UN sent in peacekeeping troops. And the situation was **calmed**.

Toronto's CN Tower is the tallest freestanding structure in the world, soaring 555.3 m high.

Figure 64.4 *Lester B. Pearson (left) accepting his Nobel Peace Prize from Dr. Gunnar Jahn, December 1957. Who was winner of the Nobel Peace Prize this year?*

Lester Pearson was given the Nobel Peace Prize because of his efforts. This was a great honour both for him and for Canada. It showed that the world recognized Canada's important role in keeping the peace.

Overall, the UN has been a success. It has helped to maintain peace in the world. But today there are many problems that could easily lead to war. In the next chapter, you will learn about these problems and how Canada deals with them.

THE FACTS

Remembering Facts

1. What is Canada's reputation in the world?
2. Explain one reason why the League of Nations failed.
3. What is the UN?
4. What happened in Korea in 1950?
5. Who was Lester Pearson?

Finding Facts

Another important organization that Canada belongs to is the Commonwealth. Read other books or encyclopedias to find out the answers to the following questions.

1. Who is allowed to join the Commonwealth?
2. Who is the symbolic head of the Commonwealth?

3. What activities do Commonwealth countries take part in together?

Name 5 member countries of the Commonwealth that you had never heard of before doing this research. Find where they are located on a map.

YOUR OPINIONS

Stating Opinions

Do you think it will ever be possible to stop all wars? Explain your opinion in a few sentences.

Discussing Opinions

Canada has often sent Canadian soldiers to be part of UN peacekeeping forces. Often these soldiers have been sent to countries that have nothing directly to do with Canada. Often these soldiers have been in danger. Some have been wounded and killed.

Do you think Canada should continue to send soldiers as part of UN peacekeeping forces? Discuss your opinions with your classmates.

NEW WORDS

Learning Words

In your notebook, write the title Vocabulary: Lesson 64. Then write down the following words in a list. Using the Glossary or a dictionary, write the meaning beside each word.

When you are finished, write a short note telling what you have learned in this lesson. Try to use all 5 of these words in your note.

calm	**contribution**	**peaceable**
reputation	**warlike**	

Examining Words

Peninsula and *canal* are words that you have probably learned in geography class. They are the names for special geographical features.

Write down as many other words as you can think of that are names for geographical features.

AN ILLUSTRATION

Find a picture of the United Nations flag. Copy this flag into your notebook. What do the symbols on the flag stand for?

Oscar Peterson

Figure 64.5 *Oscar Peterson with Anne Murray at the 1985 Order of Canada award ceremonies*

Claim to fame: He is the world's most famous jazz pianist.

Born: 1925 in Montreal, Quebec of West Indian parents

Married: 1966 to Sandra King. They have 5 children. Peterson has another son by his second wife, Charlotte.

Career: Peterson's family was very musical. When he was only 5 years old, he was playing trumpet in the family band. However, when he was 7, he came down with tuberculosis. The doctor said he should not strain his lungs. So he switched from trumpet to piano.

Peterson left high school early to study piano at the Conservatory of Music in Montreal. After winning an amateur contest, he was given his own radio show. Then he formed a jazz trio that played in Montreal.

In 1945, Peterson cut a jazz record for RCA. It was the first of more than 100 records that he has made in his career.

Then in 1949, Peterson gave his first concert in the United States. He was an instant hit. Soon he was giving concerts all over the world in countries like Japan, Czechoslovakia, Mexico, and Holland. In 1974, he even toured the Soviet Union.

Peterson is an international celebrity. Millions of people around the world know and love his music. He has received countless awards from many countries. But he has kept Canada as his base. He has always kept his home in the country where he was born.

- **Where are 2 places you can go to study music in Canada?**
- **Many Canadians don't know about Oscar Peterson. Why do you think Canadians often ignore their own stars?**

QUIZ 9

The following questions are based on the lessons in Chapter 9. **DO NOT WRITE YOUR ANSWERS IN THIS TEXTBOOK.** Instead, you should write the answers in your notebook or on a separate sheet of paper.

1. There are 12 blanks in the following paragraphs about the two World Wars. They have been labelled from (a) to (l). Write down the 12 answers in a list on your paper. Then beside each answer write the letter of the blank where it belongs.

weapons	recycling	Britain
food	air force	battle front
convoys	interned	war profiteers
trenches	rationed	no man's land

In World War I, thousands of Canadians served in the army. They were sent to the (a) ______ in order to fight enemy soldiers. They had to live in muddy (b) ______. To fight, they would crawl "over the top" into (c) ______. Many were wounded or killed.

In World War II, many Canadians served in the (d) ______. Their job was to protect the (e) ______ that carried supplies across the Atlantic to (f) ______.

Canadians at home during World War I did their best to help the war effort. The soldiers in Europe needed (g) ______, so Canadian farmers worked longer hours. The soldiers needed (h) ______, so Canadian businessmen built factories. Unfortunately some were (i) ______ who charged unfair prices.

In World War II, life in Canada was difficult. Householders were asked to save items like tins cans for (j) ______. Food was (k) ______. Japanese Canadians had the worst time. They were (l) ______ and forced to live in special camps.

2. Write the letters from (a) to (e) on your paper. Then write a T if the statement is TRUE. Write an F if the statement is FALSE.

(a) All Canadian workers were paid high wages during the Roaring Twenties.
(b) Sports were very popular in the Roaring Twenties.
(c) When people bought stocks in the Roaring Twenties, they always paid for them right away.
(d) The crash of the United States stock market also affected Canada and Europe.
(e) During the Depression, weather conditions on the prairies made life even harder.

3. Match the person in the list on the left side with the correct item from the list on the right side. For each one, write the letter and the number together on your paper.

(a) Mackenzie King	(1)	the German leader who started World War II and who was responsible for the Holocaust
(b) Lester Pearson	(2)	the prime minister of Canada during World War II
(c) Igor Gouzenko	(3)	the person who gave proof that there was a Cold War between the Soviets and the other Allies who had fought in World War II
(d) Adolf Hitler	(4)	the Canadian who won the Nobel Peace Prize for his work in the United Nations

4. Match the item in the list on the left side with the correct description from the list on the right side. For each one, write the letter and the number together on your paper.

(a) Warsaw Pact	(1)	the group of countries that tried to keep peace in the world after World War I, but failed
(b) NATO	(2)	the group of countries, led by the Soviet Union, that have promised to protect each other in case of attack by Western countries
(c) United Nations (UN)	(3)	the group of countries, led by the United States, that have promised to protect each other in case of attack by Eastern countries
(d) League of Nations	(4)	the group of countries that joined together after World War II to try once more to bring peace to the world

CHAPTER TEN

Into the Twenty-First Century

There are many important problems in the world today. Recently, the Canadian government asked Canadians to name the problem they thought was most important. The 10 problems that were mentioned most often are given here. Note that they are in alphabetical order, not order of importance.

- danger of nuclear war
- emergencies caused by natural disasters
- energy and resource shortages
- human rights violations in other countries
- pollution
- population growth
- poverty of underdeveloped nations
- refugees around the world
- wars now being fought
- world hunger

The lessons in this chapter discuss many of these problems. Before you begin studying, try the following experiment.

Decide which of these problems you think is the most important. Then rewrite the list of problems according to the way your class rates them. The first problem should be the one chosen by the most students. The second problem should be the one chosen by the next greatest number of students, and so on.

When you have finished studying this chapter, repeat the experiment. Did you change your mind about what is the most important problem in the world today? Did the class list change?

65 The Arms Race

It was the night of September 1, 1983. Korean Airlines Flight 007 was flying from Alaska to Seoul, South Korea. The passengers on the jumbo jet were mainly Korean tourists. There were also some Canadians.

Mysteriously, the jet began to stray from its regular flight path. It gradually moved northwards until it had crossed over the Kamchatka Peninsula. This peninsula is part of the Soviet Union. The Soviets have many important military bases there. Naturally, they want to keep foreigners away.

Quickly, Soviet fighter planes flew up to meet the jumbo jet. They signalled the pilot to land. But he did not seem to notice them. Instead, he changed the plane's altitude.

Drop in the Bucket

"Doesn't it seem kind of academic to be debating whether WE should have nuclear weapons?"

Figure 65.1 *This cartoon was first published in the 1960s. But it is still relevant today. How do you think this cartoonist would feel about people who want to stop missile testing in Canada today?*

The Soviet officers on the ground decided that the jumbo jet was a spy plane. They ordered the fighter pilot to shoot. And the KAL jumbo jet was blasted from the sky. Not one of the 269 people aboard survived.

The destruction of the jumbo jet shocked the world. Everyone was horrified that the Soviets would attack a **civilian** plane. It was almost impossible to believe it had happened.

But the destruction of the jet was no accident. It was a sign of growing tensions in the world between the 2 superpowers — the United States and the Soviet Union.

Since the early 1960s, the 2 superpowers have been involved in a deadly arms race. They now have enough nuclear missiles to destroy the world. But that has not stopped them from trying to develop bigger and more powerful weapons.

During the 1970s, there was some hope that the arms race could be slowed down. Representatives from the United States and the Soviet Union met in Geneva, Switzerland. They talked about cutting down the number of missiles each country owned.

These meetings were known as SALT. SALT is short for **S**trategic **A**rms **L**imitation **T**alks. And for a while, the SALT meetings were successful.

Canadian Joe Shuster was the creator of the world-famous comic book hero, Superman.

Note: You can read more about the tension between the United States and the Soviet Union in Lesson 63.

Figure 65.2 *Scientists warn that a nuclear war could destroy all life on this earth. The real problems come* after *the bombs have exploded.*

(65.2.a.) *Nuclear bombs explode, destroying major cities in the northern part of the globe.*

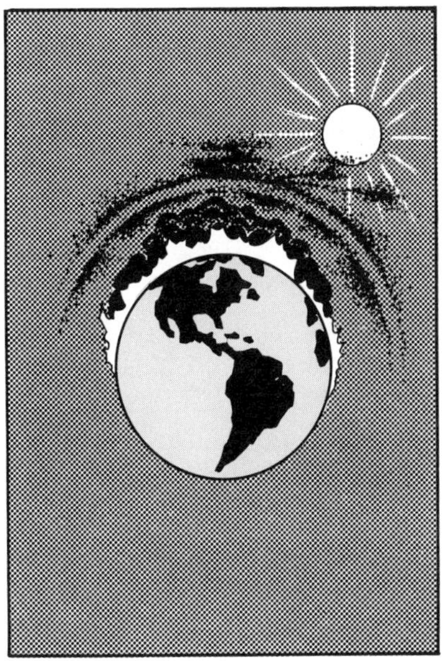

(65.2.b.) *Debris such as asphalt rises up and collects in the atmosphere, forming a black cloud.*

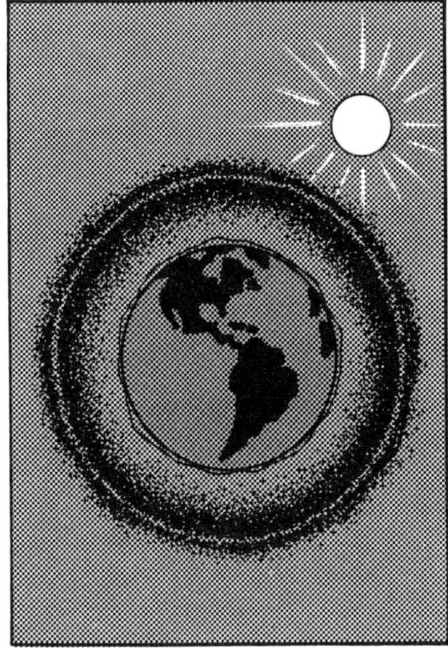

(65.2.c.) *The sun's rays cannot break through the cloud. The earth below is trapped in a nuclear winter for several years.*

Figure 65.3 *Nuclear power has a good side as well. Here Canadian scientists stand in front of the fuel rods of a Candu nuclear reactor. Canadian reactors like this are used around the world to bring electricity into people's homes.*

In 1972 the Soviet and American governments both accepted SALT I. This was an agreement to limit the number of places on both sides where missiles could be **launched**. Then in 1979, the representatives in Geneva agreed on SALT II. This was an even better agreement. SALT II put a limit on the actual number of bombers and missiles on both sides.

SALT II was accepted by the Soviet government. But it was never accepted by the United States government. Part of the problem was that the Soviet Union invaded the country of Afghanistan in 1979. The American politicians were very angry at this move. They felt it showed that the Soviets did not want peace. So they turned down SALT II.

Canada has won more gold medals for Olympic hockey than any other country.

During the early 1980s, new talks began. But they seemed **doomed** from the beginning. The United States was planning to set up, or **deploy**, missiles in Western Europe. These missiles could reach targets in the Soviet Union in just 10 minutes. The Soviets said that they would leave the talks if these missiles were set up.

In December, 1983, the United States went ahead with the plan. Nearly 600 new missiles were deployed. As they had threatened, the Soviets walked out of the talks.

The Soviets weren't the only ones who did not want the new missiles to be set up in Europe. Thousands of ordinary people across Europe and North America protested against the missiles, too. They were part of something called the peace movement.

The peace movement is made up of hundreds of different groups around the world. What these groups have in common is that they want nuclear disarmament. In other words, they want the governments on both sides to stop the arms race and get rid of their nuclear weapons. Only this way, they say, can we prevent nuclear war.

Those who are against the peace movement argue that the Soviet Union will never give up its nuclear weapons. So they say that the United States must keep its own weapons for defence and also as a deterrent. The Soviet Union won't dare to start a war as long as the United States has nuclear weapons of its own.

The Canadian government seems to agree in part with both sides. In 1983, the Canadian prime minister at the time, Pierre Trudeau, started a **global** peace mission. He travelled around the world talking to important leaders. He wanted them to agree on a new plan for peace.

But also in 1983, the Canadian government let the United States start testing the cruise missile on Canadian soil. In 1985, there was some talk of Canada being involved in the American Star Wars program.

The Star Wars program is supported by the president of the United States, Ronald Reagan. It is a plan for putting nuclear missiles in outer space. Many people feel this is the most dangerous plan of all.

In 1985, the Americans and Soviets did start peace talks once again. But if these talks are ever going to work, the governments on both sides are going to have to start trusting each other. And that is the most difficult task of all.

The first Canadian artist to have a painting hanging in the Vatican Museum is Garth Speight. It was accepted in 1979.

Note: You can learn more about Canadian involvement with American defence in Lesson 56.

World-famous Canadian bacon is leaner than side bacon, being cut from a boned strip of pork loin.

THE FACTS

Remembering Facts

1. What is SALT?
2. Why was SALT II not accepted?
3. Why did the arms talks stop in 1983?
4. What is the peace movement?
5. Why are some people against the peace movement?

Finding Facts

The state of the arms race is constantly changing. Much will have happened since this lesson was written. Read the latest newspaper and magazine articles about the arms race. Listen to the radio or television for the most up-to-date news.

Can you find the answers to the following questions?

1. Are the United States and the Soviet Union still talking together about cutting down their nuclear weapons?
2. Have the United States and the Soviet Union reached any new agreements about arms control?
3. Is the Soviet Union still fighting in Afghanistan?
4. What has happened to Reagan's Star Wars plan?
5. Is the cruise missile still being tested in Canada?

YOUR OPINIONS

Stating Opinions

In Canada, thousands of ordinary citizens went on peace marches to "refuse the cruise". Would you go on a peace march if one was held near where you live? Explain your opinion in a few sentences.

Discussing Opinions

Thousands of people have gone on marches and signed petitions in order to protest nuclear weapons. But some protestors have used more extreme methods.

For example, 50 English women lived for 3 years in tents outside an air force base where nuclear missiles were kept. In Canada, 5 protestors exploded a bomb in a factory where parts were made for the cruise missile.

What is your opinion of these extreme methods for protesting nuclear weapons? Can you think of better ways that ordinary people could use to stop the arms race?

NEW WORDS

Learning Words

In your notebook, write the title Vocabulary: Lesson 65. Then write down the following words in a list. Using the Glossary or a dictionary, write the meaning beside each word.

When you are finished, write a short note telling what you have learned in this lesson. Try to use all 5 of these words in your note.

civilian **deploy** **doomed**
global **launch**

Examining Words

The Soviets do not use the same alphabet that we do. For example, the first word in their country's name is written like this: С О Ю З

In fact, many languages in the world use writing systems that are different from the one we use in English. See if you and your classmates can find examples of writing in the following languages. (**Hint**: Search for labels on imported foods and other products.)

Danish Hebrew Hindi Korean

AN ILLUSTRATION

Table 65.1 lists the amount of money that has been spent in the world on weapons and wars from 1950 to 1980. The table is given in constant 1980 American dollars. In other words, $1 spent in 1950 is exactly the same value as $1 spent in 1980.

Make a graph using the information in this table. What does your graph tell you about military spending in the world?

Year	Approximate Billions of U.S. $ spent	Year	Approximate Billions of U.S. $ spent
1950	221	1966	330
1952	272	1968	374
1954	253	1970	369
1956	249	1972	381
1958	252	1974	403
1960	260	1976	422
1962	291	1978	451
1964	301	1980	500

SOURCE: CUSO Journal 1983, Yearbooks of the Stockholm International Peace Research Institute

Table 65.1 *World military expenditures 1950-1980 (1980 constant prices)*

George Ignatieff

Figure 65.4 *George Ignatieff receiving the Pearson Peace Award from Governor General Jeanne Sauvé, 1984*

Claim to fame: He is an important Canadian diplomat who has always been active in the peace movement.

Born: 1913 in St. Petersburg (now Leningrad), Russia

Married: 1945 to Alison Grant. They have 2 sons.

Career: George Ignatieff was born in Russia before the communist revolution. He was the son of a nobleman. Therefore, when the communists took power, life was difficult for the Ignatieffs. They managed to escape to England in 1920. Then they came to Canada in 1922.

George Ignatieff went to several Canadian high schools. He did so well that he earned scholarships to study at the University of Toronto. Later, he earned a Rhodes Scholarship to study at Oxford University in England.

In 1939, Ignatieff wrote the special exams taken by all people who want to be diplomats. These are people who want to represent Canada in foreign countries. Ignatieff wrote one of the best exams. And so he became the first foreign-born Canadian to be a diplomat.

Ignatieff has had a long and important career as a diplomat. He was the Canadian Ambassador to Yugoslavia. He was also Canada's representative to NATO, to the United Nations, and to the Geneva Disarmament Conference.

Presently, Ignatieff is Chancellor of the University of Toronto. He continues to travel and give speeches in support of the peace movement.

- **When was the communist revolution in Russia? Who was it against?**
- **What sort of person would make a good diplomat? What abilities and what kind of personality should a diplomat have?**

The Third World

66

Have you ever been thirsty because there wasn't any water to drink? Have you ever been hungry because there was no food available? Have you ever missed school because there weren't enough teachers for everyone?

Almost every Canadian would answer no to these questions. Canadians don't go thirsty. Canadians don't starve to death. Canadians don't have to go without an education. But this is not true for millions of other people around the world. These are the citizens of the Third World.

When people speak about the Third World, they mean countries in Africa, Asia, Latin America, and the Caribbean. In nations with the lowest incomes, the average person only lives to be 50 years old. The average person earns no more than $245 a year.

Figure 66.1 The Third World *This map shows the areas that are part of what is called the Third World. There is another way of expressing the differences between developed nations and developing nations. This is the term* North-South relations. *Study this map carefully. In general, what kind of nations are the "North" nations. What kind of nations are the "South" nations?*

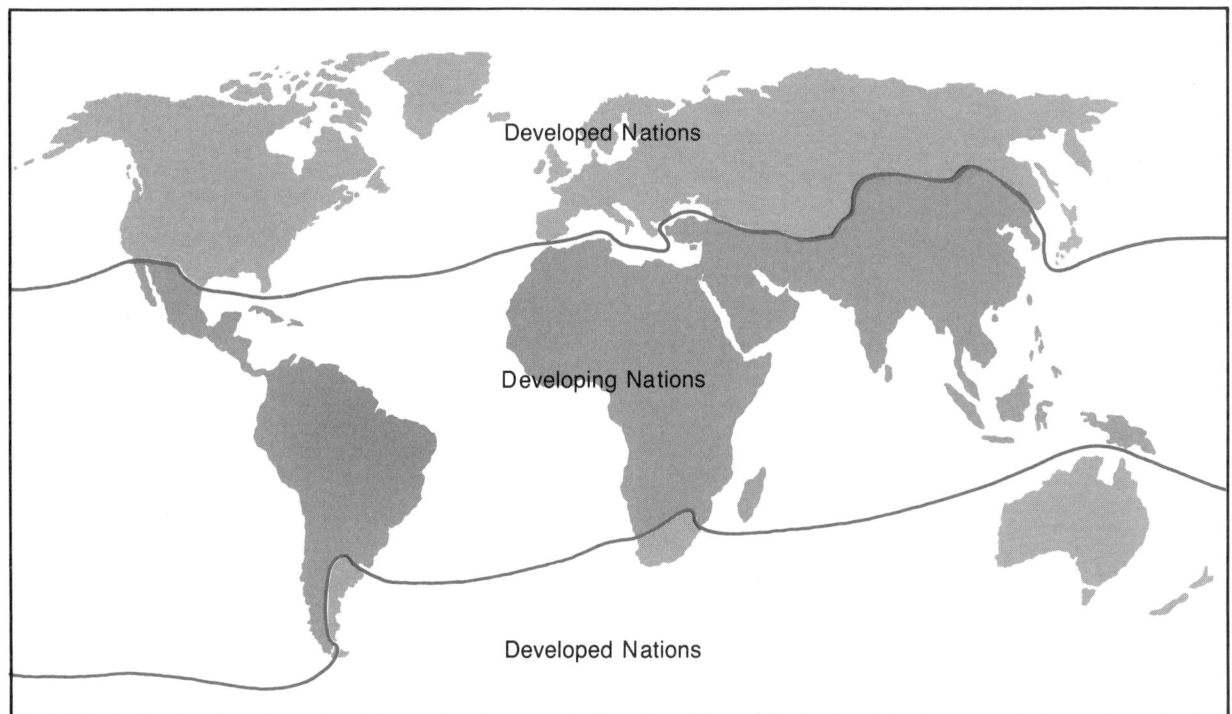

Figure 66.2 *Two boys in Sri Lanka drink at a precious water supply.*

Most Third World nations depend on farming and fishing. There is very little modern **technology**. In other words, there are very few machines or factories. That is why Third World nations are often called "**developing**" nations. They are still developing the kinds of technology that we take for granted in Canada.

Because Canada and the other developed countries are so rich, they can afford to help these developing nations. In fact, the Canadian government gives them about a billion dollars each year. This money is called foreign **aid**. A billion dollars may sound like a lot of money. But it is only a tiny part (0.5%) of all the money Canada makes in a year.

Most of this money is given through the Canadian International Development Agency. This government department is called CIDA for short. The people who work in CIDA decide on which projects they will support each year.

One project that CIDA gives money to was started by the United Nations. The UN declared the 1980s as the International Drinking Water Supply and **Sanitation** Decade. The UN goal is for everyone in the world to be able to get safe water by 1990.

Canadian-developed hard red spring wheat is now the major breeding wheat in Russia and China.

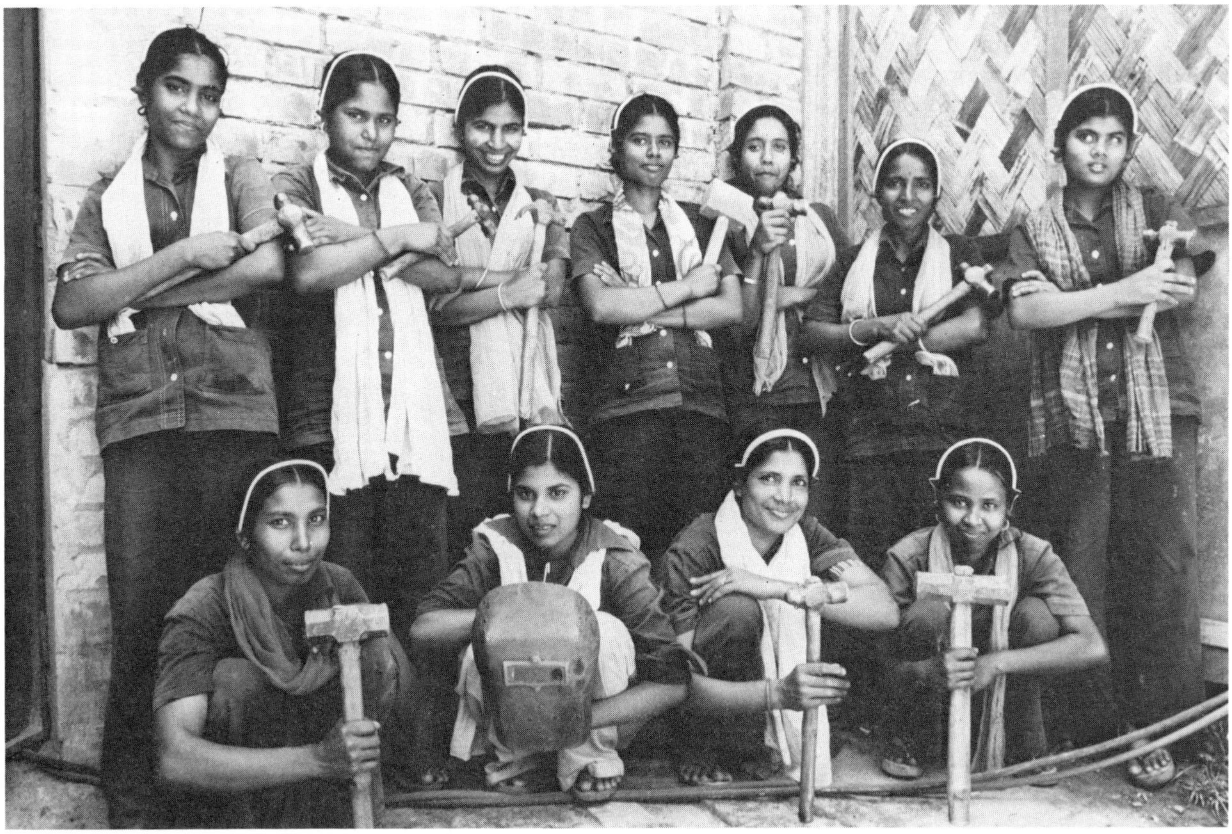

Figure 66.3 *Women in Asia work to improve their communities. These women are holding tools provided by Canada.*

This may seem a strange goal. After all, three-quarters of the earth's surface is covered with water. The trouble is that most of the water in the world is either salt water or frozen. Only 0.8% of all the water is fresh. And even then, a lot of the fresh water is polluted.

In Canada, we have lots of fresh, clean water. But more than half the people in the Third World have trouble getting fresh water. Even worse, 1 in every 4 people cannot get clean water. These people *have* to drink polluted water to survive.

Drinking polluted water is more than unpleasant. It causes diseases like dysentery. These diseases can kill. It is hard to imagine, but about 30 000 people die *every day* because they cannot get clean water.

Thousands of people in the Third World also die every day from malnutrition. In other words, they are starving. CIDA spends a lot of money on supplying these people with food.

Sometimes this means that Canada actually sends food like wheat and powdered milk. But it also means that Canada supports projects to help the people get their own food.

Figure 66.4 *A scientist in India studies grain samples in a multi-million dollar project partially sponsored by* CIDA.

For example, in an African country called Zambia, there are 2 lakes that are filled with fish. The trouble is that these lakes are difficult to reach. They are far away from where the people live. So in 1981, CIDA started a project to build roads. In this way, fish can be carried to the people who are starving.

The people in the Third World also need energy to cook their food. In many parts of India, women walk for hours searching for wood to burn. CIDA now helps villages buy special units. These units turn animal waste into something called biogas. This biogas can be used for both cooking and lighting.

The major goal of organizations like CIDA is to help Third World nations help themselves. That means that the Canadian government spends a lot of money on education. People from developing nations are given **scholarships** to study in Canada. And Canadian scientists, engineers, and educators go to teach their skills in the Third World.

This foreign aid is becoming more and more important for Third World nations. Their populations are growing very rapidly. Each year there are more people to feed and care for.

One problem is that developed countries like Canada do not give as much as they could. Some people think that there is a lot of foreign aid. But a very sad fact shows this is not true: for every $1 that is spent in the world on foreign aid, another $25 are spent on making weapons.

Electric kettles are popular in Canada. But you won't find many in other parts of the world. They are uniquely Canadian.

THE FACTS

Remembering Facts

1. What is the Third World?
2. Why are Third World nations called "developing" nations?
3. What is CIDA?
4. What is the United Nation's goal for 1990?
5. Describe one of the ways CIDA helps people in the Third World.

Finding Facts

In the Third World, people don't just turn on the tap to get water. Millions of women and children spend half their days carrying water in buckets over long distances.

How many times a day do you use running water? This means more than just getting a glass of water. Think of making a pitcher of lemonade, or boiling an egg, or brushing your teeth.

For 1 full day, keep a record of every single time you use running water. If you had to carry all the water you use would you change your habits? How?

YOUR OPINIONS

Stating Opinions

CIDA is not the only Canadian organization that helps in the Third World. It is just the main government organization.

There are more than 50 private organizations in Canada that also give aid. These are groups like churches. There are also groups you may have heard of like CARE Canada, Foster Parents Plan of Canada, and The Canadian Red Cross Society.

After reading this lesson, would you like to get involved in one of these private groups? Would you like to get involved personally in helping the Third World? Explain your opinion in a few sentences.

Discussing Opinions

One of the biggest problems in giving foreign aid is that so much is needed. It is very hard to decide which nations and which projects should get money. They all seem to deserve help.

Do you think it would be better if Canada gave all its money for aid to just 1 or 2 nations? Or do you think it is better to spend the money on hundreds of different projects in many different nations?

NEW WORDS

Learning Words

In your notebook, write the title Vocabulary: Lesson 66. Then write down the following words in a list. Using the Glossary or a dictionary, write the meaning beside each word.

When you are finished, write a short note telling what you have learned in this lesson. Try to use all 5 of these words in your note.

aid	**develop**	**sanitation**
scholarship	**technology**	

Examining Words

Biogas is made up of 2 parts: *bio* and *gas*. *Bio* comes from the Greek word meaning "life". Does this help you to explain what a *bio*graphy is? Do you know any other words that use *bio* meaning "life"?

AN ILLUSTRATION

The graph in Figure 66.5 shows 2 things. First, it shows how much income different parts of the world have. Second, it shows what percent of the world's population lives in these different areas. Study this graph. Then answer the following questions:

1. What area of the world has the highest income?
2. What arca of the world has the lowest income?
3. What area of the world has the most people?
4. What area of the world has the smallest number of people?
5. What is the balance like between income and people in the world?

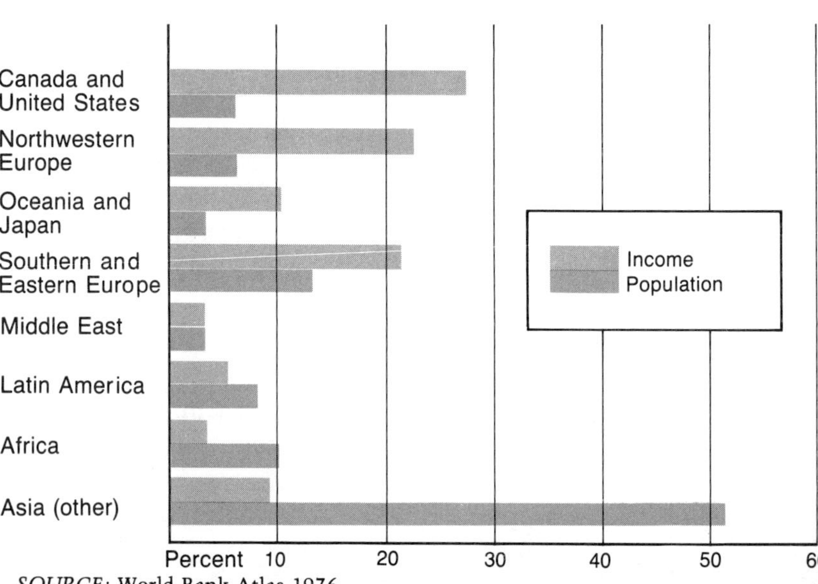

SOURCE: World Bank Atlas 1976

Figure 66.5 *Distribution of world population and income, 1975*

Sandra Simpson

Figure 66.6 *Sandra Simpson with two of her adopted children, Xalima Hassan Jama (left) from Somalia, and Manu Simpson (right), from India*

Claim to fame: She is volunteer head of Families for Children.

Born: 1937 in Baranquilla, Colombia, of Canadian parents

Married: 1955 to 1963 to Gerald Crotty. Their daughter, Kimberly, now works as a nurse in the Third World.

In 1965, Sandra married Lloyd Simpson. They have had 3 children of their own. They have also adopted more than 20 children from Third World countries. Many of these children had handicaps and needed special care.

Career: When World War II began, Sandra Simpson's parents left South America and returned to Quebec. Three-year-old Sandra could speak only Spanish. But she soon learned English at her new school.

Perhaps because she was born in South America, Simpson was always interested in the Third World. In the 1960s, there was a war in Vietnam. Simpson wanted to help the children whose parents had died in the fighting.

Simpson started an adoption agency. This agency helped people in rich countries to adopt the Vietnam orphans.

Soon Simpson started work in other parts of the Third World. She set up orphanages in countries like Bangladesh, India, and Somalia. Today, these orphanages are run by 250 paid workers and 18 volunteers. They have helped find homes for more than 3000 Third World orphans.

Simpson is not paid for all this. She is a volunteer. The government recognized how important her work is when she was made a member of the Order of Canada in 1984.

- **Where is Vietnam? Who was fighting in Vietnam in the 1960s?**
- **Do you think you might ever adopt a child? Why or why not?**

67 Shifting Power

It is easy for people in developed countries like Canada to think that they have more power than the people in Third World nations. After all, the people in Third World nations do not have the money and machines that we have.

But people in the Third World can have a big effect on what happens in countries like Canada. This was made very clear in 1973: the year of the oil crisis.

Oil is very important for developed countries like Canada. Oil is used to heat homes. Oil is used to make machines run smoothly. Oil is turned into gasoline to drive cars, trucks, and planes. Oil is turned into plastics and other modern materials. In other words, without oil, many of the things that go on in developed countries would stop.

Canada produces a lot of its own oil. This oil comes mainly from western provinces like Alberta. For many years it cost too much to send oil from Alberta to eastern Canada. It was actually cheaper to buy oil from Third World nations. Then this oil came by ship to Quebec and the Maritimes.

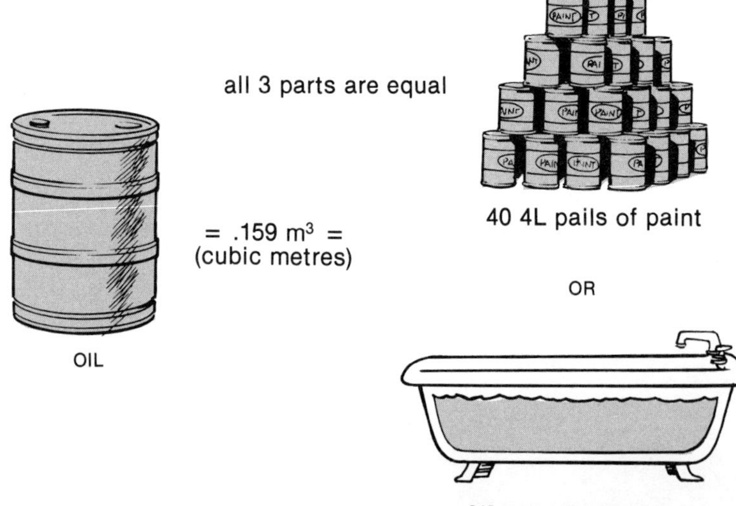

Figure 67.1 *How much is a barrel of oil?*

The Third World oil was cheap because there was so much of it. There was more oil than Canada and all the other developed countries could use. Therefore the nations that exported the oil could not get a fair price for it. In the 1960s, they were only getting about $1 for every **barrel** of oil.

However, countries like Canada started to use this cheap oil more and more. By the early 1970s, developed countries were using the oil as fast as it could be pumped out of the ground.

Then the Third World nations that produced the oil decided to get together. They wanted a fairer price for the oil. So they formed a group called OPEC. This is short for the **O**rganization of **P**etroleum **E**xporting **C**ountries.

In 1973, the OPEC nations decided to cut the amount of oil they would sell. Suddenly, there was a lot less oil available. People in the developed countries had to compete with each other to buy the oil. This caused the price to rise. By the end of the year, oil cost $23 for each barrel.

In the 1984 Summer Olympics, Canada collected 44 medals: more than all the medals won by Canadians in all the Summer Olympics since 1932.

Figure 67.2 Pilgrims arrive at Mecca *The main religion of many of the OPEC nations is Islam. The people in this photograph are pilgrims travelling to the Islamic holy city called Mecca (or Makkah). Find Mecca on a map of the Middle East. Look up the Islamic religion in an encyclopedia. Why is Mecca important in the Islamic religion?*

Figure 67.3 A bucket-wheel excavator at Fort McMurray, Alberta *There is lots of oil in Canada. But much of this oil is expensive to collect. For example, the tar sands in western Canada are filled with oil. But huge machines such as the one in this photograph are needed to separate the oil from the sand. If the man standing on the excavator is 180 cm tall, how high do you think the excavator is?*

This rise in price had a big effect in Canada. Home owners had to pay a lot more to heat their homes. Car drivers had to pay a lot more money for gasoline. Everything that had to be carried by truck suddenly cost more. For example, the price of food went up quickly.

In fact, the price of almost everything went up. As a result, workers started to ask for higher wages. But that also made prices rise. Things like appliances and cars cost more to buy because the workers who made them were being paid more.

This kind of quick rise in prices is called **inflation**. Soon many people could not afford to pay for the appliances and cars. They stopped buying them. And as a result, the manufacturers had to lay off many of their workers. Unemployment became a real problem.

The problems in Canada happened in other countries, too. Developed countries like the United States and Britain also had high inflation and unemployment.

MP Lincoln Alexander became the first Black Cabinet minister as Minister of Labour in 1979. In 1985 he became the Lieutenant Governor of Ontario.

Figure 67.4 *During the 1970s, many plans were made to build oil pipelines like this one. The plan was to bring oil from Alaska and the Northwest to the rest of Canada and the United States. These were expensive projects. Once the price of oil dropped, they were no longer worth building. How do you think a pipeline affects wildlife in the area?*

The trouble was that most countries kept on using as much oil as they had used in the past. In fact, countries like the United States actually used more oil than they ever had before. This meant that the OPEC nations could ask for higher and higher prices. By 1981, oil cost $35 a barrel.

But gradually, people began to **conserve** oil. They learned to use less. They drove smaller cars. They drove at slower speeds. They didn't drive as much. They turned down the heat in their houses. And they used more insulation.

Soon there was an oil **glut**. The OPEC nations had more oil to sell than people needed to buy. That meant that they could not charge such high prices. So the price of oil began to go down. In July of 1984, a barrel of oil cost $29.

This was a sign that the oil crisis was over, at least for the time being. But there was an important lesson from the oil crisis. It showed how small this world is. Things that happen in far-off places can have a big effect here at home.

In addition, the oil crisis taught us that Third World nations are important to our **economy** and way of life. Just because they are poorer does not mean that they cannot affect what happens to us.

The people of the Third World depend on us. But you can see that we also depend on them.

Launched in 1962, Canadian satellite *Alouette I* was the first satellite to be built outside the U.S. or Soviet Union.

THE FACTS

Remembering Facts

1. Why is oil important for developed countries?
2. Where does Canada get its oil from?
3. Why was OPEC started?
4. How did the rise in oil prices affect life in Canada?
5. Why did the price of oil go down after 1981?

Finding Facts

Several leaders of OPEC nations have had a big effect on world politics. Find out about one of the following leaders. Who was (is) this leader? What country did (does) he run? Describe a situation in which his actions had an effect on the rest of the world.

Shah Mohammad Reza Pahlavi
Colonel Muammar Qaddafi
Ayatollah Khomeini

YOUR OPINIONS

Stating Opinions

During the oil crisis, the United States government passed a law saying that drivers could not go faster than 80 km/h. Because they had to slow down so much, motorists saved on gas.

Do you think our government should pass the same law? Explain your opinion in a few sentences.

Discussing Opinions

When the OPEC price for oil started to rise, Alberta wanted to raise the price of its oil. If OPEC could get $35 for a barrel, Alberta thought that it should be able to get $35 for a barrel, too.

But the federal government wanted to keep the price of oil down for all Canadians. The federal government thought that if the prices could be kept lower, then there wouldn't be as much inflation and unemployment.

Therefore the federal government refused to let Alberta charge the OPEC price. Alberta was very angry about this. The premier of Alberta, Peter Lougheed, even cut back on the amount of oil that was produced.

Do you think that the federal government did the right thing? Or should Alberta have been allowed to sell its oil to other Canadian provinces for the OPEC price?

NEW WORDS

Learning Words

In your notebook, write the title Vocabulary: Lesson 67. Then write down the following words in a list. Using the Glossary or a dictionary, write the meaning beside each word.

When you are finished, write a short note telling what you have learned in this lesson. Try to use all 5 of these words in your note.

barrel	**conserve**	**economy**
glut	**inflation**	

Examining Words

Insula is a Latin word that means "island". Our English word *insulation* comes from this Latin word.

Can you explain the relationship between insulation and an island?

AN ILLUSTRATION

The price of a barrel of oil is given 4 times in this lesson. Find these 4 references. Then make a graph that shows the changing price of oil from 1960 to 1984. Use 1960 as the first year and $1 as the price.

Garth Taylor

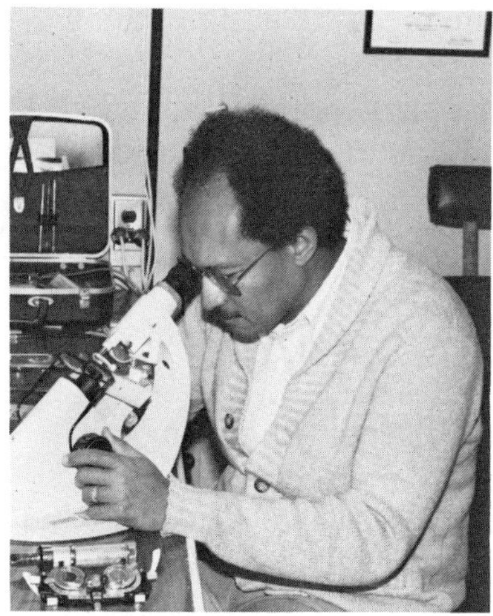

Figure 67.5 *Garth Taylor at work in his office.*

Claim to fame: He works three months a year helping to cure eye diseases in the Third World.

Born: 1944, Montego Bay, Jamaica.

Married: 1970 to Beverly McGill. They have a daughter and a son.

Career: As a boy in Jamaica, Dr. Taylor suffered from an eye disease. He decided to become an eye doctor to help other people like himself. He studied medicine at universities in Jamaica, Canada, and the United States. He is now chief of ophthalmology at Cornwall General Hospital in Ontario.

In 1982, Dr. Taylor was asked by a friend to join a team of doctors who were flying to Jamaica. They were members of Project Orbis, a group of doctors who volunteer their time to help cure eye diseases in the Third World. They work on board a DC-8 plane that has an operating room.

Since that first trip, Dr. Taylor has performed eye operations in over 16 different countries in the Third World. He finds this work very rewarding. For example, in Swaziland he operated on two children from a school for the blind who were later able to see. All the students from the school performed a traditional dance to thank him.

An important part of Dr. Taylor's work is to teach doctors in these countries to do the surgery themselves with their own instruments. In doing this, he finds he learns things which help him with his own patients at home.

- **Look up the word "orb" in the dictionary. Does this help explain the name "Project Orbis"?**
- **What other things can people do to help bring all the countries of the world closer together?**

Human Rights

68

Under the blazing African sun, a young boy, Adolfo, sits writing a letter. It is addressed to a stranger, a man Adolfo has seen only once in his life. But there is a faint chance that the man might help. And all Adolfo has left to live on is hope.

Adolfo asks the stranger for $50. This is not a huge sum of money. But for Adolfo it is an impossible amount. He has to have the money to pay for his education. Adolfo desperately wants to go to high school. But if he cannot pay, he cannot go.

Adolfo is a **refugee**. He is one of nearly 5 million refugees living in Africa today. One out of every 2 of these refugees is a child. Many of them, like Adolfo, are orphans.

Refugees are people who have fled from their homelands. They had lost their human rights in their own countries. If they had stayed at home, they would probably have been imprisoned, tortured, or even killed. They would have been **persecuted** like this because of their race, or their religion, or their politics.

Figure 68.1 *Over the years, Canada has accepted many refugees. These young children were sent from Britain in 1940 to escape the bombs in World War II. How do you think you would feel if you were in the situation of these children?*

To win a part in the musical *Oliver*, Karen Stolman of Burlington, Ontario, pretended to be a boy. She kept the secret for 3 months.

Sadly, there have been refugees all through history. The Bible tells of how the Jews were forced out of Egypt. Some of the first British settlers in North America came because they did not have religious freedom at home. Even the United Empire Loyalists who came to Canada were refugees. They were persecuted after the American Revolution because they were loyal to Britain.

There have always been refugees. But the fact is that there have been more refugees in this century than at any other time in history. Historians have named the twentieth century the "century of the refugee".

The numbers are awesome. During World Wars I and II, 70 million people were forced to leave their homes. Luckily, most of these people were able to return after the fighting was over.

However, several million of these refugees could not go back home. Some found new homes in countries like Canada. Others, like the Palestinians, are still waiting to find permanent homes.

To make matters worse, there have been many wars since World War II. Battles have been fought in far-off countries like Korea, Pakistan, Uganda, Vietnam, and El Salvador. These wars have added to the number of refugees. In fact, it is estimated that there are 10 million refugees in the world today.

Figure 68.2 *Both these dancers are refugees. Chinese ballet dancer Xing Bang Fu is on the left. He defected from China to the United States. On the right is Vietnamese Thanh Huynh (Dennis Wong). He was one of the thousands of "boat people" who escaped from Vietnam in 1979. Since coming to Canada at the age of 17, he has developed a whole new career for himself as a dancer and choreographer. Find out more about the boat people and the hardships they suffered trying to find a new country.*

It is very difficult to know how to help these refugees. The most common solution is to put them in camps. For example, Adolfo, the young boy described at the beginning of this lesson, lives in a refugee camp for boys in Africa.

The conditions in these camps are usually terrible. People are crowded together. They sleep in long rows on mats inside tents or huts made of sticks and leaves. All they are given to eat each day is 350 g of rice. Once a week, they are given an extra 200 g of fish or meat. There are only a few medical supplies and almost no doctors.

The main problem with refugee camps is that they are meant to be temporary. The people who live in these camps wait for the day when they can leave. But the question is, where can they go? Almost all of the refugee camps are in developing nations. Sometimes the citizens of the country where a camp is located are almost as poor as the refugees in the camp.

Blissymbolics, used for communication by more than 30 000 disabled people in the world, was created by Canadian Shirley McNaughton.

Figure 68.3 Ethiopian refugees waiting for food and medical aid *In 1984, the world suddenly woke up to the crisis in Ethiopia. Hundreds of thousands of Ethiopians were dying of starvation. Canadians opened their hearts to these people and donated money, clothing, food, and medical supplies. Is there still a problem in Ethiopia today?*

The longest covered bridge in the world is at Harland, New Brunswick. It is 390.7 m long.

One solution is to send the refugees to developed countries where they can start a new life. But this means that developed countries have to be willing to let these people come in.

Canada is very generous about accepting refugees. According to the 1983 *World Refugee Survey*, 1 out of every 70 people living in Canada is a refugee. The only country in the world where there are more refugees per person is Australia.

Normally Canada sets a **quota** for the refugees it will accept. In other words, the government will only accept a certain number of refugees each year.

The trouble is that it costs money to accept refugees. The refugees have to be flown here. They need to be housed, clothed, and fed for the first few months until they can support themselves. And usually they have to be taught English or French.

Another problem is that many refugees have a hard time **adjusting**. Getting used to the cold weather or strange foods can be a big problem for some refugees. Some find it hard to accept Canadian ideas about how people should behave.

Of course most refugees would like to go back to their homes. But this will not happen as long as governments **repress** people. We will always have refugees while there are countries that do not protect the human rights of all their citizens.

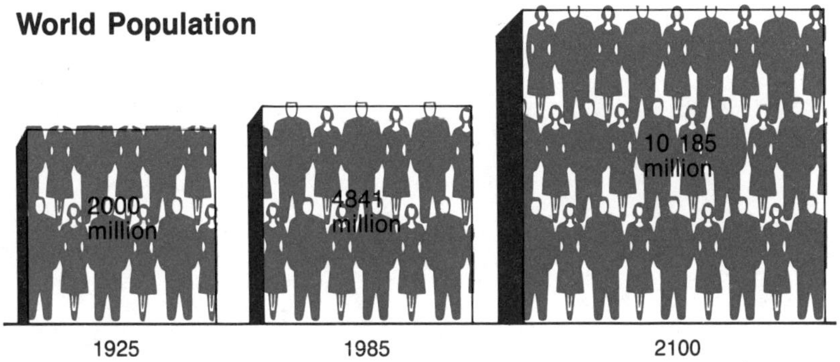

World Population

2000 million — 1925

4841 million — 1985

10 185 million — 2100

Figure 68.4 *This century has seen the largest rise ever recorded in the number of people in the world. The United Nations predicts that this growth will continue right into the twenty-first century. Most of the population increase has taken place in Third World countries. How will this affect the refugee problem?*

In 1924, English Canadian Professor John Squair won the Legion of Honour, France's highest award, for his work in bilingualism.

THE FACTS

Remembering Facts

1. Why do refugees leave their homes?
2. Why is this century called the "century of the refugee"?
3. How many refugees are there in the world today?
4. What is life like in refugee camps?
5. Why does Canada set a quota for accepting refugees?

Finding Facts

Many people in the world have had their human rights taken away from them. A few of these people have become world famous.

Find out about 1 of the following people. When and where did this person live? Who took away this person's human rights? Why did this person lose his or her human rights? What happened to this person? Why is this person famous?

Steve Biko
Anne Frank
Paul Robeson
Alexander Solzhenitsyn

YOUR OPINIONS

Stating Opinions

Imagine that you suddenly became a refugee and went to a country where they didn't speak English. How do you think you would feel about not being able to speak in English all the time?

Explain your opinion in a few sentences.

Discussing Opinions

What do you think it would be like to be a refugee in your community? Would it be easy or difficult? Would there be people or groups who would help you adjust to life in Canada? Or would you be left on your own?

Discuss these questions with your classmates. When you have finished, do some research to find out what *does* happen to refugees in your community.

NEW WORDS

Learning Words

In your notebook, write the title Vocabulary: Lesson 68. Then write down the following words in a list. Using the Glossary or a dictionary, write the meaning beside each word.

When you are finished, write a short note telling what you have learned in this lesson. Try to use all 5 of these words in your note.

adjust	**persecute**	**quota**
refugee	**repress**	

Examining Words

The word *awesome* means ''overwhelming'' or ''terrifying''. Something that is *awesome* fills you with awe or fear.

One of the following words also comes from the word *awe*. Can you tell which one?

away awful awkward

Figure 68.5 is a graph showing the rise in Canada's population. The graph was produced in the early 1970s. The line up until 1973 is accurate. The lines after 1973 are estimates. The *actual* population of Canada in 1981 was 24 343 181 million. Was the estimate on this graph correct for 1981?

Compare this graph with Figure 68.4. Is Canada's population rising more quickly or more slowly than the world's population as a whole? Why do you think this is so?

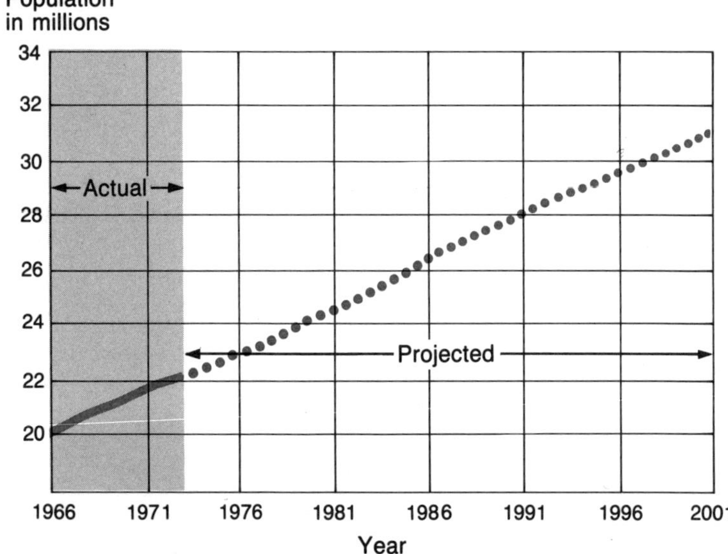

SOURCE: Adapted from Canada Year Book 1967-77

Figure 68.5 *Projections for Canada's population to the year 2001*

Sandra Lovelace

Figure 68.6 *Sandra Lovelace*

Claim to fame: She fought Canada in front of the United Nations Human Rights Committee.

Born: 1948 on the Tobique Indian reserve in New Brunswick. Her grandfather had been chief on the reserve for 22 years.

Married: 1970 to a non-Indian. They were divorced in 1976.

Career: Sandra Lovelace met and married her non-Indian husband at the American Air Force base just across the border in Maine.

After their divorce, Lovelace tried to go back to the reserve. But to her surprise, they wouldn't let her live there. She found out that by marrying a man who wasn't an Indian she had lost her status as an Indian. According to Canadian law, she no longer had the legal rights of an Indian.

Many other Indian women had gone through this. They were angry because Indian men who married non-Indian women were not treated the same way. The men were allowed to keep their rights as Indians. And their wives were also given the rights of Indians.

The Indian women had made many protests. Some of them had even taken the government to court. But the situation did not change.

As a last resort, Lovelace took her case to the United Nations Human Rights Committee. The case was embarrassing for Canada and the UN. But after 4 years, the UN Committee passed judgement. It said that Canada was guilty. It said that Indian women had been denied their human rights and should get them back.

- **Is it still true that an Indian woman will lose her rights if she marries a non-Indian? Or has this law finally been changed?**
- **Why do you think Lovelace's case was embarrassing for Canada?**

69 This Planet Earth

Figure 69.1 *Marshall McLuhan was the world-famous Canadian philosopher who coined the phrase "global village". He was one of the first people to recognize how much inventions like television and computers were changing our lives. Could you imagine living in a world without these inventions? How important are they to your life?*

Montreal singer France Joli won 2 gold medals at the 1984 Popular Song Festival for her performance of *Party Lights*.

In 1867, when Canada came into being, the world was a very different place from what it is today. Journeys to other countries were usually difficult and dangerous. Letters could take several months to be delivered.

Today, tourists can fly to countries on the other side of the earth in just a few hours. Places like India and China are just a quick phone call away. Through satellites and television, we can even watch live events from half way around the globe.

You could say that the world has become a much smaller place since 1867. The earth has become a "global village". We have all become close neighbours on this planet because of **technological** advances. **Inventions** like airplanes and cars and television and **satellites** have brought us all into close **contact**.

Unfortunately, these technological advances are not all for the good. They have also brought problems that threaten people's lives. For example, technology has brought us modern weapons. As you have learned, millions of people have been injured and killed with these weapons. A nuclear war could destroy all life on earth.

Technology has also brought us pollution. For example, in Lesson 52, you learned about the problems of acid rain. This problem is serious. It affects our whole environment and our health.

But at least Canada and the United States are rich nations. They have the power and the money to be able to cure this problem. All they need to do is to agree on its importance. It is not so easy for people in developing nations.

For example, think of Mexico. This country lies along the other side of the United States border. It is just as close to the United States as Canada is. But Mexico is a developing nation. Life there is totally different.

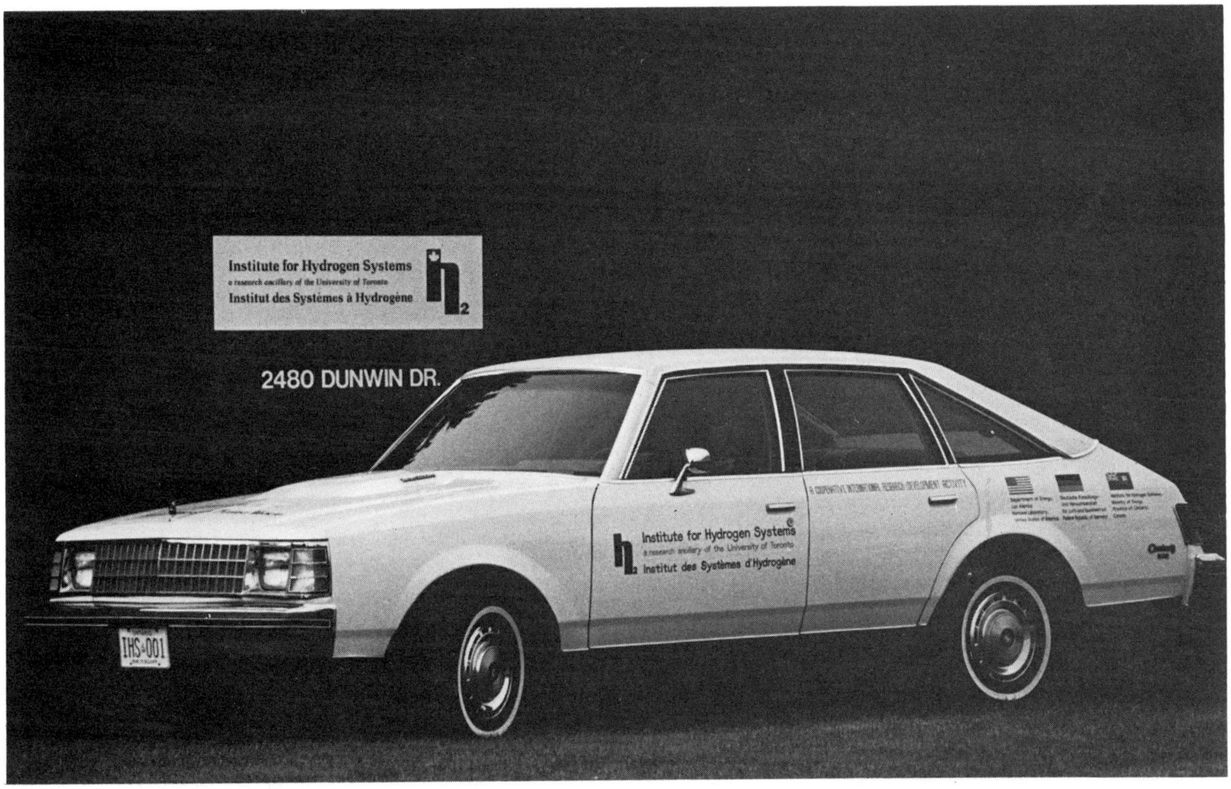

Figure 69.2 *This car looks no different from any other. But it is actually powered by hydrogen rather than by gasoline. The large tank needed for the hydrogen is hidden in the trunk. The Canadian scientists who developed and tested this fuel system want people to stop burning fossil fuels like regular gasoline. Fossil fuels give off gases that trap the earth's air. This creates a "greenhouse effect", making the earth hotter and hotter. Scientists predict that at the current rate of using fossil fuels, the earth will heat up to unbearable temperatures by the year 2035.*

There are 17 million people living in Mexico City, the capital of Mexico. The pollution from factories and cars in Mexico City is almost unbearable. Every year this pollution kills 70 000 adults. Another 30 000 children are also killed.

Every day, 4000 tonnes of garbage are thrown on the streets. The Mexicans do not have the money or the trucks to take it away. Instead it lies there to rot. The flies and rats that feed on the garbage spread disease throughout the city.

Twelve million people live in Cairo, the capital of Egypt. The pollution there is even worse. It is 4 times what is considered dangerous for human health. Millions of the people living in Cairo have no way to get rid of garbage or sewage. All they can do is to throw it in the streets.

There are many other cities in the world like Mexico City and Cairo. This should make you happy that you live in a country like Canada. But it should also make you think. How long can we ignore the problems facing the other nations in the world?

Organizations like CIDA and the UN can help. But this is not enough. Technology has left too big a **gap** between the poor and the rich nations. In the future, countries like Canada will have to work to close this gap.

It's safer to be born in Canada than in the United States (12% more babies die at birth) or Britain (16% more die).

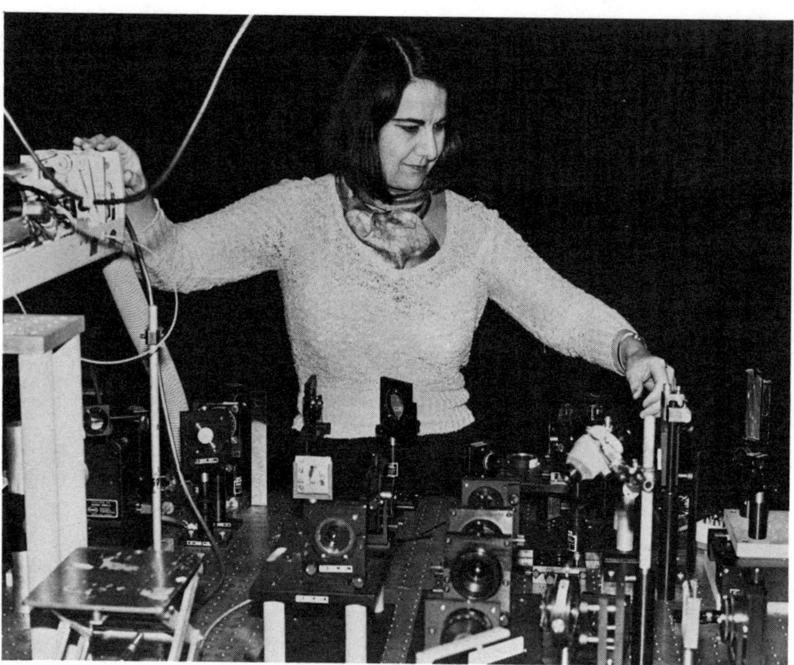

Figure 69.3 *Canadian scientist Dr. Geraldine Kenney-Wallace is one of the world's top experts on lasers. In this photograph she is conducting an experiment using a beam of laser light. She is measuring its speed in trillionths of a second. Lasers are already used in hundreds of different fields, from communications to medicine. But more scientific research of this kind is necessary if Canada is to keep pace with the rest of the developed world.*

This is something that we *should* do. But it is also something that we *have* to do. Because we live in a global village, we can now see the suffering of the poorer nations. And more and more of the world's poor know about Canada's wide open spaces, rich crops, fresh water, and natural resources.

In Lesson 67, you learned how the OPEC nations controlled the world's oil supply. This power meant that they could raise the price of oil. And they used their power to get some of the wealth from the developed nations for themselves.

Other developing nations may some day have different kinds of power. For example, it is possible that they will get physical power in the form of nuclear weapons. They might use this power to take a greater share of the world's wealth.

Canada will have to face these and other problems in the future. Our history shows that we can face difficult problems and find solutions to them. But we will have to use all our experience and resources to meet the new challenges that lie ahead.

Canadian scientist David Strangway worked for 3 years training American astronauts to conduct experiments on the moon.

THE FACTS

Remembering Facts

1. Why is the earth called a "global village"?
2. What is 1 problem that has been caused by technological advances?
3. Why is pollution not as big a problem for Canada as it is for developing nations?
4. How many people live in Mexico City?
5. How bad is the pollution in Cairo?

Finding Facts

External Affairs is a department of the Canadian government. This department takes care of dealings with other countries.

Canada didn't even have a department of External Affairs until 1909. There were only 5 employees that first year. Their office was above a barbershop on Bank Street in Ottawa. And the total budget was only $13 350.

Today, External Affairs is a huge operation. Use encyclopedias or write directly to External Affairs to find out about how it is run. How many people work for External Affairs today? What sorts of things do these people do? What is the yearly budget of External Affairs?

YOUR OPINIONS

Stating Opinions

In the near future, ordinary people will probably be taking trips in space. Would *you* like to travel in space some day? Explain your opinion in a few sentences.

Discussing Opinions

One thing that stops people from different countries from working together is the language barrier. It is difficult to get together when you do not speak the same language and have to use interpreters.

In 1887, a language scholar invented a new language called Esperanto. It was made up of parts taken from the main European languages. The scholar hoped that Esperanto would become a universal language. He hoped that everyone would learn it.

Do you think it would be a good idea for all school children to learn Esperanto? Can you think of any other solutions to the language barrier?

NEW WORDS

Learning Words

In your notebook, write the title Vocabulary: Lesson 69. Then write down the following words in a list. Using the Glossary or a dictionary, write the meaning beside each word.

When you are finished, write a short note telling what you have learned in this lesson. Try to use all 5 of these words in your note.

contact	**gap**	**invention**
satellite	**technological**	

Examining Words

The short form for television is TV. Many modern appliances and inventions have short forms. Do you know what the following short forms stand for?

LED VCR RAM K VHS

AN ILLUSTRATION

Figure 69.4 shows the world's top 12 languages according to the number of people who speak them. What is the language spoken by the most people? How many people speak English? How many people speak French? Do any of these figures surprise you?

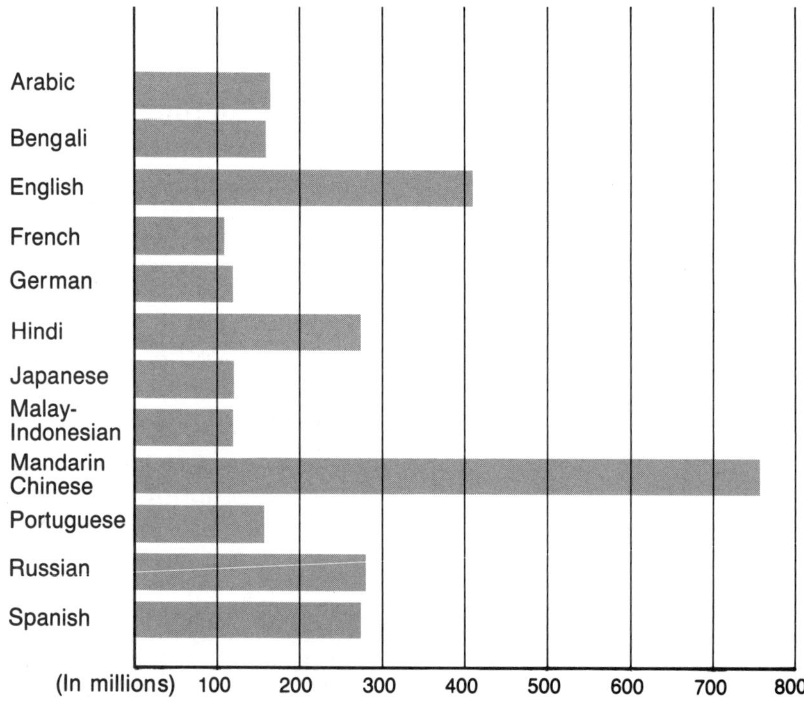

SOURCE: The World Almanac and Book of Facts 1985

Figure 69.4 *The top 12 languages spoken in the world today.*

Marc Garneau

Figure 69.5 *Marc Garneau appears to be upside down as he is photographed on board the Space Shuttle* Challenger. *Beside him is American astronaut David Leeshma.*

Claim to fame: He was the first Canadian astronaut to go into outer space.

Born: 1949 in Quebec City, Quebec

Married: 1973 to Jacqueline Brown. Marc was in space on the day of their eleventh wedding anniversary. Their children, Yves and Simone, are twins.

Career: Garneau's father was a brigadier general in the Canadian army. That meant the family was always on the move, living on military bases in Germany, Canada, and England.

Marc loved the military life. So it wasn't surprising when he decided to attend the Collège Militaire Royal in Quebec. Afterwards, he went on to earn a Ph.D. in electrical engineering in London, England.

Garneau then joined the navy, eventually becoming a commander on the Canadian destroyer, HMCS *Algonquin*. As well as sailing the seas on the big destroyer, Garneau has also crossed the Atlantic twice in a small sailboat.

In 1981, the government announced plans to send a Canadian into space. There were more than 4000 applicants for the job. Garneau was one of 5 Canadians who were chosen for training as astronauts.

After months of intensive training, Garneau was chosen to be the very first Canadian in space. He was part of a 7-member crew aboard the United States space shuttle, Challenger.

At precisely 07:03 on Friday, October 6, 1984, Garneau blasted off into space and into Canadian history. Among the items he carried with him were a Canadian flag and a hockey puck from the National Hockey League.

- **Who were the other 5 Canadian astronauts chosen in 1981?**
- **Would you enjoy being in a military family and moving to different bases in a number of countries?**

QUIZ 10

The following questions are based on the lessons in Chapter 10. **DO NOT WRITE YOUR ANSWERS IN THIS TEXTBOOK.** Instead, you should write the answers in your notebook or on a separate sheet of paper.

1. There are 6 blanks in the following paragraphs about Canada. They have been labelled from (a) to (f). Write down the 6 answers in a list on your paper. Then beside each answer write the letter of the blank where it belongs.

deployed	limitation
superpowers	jumbo jet
peace movement	nuclear

In 1983, Soviet pilots shot down a (a) ______ that was flying over secret Soviet bases. This was a sign of tension between the two (b) ______: the United States and the Soviet Union. Just a few months later, the United States (c) ______ nearly six hundred missiles in Europe. This caused the Soviets to break off the arms (d) ______ talks. Thousands of ordinary people across the world joined the (e) ______ because they wanted to stop the spread of (f) ______ weapons.

2. Match the item in the list on the left side with the correct description from the list on the right side. For each one, write the letter and the number together on your paper.

(a) SALT	(1)	the group of developing nations that sell oil and worked together to raise the price
(b) CIDA	(2)	the poor countries in the world that do not have the kind of technology Canada has
(c) OPEC	(3)	the world organization that tries to help the people living in developing nations
(d) UN	(4)	the Canadian government agency that gives aid to developing nations
(e) the Third World	(5)	the talks held between the United States and the Soviet Union to try to limit nuclear weapons

3. Write the letters from (a) to (e) on your paper. Then write a T if the statement is TRUE. Write an F if the statement is FALSE.

   (a) For every $1 that is spent on foreign aid in the world, another $25 are spent on making weapons.
   (b) Canadians use only oil that comes from provinces out west such as Alberta.
   (c) One out of every 2 refugees in Africa is a child.
   (d) Canada allows in as many refugees as want to come here.
   (e) Pollution is a big problem in some developing nations.

GLOSSARY

A glossary is a kind of dictionary. It explains the meanings of important terms. In this glossary you will find all the words that appear in the "Learning Words" activities. The lesson each word comes from is shown in brackets at the end of the explanation.

A glossary is also different from a dictionary. It does not explain all the meanings of a single word. For example, look up the word "right" in this glossary. Of course the word "right" has many more meanings than the one given here. However, this glossary only gives the meaning of "right" according to the way it is used in Lesson 16.

For this reason, it would be a good idea to compare the meanings given in this glossary with the meanings given in a regular dictionary. In this way, you can see whether the word has any other meanings that would be useful for you to know.

A

abolish end; put a stop to (5)
absolute complete (61)
abuse damage; harm (30)
accommodate make room for differences between groups (32)
adjust fit in (68)
advance move forward (57)
adversary someone on the opposite side (19)
agricultural having to do with farming (40)
aid help (66)
ally a nation that helps another, especially in war (55)
amendment change; addition (2)
ammunition bullets (58)
ancestor parent, grandparent, etc. (Introduction)
appeal ask for a second opinion (22)
appointment assignment (5)
arbitration settlement by a judge (50)
arbitrator person who decides an argument between two or more parties (25)
argument reason (49)
arrest take prisoner (18)
artist performer (56)
assassination murder of an important person by someone disloyal (57)
assault violent attack (30)
assembly meeting (7)
assess decide the amount of (9)
asset something of value (26)
assimilate to absorb one group completely into another (32)
association group; connection (43)
asylum shelter (63)
attitude way of thinking (56)
automatic held at regular set times (12)

B

bail deposit allowing a person charged with a crime to go free until trial (29)
balance the relationship between the money coming in and the money going out (53)
ballot paper marked in voting (14)
bargain to work out a deal or an agreement (25)
barrel an amount of oil equal to about 35 four-litre pails of paint (67)
base main location (45)
battery beating or hitting someone again and again (30)
benefit profit (9)
betray give over to an enemy (40)
bill a proposal for a law (4)

border boundary line between two areas (6)
branch smaller part of division (54)
breakthrough important or dramatic change in a situation (44)
broker person who arranges the buying and selling of stocks and bonds (60)
business trade; buying and selling (41)

C

calm quiet (64)
campaign pre-election activities (13)
cancel take back; cross out (34)
candidate person applying for or running for office (11)
capacity ability (23)
capital centre of government (6); the basic amount of money used to start a business or to earn interest (54)
capture take by force (31)
citadel fortress (48)
civilian not in the armed forces (65)
claim demand (23)
clash fight (45)
clerk record-keeper (14)
collect take in (9)
collective as a group (25)
colony settlement in a new country that is ruled by the old country where the settlers first came from (31)
commercial advertising (56)
commission group of people having the legal power to do certain things (51)
common based on earlier law cases (20)
compromise agreement in which each side gives up a little (37)
condemn sentence (36)
conference meeting (49)
confidence faith; trust (12)
confident sure (27)
conflict disagreement (16)
connection relation (44)
conquest victory (32)
conscription being forced by law to join the armed forces for a set period of time (38)
consent agree (23)
consequence result (46)
conserve save (67)
consideration something of value (23)
constitution set of laws for running a country (2)
contact being in touch (69)
contract legal agreement between two parties (23)
contribution amount given (64)
control power (18)
convince persuade (13)
convoy group of ships (61)
corrupt dishonest (40)
council group of political advisors (33)
crisis turning point (38)
criticize find fault with (63)
culture language and customs of a group of people (32)
cure preserve (46)
custody care (26)
customs taxes paid on things brought in from a foreign country (50)

D

deadlock at a standstill; unable to come to agreement (35)
debate formal argument (1)
declare announce (47)
defence protection (55)
defendant person or party who has been charged with breaking the law (19)
deform ruin the shape of (52)
demand insist on (10)
democracy society in which the government is elected by the people (4)
deploy set out in a battle line (65)
deposit money given as a sign of serious intention to run for election (11)
deputy assistant (14)
descendant child, grandchild, etc. (Introduction)
deterrent something that prevents (22)
develop become more industrialized (66)
dictator a person who acts with total authority (61)
dilemma situation involving a different choice (37)
disagree have a different opinion (37)
discuss talk about (4)
dispute argument; disagreement (50)
division separation into two or more parts (34)
divorce legal ending of a marriage (26)
domestic having to do with the home (30)
donate give (13)
doomed fated to fail (65)
dose quantity of medicine (28)
drug substance that affects the body or mind (28)
duty an action that has to be done (3)

E

economy the state of wealth in a community (67)
eligible qualified (12)
emission something given off into the air (52)
encourage urge on (47)
enforce uphold (6)
enlist become a member of the armed forces (38)
enumerator person who counts and lists voters (12)
espionage spying (62)
essential very important; necessary (58)
ethnic having to do with a national group (Introduction)
evict force out (24)
evidence proof (20)
exaggerate say or think something is greater than it really is (42)
exception something not included (17)
excuse free; allow to go (21)
exile being forced to live away from your home or country (31)
export send goods to another country (53)

F

federalist in Canada, a person who thinks a strong central or federal government is best (44)
federation union; joining together to act as one (35)
Fenian member of an Irish secret organization (49)
fierce intense; violent (31)
flare burn hot (44)
foreigner person from another place or country (40)
formula system for doing something (2)
furious very angry (45)

G

gap distance (69)
generation people born around the same time (Introduction)
global having to do with the whole world (65)
glut having too much of a supply (67)
goal something aimed at (43)
goods items or property that can be moved (29)
grand large; major (29)

H

harass bother or annoy someone again and again (25)
headquarters main location (15)
Holocaust the killing of more than 6 million Jews in World War II (62)
host someone who receives others as guests (7)
humiliate make someone feel embarrassed or ashamed (61)

I

ignore pay no attention to (10)
immigrant someone who moves to a country from somewhere else (Introduction)
impaired drunk or on drugs (27)
impartial not taking sides (51)
import bring in goods from another country (53)
income money earned (9)
independent not relying on another (2)
industry manufacturing (41)
inflation increase in prices (67)
inform tell (6)
infringe trespass on; cut into another's rights (16)
insult treat someone rudely (35)
intend mean to; plan on (30)
interfere disturb (37)
intern keep in a place by force (62)
interpret explain the meaning of (18)
invade enter with force (39)
invention something newly made or discovered (69)
investment amount of money laid out in hope of earning interest (54)
investor person who hopes to earn interest on money lent (60)
isolate place someone or something alone (39)
issue subject or topic on which people have different opinions (13)

J

jury group of people (usually 12) in a trial who hear the evidence and decide whether a person is guilty (21)

K

kidnap carry off and hold by force (42)

L

landlord person who rents a place to someone else (24)
launch set off (65)
league group or association for helping one another (59)

lease rental agreement (24)
legal allowed by law (10)
legislate pass a law (17)
legislature group of people who make laws (7)
leisure free time (59)
licence paper or legal document that gives permission to do something (16)
limit restriction (27)
lockout act of keeping workers out of their workplace until they agree to terms (25)
lodging a place to stay (60)
loot rob (33)
loyal faithful (49)

M

majority more than half (4)
margin extra amount (15)
maritime having to do with the sea (35)
market group of people who buy goods (53)
massive huge (51)
merchant someone who buys and sells (33)
Métis people who are part European and part North American Indian (36)
military the armed forces (38)
minority smaller of 2 parts of a group (15)
missile rocket containing explosives (55)
modify make different; change (17)
monarch ruler; king or queen (5)
mortgage loan agreement for borrowing money to buy a house or other such property (60)
motto saying that is linked to a person or group (1)
multiculturalism having many different cultures side by side (56)
municipal having to do with the government of a city or local district (8)

N

negotiator one who arranges terms of an agreement (46)
neutral not taking sides (45)
nominate suggest for office (11)
nuclear having to do with atomic energy (55)

O

obstacle something in the way (51)
occupy take over (63)
offence crime (21)
official used as part of a person's office in government (6)
Opposition political party with the second highest number of elected members (4)
overlap partly cover (3)
overseas countries on the other side of the ocean (39)
overthrow take power from; defeat (63)

P

pact agreement (63)
pardon forgive (36)
partner one who shares (44)
party people acting together in politics for particular aims (11)
peaceable preferring peace to war (64)
peaceful calm (17)
penalty punishment (20)
permanent lasting forever (5)
permission consent (2)
persecute do harm to (68)
petty minor; small (29)
pioneer someone who opens up new land (46)
plaintiff person or party who starts a lawsuit (19)
plaque flat wall plate, often with writing on it (51)
plebiscite vote of all the people (39)
poll voting place (12)
pollute make dirty or poisonous (52)
possession having or carrying a drug when it is illegal to do so (28)
power ability to act or control (3)
practical concerned more with action than with thought (41)
precaution something done beforehand to prevent problems (14)
precedent example from before (20)
precious valuable (58)
predict tell beforehand (40)
premier chief officer (7)
prescribe give medical directions (28)
private not in public (14)
probation time when close watch is kept on a lawbreaker who is free from jail early (22)
procedure course of action (26)
proclamation an official announcement (32)
profit gain (54)
profiteer make an unfair profit from business (58)
property housing or land; possessions (5)
prosperity good fortune (59)
protect keep from harm (17)
protest object to (59)

Protestant a branch of the Christian church (often used to mean those Christians who are neither Roman Catholic nor Orthodox) (36)
publicity public notice; advertising (13)
pursuit chase (18)

Q

qualification requirement (10)
qualified licensed (27)
quota allowed amount (68)

R

radar system that can tell distance and speed of objects too far away to be seen (55)
radical person with extreme views (42)
raid sudden attack (48)
rally meeting; assembly (61)
ration allowance (62)
rebellion armed revolt against those in power (33)
reciprocity exchange of privileges, especially between countries which trade with each other (50)
recognize come to see (56)
recommend suggest; speak or write in favour of (42)
referee judge (50)
referendum vote on a question by all the voters, not just by their government representatives (43)
refugee person who has fled from trouble in his or her homeland (68)
regulate control (8)
regulation rule (26)
rehabilitate change for the better (22)
release let go (39)
relief assistance (60)
rely depend (15)
representative someone who stands for a larger group (1)
repress put down (68)
reputation how a person is thought of by others (64)
request something asked for (46)
requirement something that is needed (11)
resource raw material such as trees or oil (3)
respect honour (59)
responsibility something that a person is supposed to do or look after (16)
responsible accountable; required to answer to the people (35)
retreat moving back (57)
revenge getting back at someone who has caused you harm (47)
revolution great change; uprising (41)
right something a person is entitled to (16)
robbery stealing by force (29)
route road; way taken (48)
rural having to do with the country (8)

S

sacrifice give up (57)
sanitation conditions for protecting health (66)
satellite human-made object orbiting in space (69)
scholarship money given to help a student pay for schooling (66)
segregate separate from others (22)
separate not together; apart (1)
sequester set apart; isolate (21)
settle deal with; get rid of (37)
share part of a company (54)
side agree (34)
slavery being the property of someone else (49)
slogan saying (41)
smelter furnace for heating metals (52)
solution answer (15)
sovereignty power and authority, especially that of a country or nation (43)
station place (48)
statute written law (20)
strategy plan for winning (43)
stunt shorten (52)
suffrage right to vote (10)
surrender give up (31)
suspension taking away for a time (27)
suspicion mistrust; doubt (62)
sympathetic understanding and sharing the same feelings (42)

T

tax charge on income or property (9)
technological having to do with machinery (69)
technology knowledge about machinery (66)
temporary for a time only; not forever (58)
tenant renter (24)
tension strain (3)
territory region (7)
timber wood (48)
trade buying and selling (53)
trafficking buying, selling, growing, or making illegal drugs (28)

traitor person who is disloyal to his or her country (36)
treaty agreement between two sides after fighting each other (47)
trench ditch (57)
trial process for deciding on a case in a law court (19)
trustee person responsible for something or for someone else (8)

U

unanimous having everyone's agreement (21)
unite bring together (34)
uprising revolt or rebellion against people in power (45)
urban having to do with the city or town (8)
utility service such as water or electricity (24)

V

versus against (33)
victory success in contest or battle (47)
volunteer offer freely (38)

W

warlike fond of fighting (64)
warrant legal paper giving permission for something (18)
wealth money; riches (1)
wealthy rich (34)
witness person who has evidence about a case (19)

CREDITS AND SOURCES

The publisher wishes to acknowledge the following sources for the use of photographs:

Introduction
Figure (1.a.). Glenbow Archives.
Figures (1.b.), (1.c.), (1.e.), (1.g.). Public Archives Canada.
Figure (1.d.). Canadian Army Photo/Public Archives of Nova Scotia.
Figure (1.f.). W.J. Sisler Collection/Provincial Archives of Manitoba.
Figure (2.a.). Ministry of Education, Ontario.
Figure (2.b.). Rudi Haas.
Figure 4. Department of Secretary of State.
Figure 5. Ministry of Citizenship and Culture for the province of Ontario.
Figure 6. The Iannucci Family and Birgitte Nielsen.

Unit One: Chapter One
Figure (1.2.a.). Notman Photographic Archives, McCord Museum.
Figure (1.2.b.). Provincial Archives of New Brunswick.
Figure (1.2.c.). Archives of Ontario.
Figure 1.4. Canadian Railroad Historical Association.
Figures 1.5, 2.1, 3.4, 4.4, 5.2, 6.1, (6.2.a.), 6.4. Public Archives Canada.
Figure (6.2.b.). D. Cameron/Public Archives Canada.
Figures 2.2, 4.2, 5.1, 7.4, 9.5. Canapress Photo Service.
Figure 2.6. Liberal Party of Canada.
Figures 3.3, 6.3. The Ottawa Citizen.
Figures 4.6, (6.2.c.). Office of the Governor General and Commander-In-Chief.
Figure 5.4. Rideau Hall, Ottawa.
Figure 5.5. City of Edmonton Archives.
Figure (7.3.a.). Imperial Oil Limited.
Figure (7.3.b.). Abitibi-Price Inc.
Figure (7.3.c.). Ford Motor Company of Canada Ltd.
Figure (7.3.d.). Transportation Railway 28/Manitoba Archives.
Figure (7.3.e.). MacMillan Bloedel.
Figure (7.3.f.). H. Barfod.
Figure 8.1. Media Club of Canada/Public Archives Canada.
Figures (8.4.a.), 8.5. City of Toronto Archives.
Figure (8.4.b.). Provincial Archives of Newfoundland and Labrador.
Figure (8.4.c.). Toronto Transit Commission.
Figure 9.1. The Toronto Star Syndicate.
Figure 9.2. The Sun, Vancouver.
Figure 9.3. Revenue Canada — Customs and Excise.

Unit One: Chapter Two
Figures 10.2, 10.3, 10.4, 11.4, 14.1, 14.2, 15.2. Public Archives Canada.
Figures 11.1, 12.2, 12.3, (13.3.a.). Canapress Photo Service.
Figure 11.3. The Toronto Star Syndicate.
Figure 12.1. Photo by Brian Willer/MacLean's.
Figures 12.4, 15.5. Liberal Party of Canada.
Figure 13.1. New Democratic Party.
Figure 13.2. Paul Regan/The Toronto Star Syndicate.
Figure (13.3.b.). Dick Darrell/The Toronto Star Syndicate.
Figure 13.4. Fred Phipps/CBC.
Figure 14.4. Flora MacDonald.
Figure 15.1. Manitoba Archives.
Figure 15.3. Bren Kenney/Provincial Archives of Newfoundland and Labrador.

Unit Two: Chapter Three
Figures 16.1, 17.2, 17.3, 20.4, 21.1. Public Archives Canada.
Figure 16.2. Chris Coderre.
Figure 16.3. The Toronto Star Syndicate.
Figure 17.1. B.H. Sterling Collection/Public Archives of Prince Edward Island.
Figure 18.1. Photo by Pringle and Booth, Toronto 1924. *Courtesy* Bell Canada Telephone Historical Collection.
Figure 18.2. Ontario Provincial Police.
Figure 18.3. Sergeant Sam Donaghey/Edmonton Police.
Figure 19.1. Ottawa Police Department.
Figures 19.2, 20.2. Miller Services.
Figure 19.5. University of Toronto.
Figure 20.1. The General Synod of the Anglican Church of Canada/Vale Photo.
Figure 22.1. W.J. Topley/Public Archives Canada.
Figures 21.2, 21.3. Canapress Photo Service.
Figure 22.2. Ontario Ministry of Correctional Services.
Figure 22.3. Whig-Standard/Canapress Photo Service.
Figure 22.5. Karsh/Public Archives Canada.

Unit Two: Chapter Four
Figure 23.1. Canadian Pacific Corporate Archives.
Figures 23.2, 24.2. The Toronto Star Syndicate.
Figure 23.3. Canadian Imperial Bank of Commerce.
Figure 23.4. Canapress Photo Service.
Figure 24.1. Vancouver City Archives.
Figures 24.3, 29.2. Uluschak/Miller Services.
Figure 24.5. Paul Rockett/Chatelaine Magazine.

Figures 25.1, 25.2, 28.1. Public Archives Canada.
Figure 25.4. McDonald's Restaurants of Canada Limited.
Figure 25.5. Canadian Union of Public Employees.
Figure 26.1. Whyte Museum of the Canadian Rockies, Banff, Alberta.
Figure 26.2. Anne Levenson/The Toronto Star Syndicate.
Figure 26.3. Office of the Registrar General.
Figure 26.4. By Betty Swords. Reprinted from Male Chauvinist Pig Calendar 1974. Copyright R/M Hurley.
Figure 27.1. Provincial Archives of British Columbia.
Figure 27.2. Vancouver City Archives.
Figure 27.3. Royal Canadian Mounted Police.
Figure 27.4. Ontario Ministry of Transportation and Communications.
Figure 27.5. Deni Eagland/Vancouver Sun.
Figure 28.2. United Church Archives, Victoria University, Toronto.
Figure 28.4. Len Sideway/The Montreal Gazette.
Figure 29.1. Foote Collection/Manitoba Archives.
Figure 29.4. Metropolitan Toronto Library.
Figure 30.1. Vancouver Public Library Photo.
Figure 30.2. Denis Brodeur.
Figure 30.4. The Toronto Sun.

Unit Three: Chapter Five

Figure IIIB. Editeur Officiel du Québec.
Figures (31.2.a.), 33.4, 34.1, 34.2, 35.1, 35.2, 35.5, 36.1, 36.4, 36.5, 37.1, 37.3. Public Archives Canada.
Figure (31.2.b.). Ministère du Tourisme du Québec.
Figures 31.3, 32.4. Canapress Photo Service.
Figure 31.4. McNally/The Montreal Gazette.
Figure 31.5. Canada Post Corporation.
Figure 32.2. Provincial Archives of New Brunswick.
Figure 32.3. Photo by Melvin Gallant.
Figures (33.2.a.), (33.2.b.). Les Editions de L'Homme.
Figure 33.3. Le Château Montebello.
Figure 34.4. Cornelius Krieghoff Collection/The National Gallery of Canada Ottawa.
Figure (35.3.a.). S. McLaughlin/Public Archives Canada.
Figure (35.3.b.). Notman Photographic Archives/ McCord Museum.
Figure 36.2. Mathers/Public Archives Canada.
Figure 36.3. James Peters/Public Archives Canada.
Figure 37.2. Glenbow Archives.
Figure 37.4. Acadia University Archives.
Figure 37.5. Ontario Ministry of Tourism and Recreation.

Unit Three: Chapter Six

Figure 38.1. APC/Public Archives Canada.
Figures 38.2, 39.3, 39.5, 40.1, 40.3, 41.2, 42.3, 43.4. Public Archives Canada.
Figure 38.3. United Church Archives, Victoria University, Toronto.
Figure 38.4. Metropolitan Toronto Library.
Figure 39.1. Canadian Pacific Corporate Archives.
Figure 39.2. Milne Studio Ltd/Public Archives Canada.
Figure 40.2. McGill University Archives.
Figures 40.4, 41.1, 42.4, 43.1, 44.3. Canapress Photo Service.
Figure 41.3. Jehane Benoit.
Figure 41.4. Denis Brodeur.
Figure 41.6. Photo by John Reeves/*Courtesy* Gabrielle Roy.
Figure 42.1. Montreal Gazette/Public Archives Canada.
Figure 43.2. Archives Nationales du Quebec/Fonds Armour Landry.
Figure 43.3. Gabor Silazi/Notman Photographic Archives, McCord Museum.
Figure 43.5. Monique Mercure.
Figure 44.1. John Chretien.
Figure 44.2. J. Haggarty/Winnipeg Free Press.
Figure 44.4. Hydro-Quebec.
Figure 44.6. Tony Bock/The Toronto Star Syndicate.

Unit Four: Chapter Seven

Figures IVD, 45.3, 46.1, 47.3, 49.5, 51.2. Public Archives Canada.
Figure 45.2. Wood Engraving on pg. 283 of *Lossing, the Pictorial Field Book of the War of 1812*, Metropolitan Toronto Library.
Figure 45.4. Metropolitan Toronto Library.
Figure 45.5. Webster Collection/New Brunswick Museum.
Figure 46.5. APC/Public Archives Canada.
Figures (47.1.a.), (47.1.b.), 47.2. Parks Canada.
Figure 48.1. The Globe and Mail, Toronto.
Figure 48.2. Provincial Archives of Alberta: E. Brown Collection.
Figure 48.3. Corps of Royal Engineers/Public Archives Canada.
Figure 48.4. Provincial Archives of British Columbia.
Figure 49.1. Sawyer/Public Archives Canada.
Figures 49.2, (49.3.b.). Archives of Ontario.
Figure (49.3.a.). James Inglis/Public Archives Canada.
Figure 50.2. Provincial Archives of British Columbia.
Figure 50.4. C. Gentile/Public Archives Canada.
Figure 50.7. Yukon Archives.
Figure 51.1. Notman Photographic Archives, McCord Museum.
Figure 51.4. Ontario Hydro.
Figure 51.5. Photo by Denis Cahill of the *St. Catherines Standard* from a donation by Mrs Clare Merritt to the St. Catherines Historical Museum.

Unit Four: Chapter Eight

Figure 52.1. Environment Canada.
Figure 52.3. The Pollution Probe Foundation.
Figure 52.5. Fred Phipps/CBC.
Figures 53.4, (55.2.b.), 55.5. Canapress Photo Service.
Figure 53.6. Elizabeth Arden of Canada Ltd.
Figure (54.2.a.). N. McConnell/Manitoba Archives.
Figures (54.2.b.), 54.4. Public Archives Canada.
Figure 54.3. IBM Canada Ltd.
Figure 55.1. Canadian Forces.

Figure (55.2.a.). Fred Phipps/Miller Services.
Figure 55.3. NASA.
Figure 56.1. Steve Behal.
Figure 56.2. Vancouver City Archives.
Figure 56.3. Provincial Archives of Alberta: Edmonton Journal Collection.
Figure 56.4. Roy Peterson/The Vancouver Sun.
Figure 56.5. The Canada Council.

Unit Five: Chapter Nine

Figures 57.1, 57.2, 57.3, 57.4, 58.1, 58.2, 58.4, 59.4, 60.2, 61.1, 61.2, 62.1, (62.2.a.), 62.3. Public Archives Canada.
Figure 57.5. National Aviation Museum.
Figure 58.3. Lucille Mulhall Collection/Manitoba Archives.
Figure 58.6. Harry Steele/E. Cora Hind Collection/ Manitoba Archives.
Figure 59.1. James Collection/City of Toronto Archives.
Figure 59.2. Glenbow Archives.
Figure 59.3. J.J. Kelso Collection/Public Archives Canada.
Figure 59.5. Canada's Sports Hall of Fame.
Figure 60.1. McGill University Archives.
Figure (60.3.a.). Provincial Archives of Alberta.
Figure (60.3.b.). McDermid, Edmonton/Glenbow Archives.
Figure 60.4. Foote Collection, Manitoba Archives.
Figure 60.6. The Ukrainian Women's Association of Canada.
Figure 61.3. Public Archives Canada/DND.
Figure 61.4. Ken Bell/Public Archives Canada/DND.
Figure 61.6. Gary McKim/Canadian Radio-Television and Telecommunications Commission.
Figure (62.2.b.). Mrs. R.C. Bartlett.
Figure 62.4. J.C.M. Hayward, Pamela B. Collins Scrapbook, Graham Metson.
Figure 62.6. Ben Fiber/Joy Kogawa.
Figure 63.1. Montreal Star/Public Archives Canada.
Figure 63.3. Miller Services.
Figure 63.4. Canadian Forces Photo.
Figure 63.5. Helena Wilson/Joseph Skvorecky.
Figure 64.1. Sergeant Paul Tomelin/DND/Public Archives Canada.
Figure 64.3. Canadian Forces.
Figure 64.4. D. Cameron/Public Archives Canada.
Figure 64.5. Canapress Photo Service.

Unit Five: Chapter Ten

Figure 65.1. Wright, *Spectator*.
Figure 65.3. Atomic Energy of Canada Limited.
Figures 65.4, 67.2, 67.3. Canapress Photo Service.
Figures 66.2, 66.3, 66.4. Dilip Mehta/Canadian International Development Agency.
Figure 66.6. Doug Griffin/The Toronto Star Syndicate.
Figure 67.4. Miller Services.
Figure 68.1. E.A. Bollinger Collection/Public Archives of Nova Scotia.
Figure 68.2. Donald Grant/The Globe and Mail, Toronto.
Figure 68.3. Robert McKerron/Canadian International Development Agency.
Figure 68.6. Stephen Homer.
Figure 69.1. Robert Lansdale.
Figurc 69.2. Institutc for Hydrogen Systems.
Figure 69.3. Reg Innell/The Toronto Star Syndicate.
Figure 69.5. NASA.

INDEX

T

U

V

W

Y

Z